PRAISE FOR
ACTS: A GLOBAL PERSPECTIVE

Would you like to read the story of the early church that is uncomplicated, reliable and scholarly? If so, read Acts: A Global Perspective, written by a missionary who sees in this New Testament book principles that can be applied in different cultural contexts. Robert Shade writes simply, and honestly about some of the interpretive challenges in the book, but he always looks beyond the text to the greater narrative of global evangelization. Read this book for your devotions or use it as a reference to grasp an understanding of the Spirit's work centuries ago and his continuing work today. I could only wish this volume had been available years ago.

—*Erwin W. Lutzer,* Pastor Emeritus at
Moody Church, Chicago

This commentary is a concise, straight forward treatment of Acts that keeps the main things Luke is doing in view. It is a useful guide to understanding the key points of this unique book of the Bible focused as it is on the earliest church.

—*Darrell L. Bock,* Executive Director for Cultural
Engagement at Hendricks Center and Senior Research
Professor of New Testament Studies

In *Acts: A Global Perspective*, W. Robert Shade III offers a fresh exploration of the Book of Acts, designed with pastors, church leaders, and small group leaders in mind. This commentary delves beyond traditional perspectives, emphasizing the universal reach and relevance of Acts for believers around the world.

Shade's insights are enriched by his extensive experiences as a missionary, combining textual analysis with real-life applications that resonate on a global scale.

- Examine key theological themes, from the Holy Spirit's role to the spread of the gospel.
- Engage with accessible, scholarly insights that reveal Acts' enduring relevance.
- Explore the book's distinct lessons for leaders seeking to inspire faith communities today.

Join Shade on a journey through Acts that combines robust scholarship with personal anecdotes and "Lessons for Life." Includes maps not found in most commentaries and highlights points of humor in the text.

—Dr. Harold A. Netland, Professor of Philosophy of Religion and Intercultural Studies at Trinity Evangelical Divinity School, Deerfield, Illinois.

ACTS

A COMMENTARY WITH A GLOBAL PERSPECTIVE

W. Robert Shade III

MEDIA.COM

Published by
Illumify Media Global
www.IllumifyMedia.com
"Let's bring your book to life!"

Paperback ISBN: 978-1-964251-39-4

Typeset by Art Innovations (http://artinnovations.in/)
Cover design by Debbie Lewis

Printed in the United States of America

Dedicated by W. Robert Shade III

To my beloved wife, **Kathleen (Kay) Shade** (1939-2008)

My companion and helper and fellow soldier

for the gospel 34 years in Japan.

CONTENTS

LIST OF MAPS

PREFACE

The first edition of this book was the result of a project birthed by Dr Bruce J. Nicholls, a missionary to India who was for many years a professor at Union Theological Seminary in Pune, India. His idea was to produce a series of inexpensive commentaries for pastors in Asia to be published by the Asia Theological Association. Different theological institutions in Asia would each be responsible for one book of the Bible. He visited Tokyo Christian University, and I suggested that TCU take the Book of Acts. Originally two Japanese colleagues were supposed to help me, but both dropped out, one early, and one later. One was supposed to add the applications and "color" pertinent to Asia. Bruce took over that part of the job. An astute textual critic will be able to discern his contributions. The first edition was published by ATA in 2007.

But then it went out of print. The Langham Global Library, a brainchild of John R. W. Stott, became a partner of ATA. One of Langham's policies was that all the commentaries be written by indigenous scholars: Asians for the Asian series, and Africans for the African series. Since neither Bruce nor I qualified as indigenous Asians, our book was allowed to lapse.

I found a certain amount of demand for the book in our church, but I ran out of copies to give or sell. So I finally decided that the book had enough merit to publish a revised version. It is no longer aimed specifically at Asia, but I left many of the references to Asia. I hope that it will be usable and profitable for pastors in any area of the world, hence the subtitle: "A Global Perspective." Bible study leaders will find it useful for any small group studying Acts.

Distinctives: This commentary is written in simple English. It is "scholarly," with plenty of interaction with the Greek text, but it also tries to get at the message of larger units of Acts, often asking "Why is this part here?" It deals with theological points raised by each passage: baptism, the

Holy Spirit, the doctrine of Christ. Where there are differences of opinion, I state my own position while trying to be charitable and understanding of those who would differ with me. I am a conservative dispensationalist who holds to the inerrant inspiration of Acts by the Spirit, while at the same time appreciating the characteristics of Luke the human author.

There are a number of illustrations and anecdotes from my 34 years of service as a missionary in Japan from 1969 to 2003. Twenty years were spent in planting two churches in Yokohama and nine years teaching Greek, Acts, and the Pauline Epistles at Tokyo Christian University in Chiba Prefecture. There is plenty of "application," some within the main text, and most in the pithy points listed after each section as "Lessons for Life." I tried to make it more interesting and engaging and readable than the average commentary. I have personally visited most of the locations mentioned in the Book of Acts in Israel, Turkey, and Greece. There is nothing like standing in the ancient theater in Ephesus and knowing that these very stone seats reverberated with the cry "Great is Diana of the Ephesians" for two hours.

If you find any mistakes, please know that some readers look only for mistakes, and I have left some for them to have the pleasure of finding them.

There are some original ideas, but any author of a commentary is standing on the shoulders of those who have gone before him. I leaned heavily on the commentaries of F. F. Bruce, John Stott, Richard Longenecker, and Ben Witherington, all of whom have mined riches in the Greek text and historical background far beyond my abilities. Thank you. The voluminous commentaries of Darrell Bock and Eckhard Schnabel appeared after the publication of the first edition; I tried to check their opinions at many points. My advice to pastors preparing sermons is to pick your three most helpful commentaries and stick with them. If you try to read too many, you will find yourself frantically composing your sermon too late into Saturday night. On some knotty issues, you may need to consult a wider set of commentaries.

I want to acknowledge with gratitude the help of Illumify Media Global, a company specializing in publishing Christian books for unknown/first-time authors like me. Mike Klassen, seminary graduate and former pastor, and now head of Illumify, was particularly helpful and encouraging. "I am very grateful to Jen Shepard for her meticulous proof-reading of the entire book."

Bon appétit!

INTRODUCTION

What if Jesus had decided not to ascend into heaven 40 days after his resurrection but stay on earth to do the task of world evangelism by himself? If he were to visit one village of India a day, starting in the year 30 AD, he would, by the year 2005, have ministered in over 750,000 villages. But today there are more than 6,000,000 villages in India.[1] At this rate it would take Jesus 14,384 more years to complete the task.

That does not take care of the rest of the world outside India. And even within India, to say nothing of the rest of the world, it would not cover the 50 or so generations (if each generation is 40 years) that would have come and gone during these 2,000 years since Jesus started his task. What Jesus did to solve this problem is the story of the Book of Acts.

He sent the Holy Spirit to indwell each of his believers in order to make each believer a very imperfect incarnation of himself, a "little Christ." By multiplying himself in each land and in each generation the problem of spreading his gospel of salvation throughout the earth would be solved.

The first believers were very ordinary people. But they were convinced by "many infallible proofs" that Jesus had risen from the dead (1:3). They received the baptism of the Holy Spirit (1:5). They believed that he would come again to consummate the kingdom (1:11).

Twenty centuries later, and in most cases thousands of miles from Jerusalem, the Lord Jesus continues to reproduce himself in his believers and endow them with his Spirit to represent him on the earth. Can there be any question about the purpose of our lives? Can there be any greater calling?

On the day of Pentecost there were only 120 disciples of Christ gathered in Jerusalem. This does not seem like a very large number for three years of

---

1   Census of India Newsletter, 2001.

miraculous powerful ministry and the greatest preaching that the world has
ever heard. But within a few years, using the "incarnation/Spirit indwelling"
strategy, there were thousands of believers and dozens of churches, not only
in Jerusalem, but as far away as the coast of the Black Sea and in the capital of
empire itself, Rome. Some Jews complained that this upstart sect was *turning
the world upside down* (17:6). How did this revolution happen? This is the
story of the Book of Acts.

The Purpose(s) of the Book of Acts

On the face of it, Acts seems to be a history of the birth and development
and spread of the early church. But a closer look reveals that, though this book
is history, it is a very incomplete history. It is called "The Acts of the Apostles,"
but only two apostles, Peter and Paul, are prominent. John is mentioned in
the early chapters, but we hear nothing of the mission of Mark, who founded
the church in Egypt, or Thomas, who founded the church of south India.
Nothing is written about the travels of Matthew, or Philip, or the rest of the
Twelve.

A better title for this book would be "The Acts of the Holy Spirit" or
"The Acts of the Risen and Ascended Christ." Notice in the very first verse that
the previous work (The Gospel of Luke) is introduced as *all that Jesus **began**
to do and to teach*. The clear implication is that this volume 2 of the two-part
series will tell of what Jesus **continued** to do and to teach through all the
"little Christs" he sent into the world. The **key message of Acts** is that Jesus is
alive, glorified, and active through his apostles and his church.

What are the primary purposes of the book of Acts? I agree with I.
Howard Marshall and Richard N. Longenecker that the primary purpose of
Acts is at once **evangelistic** and **apologetic**.[2] That is, to persuade readers to
believe in Christ and to follow him. The author himself tells us that in Luke
1:1-4 of this two-volume work. The author wants Theophilus *to know the
certainty of the things you have been taught* (Luke 1:4). A number of words and
phrases are piled up to drive home the point of **certainty**: *eyewitnesses from
the beginning, handed down to us, carefully investigated*, and *an orderly account*.

---

2   I. Howard Marshall, *The Acts of the Apostles: An Introduction and Commentary*
(InterVarsity Press, Leicester, England, 1980), 20 and Richard N. Longenecker, *Acts, The
Expositor's Bible Commentary*, Vol 9, (Grand Rapids: Zondervan, 1981), 217.

This is true not only of the Gospel of Luke, one of the four records of the facts of Jesus' birth, life and ministry, death, and resurrection, but also of that which Jesus continued to do through his apostles and believers. This certainty builds faith both in inquirers and believers. Thus the overall purpose of Luke/Acts is both apologetic **and** evangelistic.

There are however obvious differences between the two volumes:

LUKE	ACTS
Jesus in person	Jesus "incarnated" in his church
In Palestine only	"To the ends of the earth"
To Jews only	To Gentiles also
The Era of the Law of Moses	Transition to the Rule of the Spirit

Seen in this light, one of the important purposes of Acts is to trace **a momentous transition in salvation history**. Today, most of us who are Gentile believers take these changes for granted. But it was not obvious to the early Jewish believers in Christ that the Gentiles were even included in the salvation plan of God or that the Law of Moses was not eternally obligatory upon all true believers. God had to do a special work to get Peter into the house of Cornelius (chap. 10). The church in Antioch was born not by apostolic strategy, but almost by "accident." The question of whether the Gentiles would be required to submit to the entire Law of Moses was a point of sharp contention in the church and was solved only by the Jerusalem Council (chap. 15).

Returning to the theme of the evangelistic/apologetic purpose, a major subset of that theme has been seen by many to be the defense of the new movement as a *religio licita* (a legal religion recognized officially by the state). Roman Law outlawed certain religions that were perceived to be a threat to the stability of the Empire and recognized others that were not perceived to be a threat. Judaism was recognized by the Roman authorities as a legal religion and at first Christianity was treated as a sect of Judaism. But the split was clearly coming, and Luke took pains again and again to point out that various civil magistrates exonerated the apostles against charges of *unlawful customs* (16:20-21), *treason against Caesar* (17:7), and *worship contrary to the law* (18:13). Always the apostles and missionaries of the gospel are vindicated and the civil magistrates often impressed. One, Proconsul Sergius Paulus, was even converted (13:6-12). This may be the chief reason that the lengthy record of Paul being vindicated five times in the trials in the latter chapters of Acts was included.[3]

Another purpose of Acts that falls under the category of apologetic is Luke's **vindication of and promotion of Paul**. Paul was a suspicious character to many Jewish Christians. He was not one of the original twelve apostles. He did not require Gentiles to keep the Law of Moses; indeed he wrote vehemently against such an idea as *another gospel* in the epistle to the Galatians. He spent most of his time preaching to the unclean Gentiles instead of to the chosen people of God, the Jews. His gospel may have had too much grace and not enough law for many. But Paul is clearly Luke's hero. More than half the book is given to the exploits of Paul (chaps. 13-28). His conversion is given in detail in chapter 9 and then repeated twice more (chaps. 22 and 26) without abbreviation.

The following table shows that Luke deliberately presented Paul as just as important as Peter. Everything that Peter did Paul did also!

	PETER	**PAUL**
Healed a lame man	3:2	14:8
Healing "at a distance"	5:15	19:12
Casts out demons	5:16	16:18
Confounds a sorcerer	8:18-24	13:6
Raises the dead	9:36	20:9
Miraculous escape from jail	Chap. 12	Chap. 16

---

3   For more on these points see Stott, *The Message of Acts* (InterVarsity Press, 1996), 25-26. Stott calls this Luke's "political apologetic."

These are too many to be accidental. Luke has a deliberate plan at work here.

One realizes the importance of "pushing Paul" if we recall that so much of our New Testament content and doctrine was given through Paul. So much so that some accuse Paul of taking the simple ethical religion of Jesus and changing it into a complex system of difficult dogma. The current style in NT scholarship is to pit one NT writer against the others and to emphasize the unique theology of each writer. While to a certain extent this is a legitimate and profitable study, we are persuaded that the NT writers were not soloists separately piping their own tunes, but under the hand of the Holy Spirit, more of an orchestra contributing to an overarching whole.

Another purpose of Luke in Acts (which is not noticed by many commentators) is to answer the question: **Why did the Jews reject Jesus?** We are so used to the fact that the majority of the Jews of Jesus' own day did reject him that we fail to appreciate the problem that must have occurred to many Gentiles like Theophilus. Put simply, their doubt may have been something like this: "The Jews are the experts on Messiah. If Jesus was the true Messiah, why did his own people, who knew him best, reject him"?

We can understand the gospels better if we realize that one purpose for their writing was to answer this unspoken question. All of the first five books of the NT show how again and again the Jews of his day rejected Jesus despite his many miracles and *many infallible proofs*. They rejected him out of jealousy and to protect their own positions in society. They rejected him because he was not a triumphant liberator but a wretched victim of the Roman cross. They rejected him in the face of the most compelling evidence such as the raising of Lazarus.

In the first five chapters of Acts, God is still appealing to the Jewish nation to repent and believe. One of the answers to the question is that many Jews, in fact thousands of them, **did** believe. Nevertheless, most did not believe, despite the fact that they could not deny the evidence of the miracles such as the healing of the lame man in the temple (3:1-11 and 4:16). Luke is demonstrating that many Jews simply refused to believe in the face of overwhelming evidence.

During the Gentile mission, Paul, almost with monotonous regularity, always visits the town's Jewish synagogue first. Always the response is the same: some believe and some do not, and those who do not believe do not refute

Paul in reasonable argument, but like unreasoning beasts, raise up fanatic mobs to harry him and his helpers out of town. The "trial" chapters (22-26) demonstrate that Paul was seized and beaten in the temple on an erroneous charge, and repeated trials or inquiries before neutral governors and kings all resulted in verdicts of "innocent." The Jews simply could not prove their case against Paul and their opposition was unreasonable.

In short, the answer to the question of why the Jews did not receive their own Messiah is twofold: 1. Many, even a fanatic persecutor like Paul, did believe. 2. Those who did not believe never presented a reasonable case but acted in fear and jealousy.

The Importance of Acts

Historical: We have said that the book of Acts is not primarily a book of history, but nevertheless it is the only record we have of what happened between the resurrection and the conversion of Paul. It explains the origin of the churches to which most of the letters of Paul were addressed. Without Acts we would know nothing of the early days of the Christian movement except for scraps of information garnered from Paul's letters. And when the book of Acts suddenly ends, the curtain goes down and we are in the dark.

Theological: Acts contributes much to our understanding of many areas of doctrine. **Natural revelation** is prominent in chapters 14 and 17. Acts is full of **pneumatology**, not so much discourses on the person of the Holy Spirit, but a record of his acts in launching the church on the day of Pentecost and following. We cannot discuss the baptism of the Spirit, the filling of the Spirit, or the gift of tongues without consulting these chapters. The Spirit was given to all believers (2:38; 10:47; 15:8; 19:2). He was the director and the power behind the Christian mission (1:8; 8:29; 10:19; 11:12; 13:2; 20:22). The filling with the Spirit enabled bold witness (2:4; 2:18; 4:31; 11:24; 19:6). Revelation was given to Old Testament prophets by the Spirit (4:25 and 28:25) and he enabled prophecy in the New Testament (11:28; 21:11). The Holy Spirit led in appointing church leaders (6:3 and 20:28) and worked in the church to resolve problems (6:3 and 15:28).

Acts also adds much to or corroborates the witness of other NT books to the doctrine of **Christology**. Though Acts presents the **humanity** of Jesus (2:22) as "Jesus of Nazareth" (3:6; 4:10; 6:14; 10:38; 22:8; 26:9), it majors much more on his exaltation and divine titles such as Messiah (the point of the sermon 2:36, and also 3:20; 4:26; 5:42 and many other places). Jesus is also **Lord**. The comparison of 2:21 where "Lord" is Yahweh and 2:36 shows that "Lord" in Acts is not merely a title of respect like "Sir" but a title of deity. The message of Acts is that Jesus is *Lord of all* (10:36) and that those who call upon his name shall be saved (2:21; 16:31). "Lord" is the most common title for Christ in Acts, being used over 90 times. Other more primitive or Jewish titles for Christ occur in Acts such as *pais theou,* the servant of the LORD from Isaiah (3:13, 26: 4:27-30). Titles unique to Acts are "the Holy One" (3:14) and "the Righteous One" (3:14 and 7:52). The title *Archēgos* (3:15; 5:31) is also "primitive" but is also mentioned twice in Hebrews (2:10 and 12:2).

The **resurrection** of Christ is a dominant theme in seven of the ten speeches or sermons in Acts (chaps. 2, 3, 4, 10, 13, 17, and 26). In the first three speeches one of the main points is that **you** killed Jesus, but **God** raised him from the dead! It is clear that without the resurrection and exaltation of Jesus there would be no Pentecost and no book of Acts.

The death of Christ is mentioned in these speeches eight times, but the doctrine of substitutionary atonement is not developed in Acts. It is not entirely absent; 20:28 says *feed the church of God which he has purchased with his own blood.* Also there are several references to Isaiah 53, the clearest reference to substitutionary atonement in the whole Bible (most directly 8:28-33; but also as we have seen in the title *Servant of the Lord* (3:13, 26; 4:27, 30).

The doctrine of the cross is not explained but for those who repent and believe in this Savior, there is forgiveness of sin (2:38; 3:19; 10:43; 13:38; 26:18). Justification is mentioned only once, appropriately, in the mouth of Paul (13:39). The death of Christ was not an unfortunate accident on the part of a helpless victim; it was foreordained by God (2:23) and was a fulfillment of prophecy (3:18).

Acts also gives us much about the **terms of salvation**, that is the answer to the question "What must I do to be saved?" Acts is a book of testimonies of salvation. First, Jesus is the only Savior; *there is no other name . . . whereby we must be saved* (4:12). One is saved by *calling on his name* (2:21), by repenting and submitting to baptism (2:38), by *repenting and being converted* (3:18), by *believing on the Lord Jesus Christ* (16:31), by *repentance toward God and faith in our Lord Jesus Christ* (20:21). In some cases, there is no time to ask the question "What must I do to be saved?"; the scales fall from the eyes and the

Spirit falls upon those listening to the word of Christ (9:18 and 10:44). These immediately received baptism.

These conditions should not be made into a list of half a dozen separate items but should be seen as the response of the heart and will in what is variously called "repenting," "calling on the name of the Lord," and "believing." The outward sign of the response of the heart is proven by submission to baptism. Is baptism essential to salvation? My conviction is that baptism is not essential to salvation but that the "faith" that refuses baptism is probably not genuine faith.

Acts also contributes much to what we call **practical theology**. We learn much about **mission methods and strategy** (chapters 13-19). We see outstanding examples of **homiletics** and what the earliest preachers said and how they said it. We notice the stark contrasts that can occur in a sermon to the Jews (chap. 13) and a sermon to Athenian intellectuals (chapter 17). We see the importance of **baptism** and even have some clues as to how they baptized. The first records of the **Eucharist or Lord's Supper** are in Acts. We listen in on the fervent **prayers** of early Christians and see the rudiments of **church polity** and its leadership by apostles, elders, and deacons. We see an early example of **church discipline** (5:1-11).

In the area of practical theology, we face a problem that confronts all serious readers of Acts: how do we apply or put into practice these examples today? Is the book of Acts **prescriptive** or **descriptive**? One problem in making it the former is that events often do not fall neatly into the same pattern. If we insist that the gift of tongues is a "second work of grace," we are confronted with the fact that the Gentiles in Cornelius' house spoke in tongues at the instant of conversion (10:44). If we insist that all Christians should sell all their real estate and give it to the church, we are faced with the fact that some people continued to own houses (12:12; 21:16).

Another caution in attempting to reproduce the phenomena of Acts is that, in terms of salvation history, the period of Acts was a period of transition (as noted above). Why do we not see so many miracles of healing today as then? Is it because our faith is lacking or our sanctification deficient or that we have not received the baptism of the Spirit? It is more likely that there were outbursts of miracle because the Risen Lord was giving a powerful push to launch his Church and to protect it from being extinguished by its enemies. We hear more reports of "signs and wonders" even today where the church is in its infancy or facing danger and persecution than in areas where the church has been established for centuries and there is no persecution. There is in Scripture an economy of miracle. When there were major transitions in salvation history—at the giving of the Law (Exodus) or at the appearance of the first prophets (Elijah and Elisha) and at the birth of Christ—there were outbursts of miracle. Even within the book of Acts we see that there are many more miracles in chapters 1 through 12 (I count 32) than in chapters 13 through 28 (18). From 21 to 27 no miracles are recorded.

The Historical Reliability of Acts

Perhaps for the majority of our readers, this is not an issue. But there has been a history of two and half centuries of persistent skepticism in some circles of NT scholarship toward the historical accuracy of Acts. One can see the interplay of detractors and defenders since the time of F. C. Baur outlined in the introduction to Marshall's commentary.[4] Interestingly the major doubters seem to be all German (Baur, Dibelius, Haenchen, and Conzelmann) and the major defenders, except for Martin Hengel, all British (Ramsay, F. F. Bruce, Sherwin-White, and Hemer).

In 1956 the first edition of Ernst Haenchen's 700-plus page commentary on Acts appeared. Marshall comments on this work as follows:

> Haenchen's method was to ask at every point in Acts 'What was Luke trying to do?' and he found that he could explain most of Acts in terms of Luke producing an edifying account of the early church that owed nothing to written sources and was based on the scantiest of oral traditions. The result was that Luke's historical accuracy was apparently torn in shreds; the narrative was claimed . . . to be basically the product of the fertile mind of a historical novelist with little or no concern with such tiresome things as facts . . . for the moment the Haenchen-Conzelmann approach appears to be dominant and largely uncontested on the Continent.[5]

There is not enough space in this work to provide a complete refutation of the attacks on the historical accuracy of Acts. Colin Hemer, before his

---

4   Marshall, 34-37.

5   Marshall, 35.

unfortunate early death, left us with a magnificent book defending the historical reliability of Acts in exhausting detail.[6] The reader is also referred to the landmark archaeological and geographic study by William M. Ramsay, now available in an updated and revised edition with color photographs.[7]

In this introduction, we content ourselves with underlining the fact, often observed by others, that Luke always got the titles of officials precisely correct. This type of detail would have been very difficult for one writing historical fiction many years after the events depicted, to get these twelve titles, four of which are those of minor local officials, exactly right.

Titles of Government Officials in Acts

The many provinces of the Roman Empire were divided into two categories: those ruled directly by the Emperor; and those under the control of the Senate. The former were those more fractious or rebellious provinces (such as Judea) that required a strong military presence to keep the populace in check. Thus Judea was ruled by a *praefect* or *procurator* (Greek *hēgemon*) like Pilate, and in the time of Acts, Felix in Acts 23:24 and Festus in 26:30. On the other hand the correct title for the Roman governors of the Senatorial provinces of Cyprus (13:7), Achaia (18:12), and Asia (19:38) was *proconsul* (*anthupatos* in Greek).

The titles of the Herods that appear in Acts are also scrupulously correct: Herod Antipas the *Tetrarch* (originally "ruler of a fourth part") of Galilee and Perea (Luke 3:19; 9:7; Acts 13:1). Herod Agrippa I was *rex* (*basileus* in Greek) of Judea and Samaria (Acts 12:1) as was his son Herod Agrippa II *rex* of Galilee and northern Palestine (25:13). The title of "king" was not used loosely in those times; it was vigorously sought and jealously guarded.

The fact that Luke gets the titles of various officials of the different cities appearing in Acts right every time is most impressive. In Philippi there were two *stratēgoi*. There were two of them, reflecting the tradition of two joint rulers of the Republican period in Rome; this was the regular practice in

---

6   Colin J. Hemer, *The Book of Acts in the Setting of Hellenistic History,* Winona Lake, Indiana, Eisenbrauns, 1990.

7   William M. Ramsay, *St. Paul, The Traveler and Roman Citizen* (Grand Rapids: Kregel, 2001, revised and updated by Mark Wilson.

Roman colonies such as Philippi.[8] In Thessalonica the correct title for the local officials was *politarchēs* (17:6, 8). There is independent attestation from inscriptions in Thessalonica to the five or six *politarchai* who formed the city council.[9] On the other hand the correct title for the city officials of Ephesus was "Asiarch" or "ruler of (the province of) Asia" (19:31) and the correct title for the town clerk was indeed *grammateus* (19:35) as Luke records.

It must be noted that the precise status of provinces and cities (and thus the titles of officials) within the Empire changed from time to time, and they could easily be mistaken by a writer not familiar with current conditions. For example, Corinth went from being a Senatorial province under a *proconsul* from 27 BC to 15 AD, to an Imperial province under a *praetor* from 15 AD to 44 AD, and then again a Senatorial province under a *proconsul* after 44, the period when Paul visited the city.[10]

Despite dealing with scores of particulars that an outsider could hardly know, what we know from secular history of that time corroborates Luke every time. There are only two problems that have not been resolved. One is the famous reference in Luke 2:2 that the census causing Mary and Joseph to journey to Bethlehem *first took place when Quirinius was governor of Syria* (NASV). The problem is that Quirinius was not governor of Syria until 6-9 AD.[11]

The second problem is the reference to a rebellion led by one Theudas mentioned by Gamaliel in Acts 5:36 as having occurred *some time ago.* However, the Jewish historian Josephus mentions a rebellion led by "Theudas" during the governorship of Cuspius Fadus (44-46 AD), **after** this speech by Gamaliel (in the mid 30's.) Those who raise this objection assume that Josephus is correct and that Luke was in error. However errors have been detected in Josephus. Bruce thinks that the most likely solution is that there

---

8   Hemer, 115. The *rhabdoukoi lictores* of verse 22 were the attendants of colonial magistrates, who bore the *fasces* and used them to beat miscreants. Bruce notes that of 32 known inscriptions bearing the word "politarch," 18 are from Thessalonica (370).

9   Walter Bower, W. Danker, W. F. Arndt, and F. W. Gingrich. *A Greek-English Lexicon of the New Testament and Other Early Christian Literature* (BDAG) (3rd Edition), 845.

10   F.F. Bruce, *The Acts of the Apostles: Greek Text with Introduction and Commentary,* (Grand Rapids: Eerdmans, 1990) 395.

11   See I. Howard Marshall, *The Gospel of Luke: A Commentary on the Greek Text* (Grand Rapids: Eerdmans, 1978, 102-104 for suggested solutions.

were two men named "Theudas" (a common name) who led a rebellion (a very common occurrence).[12]

That we might have only two "errors" by Luke, and those not certainly "errors," but possibly unsolved problems that might someday yield to further information and clarification, still allows for a very high view of his accuracy and reliability in historical details.

The Date of Acts

Like so many books of the New Testament, there is no certainty as to the exact date of the book of Acts. Any discussion of the date of this book is inseparably linked with the date of the Gospel of Luke, since there are very few scholars who doubt that the same author wrote both volumes, as is explicitly stated in the prologue to Acts (1:1-4). Roughly speaking, the estimates of the date of Acts fall into three periods: after 100 AD, 80-95 AD, and between AD 62 and 70.[13] The first option, a second century date, is now out of fashion. It was largely built on the now discredited theories of F. C. Baur who thought that Acts represented an attempt to smooth over a split in the church between a "Peter" faction and a "Paul" faction in the middle of the second century. "Few scholars now think that Acts is a second century document."[14]

Many current scholars opt for the 80-95 AD period. Those who hold to this date believe the gospel of Luke had to be written after the fall of Jerusalem in 70 AD which is described in Luke 21:20-24. (It is assumed that this passage is history, not prophecy.) It cannot be later than 95 AD when empire wide persecution broke out against the Christian church, because the attitude toward Roman authorities and the good will (at least neutrality) of the Romans does not reflect the situation after the mid-90s.

As for the latter point, however, the same argument would just as well fit the savage persecution by Nero in 64-65 AD which broke out in Rome. There are other factors that point to a date prior to 64. Luke says nothing of the death of Paul in the Neronian persecution about 67 and this seems a very

---

12   Bruce, 176.

13   I drew much of this material on the dating of Acts from *An Introduction to the New Testament* by D. A. Carson, Douglas J. Moo, and Leon Morris (Grand Rapids: Zondervan, 1992).

14   Ibid., 191.

strange omission since Paul has been the main character in the latter half of the book. No mention is made of the Neronian persecution. The vivid account of voyage and shipwreck in chapters 27 and 28 suggests a recent experience. These points and many more are thoroughly discussed by Hemer.[15] After an exhaustive discussion from many angles, Hemer dates the writing of Acts at **62 AD**.[16]

We agree that the best guess as to the date of Luke-Acts is 62 AD, the end of "two whole years" of imprisonment mentioned in 28:30.

The Author of Acts

For those who date Acts in the second century, the traditional author cannot be Luke the companion of Paul mentioned in Philemon 24 and 2 Tim 4:11 and "Luke the beloved physician" of Col 4:14. Neither the gospel nor its sequel Acts anywhere mention the author by name as is typical of so many NT writings. However, early church tradition assigns the authorship of both books to Luke the companion of Paul: the Muratorian Canon (190 AD), Ireneus (*Against Heresies* 3.1; 3.14.1-4; about 185), and other sources later into the third century including Clement of Alexandria, Tertullian, and Eusebius. This tradition survived unchallenged at that time or any time until the rise of radical criticism at the end of the eighteenth century.

What we can know about the author from the evidence of Luke-Acts (internal evidence) is the following:

1. He was well educated and wrote in Greek of good style.
2. He was not among the first generation of Christians or disciples because he writes about those things *handed down to us by those who from the first were eyewitnesses and servants of the word* (Luke 1:2).
3. He was a participant in many of the events of the books of Acts because he uses the word "we" when he was a participant (16:8-17; 20:5-15; 21:1-18; and 27:1-28:16).
4. His use of more technical medical vocabulary than the other gospel writers supports (but does not prove) the idea that he was indeed a physician.

---

15   Hemer, 365-410.

16   Ibid., 408.

We know little else about Luke. Most likely he was a Gentile because Col 4:10-14 does not include him among Paul's Jewish companions. Eusebius and Jerome thought that he was from Antioch of Syria.[17] We do not know how long he lived, though he was a companion and helper of Paul as late as the writing of 2 Timothy (4:11 *Only Luke is with me.*)

The Structure of Acts

There has been a healthy emphasis among scholars in recent decades away from focusing exclusively on individual verses ("texts") to seeing the overall picture in not only paragraph units but also paragraphs within a larger context that constitutes broad segments of a given book of the Bible.

Many agree that 1:8 *But you will receive power when the Holy Spirit comes on you; and you will be my witnesses in Jerusalem, and in all Judea and Samaria, and to the ends of the earth* is the theme verse of the entire book. In chapters 1-7 we have the birth of the church on the day of Pentecost in Jerusalem, its growth, and the development of opposition. In chapters 8-12 we have the spread of the gospel through Philip and Peter to Samaria and Judea. This section also includes two important preparations for the third movement: the conversion of the Apostle Paul in chapter 9 and the conversion of a household of Gentiles in chapter 10. Then from chapters 13 through 28 there is a movement to the ends of the earth.[18] This section falls into two parts: the three missionary journeys in chapters 13-20, and the trials of Paul in chapters 21-28. Others have pointed out that Acts continues a geographic movement of the Gospel of Luke from Galilee to Perea to Jerusalem, and now Acts moves the reader from Jerusalem to Samaria to Rome.[19]

One can also divide Acts according to its two main protagonists, Peter in chapters 1-12 and Paul in chapters 13-28. Longenecker sees the structure of Acts indicated in the "summary statements" of the book: 6:7; 9:31; 12:24;

---

17   Joseph Fitzmyer supports this tradition in his introduction to his commentary on Luke (*The Gospel according to Luke, I-IX*, Doubleday, 1981, 45-47.

18   Tannehill correctly points out that Rome is not the "end of the earth" and that this phrase denotes an "outline of the mission but only in part an outline of Acts." Robert C. Tannehill, *The Narrative Unity of Luke-Acts: A Literary Interpretation, volume two: The Acts of the Apostles* (Minneapolis: Fortress Press, 1990), 18.

19   For example, Longenecker, 233; Ben Witherington III, *The Acts of the Apostles: A Socio-Rhetorical Commentary* (Grand Rapids: Eerdmans, 1998), 69.

16:5; 19:20; and 28:31. This divides the book into two parts of three panels each:

Part I   The Mission to the Jews 1-12

Panel 1   The Birth and Growth of the Church in Jerusalem 1:1-6:7

Panel 2   The Spread of the Church into Samaria, Judea and Damascus through Stephen, Philip, and Saul. 6:8-9:31

Panel 3   The Spread of the Gospel as far as Caesarea and Antioch 9:32-12:25.

Part II   The Mission to the Gentiles 13-28

Panel 4   The Mission to Galatia and the Jerusalem Council 13:1-16:5

Panel 5   The Mission to the Greek World 16:6-19:20

Panel 6   The Journey to Jerusalem and then to Rome 19:21-28:31[20]

One feels some discomfort at breaking into the middle of chapters such as the break at 6:7 or "breaking up" the three missionary journeys. Nevertheless, we must remember that our chapter divisions were unknown to the author, and indeed for much of the history of the Bible. What seems to be the author's scheme does highlight his thinking about geography and even peoples. For example, though the second missionary journey starts at 15:36, in Luke's mind the main point of that journey is the crossing into Macedonia, a process that begins in 16:6. The return to Antioch in 18:22, which divides the second and third missionary journeys, is not seen as a major break by the author who sees the return to Antioch and then the journey through central Anatolia as a brief interlude to the main point of Panel 5, the mission to the heartland of Greek civilization, which in those days included Macedonia, Achaia, and eastern Anatolia, the center of which was the province of Asia and the major city of Ephesus. So in Luke's mind Panel 4 was the mission to the Galatians and Panel 5 the mission to the Greeks. (The Galatians were not really Greeks; though many of them no doubt spoke Greek, they had their own languages

---

20   I have reworded this basic outline taken from Longenecker, 234.

(14:11) and were in a "more primitive" state than the subjects of the Panel 5). Extending this line of thought we may see the long Panel 6 as a mission (really a witness) to the Roman world.

A Chronological Table of Acts

Here we are heavily dependent on the work of others who have meticulously researched the dates of the events of Acts and the life of Paul. A problem any chronologist of this period faces is that though Luke gives us fairly precise information about the beginning of the ministry of Jesus (Luke 3:1), he does not give similar information about the events of Acts. Nevertheless, an approximate timeline can be worked out based on information in the epistles, particularly Galatians 1 and 2, and the few time notices given in Acts. We are greatly helped by five benchmarks from extra-biblical history from which we can estimate the approximate years in which various events of Acts took place:[21]

1. The death of Aretas IV King of Nabatea was no later than 40 AD (2 Cor 11:32-33; Acts 9:23-25).
2. The expulsion of the Jews from Rome by Claudius in 49 AD (Acts 18:2).
3. The beginning of Gallio's proconsulship in Achaia in May/June 51 AD. This pinpoints the time when Paul appeared before the judgment seat of Gallio (Acts 18:12).
4. The replacement of Felix by Festus for the procuratorship of Judea in May 59 AD (Acts 24:27).
5. The death of Herod Agrippa I in March 44 AD (Acts 12:23).[22]

Unfortunately, we have very little to go on to determine dates in the first twelve chapters of Acts. That chronology is complicated by the uncertainty of the date of the crucifixion and the Day of Pentecost in Acts 2 that followed immediately upon it. We are helped in that there is a general consensus among Bible chronologists now that the crucifixion occurred on April 7, 30 AD,

---

21   These are taken from John McRay, *Paul: His Life and Teaching* (Grand Rapids: Baker, 2003), 61. McRay calls them "pinpoints." The documentation and explanation for each point is given on pages 62-66. Bruce gives detailed information on how these dates were arrived at in his comments on each of these passages.

22   Witherington, 80, citing Josephus, *Antiquities* 19.8.2.

though some prefer 33 AD. The events soon following the crucifixion of Acts 2 through 5 flow seamlessly together but after that we know very little about dating the events of Acts 6-12. How long after Pentecost, for example, did the martyrdom of Stephen of chapter 7 and the subsequent persecution of 8:1 occur? Or Philip's evangelistic ministry in Samaria in chapter 8? When we move into the missionary journeys and the trials of Paul in the rest of Acts, we can date events within a year or two, and in many cases make good guesses as to what time of year the events occurred.

The following table is a combination of the chronologies of F. F. Bruce and Colin Hemer.[23] They are in remarkably close agreement.

Event	Date
Crucifixion, Resurrection, Ascension, Pentecost	April 30
Conversion of Saul (Acts 9)	33 or 34
Paul's first visit to Jerusalem (Acts 9:26-30; Gal 1:18-20)	c. 35
Death of Herod Agrippa I (Acts 12:20-23)	44
Famine in Judea (Acts 11:28)	45 to 48
Barnabas and Paul visit Jerusalem (Acts 11:30; Gal 2:1)	46
First Missionary Journey (Acts 13 and 14)	47 to 48
Letter to the Galatians	48
Jerusalem Council (Acts 15)	49
Second Missionary Journey (Acts 16:9-18:18)	49 to 52
Paul in Corinth (Acts 18:1-18; 1 Cor 2:1-5)	Fall 50 to Summer 52
Letters to the Thessalonians	50/ 51
Paul's Trip to Jerusalem and Antioch (Ac 18:22)	Summer 52

---

23   Bruce, 92-93; Hemer, 251-76.

Event	Date
Third Missionary Journey (Acts 18:23-21:15)	52-57
Paul in Ephesus (Acts 19:1-20:1)	Autumn 52-Summer 55
First Corinthians	early 55
Paul in Macedonia (Acts 20:1 f.)	Winter 55/56
Second Corinthians	56
Paul in Corinth (Acts 20:2 f; Rom 15:25 f.)	Winter 56/57
Letter to the Romans	early 57
Paul's Arrest in Jerusalem (Acts 21:15-33)	April/May 57
Paul in Custody in Caesarea (Acts 23:23-26:32)	57 to 59
Paul's Voyage to Rome (Acts 27)	Sep 59-Spring 60
Paul in Custody in Rome (Acts 28:16-31)	60 to 62
Prison Epistles: Colossians, Ephesians, Philemon, Philippians	
Great Fire in Rome	July 64
Nero's Persecution and Martyrdoms of Peter & Paul	65 (?)
Outbreak of the Jewish War	Sep 66
Destruction of Jerusalem	Aug/Sep 70

ACTS 1

THE PROMISE OF THE SPIRIT AND THE REPLACEMENT OF JUDAS

Acts 1:1-5

Introduction:

A Continuation of the Ministry of Jesus

ᘒᕉᕉᕉ

1 In the first book, O Theophilus, I have dealt with all that Jesus began to do and teach, 2 until the day when he was taken up, after he had given commands through the Holy Spirit to the apostles whom he had chosen. 3 He presented himself alive to them after his suffering by many proofs, appearing to them during forty days and speaking about the kingdom of God. 4 And while staying with them he ordered them not to depart from Jerusalem, but to wait for the promise of the Father, which, he said, "you heard from me; 5 for John baptized with water, but you will be baptized with the Holy Spirit not many days from now."

1:1 *The first book* is of course the gospel of Luke. The book of Acts makes the gospel of Luke unique by making it the only gospel with a sequel. The Greek word is "first" (*prōton* [comparing three or more] not *proteros* [comparing two]). Some have therefore suggested that Luke really intended to write three volumes. This is a fascinating possibility, and the abrupt ending of Acts would support it, but the majority of scholars point out that though the two words were carefully distinguished in classical Greek, the Greek of NT times (Koine Greek) had abandoned the distinction and often used *prōton* even when comparing two things.

Volume I, the Gospel of Luke, is the record of what *Jesus* **began** *to do and to teach.* Volume II, the Book of Acts, is therefore the record of what Jesus **continued** to do and to teach. It is labeled "The Acts of the Apostles," but as many have commented, it would better be called "The Acts of the Risen Christ," or "The Acts of the Holy Spirit."[1]

Though the current tendency is to contrast "the theology of Matthew," with "the theology of John" and then to find further distinctions with the "theology of Paul," this verse reminds us that Jesus taught not only on earth but also from heaven through his chosen apostles. Though the various authors have their distinctive emphases, it is all "The theology of Jesus." One of the great central truths of Acts is that Jesus is still alive and active through what Paul will call his Body, the Church, and **continued to teach** through his apostles. The result is what we call the New Testament.

The second volume is dedicated, as was the first volume, to one Theophilus. It was quite common in NT times for a writer to dedicate his work to someone much as the King James Bible was dedicated to the king of England. We do not know who Theophilus was. Some have thought Theophilus was an address to any Christian "Dear to God" (the literal meaning of the name). But "Theophilus" was not an uncommon name in those times. In Luke 1:3 he is called *kratiste Theophile* "most excellent Theophilus." The best explanation is that this volume was dedicated to an actual but unknown official of some high rank whose name was Theophilus. *Kratiste* is also used for Governors Felix (Acts 23:26 and 24:3) and Festus (26:25).[1]

1:2 Among the gospels only Luke mentions Jesus' ascension, here and in Luke 24:44-51. The word *commands* refers to Luke 24:47-49 where there are two instructions, *that repentance and remission of sins should be preached in his name among all nations* (the Lukan Great Commission), and the command to *wait*

---

1   Josephus uses the word *"Kratiste"* to dedicate his work *Against Apion* to his patron Epaphroditus.

for the promise of my Father (the baptism of the Holy Spirit). The main themes of Acts are the beginning of the worldwide proclamation of repentance and forgiveness and the provision of enabling power for that stupendous task, the indwelling Holy Spirit.

1:3 Luke continues to give assurance of the truth of these amazing reports of Jesus to Theophilus (Luke 1:3-4), citing the many convincing proofs that the unbelievable resurrection of Jesus was indeed compellingly believable.[2] Jesus appeared some ten times over forty days (the precise time period is mentioned only here) to many of his disciples (I Cor 15:6 mentions five hundred at one time). The tomb was empty and the body gone!

These things happened not "after his crucifixion" or "after his death," but *after his suffering* (hinting at the redemptive value of all of Jesus' suffering). His suffering was a passing phase and though he did actually die, he is now very much alive.

The forty-day period between Resurrection and Ascension is found only here. The other forty-day period mentioned in Jesus' life was the forty days of temptation in the desert. That was a time of testing and proving, and so was the post-resurrection period of forty days; during that time he appeared ten times to prove the reality of his resurrection.

Speaking about the kingdom of God. In verse 6 the disciples ask about the coming of that kingdom. What did that word mean here? Though many books and dissertations have been written on the "kingdom of God", the precise meaning here is not clear. In our thinking, the kingdom of God (or "the kingdom of heaven" in Matthew) in the gospels "came" or "was at hand" (Mark 1:15; Luke 10:9; 11:20) with the presence of the King, Jesus Himself. In the times of the end, predicted extensively by Jesus in the Olivet Discourse (Matt 24-25; Mark 13), it would mean not only **the presence** of Messiah but also **the actual rule** of Messiah. The phrase "kingdom of God" is used thirty-two times in Luke but only eight times in Acts, the beginning of an in-between time when the King is very active but not personally present. The dominant meaning of "kingdom of God" in the book of Acts seems most often to refer to the progress of the gospel and the building of the church.

---

2   Aristotle defined the word for "proofs" (*tekmērion*) as "a compelling sign."

Jesus, after giving his disciples a three-year seminary course of practical work and teaching, now, over a period of forty days, finishes the course with explanations of prophecy that could be fully understood only **after** his crucifixion and resurrection. It was just after His resurrection that He opened their minds to understand the Old Testament prophesies (Luke 24:44-46).

1:4-5 The command to wait in Jerusalem repeats Luke 24:49. The promise of the Spirit was given first in these exact words by John the Baptist (Mark 1:8; Matt 3:11-12; Luke 3:15-17). It is interesting that Acts, like the reference in Mark, omits the mention of "baptizing with fire." The promise of the baptism of the Spirit was fulfilled ten days later on the day of Pentecost. John did not introduce Jesus as a miracle worker and teacher but as one who would baptize with the Holy Spirit.

Lessons for Life

1.   Our faith is founded, not on legends and myths, but on many "compelling signs," the greatest of which were the appearances of Jesus after his resurrection to hundreds of witnesses. God holds men responsible, even after the lapse of 2000 years, to believe those witnesses.
2.   God equips for what he commands. The apostles were commanded to preach the gospel. For this they were equipped by: being chosen (v. 2), given proof of Jesus' claims by many *compelling signs* (v. 3), and promised the power of the Holy Spirit.

Acts 1:6-11

The Final Departure of Jesus

6 So when they had come together, they asked him, "Lord, will you at this time restore the kingdom to Israel?" 7 He said to them, "It is not for you to know times or seasons that the Father has fixed by his own authority. 8 But you will receive power when the Holy Spirit has come upon you, and you will be my witnesses in Jerusalem and in all Judea and Samaria, and to the end of the earth." 9 And when he had said these things, as they were looking on, he was lifted up, and a cloud took him out of their sight. 10 And while they were gazing into heaven as he went, behold, two men stood by them in white robes, 11 and said, "Men of Galilee, why do you stand looking into heaven? This Jesus, who was taken up from you into heaven, will come in the same way as you saw him go into heaven."

1:6 This "foolish" question prompts many commentators and preachers to "beat up" on the dim-witted disciples. "They still don't get it! The kingdom is not national, it is international! It is not physical, it is spiritual! The church has replaced Israel!"[3] This is the currently dominant "replacement theory" which says basically that the Christian Church has permanently replaced the Jewish nation as God's chosen people. This idea goes back to the great Augustine and has been continued since his time in the Catholic Church to this day and in many Protestant denominations, particularly of the Reformed tradition.

At the risk of getting "beat up" ourselves, may we suggest that maybe the disciples' question was not so stupid. The Hebrew Scriptures are filled with numerous prophecies which promised to Israel a land and a Messiah

---

3   These are not John Stott's words, but he discusses this view favorably in *The Message of Acts*, pages 41-44. Bock counters Stott's view: "Jesus's reply does not reject the premise of the question, that the kingdom will one day be restored to Israel." "There is no indication in Jesus's reply, however, that anything they said was wrong except that they were excessively concerned about when all of this would take place." Darrell L. Bock, *Acts*, (Grand Rapids, Baker, 2007), 62.

who would reign over the nations with Jerusalem as the center.[4] The concept of delivering Israel from all her enemies, restoring her to her promised land, and "restoring the fortunes" of Israel occurs again and again in the prophetic books. The ancient Jewish prayer Shemoneh Esrei, repeated in synagogues weekly throughout the world, called upon God "for the restoration of the kingship to Israel and the throne of David."

1:7 Note that Jesus does not rebuke them for their "foolish" question. If their question was misconceived or mistaken, surely this would be the time to correct their mistake perhaps by saying something like he said on other occasions: *Are you still so dull?* (Matt 15:17; Mark 8:17 NIV). He does not deny that the kingdom will be restored to Israel. Indeed, he seems to affirm it by saying that the time of those end-time events is not yet. *It is not for you to know times or seasons that the Father has fixed by his own authority.*

The Greek phrase for "times and seasons" (*chronoi kai kairoi*) is used in the Greek OT in Dan 2:21 and 7:12, and in the NT in 1 Thess 5:1, all referring to the end times. Jesus is not telling his disciples that these things will **not** occur, but that they will occur in the end times. Meanwhile they have a job to do. A big job.

1:8 This verse has rightly been seen by many expositors to be the thematic summary of the entire book of Acts. There is the witness in Jerusalem in chapters 2-7, the witness in Judea and Samaria in chapters 8-12, and the beginning of the witness to the ends of the earth in chapters 13-28.

The *baptism of the Spirit* referred to in v. 5 is here called *the Holy Spirit comes upon you.* Without his power there can be no testimony. The rest of the book of Acts is a demonstration of that power.[5]

---

4   My top ten: Isa 2:2-4 (parallel to Mic 4:1-3; Isa 9:7; 25:6-9; 60:1-5; Jer 33:7-16; Ezek 39:25-29; Joel 3:1; Amos 9:14; Zech 8:3-8; 14:4-19. Christian interpreters since Augustine generally have taken these passages to apply spiritually to the Christian church, but the Jews of Jesus' time, including the disciples, seem to have taken them literally.

5   Preachers who know a little Greek love to point out that the Greek word for "power" here is *dynamis*, "from which we get the word dynamite"! Let's give this one a long vacation. The meaning of a Greek word in the first century is not established by a derivative word in a different language twenty centuries later. The word simply means "power" or "ability." The fact that it is the power of **God** is power enough!

The result of that empowerment will be worldwide witness. Note that the Lord does not say "you must become witnesses" or "you must convert people" but *you **will be** my witnesses*. This is an encouraging certainty—the believer filled with the Spirit **is** a witness; he does not need to strive or struggle to be a witness. There will be hardships and opposition and a need for diligence, but it will happen. He is not responsible for the results of the witness. Not all believe the testimony, as is shown repeatedly in the rest of Acts.

1:9 It was not necessary for Jesus to go up into the sky (in Greek the same word as "heaven") to return to heaven. He could have simply disappeared to enter a different dimension of existence as he had done repeatedly during the forty days since his resurrection.[6] But the ascension, enshrined in the Apostles' Creed, marks the beginning of a new era in which Jesus will no longer appear on earth until he comes again. This is the final farewell. It is the first step in assuming the Throne at the Right Hand, the first step in the exaltation and enthronement. *God has also highly exalted Him* (Phil 2:9). The going up was the beginning of the exaltation.

He does not ascend by himself; he is *lifted up*. This is an instance of the "divine passive." God the Father takes him up. Jesus is the first fruits, not only in resurrection but also in being raptured into heaven as all believers will be taken up (I Thess 4:11-18; 1 Cor 15:50-54).

Luke has already told Theophilus that this happened at Bethany, just over the ridge on the east side of Jerusalem known as the Mount of Olives (Luke 24:50). It is most interesting that Zech 14:4 pinpoints the Mount of Olives as the location of his return.

A cloud took him out of their sight. We must not imagine that Jesus ascended to 30,000 feet before he finally disappeared from their sight as an almost invisible speck. Jesus was not diminished in their sight as he rose. I used to live next to a military exercise ground in Japan that was used only for practice paratroop drops. It was always interesting to watch them drop the paratroopers. The planes were at low altitude, certainly no more than 1000 feet, but even at that altitude a man jumping from a plane appears so tiny it is hard to see him until his parachute opens. We believe that Jesus did not

---

6   C. S. Lewis in his *Chronicles of Narnia* has popularized the attractive concept that the spiritual world is all around us.

disappear into a barely visible speck but that the cloud veiled his disappearance into the heavenly dimension at a much lower altitude.

1:10-11 While the astonished disciples are gazing into the sky where the cloud had received Jesus, two men dressed in white robes suddenly appeared beside them. These are certainly angels, but it is interesting that they are called as they appeared: *men*. We must not imagine that they had wings as is so often depicted by Medieval artists. Men do not have wings. Angels here accent a special event in the life of Jesus. Angels appeared for the big events in his life: his birth, his temptation, his resurrection, his return, and now his ascension. This puts the ascension on the same level of importance as the other events. Why then is there so little preaching or theological reflection on the ascension?

Perhaps there is another reason for the appearance of angels. The return of Jesus is explicitly described in this passage as the reverse of his ascension. At the second coming there will be not just two angels, but myriads of angels (Matt 16:27; 24:31; 25:31; Luke 9:26; 2 Thess 1:7). As a cloud received him up so he will come *in the clouds* (Matt 24:30; 26:64; Mark 13:26; 1 Thess 4:17; Rev 1:7). *This same Jesus* will come back *in the same way* as he departed. He ascended visibly, bodily (not as a spirit or invisible presence); so will he return visibly and bodily.

Lessons for Life

1. There is a time in the *times and seasons* of the end times when the kingdom will literally be *restored to Israel,* a converted and repentant Israel.
2. In any case we have a job to do. As someone has said "The whole task of the whole church for the whole age" until our Savior comes again is being witnesses to him *to the uttermost parts of the earth.*
3. This task, even the little part of it that we may share, cannot be done without the Power, the power of the Holy Spirit.
4. Our doctrine of the return of Christ must hold unswervingly to the limits imposed by Acts 1:11: visibly, bodily, personally.

Acts 1:12-26

Judas' Replacement

Then they returned to Jerusalem from the mount called Olivet, which is near Jerusalem, a Sabbath day's journey away. 13 And when they had entered, they went up to the upper room, where they were staying, Peter and John and James and Andrew, Philip and Thomas, Bartholomew and Matthew, James the son of Alphaeus and Simon the Zealot and Judas the son of James. 14 All these with one accord were devoting themselves to prayer, together with the women and Mary the mother of Jesus, and his brothers.

15 In those days Peter stood up among the brothers (the company of persons was in all about 120) and said, 16 "Brothers, the Scripture had to be fulfilled, which the Holy Spirit spoke beforehand by the mouth of David concerning Judas, who became a guide to those who arrested Jesus. 17 For he was numbered among us and was allotted his share in this ministry." 18 (Now this man acquired a field with the reward of his wickedness, and falling headlong he burst open in the middle and all his bowels gushed out. 19 And it became known to all the inhabitants of Jerusalem, so that the field was called in their own language Akeldama, that is, Field of Blood.) 20 For it is written in the Book of Psalms,

'May his camp become desolate' and 'let there be no one to dwell in it'; and 'Let another take his office.'

21 So one of the men who have accompanied us during all the time that the Lord Jesus went in and out among us, 22 beginning from the baptism of John until the day when he was taken up from us—one of these men must become with us a witness to his resurrection." 23 And they put forward two, Joseph called Barsabbas, who was also called Justus, and Matthias. 24 And they prayed and said, "You, Lord, who know the hearts of all, show which one of these two you have chosen 25 to take the place in this ministry and apostleship from which Judas turned aside to go to his own place." 26 And they cast lots for them, and the lot fell on Matthias, and he was numbered with the eleven apostles.

When I taught 28 chapters of Acts in ten sessions at Tokyo Christian University, I confess I treated this section lightly. Not much seems to be happening here that advances the story. Let's get on with the main events! Why did Luke include it? He is capable of severe abbreviation, as we shall see in the rest of the book of Acts. And if he had to include it, why did he make it so long? The point of this section is the replacement of Judas, but the replacement apostle Matthias is never mentioned again either in this book or in the rest of the NT. Why is it necessary to replace Judas? Why the use of lots to choose an apostle? *All Scripture is profitable* (2 Tim 3:16), and as we try to answer some of these questions, this section becomes more profitable than we first thought.

1:12-14 These verses give us a fascinating glimpse into the embryonic church. Theophilus has evidently never been in Jerusalem (and probably not in Palestine) or he would not need an explanation of the location of the Mount of Olives. *A Sabbath day's journey* was set by the Jews of the time at 2000 cubits (3000 feet or less than a mile). Bethany is just over the crest of the Mount of Olives to the east.

The precise location of *the upper room* is unknown, though present-day tourists to Jerusalem are shown to a large second floor room called Coenaculum near the tomb of David on Mount Zion on the southwest corner of the old city. This building dates from later times but it does give an idea of what such a second-floor room might have looked like. It was big enough to accommodate 120 people.

Next we have a list of the remaining eleven apostles with Peter, James, and John at the head of the list. The others do not appear at all in "the Acts of the Apostles." The reader was supposed to know the apostles well enough to realize that one name is missing—Judas Iscariot.

Among the 120 are *the women* including Mary the mother of Jesus and Jesus' brothers. These are no doubt the same group of women (note the article *the*) Luke mentioned in 8:2-3 of his gospel and included Mary Magdalene and Joanna and Suzanna and many others. *They provided for them out of their own means.* Luke, more than the other gospel writers mentions women and their part in the ministry. Women as well as men were among those who received the Spirit and prophesied in tongues.

The only woman here mentioned by name is Mary the mother of Jesus, who appears here for the last time in the NT. Mary has gone from the agony of watching her son die on the cross to the ecstasy of his resurrection. One wonders if Jesus appeared to his mother after his resurrection to reassure and comfort her. That would have made a wonderful scene for later artists to paint! But Scripture is silent on any such reunion.

Those churches that insist on the eternal virginity of Mary must take the mention of Jesus' *brothers* to mean "cousins" or "adopted siblings." This is a possible meaning of the word *adelphos,* but a bit of a stretch; the plain meaning of the word is that Mary bore other children after Jesus. We are given the names of four of them in Mark 6:3 (Matt 13:55-56) and sisters are also mentioned. Jesus came from a large family! John 7:5 tells us that *even his brothers did not believe in him.* They must have had a change of heart for here they are praying and waiting for the Spirit. Let those who are the only believers in their family take comfort that Jesus himself for a long time also endured a similar situation.

All these with one accord were devoting themselves to prayer. What did they pray? Did they mechanically repeat "Send the Spirit O, Lord!" like a Tibetan prayer wheel? Jesus warned against *vain repetition* in prayer. Pastor James M. Boice (unfortunately now deceased) in his commentary on Acts speculated about the content of their prayers.[7] He refers to the well-known acronym ACTS which stands for Adoration Confession Thanksgiving and Supplication. We agree with him that they probably spent much time studying and memorizing the Scriptures that Jesus had taught them (Luke 24:27 and 45). They must have had times of worship and thanksgiving with joy overflowing their hearts. They must have confessed their cowardice and unbelief at the crisis of the crucifixion. They may have had resentments or offences to confess to one another. There may have been supplication for various needs within the group or for the conversion of unbelieving Jews, especially the Sanhedrin who had voted to condemn Jesus. They may have prayed for their enemies the Romans, beginning with Pontius Pilate. And of course they must have prayed concerning the promise of the Spirit, maybe as David prayed after he had received a great promise from God, *LORD, do as you have said* (2 Sam 7:25).

For those of us who now live in a hurry-up hurry-on world of clocks and

---

7   James Montgomery Boice, *Acts: an Expositional Commentary* (Grand Rapids, Baker, 1997), 34.

schedules, warp-speed computers, mobile phones, and an infinite variety of entertainment, who have trouble spending ten minutes in prayer; spending ten days in prayer must seem like an eternity. But for these who lived at a slower pace, and more important, were electrified with the joy of having seen the risen Lord, time must have stood still. What must we do to unplug the wires, turn off the TV, and recover something of the peace and power that they knew?

1:15-17 There was not only prayer, there was organizational preparation. If God was going to pour out his Spirit, there must be sufficient leadership capacity to handle the harvest. Jesus had spent three years preparing the apostles for this time, but now one was missing. One might ask why it was really necessary to have exactly twelve apostles. Later when the Apostle James was martyred, (Acts 12:1-2) there was no replacement. Most all commentators agree that the number twelve represents the twelve tribes of Israel. Jesus had told his disciples that in the *palingenesia* (regeneration) they *would sit on thrones, judging the twelve tribes of Israel* (Matt 19:28; Luke 22:30). Now one tribe would be without its judge! Not only that, but for the witness to Israel, which is the content of chapters 2 to 7, having twelve apostles would lend credibility and validity to their witness.[8] The Qumran community, who considered themselves the true Israel, appointed twelve leaders. This might explain why, when the main period of testimony to the Jews was finished, that the Apostle James did not need to be replaced.

Peter's explanation was from two passages in Psalms. Notice that for Peter these Scriptures were not just some poems that David wrote but were the speech of the Spirit. David was simply a *mouth*. There is a tendency today in evangelical preaching, in a basically correct zeal to follow grammatical historical interpretation; to constantly mention the human author but neglect the divine author. I once challenged a NT scholar to preach a sermon from one of Paul's epistles without using a certain word. "What word?" "Paul." He looked at me as if I were daft. I recommend that we restore the balance by mentioning the divine author as much as we do the human author.

He (Judas) was numbered among us and was allotted his share in this ministry.

---

8   "The twelve-fold witness was required if early Jewish Christianity was to represent itself to the Jewish nation as the culmination of Israel's hope and the true people of Israel's Messiah." (Longenecker, 265.)

We can cheerfully endure the opposition of outsiders; it is the defection and betrayal of insiders that is unbearable. Ajith Fernando, commenting on this passage, writes:

> Sometimes our biggest anger about betrayal by friends has to do with the humiliation it causes us. All this should give us hope. Several years ago I suffered deep shock and pain when I found out that one of our workers had lied to us and been dishonest with money. Around this time I read John 12: 6 about Judas: 'He was a thief; as keeper of the bag of money he used to help himself to what was put into it.' This ministered to me a most unusual way. When I realized that even the greatest leader, Jesus, faced the same problem, I was comforted--and comfort is one of the greatest antidotes to bitterness.[9]

1:18-19 The ESV puts these verses in parentheses, thus indicating that this is the explanation of Luke for his reader, not the words of Peter, who would not have needed to explain to the believers something they already knew too painfully well. The trouble is that this account of the death of Judas differs quite a bit from that of Matthew (27:3-10). Both agree that there was a "Field of Blood" but in Matthew it is the priests who bought it and in Acts it is Judas who "acquired a field." This could mean that the priests used Judas' money to buy the field, so that it could be said that it was Judas' acquisition. Even more in seeming contradiction, in Matthew Judas *went out and hanged himself*, in this passage Judas *falling headlong he burst open in the middle and all his bowels gushed out*. Literally the Greek says: "He then acquired a field from the reward of his unrighteousness and **becoming prone** (*prenes* genomenos), cracked open in the middle and all his entrails were poured out." We are attracted to the opinion of F. H. Chase that the phrase *prēnes genomenos* does not mean "fall prostrate" or "fall headlong," but "became swollen."[10] This replaces a weak and incomprehensible expression with an understandable rendering and explains why he burst open. Bodies do not usually burst open even if they fall

---

9   Ajith Fernando. *The NIV Application Commentary, Acts* (Grand Rapids, Zondervan, 1998), 83.

10   F. H. Chase. "On PRHNHS GENOMENOS in ACTS 1:18," Journal of theological Studies (1912), 278-85. Modern English translations do not follow Chase's suggestion (with the exception of the RSV margin and J. B. Phillips) but the Liddell-Scott classical Greek lexicon says the translation "became swollen" is possible.

off a cliff and especially not if they just stumble and collapse. Notice that it does not say he died in the field he had purchased nor is there a word for "fall" in the Greek text. "The middle" (*mesos*) then would be the middle of his body, not the middle of the field.

We suggest what we think is not an unreasonable harmonization: Judas, as Matthew says tersely, *went out and hanged himself.* It could have been on a tree in the *Field of Blood,* but the text does not say that explicitly. Nobody cut him down (because of the Jewish abhorrence of the defilement of a dead body, especially a suicide) and the body putrefied and swelled, and after several days, burst open and all his entrails spilled out.

Everyone in Jerusalem heard about this. How fast sensational gruesome news spreads in a relatively small city! How one dies, in many cultures, is a sign of the favor/disfavor of the gods. Such a disgusting and horrible death was seen as the fitting end of the betrayer of the Son of God and thereby a testimony to the innocence of Jesus, a verification of his claims, and a warning to all the inhabitants of Jerusalem. The warning remained for a generation or so because the Potters' Field was renamed *Akeldama,* "Blood Field." The traditional site is on the south side of the ancient city where the Kidron and Tyropoeon Valleys meet.

1:20-21 Peter's speech continues after the parenthetical explanation of 1:18-19. He first quotes two psalms. The first, Psalm 69:25, concerns Judas' defection, and the second, Psalm 109:8, concerns the fact that another must fill the vacancy created by the defection. To pious Jews of the time any argument or major decision had to be buttressed by quotation of Scripture.

Modern expositors may raise their eyebrows at Peter's exegetical method in quoting these psalms. On the face of it they have nothing to do with Judas who is of course not named. Both psalms 69 and 109 are psalms of complaints to God of a man who is being reviled by enemies who is crying for justice. But the early church used these psalms as part of the *Testimonia,* collections of OT portions that predicted the sufferings and glory of Messiah for use in evangelism. We suspect that Jesus himself taught the apostles these passages when he *opened their minds that they might understand the Scriptures* (Luke 24:45). Psalm 69 is quoted five times in the NT (besides this passage, 69:4 in John 15:25, and 69:9 in John 2:17 and Rom 15:3, 69:22-23 in Rom 11:9-10) and as such Psalm 69 was cited as a prediction of the sufferings of the Christ.

The verse Peter quotes (69:25) is in a section of the psalm (verses 22-28) which is a prayer for the punishment of his tormentors: *May their camp be a desolation; let no one dwell in their tents.*

Likewise, Psalm 109 is a complaint to God against those who *in return for my love accuse me, even as I make prayer for them* (RSV). Verses 6-15 are a prayer for a curse on the accuser. The portion Peter quotes is the latter half of 109:8: *may another take his office!*

1:21-22 Peter outlines here the qualifications for being a member of the twelve apostles:
1) a male (*andros*), 2) one who had accompanied Jesus during his whole earthly ministry, 3) a witness of the resurrected Jesus, and 4) one chosen by the Lord himself (v. 24). There was a much larger group than the twelve disciples that accompanied Jesus regularly. Luke in Chapter 10 of the gospel mentions seventy who were sent out.

Why didn't Jesus take care of this problem by designating a replacement before he went home? We do not know. Perhaps he wanted the apostles to make a major decision without his presence.

1:23-26 The process of selection was to pick two eligible men and cast lots. It is not clear why they did not pick more than two. There may not have been more than two who met the first three qualifications. The *they* in *they put forward two* was most likely the eleven apostles, which presumes a meeting to decide the candidates. *They* could also mean the entire body by some kind of consensus decision. We know nothing about the two candidates Joseph Barsabbas ("son of Sabbath") or Matthias.

They prayed and asked the Lord (the Risen Jesus) who is *heart-knower of all*[11] to indicate his choice by lot to take the place of Judas *who went to his own place,* no doubt a euphemism for Hades. It is a hard truth, but Hades was where he belonged.

Precisely what the *lots* looked like or how it was done we do not know. The lots may have been pebbles of different color or marking. The *casting of lots* was used quite commonly in the OT (141 times!) to determine the will of God for division of land (Joshua 14-17), the choice of the scapegoat (Lev 16:8-10), and more like Acts 1:26, for assignment to serve God in the temple (1 Chron 24:7f.). The Hebrews believed that there is no such thing as blind

---

11   Greek *kardiognosta pantōn.*

chance; *the lot is cast into the lap, but its every decision is from the LORD* (Prov 16:33). Thus the replacement apostle was chosen by God himself.

We understand the providence of God as his control of all things without using direct intervention. Miracle is a direct act of God which displaces natural law. I make a distinction between God's providence and his miracles. The providence of God, which we understand as his control of all things without using direct intervention; miracle is a direct act of God which overcomes natural law.[12] This is a fruitful subject for meditation and marvel. In my opinion providence is more remarkable than miracle, for in miracle God can control the situation directly, whereas in providence he is "confined" to using trillions of inanimate agents each moving by the dictates of natural law, and the unpredictable actions of animate beings such as donkeys and human beings who may even be trying deliberately to thwart his purposes. Did God pull invisible strings to cause Matthias to get the lot? We do not think so. Somehow the lot, manipulated only by human hands, fell to the one the Lord Jesus had chosen.

Should we choose our church leaders this way today? The Amish, a German sect who preserve the pre-modern life of the times of their ancestors in seventeenth century Germany,[13] on the basis of this passage, choose their pastors by lot. When the pastor must be replaced, a number of eligible men are selected, lined up and required to choose a Bible from the table. One Bible has a slip of paper in it and the man who draws it is the next pastor. If we would challenge this procedure, they would point to this passage and retort "Here it is in the Bible!"

This introduces a problem we will encounter often in the book of Acts and that is "to what degree should we copy or reproduce the procedures of the Book of Acts in our own churches today?" Should we speak in tongues? Should we practice communal living and sharing of possessions? Should we be able to heal? If we are spiritual enough, should we be able to raise the dead? Should we choose our pastors by lot? Can we discern a pattern of church government in Acts that we should follow? We will try to address such problems as they arise. As a general rule we must remember that the Book of Acts describes the

---

12   I cannot find this distinction made in any writings on providence. John Piper in his magisterial 750-page tome titled "Providence" (Crossway, 2020), does not mention miracle as a part of his understanding of providence, but the governing of "all creatures, actions, and things" he cites from the Westminster Confession (page 34) must include direct acts of God such as miracles.

13   The Amish, on religious grounds, forbid the use of electricity, outside water supply, and automobiles. They use horse and buggy and their clothing styles are strictly prescribed.

church in a period of transition. The transition from Judaism to Christianity, from the OT people of God in the land of Palestine to the worldwide church, from the age of the Mosaic Law to the age of the Law of Christ. Therefore, we must be cautious about making a transitional book of **description** (of how they did it then) into a book of **prescription** (how we must do it now). We may wisely choose to follow their example in many points, but we must ourselves be led of the Spirit as to how to apply this book.

In the case of casting lots to select church leaders, we find that it never happens again in the record of Acts, and it was not normative in the early church of the post-apostolic period or in any period of church history. Why? We believe that Acts 1 is still in the Old Testament era. The Spirit had not yet been given. After this chapter, when leaders are selected, the Spirit will guide.[14] One thinks immediately of Acts 13:2: . . . *the Holy Spirit said, 'Set apart for me Barnabas and Saul for the work to which I have called them.* The Holy Spirit's guidance has replaced the OT casting of lots.

John Stott aptly comments on the end of Acts 1: "Though the place left vacant by Judas had been filled by Matthias, the place left vacant by Jesus has not yet been filled by the Spirit."[15] That comes in chapter 2.

Lessons for Life

1. Prayer and confession have always been the conditions for revival.
2. If God sends revival or a large ingathering, will we have a leadership structure adequate to handle the harvest?
3. It is a fearful thing to betray Christ.
4. The apostles made decisions based on the Scriptures. We should not be intimidated by those who accuse us of "proof-texting."
5. The providence of God is a marvelous thing, more remarkable than miracle.

---

14   This explanation is at least as old as Chrysostom (fourth century) and is followed today by John Stott.

15   Stott, 59.

ACTS 2

THE DAY OF PENTECOST

Acts 2:1-13

The Coming of the Holy Spirit

1 When the day of Pentecost arrived, they were all together in one place. 2 And suddenly there came from heaven a sound like a mighty rushing wind, and it filled the entire house where they were sitting. 3 And divided tongues as of fire appeared to them and rested on each one of them. 4 And they were all filled with the Holy Spirit and began to speak in other tongues as the Spirit gave them utterance.

5 Now there were dwelling in Jerusalem Jews, devout men from every nation under heaven. 6 And at this sound the multitude came together, and they were bewildered, because each one was hearing them speak in his own language. 7 And they were amazed and astonished, saying, "Are not all these who are speaking Galileans? 8 And how is it that we hear, each of us in his own native language? 9 Parthians and Medes and Elamites and residents of Mesopotamia, Judea and Cappadocia, Pontus and Asia, 10 Phrygia and Pamphylia, Egypt and the parts of Libya belonging to Cyrene, and visitors from Rome, 11 both Jews and proselytes, Cretans and Arabians—we hear them telling in our own tongues the mighty works of God." 12 And all were amazed and perplexed, saying to one another, "What does this mean?" 13 But others mocking said, "They are filled with new wine."

2:1 The Day of Pentecost fell on the fiftieth day (seven weeks plus one day) after the Passover. The rites of Pentecost, known as the Feast of Weeks in the Old Testament, are set out in Lev. 23:15-21; Num 28:26-31; and Deut 16:9-12. Two loaves of bread baked from the grain of the spring wheat harvest were waved before Yahweh as a symbol of thanksgiving, and the stipulated sacrifices were to be offered. In later times the Book of Ruth was also read. Pentecost was one of the three annual feasts when every male Jew had to *appear before the Lord* at the temple in Jerusalem (Deut 16:16-17), and it was second in importance only to the feasts of Passover and Tabernacles. The Jews of Jesus' time regarded Pentecost as the anniversary of the giving of the Law on Sinai (Bruce, 114). For the first believers in Christ, it marked the inauguration of the new covenant, *the Law written in their hearts* (Jer 31:31f.)

It is usually assumed that the band of 120-some believers gathered in *the upper room* (1:13) but this is not necessarily the case. As a matter of fact, fitting 120 people into the Upper Room might have been a bit tight. They may have been in a courtyard of a large residence with ready access to the outside.

2:2 Notice it was not a wind that filled the house but the **sound** of a wind. Without the wind itself this must have been a mysterious and unnerving experience. The word *biaias* describing the wind is used in the Greek OT several times. In Exod 14:21 it is *a strong east wind* which divided the waters of the Red Sea. In Psa. 47:8 LXX (MT 48:7), it is the east wind that *shatters the ships of Tarshish.* The Spirit came, not with the soothing sound of a gentle breeze, but with the roar of a powerful storm.

2:3 First there was an awesome sound and now an awesome sight. It was not fire but something **like** fire which they saw dividing itself and resting upon each of them. Since the Holy Spirit is invisible, he must use these appearances to the senses of sight and sound to make his presence unmistakably clear. He came not just upon the apostles, but also upon every believer; male and female, older and younger, lesser and greater. This had never happened in the Old Testament dispensation.

2:4 The Greek word for *filled* has now occurred two times in four verses. This filling was the same as the *baptism of the Spirit and fire* promised by John the Baptist (Matt 3:11; Luke 3:16; John 1:33) and the Lord Jesus himself just before his ascension (Acts 1:5). It is also called a *baptism* in Acts 11:15, 16. To be filled with the Spirit or to be baptized in the Spirit is to be taken over and controlled by the Spirit. That was manifested by the speaking in tongues. Spirit filling in Acts always results in speaking for God.

The *tongues*, whatever they are in 1 Corinthians 12-14, are here clearly **known languages**, as the following context makes indisputably clear. The word for *languages* in verse 6 and 8 is *dialektoi*. Our English word "dialect" means a regional version of a language, but in those days it simply meant "language." It was not a miracle of hearing, as some suppose, for the text says that they *began to speak* with other tongues.

Whether they knew what they were saying is not clear. The content, as we learn in v. 11, was *the wonderful works of God*. The gift of tongues on this occasion was also a kind of prophetic gift. First the word *prophesy* occurs in the Joel passage cited to explain this incident (v. 17). Second the word translated *utterance (apophthegesthai)* is not just "to utter" but to "utter in an oracle."[1] Here this oracular proclamation was given by the Spirit.

The twentieth century church has been much divided over the issue of "speaking in tongues." The Pentecostal churches and later charismatic groups have found in this passage their inspiration and chief doctrinal distinctive. Many seek to duplicate this marvelous experience in our day. But whatever manifestations of the Spirit occur in later ages, we must be aware that the events of this unique day of Pentecost cannot be **completely** duplicated. Where is the *sound of a mighty rushing wind* and the *tongues of fire* in modern meetings? Just as Calvary happened only once, so Pentecost happened only once.

2:5 It might be supposed that these Jews from the diaspora were temporarily in Jerusalem for the feast of Pentecost, but the Greek word *dwelling* makes clear that these were permanent resident foreigners, not visitors. They were *devout* men. One of Luke's themes is that the devout are rewarded by experiencing the fulfillment of prophecy and are entrusted with critical tasks.[2] Here they are important witnesses to the phenomena of the coming of the Spirit.

---

1   It is used of prophecy in I Chron 25:1 and of soothsaying in Mic 5:12 and Ezek 13:9. However in Acts 26:25 it simply means "proclaim." We meet the same word in Acts 2:14.

2   The word for *devout* is *eulabēs*. It is used only by Luke in the NT. He uses it for Simeon (Luke 2:25), the youths who buried Stephen (Acts 8:12), and Ananias (Acts 22:12).

2:6-8 Luke does not make clear where this crowd comes from. Or how the band of believers has moved to where a crowd can hear them. Nor whether they spoke all at once or whether they took turns. Speaking all at once in a confined area would have produced an incomprehensible din, so it is more likely that they either took turns or scattered, perhaps in the temple area. One recognizes one's native language instantly, even in the midst of the babble of another language. I have heard American English, my native language, clearly from the far end of a crowded train car in Japan.

It is characteristic of Luke to emphasize the amazement of the crowd. Here he outdoes himself by using three verbs for surprise. The first, *sugcheō*, denotes not only surprise but fear or consternation.[3] The second, *existēmi*, is literally to "be outside oneself," "to be greatly astonished, to be astounded." The third is the ordinary word for "marvel" used so often in the gospels. The first two verbs in the aorist denote their initial reaction and the third, *ethaumazon*, in the imperfect tense, shows their continuing astonishment.

2:9-11 Further stress is put on the point of the different languages being spoken, by listing them in detail. The list starts with nationalities, switches to nations, and then reverts to nationalities. Not every country is mentioned (Greece for example) but this is an almost complete list of the countries of the Jewish diaspora. Each area had its own regional language, most of which would be unintelligible to those not raised in that area. In the middle of the list are the words *Jews and proselytes*. This shows that some of these witnesses were Jews by birth and some by conversion. It may be that these words describe only the Roman contingent and would appear in modern versions in parentheses. Then the list reverts to nationalities, *Cretans and Arabians*.

The most important function of this detailed list of regions in the purpose of the book of Acts is **to underline the theme of worldwide mission** *to the uttermost parts of the earth.* The main purpose of the coming of the Spirit, the birth of the Body, and the gift of tongues, is worldwide witness to the crucified and risen Christ. Though Israel had been a witness to surrounding nations in the Old Testament dispensation, they were never given an explicit "great commission." But now the era of worldwide witness has dawned at Pentecost

---

3   "To cause such astonishment as to bewilder and dismay," "to cause consternation, to confound" (Acts 9:22, 21:27). Louw and Nida, *Greek-English Lexicon of the New Testament Based on Semantic Domains* (New York: The United Bible Societies, 1989).

and is still expanding in our day.[4] Further, this account suggests something of the initial method of mission: the gospel train will initially run on a network of rails already laid out by the Jewish diaspora. The first thing Paul did in every new town was to visit the Jewish community.

The content of the messages in tongues was *the mighty works of God.* This probably was a recitation of the marvelous events of the life, death, and resurrection of Jesus of Nazareth. It is important in the context of the modern tongues controversy to note that at least here in Acts 1 the tongues were not meaningless utterances but had a clear content.

2:12-13 Luke ends this paragraph by again stressing the astonishment of the crowd.[5] He introduces the question that was the occasion for Peter's speech, *What does this mean?* He also indicates that not all in the crowd were impressed. Some mocked and said these people were drunk, on grape juice![6]

Where did the mockers come from? Were they from among the pious expatriates, or were there others who had gathered? No matter how overwhelming the testimony of the acts of God, there will always be an unbelieving element that mocks that testimony. *And some doubted* (Matt 28:17). Throughout the book of Acts there will be the same pattern of proclamation, glad reception on the part of some, and rejection on the part of others.

Lessons for Life

1. The coming of the Spirit marks the inauguration of a new age: the birth and growth of the church of Christ. Pentecost was the birthday of the Body.
2. The chief task of that church in this age is worldwide witness in every language known to man. Only the power of the Spirit enables the fulfillment of that task.

---

4   Hans Boer expounded this theme at book length in *Pentecost and Missions* (London: Lutterworth, 1961).

5   Yet a fourth word for surprise is used, *diaporeō,* "be perplexed." Luke also uses it in Luke 9:7; Acts 5:24; and 10:17.

6   On *gleukos* (grape juice!) This is a joke. The jokers knew the tongues-speakers were not really drunk; they just wanted to "put them down."

3. Tongues in Acts 2 were the miraculous ability to speak real human languages with real content, "the wonderful works of God."

4. Even if some claim to reproduce the tongues-speaking of the Day of Pentecost, the other phenomena of that day occurred only once.

5. No matter how powerful the evidence of God at work, some will only mock.

⤮

Acts 2:14-36

Peter's Speech

2:14-21 The Spirit's Coming was Predicted by Joel

Peter's first point in answering the question 'What does this mean?' is that the phenomena are a fulfillment of the prophecy of Joel 2:28-32. He quotes the passage in full without exposition. Throughout this apologetic discourse, the appeal to Scripture in general and the appeal to prophecy in particular are very instructive, both as to the apostolic homiletic and apologetic methodology with Jewish audiences and as to how we might preach the gospel in our day. It was not enough that miracles had occurred. They were only authentic if they could be interpreted in the light of the prophetic Word.

14 But Peter, standing with the eleven, lifted up his voice and addressed them: "Men of Judea and all who dwell in Jerusalem, let this be known to you, and give ear to my words. 15 For these people are not drunk, as you suppose, since it is only the third hour of the day. 16 But this is what was uttered through the prophet Joel:

17 "And in the last days it shall be, God declares, that I will pour out my Spirit on all flesh, and your sons and your daughters shall prophesy, and your young men shall see visions, and your old men shall dream dreams; 18 even on my male servants and female servants in those days I will pour out my Spirit, and they shall prophesy. 19 And I will show wonders in the heavens above and signs on the earth below, blood, and fire, and vapor of smoke; 20 the sun shall be turned to darkness and the moon to blood, before the day of the Lord comes, the great and magnificent day. 21 And it shall come to pass that everyone who calls upon the name of the Lord shall be saved.'

2:14-21 *This is what* is a *pesher* style introduction of an interpretation typical of the Dead Sea Scrolls (Longenecker, 275).[7] Peter, by using this quotation, makes three points: 1) The Pentecost phenomena are a result of the outpouring of the Spirit. 2) The last days of God's redemptive program have begun. 3) The validation of all this is the sign of prophecy.

Instead of Joel's *afterwards* (ESV) Peter substitutes *in the last days.* This is his Spirit inspired interpretation of the vague *afterwards* of Joel. This precise phrase *in the last days* is found in Isa 2:2 (and the parallel passage Mic 4:1) where it introduces the worldwide peace of verse 4. *He will judge between the nations . . . they will beat their swords into plowshares and their spears into pruning hooks . . .* Peter announces the arrival of the last days and seems to expect the soon fulfillment of Joel's prediction of the cosmic signs of judgment (blood, fire, smoke) and maybe the worldwide peace predicted by Isaiah and Micah. "Peter regards Joel's prophecy as applying to the last days, and claims that his hearers are now living in the last days" (Marshall, 73).

Why does Peter continue his quotation of Joel past *I will pour out my Spirit, and they shall prophesy? Signs on the earth beneath* might be the wind, fire, and tongues of the Day of Pentecost. But why include seemingly "irrelevant" elements about the wonders in heaven of *blood and fire and smoke* and the darkening of the sun and the moon turning to blood? Some have thought Peter just wanted to get to verse 21 *all who call upon the name of the Lord shall be saved,* and that the material in between is irrelevant. Others have seen a fulfillment in the darkness (producing a blood red moon) at the time of crucifixion (Bruce, 121). Perhaps Peter saw *the Day of the Lord,* that day of

---

7   *Pesher* is an Aramaic word meaning "solution." It was an interpretation, supposedly inspired by God, to explain a difficult text, and was introduced by the words "this is that." It was used by the Qumran community to appropriate certain OT texts to their specific situation. See R. N. Longenecker's *Biblical Exegesis in the Apostolic Period* (Grand Rapids: Eerdmans, 1975), 39-45.

judgment mentioned again and again in OT prophecy, as imminent.[8] "Peter might not have known what to make of the more physical and spectacular elements of Joel's prophecy, though he probably expected them in some way to follow in the very near future" (Longenecker, 276).

With verse 21 Peter concludes his citation of Joel because he wants to expound on the promise *whosoever shall call upon the name of the Lord shall be saved.* What must I do to be saved? "Call upon the name of the Lord"! Whereas in Joel *the name of the Lord* refers to the name of Yahweh, in Peter's usage it will refer to the name of Jesus, a subtle point of evidence for the deity of Christ.[9]

2:22-32 The Resurrection of Jesus was Predicted by David

22 "Men of Israel, hear these words: Jesus of Nazareth, a man attested to you by God with mighty works and wonders and signs that God did through him in your midst, as you yourselves know— 23 this Jesus, delivered up according to the definite plan and foreknowledge of God, you crucified and killed by the hands of lawless men. 24 God raised him up, loosing the pangs of death, because it was not possible for him to be held by it. 25 For David says concerning him,

"'I saw the Lord always before me,
for he is at my right hand that I may not be shaken;
26 therefore my heart was glad, and my tongue rejoiced;
my flesh also will dwell in hope.
27 For you will not abandon my soul to Hades,
or let your Holy One see corruption.
28 You have made known to me the paths of life;
you will make me full of gladness with your presence.'

29"Brothers, I may say to you with confidence about the patriarch David that he both died and was buried, and his tomb is with us to this day. 30 Being therefore a prophet, and knowing that God had sworn with an oath to him that he would set one of his descendants on his throne, 31 he foresaw and spoke about the resurrection of the Christ, that he was not abandoned to Hades, nor did his flesh see corruption. 32 This Jesus God raised up, and of that we all are witnesses.

---

8   In Isa 9:5 similar words portray the sacking of a conquered city. They are thus dire signs of disaster and catastrophe (Rev 6:12).

9   Compare Phil 2:10, 11 quoting Isa 45:23.

Peter now moves from an explanation of the immediate phenomena of the Spirit's coming to what lies behind them, the resurrection and exaltation of Jesus of Nazareth, the Messiah of Israel. Again, the proof from prophecy is necessary. This time he cites David from Psalm 16.

2:22 "Gentlemen Israelites, listen to these words" (literal translation) is both a rhetorical device to capture their attention and a marker of a new theme in the speech. Then the subject *Jesus of Nazareth* is introduced; not just "Jesus," because "Jesus" was a very common name among the Jews. They pronounced it "Yeshua." In Greek it was "Iēsous."

There were no surnames or family names among the Jews in Bible times. The individual was specified either by naming his hometown, as here, or his father, as in "James, son of Alphaeus."

With miracles and wonders and signs denotes the means of the attestation of Jesus. These three words, essentially the same in meaning, seem to be piled on for effect. The miracles of Jesus in the gospels are too numerous to be recounted. The second word *wonders* is often used for portents in the heavens. Perhaps Peter has in mind the star of Bethlehem or the darkness of the sun at the crucifixion or the earthquake. The word *sign* draws attention to the significance of the miracle, the attestation of Messiah.

With the words *in your midst as you yourselves know* Peter appeals to the fact most in his audience had seen the miracles of Jesus. Everybody knew about them. No one present at the time could possibly dispute that many miracles had occurred. Denial of the historicity of the miracles of Jesus did not happen until the eigtheenth century.

2:23 *This one, by the predetermined plan and foreknowledge of God given over, through the hands of lawless men, by crucifying you killed* (literal translation). With this thunderbolt Peter plunges boldly into the heart of the matter. He must bring conviction and repentance of their terrible sin of killing their own Messiah, or the gift of the Spirit will profit them nothing. The first and last words in the Greek text are emphatic by position: ***this one . . . you killed***. Peter is not afraid to accuse them to their face. "Even though you saw his many miracles, you murdered him with such an unspeakable death."[10] There is in the cause of the crucifixion of Jesus an exquisite balancing of the sovereignty of God (it was his plan), and the responsibility of man. Who killed Jesus? God

---

10   *Prospeixantes (prospeignumi)* "put on a stake" is more stark than the usual word "crucify."

planned it but wicked men executed him. The phrase *lawless men* refers to Pilate and his executioners, which is ironic because the responsibility of the Roman authorities was first to maintain "law and order." But Peter leaves no doubt about who was primarily responsible: the Jewish authorities.

2:24 The word "God" is in the emphatic position in the Greek text. The contrast "whom **you** killed **God** raised" is sharp. Compare Acts 3:13. 14. The phrase *loosing the pangs of death* could be temporal: "**after** releasing from the pangs of death," or instrumental, "**by** releasing from the pangs of death." The *pangs* ("pains" in more modern English) seem to refer to the sufferings of death on a cross. The *loosing* was supernatural: Jesus dismissed his spirit at the sixth hour. Ordinarily the death of the cross took two or three days.

Because it was not possible for him to be held by it. "The abyss can no more hold the Redeemer than a pregnant woman can hold the child in her body" (G. Bertram, TDNT 9, 673). The word "pangs" is regularly used for "birth pangs."

2:25-31 Peter now cites the last four verses of Psalm 16 as prophetic testimony to the resurrection of Jesus. Psalm 16 was a very important proof text for the apostolic church (Compare Paul's similar use of this passage in the sample sermon before a Jewish audience in Acts 13:34-37.) Peter's argument is that this psalm, though written by David in the first person singular, cannot refer to David, but must refer to Jesus of Nazareth. His line of reasoning is as follows: a) the psalm speaks of "not seeing corruption," b) David died and was buried and his body decomposed, c) therefore David was speaking of someone else, d) the "someone else" was the Messiah whom God had promised would be a descendant of David. e) Jesus **did** rise from the dead--we are witnesses. f) Therefore, Jesus of Nazareth is the promised Messiah.

Hades in both Old (Hebrew *Sheol*) and New Testaments and among the pagan Greeks, was the underground (Matt 12:40) abode of the dead.[11] In Jesus' story of Lazarus and the rich man (Luke 16:20-31), though all souls were in Hades, torment was reserved for the wicked, and the righteous were

---

11   *Hades,* the abode of the dead, must be distinguished from *Gehenna,* the final abode of the wicked. See J. Jeremias' article "Hades" in TDNT vol 1, 146-149 for the concept of Hades in the Bible.

in *Abraham's bosom,* which Jesus called *paradise* in his promise to the repentant thief (Luke 23:23).

David's Tomb (2:29) was located on the slope of Ophel near the pool of Siloam (Bruce, 126). Herod had built a monument of white marble at its entrance. It must have been one of the landmarks of Jerusalem, well known to every inhabitant and pilgrim.

2:32-35 *This Jesus* (again in emphatic position) *God raised up* resumes the claim of v. 24 and summarizes the main point of the long quotation from Psalm 16. *Of which (fact) we all are witnesses.* The *we all* certainly includes the Twelve as official witnesses of the resurrection (1:22), but also in this context includes all of the 120 followers of Jesus present on this occasion (cf. I Cor 15:6). One would think Peter would spend more time on this point and less on the proof from scripture. It could be that Luke has condensed his speech at this point since he had already given the details of the eye-witness testimony to the resurrection of Jesus in his gospel.

2:33-35 David also Predicted Messiah's Exaltation

2:33-35 Verse 33 gives the preliminary conclusion. This is the final explanation of the phenomena of Pentecost. Jesus has been exalted to the Right Hand of God the Father and has poured out the Holy Spirit. All three members of the Trinity have their parts: Jesus, risen to the right hand, has received the promised Holy Spirit from the Father and has poured out these things you are experiencing. The outpouring of the Holy Spirit proves that Jesus has not only been resurrected but given the seat of all authority at the Right Hand.

But more proof is necessary. Peter has proved the resurrection from scripture but what about the exaltation? That is found in one of the OT texts most used by the apostolic church, Psalm 110. It is quoted six times in the NT[12] and there are numerous other allusions to the concept of Jesus' session *at the right hand.* Peter again makes the point that David could not have been speaking of himself in Psalm 110.

---

12   Psalm 110:1 is quoted in Matt 22:44 (parallels Mark 12:36 and Luke 20:42) and Heb 1:13. Psalm 110:4 is quoted in Heb 5:6.

To the Jews of that day Psa 110:1 was a riddle. Some applied it to the Hasmonean rulers but some, like Rabbi Akiba, applied it to Messiah.[13] Later rabbis also interpreted it as Messiah. The early church may have used this psalm so much because Jesus himself quoted it in posing the riddle to the Pharisees at one of the most critical times in his life (Matt 22:44 and parallels). How can David call his descendant "Lord"? How can there be two "lords"? If David's descendant is a human being, how can he be exalted to the right hand, the position of supreme authority next to Yahweh? No doubt some in Peter's audience had heard Jesus stump the Pharisees with this riddle.

But now the meaning is clear. David was not speaking of himself but of his descendant the Messiah. He has already established that this one will sit on his throne. Now that throne is seen to be *the right hand*. The ascension (Acts 1:9-11) and exaltation of Jesus (Acts 2:33-35) are just as important doctrines as the doctrine of his resurrection.

2:36 The Conclusion and Main Point of the Sermon

Let all the house of Israel therefore know for certain that God has made him both Lord and Christ, this Jesus whom you crucified. This is the central point of the whole sermon in a nutshell. It must have fallen upon these people like a bolt of lightning. Peter says nothing more but lets the enormity of the charge sink into the hearts of his stunned hearers. Jesus is *Lord* according to Psalm 110 and *Christ* according to Psalm 16, the son of David who would rise from the dead.

The chief Jewish objection to the messianic claim of Jesus of Nazareth was (and still is) "How can Messiah suffer such a shameful death. If he really is the Messiah, why did he not save himself?" (Luke 23:35). The answer is "Yes you crucified him (and even that was in the plan of God) but God raised and exalted him."

As yet, there is no explicit teaching about the eternal deity of Jesus or a complete explanation of his death as an atonement for sin. For the house of Israel it is now enough to know that this Jesus is Messiah and Lord. The time when God *made* him Lord is not the time of his resurrection and ascension. He

---

13   See D. M. Hay *Glory at the Right Hand* (Nashville: Abingdon, 1973), 26.

always was both Lord and Messiah. But now the resurrection and ascension, as prophesied by scripture, constitute a certain proof of both his lordship and messiahship.

Lessons for Life

1. "Signs and wonders" are not enough. They must be backed up by the testimony of the Word of God.
2. The Old Testament predicted that Messiah would be LORD, God Himself. This is proved by Psalms 16 and 110.
3. Both the resurrection of Christ and the exaltation of Christ to the right hand are vital elements in the gospel proclamation.
4. The Jewish leaders of those days were responsible for killing their own Messiah. But in the providence of God, his death, resurrection and exaltation provided salvation for the whole world.

ↄↁↄ

Acts 2:37-41

The Call to Repentance and the Baptism of 3000

What were the results of Peter's sermon? Would they stone him, ignore him, or receive his message? The powerful witness of the Spirit alone is not enough to convert. There must be the response of the heart.

37 Now when they heard this they were cut to the heart, and said to Peter and the rest of the apostles, "Brothers, what shall we do?" 38 And Peter said to them, "Repent and be baptized every one of you in the name of Jesus Christ for the forgiveness of your sins, and you will receive the gift of the Holy Spirit. 39 For the promise is for you and for your children and for all who are far off, everyone whom the Lord our God calls to himself." 40 And with many other words he bore witness and continued to exhort them, saying, "Save yourselves from this crooked generation." 41 So those who received his word were baptized, and there were added that day about three thousand souls.

Peter did not give an "invitation." But he did not have to wait long for them to respond. The key phrase in the sentence is *cut to the heart (katenugēsan, stabbed).*[14]

2:38 What is repentance? Some, seeking to avoid an exclusive emphasis on the emotional aspect of repentance, claim that the Greek word for repent *metanoeo* simply means to "change one's mind." But the meaning of a word must be determined by its usage, not by its etymology. True, there is the cognitive element; one must realize that one has sinned. But there is also an emotional element of feeling regret or remorse for one's sin, not just for the damage it causes oneself, but also the damage it is causing to others and to God. This is expressed by one of the Hebrew words for repentance *nacham.* The external manifestations of this sorrow will vary according to the individual's situation and temperament. But without the third element, the volitional element, a change of behavior, what John the Baptist called the *fruits of repentance* (Luke 3:8 with examples given 3:10-14), there is no true repentance. This volitional element is well expressed by the frequent use of the Hebrew word *shuv* "turn" for repentance. That is a turning, or a returning to God, a constant theme of the OT prophets.

In this context the repentance demanded had a very specific object: "repent of crucifying the One whom God made Lord and Messiah." It is unlikely that the apostles had each candidate for baptism here confess a long catalog of sins. Nevertheless, the result of repentance is not just forgiveness of this one enormous sin, but the forgiveness of sins (plural).

The convicted Jews want to know what they must do to show their repentance. The answer is *be baptized.* They were familiar with the baptism of converts to Judaism, and no doubt many of them knew or had even received

---

14   The Septuagint use of the word is very instructive. It is the sting of remorse (Sirach 12:12; 14:1; 20;21. It denotes conviction of sin. Ahab was convicted at the word of Elijah accusing him of stealing Naboth's vineyard (1 Kings 20:27 LXX, 21:27 MT). Isaiah was convicted of sin when the Lord appeared to him (Isa 6:5). The word is also translated "be silent" with the connotation "shocked into silence." When Aaron witnessed the judgment of the Lord on his sons Nadab and Abihu, he was shocked into silence (Lev 10:3 NIV).

the baptism of John, but this baptism is a new baptism *in the name of Jesus Messiah for the forgiveness of your sins.* To be baptized *in the name of Jesus Messiah* is to confess by the act of baptism one's faith in and allegiance to Jesus the true Messiah.

The promised result is that they will receive the gift of the Holy Spirit. Why does Peter not say, "and you will be born again" or "and you will be saved"? The focus of attention on this day was the work of the Holy Spirit, so the focus was not on regeneration, but on receiving the Spirit. Both concepts are linked in Ezekiel 36:26-27. Though "receiving the gift of the Spirit" is seldom mentioned in modern gospel presentations, it was an important part of evangelistic appeals in the apostolic church.[15]

Many quote verse 38 to prove that baptism is essential for salvation. But how can one claim from this text alone that baptism is an absolute condition for receiving the Spirit or regeneration without also considering Acts 8:12-17 and 10:44-48?[16] Note also that this text does not support the idea that reception of the Spirit is a "second blessing" or a second work of grace, for the promise of the Spirit was to **all** who would repent and be baptized. Note also that the gift which is the Spirit promised in 2:38 would be a sharing in the baptism that the 120 had experienced in 2:1-13.

2:39 *To you* is stressed. "To you particularly." That the promise should be made available to these Messiah killers is truly amazing grace. The promise of the Spirit was given "to the Jews first."[17] *The promise* is not just the promise of the Spirit but also the promise of forgiveness.

For all who are far off refers in this context to Jews of the diaspora. This crowd, as later events in the book of Acts make very clear, would never have

---

15   Acts 5:32; 8:15; 9:17; 10:44; 11:17; 15:8; 19:2; Rom 8:15; 1 Cor 2:12; 2 Cor 11:4; Gal 3:2,14.

16   In the first case, the Samaritans received the Spirit sometime **after** baptism, and in the second case, the Gentiles were baptized after receiving the Spirit. In both cases, the reception of the Spirit and baptism were separate. We today must beware of a casual attitude toward baptism. In the early church there is no record of "going forward" or "the sinner's prayer" or "the prayer to receive Christ." These may be useful tools today, but in the early church **the** outward sign of one's inner faith and the **expected response** to indicate that faith was receiving baptism.

17   The Spirit was promised to the Jews in Joel 2 and Ezek 36:26-27. Other OT promises of the Spirit were Isa 32:15; 44:3; Ezek 37:14, 29; 39:29.

dreamed that the Spirit could be given to the Gentiles. We must remember that we are in a very Jewish setting in the first seven chapters of Acts. However, in Luke's mind (Acts 1:8) and in his readers' minds, Peter's words imply more; the promise is for the Gentiles also, to "the uttermost parts of the earth."

As many as the Lord our God shall call. This limits the promise. Otherwise one might think that all succeeding generations would automatically inherit the promise. Luke is not shy about declaring the sovereignty of God in salvation right alongside the appeal for human response.[18] *Proskalesetai* is to call to, to summon, with a possible implication of a reciprocal relation (Louw & Nida). The future tense shows that this movement is not limited to that immediate time. Just how far into the future this promise has reached and to how many lands and peoples it has come neither Peter nor his audience could have imagined in their wildest dreams!

2:40 Luke here plainly indicates that he is not relating all that Peter said on that day and it is reasonable to assume that he has only given an outline of his sermon. The verb *diamarturomai* can mean "to declare" or "to insist" or "to warn." All three seem to fit this situation, but perhaps "warn" fits the context best. *And he continued to exhort them.*[19] There was passion and real concern in Peter's appeal. His evangelism was not in a cool "Here it is, take it or leave it."

In *Save yourselves from this crooked generation* there is an echo of Joel's prophecy quoted in 2:21. One is saved by *calling on the name of the Lord (Jesus).* The word "crooked" in the metaphoric sense means "unscrupulous, dishonest." They have seen the truth but are unwilling to acknowledge him. The phrase *crooked generation* also occurs in Phil 2:15 and several Old Testament passages.[20] The perverse generation had rejected Messiah and would be judged, maybe by the terrors of the Day of the Lord mentioned by Joel; they must disentangle themselves from the influence of the unbelieving mass surrounding them. The first church was truly an *ekklesia,* "called out" from the unbelieving world around them.

2:41 With this note of triumph Peter's appeal is concluded. The word for *received (apodechomai)* means "to come to believe something to be true and

---

18   Compare Acts 13:48.

19   The imperfect tense (past continuous) of *parakaleō,* to urge or to encourage.

20   Deut 32:5 and Psa 77:8 (LXX) 78:8 in Hebrew.

respond accordingly, with some emphasis upon the source" (Louw & Nida). *Were added* is a favorite word of Luke to describe the numerical increase of the church.[21] The increased numbers were the result of the work of God and were thus to the glory of God. 3,000 people is a remarkable number by any reckoning, and that in one day! The later custom of requiring a long period for baptismal preparation was not yet in place. However, Acts must be read not as a manual of prescription but as a record of description. We cannot mechanically imitate all of the practices of the early church, but we must take their practices into account in formulating our own. There is no clue as to the mode of baptism. If they went down into water, there were plenty of ritual baths (*mikvoth*) in the temple area.

Hardly any details are given about the organization of the early church, but there must have been lists of names and that implies membership. *They were added* means not only added to the spiritual body of Christ but also added to a local body on earth.

Lessons for Life

1. Repentance is an essential element of true faith. True repentance includes 1) knowledge that one has sinned, 2) remorse for the sin, and 3) a commitment to turn away from sin and return to God.
2. Baptism is not essential for salvation but normally soon follows true conversion and is not to be taken lightly or neglected.
3. We talk mostly about being "being born again." They talked about conversion as "receiving the Holy Spirit." We receive the Spirit at the time of conversion, not in a "second blessing."
4. Turning to God means turning away from "a perverse and wicked" world.

---

21   Acts 2:47; 5:14; 11:24.

Acts 2:42-47

A Summary of the Life of the Newborn Church

42 And they devoted themselves to the apostles' teaching and the fellowship, to the breaking of bread and the prayers. 43 And awe came upon every soul, and many wonders and signs were being done through the apostles. 44 And all who believed were together and had all things in common. 45 And they were selling their possessions and belongings and distributing the proceeds to all, as any had need. 46 And day by day, attending the temple together and breaking bread in their homes, they received their food with glad and generous hearts, 47 praising God and having favor with all the people. And the Lord added to their number day by day those who were being saved.

The first section of Acts (1:1 to 6:7) has three short summary paragraphs (2:42-47; 4:32-35; and 5:12-16). All three paragraphs are descriptions of life in the early Jerusalem church. Each summarizes the situation as a result of the preceding events and introduces the narrative that follows, acting as a bridge to tie the sections of the story together. Acts 2:42-47 summarizes the results of the day of Pentecost and introduces the first panel (2:42-6:7).

2:42 The converts of the Day of Pentecost were not simply saved and that was the end of it; their daily life changed radically. The word *devoted* means "to continue to do something with intense effort, with the possible implication of "despite difficulty" (Louw & Nida). The word is used of tax collectors in Rom 13:6! The word is also used "to attend, to wait upon" (Mark 3:9; Acts 10:7) and that nuance fits this situation perfectly as the first Christian believers eagerly served one another and waited upon the Lord together.

Since the days of the Pietist movement much of evangelical Protestantism in the West has been marked by a zeal for individual devotional exercises, sometimes to the extreme of forsaking or neglecting church worship services. Many non-western cultures are group-oriented and naturally fit the biblical pattern. None of us must fall victim to an over-emphasis on individualistic Christianity.

These four activities are all preceded by the definite article and so even in the case of "vague" words like "fellowship" and "prayer," the author had something fairly specific in mind. These four religious exercises are four basic things we should be doing in our churches today. Other vital activities such as evangelism, mission outreach, and works of charity must be built on this foundation or they will either wither or suffer distortion.

The apostles' teaching. There soon emerged a definite body of doctrine as the apostles taught. The current trend in NT theology is to exaggerate the distinctive theology of each apostle, but there is no hint of diversity here. The early church had no books and no classrooms and no audio-visual tools, but the church was first and foremost a school. The people of ancient and medieval cultures were good listeners and had highly developed auditory memory such as we still find in "primitive" cultures today. This body of doctrine was probably not organized the way our systematic theologies are today, but was most likely taught in narrative style. The content most likely consisted of the life and especially the teachings of Jesus; and may have formed the core content of what later became the synoptic gospels. They probably also taught a body of Old Testament proof texts and their interpretation (cf. Acts 8:35). Those who were taught were no doubt expected to use these *testimonia* to witness to others.

It is not clear exactly what is meant by *the fellowship.* It was something more definite and probably something quite different than what we mean today by "fun, food, and fellowship." The basic meaning of the word *koinonia* is "sharing, holding in common." This is the first use of the word in the NT. But **what** was shared in various New Testament contexts where this word and its cognates occur was specific: 1) Sharing goods and possessions (same root word in 2:44 and 4:32) 2) Offering of funds, usually to meet the needs of other saints (Rom 15:26 and seven other references in the Pauline epistles). 3) The Lord's supper (1 Cor 10:16). 4) Sharing with Christ in suffering (Phil 3:10). The modern church use of the word "fellowship" to mean only "social interaction, conversation" is not found at all. Since number 3 is mentioned separately and number 4 is usually clear from context, it is best to interpret *the fellowship* mentioned here as 1) Sharing goods and 2) Giving funds or resources, some people giving (taking an offering?) and some receiving. As yet there does not seem to be charity beyond the church or collections for mission work. Both will come later.

The breaking of the bread most likely refers to the Lord's Supper. See Acts 20:7, 1 Cor 10:16; 11:24; Luke 22:19). Since the other three in the list are "religious" activities, it is most likely that *The breaking of bread* was what we know today as Communion or the Lord's supper.[22] One of the very first acts of the new community was obedience to their Lord's command *this do in remembrance of me.*

The prayers. Here again the use of the article and the plural form *prayers* indicate that these were sessions of joint prayer, not private devotions. Probably there were both formal prayers and extemporaneous prayers. Some were no doubt Jewish prayers. These people are still firmly within the Jewish faith. From Acts 3:1 we see that they no doubt also attended the temple prayers, as they were able. The temple worship consisted of twice daily burnt offerings, with rote prayers. However, this is not to exclude extemporaneous prayer such as we see in the *Magnificat* (Luke 1:46-55) and Simeon's *Nunc Dimittis* (Luke 2:28-32). Their prayers and *praising God* (2:47) probably included the singing of hymns. The modern equivalent to *the prayers* is "the worship service."

2:43 *And awe came upon every soul, and many wonders and signs were being done through the apostles.* There was a constant awe at the presence of continuing miracles and the power of God in their midst. One sample of these miracles is given in the next chapter. At this point only the apostles are doing miracles. Miracles served to draw people and to authenticate the teaching of the apostles.

2:44-45 The believers *had all things in common. All things* can hardly be taken in the absolute sense of "all" down to the last toothbrush. Later descriptions of this communal life indicate that the sale of property was voluntary and happened from time to time. If they had all things in common and were in the same place, does this mean that they set up a commune? The *ta ktēmata kai tas huparxeis* of v. 45 both mean "possessions," but the former can have the connotation of "real estate" (see 5:1; Bruce, 132). They had ample precedent for community living in the Essene sects mentioned by both Josephus and Philo and also the now famous Qumran Community. But it is unlikely that they built their own enclave because according to verse 26, they met as a body in the temple daily.

---

22 The phrase *break bread* also occurs in verse 46, but without the article "the" and no doubt means simply "to eat."

Did they do anything to earn a living? Is it possible that they expected the beginning of the Day of the Lord and imminent return of the Lord Jesus? They could live off the proceeds of the sale of goods and property for quite some time. Does this help us to understand the poverty of the *saints in Jerusalem* for whom Paul spent so much effort soliciting aid (Rom 15:25-31)? This passage has inspired many attempts at communal living, some of which exist down to the present day. It was also the inspiration for the monastic communities of the Middle Ages.[23]

2:46 They met in the temple daily, but they also split up into smaller groups (indicating some kind of organization) and *broke bread* from house to house, as it was impractical to feed the entire group in one place. In line with the discussion of the phrase *break bread* above, some think that they practiced the Lord's Supper daily. That may be, but the definite article before *bread* is absent, so it likely means simply eating together. These early believers were so full of spiritual enthusiasm that they could not get enough of sharing and worshiping together. They ate their bread (= food) *with glad and generous hearts.* What a wonderful picture of what the church in any age ought to be: faithful in attendance, harmonious, joyous, and single-minded in love and praise.

2:47 The idyllic picture of the new-born church continues. As yet no problems appear to mar the millennial conditions. *Praising God:* Whether the praise took the form of spontaneous ejaculations of praise or songs of praise or more formal worship, delighting in God was now their life. Joy at the wonderful work of God is a constant theme of Luke.

Having favor with all the people. This will change. Again *all* cannot mean "absolutely all" for there were enemies among the Jewish leadership.

And the Lord added (better "was adding") *to their number day by day those who were being saved.* It is not clear in the Greek text which word *'day by day'* modifies. Most translations render "adding daily," but it could just as well be *being saved daily. Day by day* in the Greek text follows *being saved,* not *adding.* It would then mean that people were being saved every day, an amazing and thrilling phenomenon.

---

23   To describe the church in Acts 2 as "Communism" is an anachronism. That word has connotations in the twentieth century that hardly fit the first century.

The words *to their number* are an interpretive paraphrase of the Greek *epi to auto* which was often used almost as a technical term to describe the church (1:15; 2:1; 1 Cor 11:20; 14:23) in formal assembly.[24] That the Lord was doing the adding shows that there was no need for coercive human solicitation campaigns; **the Lord** brought them in. *The Lord* of course is the exalted Lord Jesus at work in a more powerful way than when he was on earth. The summary ends on a triumphant note with the emphasis on the acts of the risen Lord.

Lessons for Life

1. The Bible nowhere requires Christians to live in communes; however, this passage is a needed corrective to our selfishness and extreme individualism.
2. The Church of Christ has many tasks in the world today. But they must all be built on the foundation of these four basic corporate responsibilities: the teaching and learning of sound apostolic doctrine, sharing of goods and financial resources, attendance at the Lord's Supper, and worshiping together as a body.
3. There is joy in serving Jesus (and one another).
4. It is the Lord who brings in the people; we have the privilege of being a part of what He is doing.

---

24 The Western text (manuscript D and its family) adds an interpretive note to *epi to auto*, *en tei ekklēsia* "in the church." This is probably the correct understanding.

*The magnificent Royal Portico, also called Solomon's Portico, extended the
entire east side of the temple courtyard (John 10:23; Acts 3:11; 5:12).
This was the meeting place of the church in the early chapters of Acts.
Photo by permission of www.HolyLandPhotos.org.*

*The Beautiful Gate (Acts 3:2), also called the Nicanor Gate, was the access from the
Court of the Gentiles to the Court of the Women. This where the lame beggar was healed.
Photo by permission of www.HolyLandPhotos.org.*

ACTS 3

THE HEALING OF A LAME MAN AND PETER'S TEMPLE SERMON

We do not know how long after the Day of Pentecost the events of chapter 3 occurred, but the impression is that there was not much lapse of time. The events of 3:1-4:31 form a connected chain of events, one leading to the other: the healing of the lame man in the temple (3:1-10), Peter's speech in the temple explaining the healing and calling for repentance for crucifying Messiah (3:11-26), provoking the alarm of the authorities who call Peter and John before the Sanhedrin, where Peter makes the "no other name" speech and they are threatened and released (4:1-22). This is followed by the rejoicing praise and prayer of the body of believers (4:23-31).

Acts 3:1-11

The Healing of a Lame Man

1 Now Peter and John were going up to the temple at the hour of prayer, the ninth hour. 2 And a man lame from birth was being carried, whom they laid daily at the gate of the temple that is called the Beautiful Gate to ask alms of those entering the temple. 3 Seeing Peter and John about to go into the temple, he asked to receive alms. 4 And Peter directed his gaze at him, as did John, and said, "Look at us." 5 And he fixed his attention on them, expecting to receive something from them. 6 But Peter said, "I have no silver and gold, but what I do have I give to you. In the name of Jesus Christ of Nazareth, rise up and walk!" 7 And he took him by the right hand and raised him up, and immediately his feet and ankles were made strong. 8 And leaping up, he stood and began to walk, and entered the temple with them, walking and leaping and praising God. 9 And all the people saw him walking and praising God, 10 and recognized him as the one who sat at the Beautiful Gate of the temple, asking for alms. And they were filled with wonder and amazement at what had happened to him.

3:1 Peter, as the leader of the apostles, does all the speaking. John says nothing until 4:19 and even then John does not give a separate speech. These two apostles were part of Jesus' inner circle, so it is fitting that they are the first through whom the healing power of the risen Christ flows to the nation of Israel. To go in pairs was the habit of the Christians in both the gospels and the book of Acts.

They *were going up* (imperfect tense) immediately brings the scene before our eyes and puts us in the action. *Going up* was both a topographical and a spiritual reality for Jews ascending to the holy place, the center of their universe, the magnificent second temple, made fabulous beyond description by the decree of Herod the Great and some half a century of labor by innumerable artisans (John 2:20). It was beautiful but corrupt at the core, the place that their master had called "a den of thieves." The temple authorities were the very people who just a short time ago had connived to crucify Jesus. His blood was still red on their hands. The same disciples who only a few days ago were in hiding *for fear of the Jews* were now entering the enemy camp. The contrast with the Qumran community is remarkable. The "covenanters" of Qumran were so disgusted with the corruption and the apostasy in the temple that they withdrew and built their own commune in the desert on the edge of the Dead Sea.

Why are Peter and John going up to the temple, apparently to worship as Jews did, at the time of the evening sacrifice? The message of Hebrews that the sacrifices are now replaced by the atonement of the cross has apparently not yet been revealed to the apostles. This narrative suggests that they had not yet abandoned the observances of the Judaism of their day in any respect, nor was this merely a public relations ploy to avoid offending the authorities.[1] The sect of the Nazarene did not abandon the temple observances until they were kicked out and the temple was destroyed. Even Paul, though he certainly knew that the cross had replaced the sacrifices, still entered the temple and sponsored a purification ceremony in the temple at the risk of his life (chapter 21).[2] Remember, Acts portrays a period of **transition**.

Prayer was held at 9:00 AM (the morning sacrifice), and again at 3:00 PM (the evening sacrifice). Luke, more than any other NT writer, relates scenes in the temple. Recall the opening chapters of Luke, and especially Luke 1:10 *and when the time for the burning of incense came, all the assembled worshipers were praying outside.* Peter and John would have been among a similar throng.

3:2 Whether the crippled man's helpers were family or friends we do not know. It must have been quite a chore to do this for more than two decades. There were no wheelchairs or special ramps or parking lot slots for the handicapped. All the disabled could do was beg. They could make no contribution to society and were just surviving until death. Is this not a picture of Israel in that day, crippled and useless to God?

My first sermon in Japan was preached in the home of Genzō Mizuno. Genzō was crippled by meningitis at age eight. His limbs were shriveled and twisted; he was totally paralyzed, and could not speak. When I met him in 1970 he had been suffering that condition for 24 years and was completely dependent on his mother's care. He had become a Christian and in later years became famous for his haiku and other poetry. He was never healed physically as this man in Acts 3, but there was an amazing triumph of the spirit through faith in Christ.

What a strategic place for begging! First this would be one of the most crowded places in the city. Second, almsgiving was a Jewish religious duty and what better place to be reminded of one's religious duty than the temple!

---

1   "Here again is clear evidence that the earliest Christians continued to live as observant Jews, probably still offering sacrifices in the temple. The implications of Jesus' death in regard to such Jewish practices was not understood in these earliest days." (Witherington, 173) Schnabel objects: "The text does not indicate whether they were 'observant' in the sense that they observed the burnt offering" (Schnabel, 192).

2   Some would object that after the cross the disciples of Christ attended just for prayer and would not take part in the morning and evening sacrifices for sin as the cross had rendered these sacrifices obsolete and unnecessary. The fact is that we do not know exactly how much the very early believers in Christ participated in Temple ceremonies.

The consensus of opinion among commentators is that *the Beautiful Gate* was the splendid solid bronze Nicanor gate between the outer court and the court of the women mentioned by Josephus as "far surpassing in value those which were plated with silver and set in gold" (Jewish Wars, 5. 201).

3:3 The beggar did not know Peter and John; they were just faces in the crowd. But perhaps they had a kindly look that encouraged him. The imperfect of *ask* could "suggest a beggar's reiterated appeal" (Bruce, 137), or, because of the participial phrase preceding, could better mean "start to ask."

3:4 Apparently the beggar habitually avoided eye contact and probably directed an unfocused gaze at their feet, an eloquent picture of hopelessness and helplessness. Why does Peter require that the beggar look at them? Could they not heal anonymously and be on their way discreetly? But then the whole opportunity for glorifying the Lord Jesus would be lost.

Peter and John gaze intently at the beggar.[3] Most almsgivers would drop a coin in the outstretched hand and, avoiding eye contact, pass by quickly. It is so important for those who minister in Christ's name to pay special attention to the object of their concern. In many cultures this will be done with eye contact.

3:5 Now they have his attention, but his expectation level is naturally very low. Occasionally he would receive a valuable coin, but he never dreamed he would get anything better than money. So are our expectations in prayer often minimal.

3:6 Did Peter have no coins in his possession at all? This seems to have been the case with Jesus, at least on the famous occasion when he asked to see a coin and asked whose inscription it was (Mark 12:15). Did he have no offering for the temple? It is more likely that Peter either had no valuable coins, or that he was speaking rhetorically, meaning that he had something better than even silver and gold. There is a delightful irony and wit in Peter's remark. The normal expectation of the beggar on hearing just this much would be that "Well, OK, I'll take copper or whatever I can get."

---

3   The word translated "gaze intently" is *atenizō*, a favorite of Luke. See especially Acts 14:9 *And Paul **looked directly** at him, and seeing that he had faith to be healed . . .*

The command to *Rise up and walk* is reminiscent of Jesus' words of healing the paralytic in Luke 5:17-26 (Matt 9:1-8; Mark 2:1-12) and the man at the pool of Bethesda in John 5 (5:8). It is very clear that the Jesus who does this miracle is the same Jesus who does the same miracle now through Peter that he did many times in his earthly ministry.

The imperative is startling. It is the voice of authority. There is no "let's have a little talk and I will tell you how you can believe in the true Messiah and he will heal you." This man did not even have time to think it over. The cognitive was overwhelmed by the imperative.

In the name of Messiah Jesus of Nazareth makes clear source of Peter's power and authority. *In the name of* means "by the authority of." When Jesus did similar healings, he did not use any such formula because he had his own authority to heal. The "name" of Jesus has a remarkable prominence in the early chapters of Acts, and especially in chapters 3-5. It occurs 33 times in Acts and 14 of these are between Acts 2:21 and 5:41.

3:7 Unlike the case of Jesus and the paralytic, this man gets a little help from Peter!

Peter stretched out his hand in a gesture of compassion and empathy with his suffering as Jesus did with Jairus' daughter (Luke 8:54). How important is a discreet touch in Christian ministry!

Many commentators say that the paralytic must have had faith to be healed because a) that is the pattern of the NT healings and b) 3:16 mentions his faith. But 3:16 does not necessarily refer to **his** faith. This man hardly had time to exercise intelligent faith. If he did exercise faith, it must have been at the intuitive instantaneous level. As for 3:16, it does not say who had faith, Peter or the lame man. At this point it was more the faith of Peter and John in the name of Jesus rather than the lame man's faith. This is an example of overwhelming sovereign grace.

It must have been a dramatic moment. This man had never stood once in all his forty miserable years. Now, like a bird that is suddenly able to fly, he can stand. There must have been healing not just of bones, sinews, and tendons, but also of neurological channels.

3:8 Peter did not have to haul up dead weight; the man responds with alacrity. His faith takes the form of instant intuitive obedience. His first act of walking was most appropriate: to accompany the apostles into the temple to praise

God, as if that were the main reason God made feet and legs. At first he walks as if in a dream, but shortly the joy that he is actually walking for the first time in his life bursts forth in leaps of exultation. Not only that but his mouth is loosed in praising God. The decorum of the holy place was shattered and people all over the vast courtyard turned their heads and stared. This was a fulfillment of Isa 35:6: *then shall the lame leap as the deer*. In the context of Isaiah this was a sign of the end-time kingdom of God when there will be universal healing and *your God will come to save you* and *they will see the glory of the LORD*, and there will be *streams in the desert*. The "kingdom of God" is mentioned only eight times in Acts but it is evident that the powers of the kingdom are here present in manifest power.

3:9, 10 Luke is particularly fond of recounting the wonder of the crowd at the miracle (compare Luke 4:36; 5:9, 26; 7:16 with the parallel passages in Matthew and Mark). *All the people* is a favorite expression of Luke's and in his usage always refers to the people of Israel, "the people" par excellence. The first word *thambos*, "the awe felt in the presence of divine activity"[4], is used only by Luke. The second word, *ekstasis,* is also a Lukan favorite and means "intense astonishment;" in some contexts in Luke it means "dream" or "trance" (Acts 10:10; 11:5; 22:17). The wonder of *the people* is important as a verification of the miracle by so many eyewitnesses who knew this man to be the cripple at the Beautiful Gate. It is also important as a means of glorifying the Lord who had given the healing.

3:11 The two apostles, after worshipping in the court of Israel, came into the inner court and proceeded to Solomon's portico, the long, covered colonnade that formed the entire eastern side of the temple. The columns were 8.2 meters high and supported a cedar roof. There were four rows of columns, forming three wide aisles.[5] This magnificent setting was to become, until persecution arose, the regular meeting place of the Jerusalem church (5:12). This was the place where Jesus had been confronted by exasperated Jews the previous December at the Feast of Dedication who said *How long will you keep us in*

---

4   Haenchen, 200.

5   Harold Stigers, "Temple, Jerusalem," Zondervan Pictorial Encyclopedia of the Bible, vol. 5, 651.

suspense? If you are the Christ, tell us plainly (John 10:24). Now Peter and John have provided powerful testimony in the same place that Jesus was indeed the Christ.

☞

Acts 3:12-26

Peter's Speech in the Temple

12 *And when Peter saw it he addressed the people: "Men of Israel, why do you wonder at this, or why do you stare at us, as though by our own power or piety we have made him walk?* **13** *The God of Abraham, the God of Isaac, and the God of Jacob, the God of our fathers, glorified his servant Jesus, whom you delivered over and denied in the presence of Pilate, when he had decided to release him.* **14** *But you denied the Holy and Righteous One, and asked for a murderer to be granted to you,* **15** *and you killed the Author of life, whom God raised from the dead. To this we are witnesses.* **16** *And his name—by faith in his name—has made this man strong whom you see and know, and the faith that is through Jesus has given the man this perfect health in the presence of you all.*

17 *"And now, brothers, I know that you acted in ignorance, as did also your rulers.* **18** *But what God foretold by the mouth of all the prophets, that his Christ would suffer, he thus fulfilled.* **19** *Repent therefore, and turn back, that your sins may be blotted out,* **20** *that times of refreshing may come from the presence of the Lord, and that he may send the Christ appointed for you, Jesus,* **21** *whom heaven must receive until the time for restoring all the things about which God spoke by the mouth of his holy prophets long ago.* **22** *Moses said, 'The Lord God will raise up for you a prophet like me from your brothers. You shall listen to him in whatever he tells you.* **23** *And it shall be that every soul who does not listen to that prophet shall be destroyed from the people.'* **24** *And all the prophets who have spoken, from Samuel and those who came after him, also proclaimed these days.* **25** *You are the sons of the prophets and of the covenant that*

*God made with your fathers, saying to Abraham, 'And in your offspring shall all the families of the earth be blessed.' **26** God, having raised up his servant, sent him to you first, to bless you by turning every one of you from your wickedness."*

3:12 None of the people were skeptical or questioned the reality of the miracle. A curious and already greatly impressed audience has gathered. This was a wonderful opportunity for Peter to preach. The heart of his message is again an appeal to repent of the terrible crime of crucifying Jesus, whom God had raised from dead. The accusation is even sharper and more severe than in the appeal on the Day of Pentecost.

Peter answered the question that was in their minds: "What is going on here"? "How could you heal this man"? In a similar situation in Acts 14:11-13, a more superstitious people were ready to worship Paul and Barnabas as gods.

3:13 Peter says in effect, "We did not do it; it was the God of our fathers." This is a Jewish audience and the appeal to *the God of Abraham, Isaac, and Jacob* was a reassuring traditional formula, and an appeal to the very deepest root of their religion and their identity as a people.

But in the next breath Peter accuses these Jews of betraying their Messiah and denying him in the presence of Pilate who was trying hard to release him. Luke gives much more space to the attempts of Pilate to release Jesus than do the other gospels, and only he and John record Pilate's judgment that Jesus was innocent. As in 2:22,23, and 36, the juxtaposition is sharp, *the one you betrayed God glorified.* He does not mention the resurrection, but the word *glorify* encompasses resurrection, ascension, and exaltation.

There are several subtle allusions to the great atonement chapter—Isaiah 53—in this speech: *my servant* in Isa 52:13 and *his servant* in Acts 3:13; *glorify* in Isa 53:13 and Acts 3:13; and *righteous one* in Isa 53:11 and Acts 3:14. Isaiah 53 is not cited here but it seems to have permeated Peter's thinking.

3:14 The first *you* is very emphatic. This refers of course to the clamor for Barabbas, a criminal guilty of murder (Mark 15:7), to be released and for Jesus, innocent of any crime, to be crucified. Peter turns the knife—again, an excruciatingly pointed contrast and a terrible irony.

The epithets *the Holy and Righteous One* are not just descriptions of Jesus, but titles of Messiah in the OT. *The Holy One* occurs in Psa 16:10 and in the

NT in Mark 1:24 where the demon cries out, *What have you to do with us, Jesus of Nazareth? Have you come to destroy us? I know who you are, the Holy One of God.* (See also Luke 4:34; 1 John 2:20.) Messiah is called *my righteous servant* in Isa 53:11 and *the Righteous One* 1 Enoch 38:2. This title may have arisen because of the constant emphasis of the OT on the righteous reign of Messiah (see 2 Sam 23:3f; Isa 32:1).

3:15 *and you killed the Author of life, whom God raised from the dead. To this we are witnesses.* Again the sharp contrast emerges, this time with even more bite and irony. In the Greek text verses 14 and 15 form an ABBA pattern called chiasm: A: God glorified him; B: You betrayed and denied him; B: you killed him; A: God raised him from the dead.

The sharpest point of irony is in the phrase *you killed the author of life.* The phrase *archēgon tēs zōēs* (Author of Life) is one of four rather primitive titles for Christ in this speech which later fell into disuse.[6] This is evidence that the speech is indeed early and very Jewish and is not a later creation by Luke. The precise meaning of the phrase is difficult. The older versions (KJV, ASV, NASV) translated it "the Prince of life." Later versions, like RSV and NIV, translate it "the author of life." The word *archēgos* means a person who as originator or founder of a movement who also continues as the leader — "pioneer leader, founding leader" (Louw and Nida). Thus the word combines two ideas 1) founder and 2) leader (thus "prince" in older translations). In the latter sense, it is used for the "heads" of the tribes of Israel in the Greek OT (cf. Num 10:4; see also Num 14:4: *Let us choose a **captain** and go back to Egypt.* RSV). Using the former idea of "founder," Darby translated "the originator of life." This is superior to "the author of life;" in modern usage only books have "authors."

But what life? Without any contextual clues, one thinks first of "the creator of (biological) life." This is true of Jesus (e.g. Col 1:16, 17) but seems out of place in this context, being as yet incomprehensible to even the most sympathetic Jew in Peter's audience. It could be the "life which is resurrection," in other words Jesus is the "firstborn from the dead," "the firstfruits." This would fit Acts 5:31 (the second of four places the word appears in the NT) *God exalted him* (as) *archēgos and savior* . . . But perhaps the best solution is to place full weight on the definite article before "life" in the Greek text "the

---

6   "Servant of God," "the Holy One," "the Righteous One," and "the Author of Life."

originator of the life" and interpret "the life" as "the salvation which brings eternal life."[7] Thus the primary meaning would be, "You have killed the Originator and Ruler of eternal life."

3:16 Peter, after his accusation of their crime, now answers their unspoken question as to how the healing took place. Though the general sense of v. 16 is clear, that faith in Jesus has healed the man, the sentence seems clumsily structured, and is, as the German commentators say, "overladen." Why is the same thing said twice? Why the unusual expression *his name has strengthened him*? Why is *name* repeated twice in the first sentence? Why does Peter say *faith has given him health* when it was really God who did the healing? Whose faith? The crippled man's faith or Peter's faith?

The syntactic awkwardness of the sentence which is not unusual in live speech, unless the speaker is reading from a carefully prepared manuscript, as transcripts of recordings of impromptu speeches even today amply demonstrate. The fact that Luke did not "clean up" the rough edges of Peter's speech hints at a degree of faithfulness to his (probably Aramaic) source. The parallelism of this verse may be an example of the Semitic parallelism common in the OT.

Both halves of the verse contain: 1) A phrase at the head of the sentence ascribing the healing to faith *And by faith* 16a; *and the faith* 16b; 2) A phrase describing this faith *in his name* 16a; *which is through him* 16b; 3) A pronoun object *this (man)* 16a; *to him* 16b; 4) A verbal clause expressing the healing *has strengthened* 16a; *has given him this perfect health* 16b; 5) A phrase emphasizing the audience as witnesses *whom you see and know* 16a; *in the presence of all of you* 16b). Peter's main thought is repeated twice: "Through faith in God this man has been healed and you are all witnesses (of that healing)."

The modern reader may feel some awkwardness in making *his name* the subject of the verb *has strengthened*. This is an example of personifying the name of God to mean God Himself. There are many examples of personifying *the Name* in the Old Testament: Psa 20:1 *The LORD answer you in the day of trouble!* **The name** *of the God of Jacob protect you!* (See also Prov 18:10; Isa 30:27). *The Name* was one of the Hebrew ways of saying "Yahweh." The Jews were reluctant to pronounce the name of God, so along with other substitutes

---

7   This meaning would also nicely fit the other two occurrences of the word in the NT: Heb 2:10 and 12:2.

they used the phrase "the Name" instead. However *the Name* referred to in Acts 3:16 (and in many places in Acts 2-5) is the name of Jesus! In Acts 5:41 the believers rejoiced that they were counted worthy *to suffer shame for The Name*. A title formerly used for "Yahweh" is now used for the Lord Jesus.

3:17 The word *brothers* marks a new section of the speech. After the accusation and explanation of the miracle, Peter moves on to mention some factors that mitigate their crime. The first factor is ignorance; *I know that you acted in ignorance*. Ignorance of the true situation is a valid reason for a less severe punishment. It does not absolve the Jews completely but does soften the blow. Compare Luke 23:34 *Father, forgive them for they do not know what they are doing*, and 1 Cor 2:8 *For had they known it, they would not have crucified the Lord of glory*. Psychologically, it offers the accused Jews some hope for mercy, which is an incentive for repentance. *But with you there is forgiveness; that you may be feared* (Psa 130:4).

3:18 The second mitigating factor is that the suffering (and by implication also the death) of the Messiah was in the plan of God, foretold by *all the prophets* hundreds of years in advance.

Again the word *all* does not mean "absolutely all." However, as Marshall points out (93), we can find such prophecies in three of the four books of the prophets, Isaiah, Jeremiah, (not Ezekiel) and the Book of the Twelve (minor prophets), and two of the Writings, Daniel and the Psalms. It may be that Peter quoted some of the prophetic passages. The apostles may have learned these prophecies from the discourse of Jesus on the Emmaus Road, when he said, *O foolish ones, and slow of heart to believe all that the prophets have spoken! Was it not necessary that the Christ should suffer these things and enter into his glory?* (Luke 24:25,26). Jesus said the same thing to his disciples in the Upper Room on Easter evening: *These are my words which I spoke to you, while I was still with you, that everything written about me in the law of Moses and the prophets and the psalms must be fulfilled. Then he opened their minds to understand the scriptures, and said to them, 'Thus it is written, that the Christ should suffer and on the third day rise from the dead'* (Luke 24:44-46). These passages certainly would have included the famous description of the suffering servant, Isa 52:13-53:12, as well as Psalm 22, and maybe Jer 11:19 and Dan 9:26. If *the prophets* also include Moses, there would be plenty of material from the typology of the Passover and the sacrifices. Luke never fails to note the mention the prophecies that Messiah must suffer (cf. Acts 17:3 and 26:23). The suffering of Messiah was the chief point of ignorance of the Jews of Jesus' day and even in our day. As in Acts 2:23, the fact that it was God's purpose that Messiah would suffer, even to death, was a powerful answer to "the scandal of the cross" in the minds of the Jews.

3:19 This blunt imperative is the heart of the message; everything leads up to the command to repent and everything following amplifies it or justifies it. *Repent*, as in 2:38, refers specifically of the sin of crucifying the Messiah. Then instead of *be baptized* as in 2:38, we have *turn*. The word *epistrepsate* is the Septuagint word for the Hebrew *shuv*, "turn," that is "turn away from what is false and wrong and turn to God." It is used countless times in the prophets and makes clear the obedience element of true repentance.

The promised result is, as in 2:38, forgiveness of sin. Here it is expressed perhaps more forcefully as a "blotting out" of their sins (again note the plural). Not only will their **sin** of crucifying their Messiah be forgiven, but also the rest of the slate will be wiped clean of their **sins.** Of the many benefits of faith and repentance like new birth and justification and cleansing, only forgiveness is mentioned by Peter. That is what his audience needs first and foremost.

3:20, 21 The second promised result of repentance is unique in the New Testament. There are of course many places where the return of Christ is promised but only here it is conditioned upon repentance. Peter says to the Jewish nation that if they repent, God will send the ascended Messiah, and there will be *seasons of refreshing* and *the restoration of all things.*

These two phrases *kairoi anapsuxeōs* and *chronoi apokatastaeōs pantōn* occur nowhere else in the Bible, or for that matter in any other literature of the time. Though some take them to have different referents, most commentators think they refer to the same thing. Since both are connected with the return of Christ, many scholars think they are eschatological and future. A minority holds that these *times and seasons* are fulfilled spiritually in the life of each person who repents. After extensive research we feel the phrase does refer to the return of Christ, but that there is indeed a present application to any person who repents and is born again.[8] The powers of the kingdom of God

---

8   See the PhD dissertation by W. Robert Shade III "The Restoration of Israel in Acts
     3:12-26 and Lukan Eschatology," Trinity Evangelical Divinity School, Deerfield, Illinois,
     USA. Available from UMI Dissertation Services, 300 N. Zeeb Road, Ann Arbor MI
     48106, USA.

are present in the heart and life of any believer; he/she partakes **now** of the *"powers of the age to come."*

What would Peter's Jewish audience understand by these phrases? The first question of interpretation must be "What did it mean to them then?" Only after answering that question should we ask "What does it mean to us now?"

We deal now with the two enigmatic phrases *times of refreshing* and *the time of restoring all things* (*kairoi anapsuxeōs* and *chronoi apokatastaeōs pantōn*). Though the noun *anapsuxis* is not found in the Greek OT, the verb *anapsuxō* is found seven times and means "to be rested in body or mind, to find relief from distress, quicken, refresh."[9] But more specifically in our context, however, it seems to refer to refreshing or quickening **given by the Spirit**. Lane pointed out that one version of the Septuagint does contain the noun *anapsuxis* in Isa 32:15 in a layout that directly parallels Acts 3:20 *Until (there) comes . . . anapsuxis* (the Hebrew text and most all translations read *Spirit from on high*) is parallel to *that times of refreshing may come from the presence of the Lord* (Acts 3:20).[10] In other words *the refreshing = the coming of the Spirit*. Lane also pointed out that this would make Acts 3:19-20 exactly correspond with Acts 2:38 except that in place of *you shall receive the gift of the Holy Spirit* we have in 3:20 *times of refreshing will come*. This admirably fits the whole context, so we conclude with Lane that "the seasons of refreshing" are the seasons when the Holy Spirit is poured out. But though the meaning of *seasons of refreshing* is thus focused, we do not want to overspecify; together with the *times of restoration of all things* a whole cluster of eschatological events is involved.

The Old Testament must be our primary source for a search for the meaning of this phrase, for it says quite plainly in v 21 that this was predicted *through the mouth of his holy prophets long ago*. The phrase *through the mouth of* is a formula for the divine inspiration of the prophets; it underlines the certainty of the promise.

The precise phrase *chronoi apokatastaeōs pantōn* is not found in the NT or OT or in any other ancient work but the verb *apokathistēmi* occurs 32 times

---

9   Exod 23:12; Jud 15:19; 1 Sam 16:23 (LXX 1 Kgdm 16:23); 2 Sam 16:14 (LXX 2Kgdm 16:14); Psa 39:14 (LXX 38:14); 2 Mac 4:46; and 2 Mac 13:11.

10   William L. Lane, "Times of Refreshment: A Study of Eschatological Periodization in Judaism and Christianity (Acts 3:19)" PhD Dissertation, Harvard Divinity School, 1962, 167-171.

in the Greek Old Testament where in six of those occurrences it is a technical term for the restoration of Israel to the land.[11] It can also refer to moral and spiritual restoration.[12] In the NT this verb occurs eight times. It refers to restoration of health or wholeness in Matt 12:13 (par. Mark 3:5; Luke 6:10) and Mark 8:25. In an eschatological context Matt 17:11 (par. Mark 9:12) is the word of Jesus that *Elijah comes and will* **restore** *all things,* a reference to Mal 4:5. But even more relevant to this passage is the question of the disciples in Acts 1:6 *Will you at this time* **restore** *the kingdom to Israel?* Jesus' answer uses the very same words of Acts 3:19, 20: *It is not for you to know* **the times and the seasons** (*chronous kai kairous*). He was not denying the kingdom to Israel, or hinting that it would be fulfilled spiritually; he simply says that they cannot know the time. Now in Acts 3:19 Peter answers the disciples' question in 1:6: **the kingdom comes when Israel repents!** Luke intends that his readers would understand that Peter is giving the answer to their question in 1:6. But the record of Acts 3-5 shows that though several thousand individual Israelites believed, the majority did not repent, and the leadership of the nation certainly did not repent, but persecuted and imprisoned the apostles. The result is that the kingdom with its *seasons of refreshing* and *restoration of all things* did not come at that time. However, for any who do repent in this present age, there is a wonderful spiritual refreshing and restoration, and participation in the future kingdom here and now.

3:22 Peter now returns to a more severe tone. After stating the rewards and blessings of repentance, he warns them what will happen if they do not repent: destruction and excommunication from the people of God. What breathtaking audacity! Peter uses the authority of the "keys" given to him by the Lord to shut out those who are unrepentant (Matt 16:19). He now quotes Moses, whom every true Jew held in the very highest esteem. The citation is almost an exact quotation of Deut 18:15-19 blended with Lev 23:29. In the midst of a passage explaining how to detect false prophets, Moses prophesied of the true prophet who would be *like Moses* and emerge from the people of Israel and have absolute authority. Peter claims that Jesus is the fulfillment of this prophecy, the prophet of whom Moses spoke. The same passage is also cited by Stephen in Acts 7:37. It was not just a Christian interpretation; the

---

11   Jer 16:15; 23:8; 24:6; 27:19 (MT 50:19); Hos 11:11.

12   Amos 5:15; Mal 3:24 (MT 4:5).

Jews who quizzed John the Baptist asked, *Are you the prophet?* (John 1:21; see also 1:25), with Deut 18:15-19 in mind.

The word *raise up* has a double meaning here; to "raise up" a prophet is to cause a prophet to appear, but this is the same word *anistēmi* that Peter has been using to refer to the resurrection of Jesus.

Then comes the warning. If they do not listen to that prophet, they will be "destroyed from among" or "cut off from" the people. Peter replaces the milder warning of Deut. 18:19 *I myself will require it of him* with the much stronger Lev 23:19 *will be cut off from the people.* In the original context these words meant excommunication from the commonwealth of Israel. In this situation it means "the true people of God recognize Jesus as Messiah. If you do not acknowledge Jesus as Messiah you will be cut off from the true people of God." This thought must have been startling to Jews in his audience, who were quite confident that they were members in good standing of the elect people.

3:24 *All the prophets* is a favorite phrase with Luke (Luke 11:50; 13:28; 24:25, 27; Acts 3:24; 10:43). This is the fifth of six times the word "prophet" occurs in this sermon. The evidence from previous revelation (the OT) was absolutely essential to establish the revolutionary claims of the first Christians. Most of the prophets *proclaimed these days.* What days? The days of the appearance and ministry of Messiah, his death, resurrection, and ascension, the days of the coming of the Spirit, and quite possibly the Messianic Age, the *seasons of refreshing* and the times of *restoration of all things.* These are the days of fulfillment, Peter warns them. You don't want to be left behind.

3:25 Peter sets forth another motivation to repent: in verse 22-23 it was the appeal to the prophet Jesus and to the threat of his punishment for disobedience. In verse 24 the motivation was a more general appeal to *all the prophets.* Now in verse 25 Peter points out their God-given relationship to the prophets: "This is your heritage: take it." Not only are they heirs of the prophets and Moses, they are also *sons of the covenant,* a very Hebrew phrase. Their covenant promises go all the way back to the grand patriarch Abraham himself and the covenant God made with him in Genesis 12. In these two speeches before the Jews Peter has touched all the bases: the prophet foretold by Moses, all the prophets, and now the greatest of them all, Abraham himself.

He quotes loosely from Gen 22:18 (as repeated in Gen 26:4): *And in your offspring (seed) all the families of the earth shall be blessed.* The "seed" (*offspring* in ESV) was seen by both Peter and Paul to be singular and to refer to Christ (Acts 13:23; Gal 3:16, 19). The true blessing of the covenant will come only through Messiah. If you reject him, you forfeit your blessing as heirs of the covenant. This Jesus is for you.

3:26 *To you first* (out of all the families of the earth) *God sent Jesus* (Greek word order). This order is maintained throughout Acts: the Jews receive the offer first (13:46; cf. Rom 1:16). "As they were first in privilege, so they were first in responsibility for their response to the offer (Rom 2:9f)" (Bruce, 146).

His servant is a messianic title referring to *the Servant of the LORD* in Isaiah. *To bless you* is a link with the promised blessing of the preceding verse. But precisely when and how does the blessing take place? Most all English versions translate the infinitive phrase *en to apostrephein hekaston apo tōn ponēriōn humōn* in the transitive sense.[13] In other words, *each* is taken as the **object** of the infinitive *turn*. "Jesus was sent to bless us by turning us from our sins." In this case the Greek infinitive phrase is understood instrumentally, that is "**by** turning each from your iniquities" (Bruce, 146; Marshall, 96; and Kistemaker, 141.[14]

But it is just as possible, indeed we think more likely, that two of the German Bibles[15] are correct to translate the phrase intransitively: "He sent him to bless you **when (or if) each turns from your iniquities**." Because the subject of a Greek infinitive is always accusative, there is ambiguity as to whether *each* is the subject or object of the infinitive "to turn." In favor of the **subject** option ("when each turns") is the fact that of the thirty-two other occurrences of the construction *en tō* + infinitive + accusative in Luke/Acts the accusative is without exception **the subject** of the infinitive, not the object. There are only two exceptions to this pattern in all the New Testament (Heb 2:8 and 8:13). The construction is temporal ("when" not "in" or "by") in

---

13   The following is a technical discussion of a point that I discovered in my dissertation research. Skip to the conclusion if you are not interested in the details.

14   The fact that God does turn us from our sin in his sovereign grace is good Calvinistic theology and good biblical theology. *The Deliverer will come from Zion, He will remove (apostrephein) ungodliness from Jacob* (Rom 11:26 quoting Isa 59:20.)

15   Luther 1912 edition and Schlachter, 1951; but not Elberfelder 1915.

94% of its occurrences in the Greek Bible. This leads us to conclude that the German versions are correct to translate "when each turns."

The translation "He sent him to bless each (person) when each turns from your iniquities" better fits the intention of Peter to bring them to repentance, the main point of the speech. The emphasis in the passage is not the sovereignty of God in bringing man to repentance, but the responsibility of man to repent. The thought then is "when you turn away from your sin, Messiah will bless you."

Summary of the Temple Sermon

The true agent of the healing was God himself, working through his risen Servant Jesus, not Peter and John. The true identity of Jesus: the risen servant of the LORD, the Holy One, the Righteous One, the Prince (or Originator) of the true life. The terrible sin of crucifying your Messiah: You are guilty of delivering him up to Pilate, of disowning him and asking for a murderer in his place, and of putting him to death. But there were two ameliorating factors: First you did it in ignorance of who he really is, and second, the sufferings of Messiah, even his death, prophesied by *all the prophets*, were in the providence of God. This all leads up to the main point: **Repent!** Inducements to Repentance: Repent of this terrible crime and God will wipe away your sin and bring in times of refreshing, both now and especially in the return of Jesus who will bring in the restoration of all things of which the prophets spoke. This is announced to you Jews first, the sons of Abraham and the sons of the prophets. Warning: If you do not repent you will be cut off from the people of God as Moses predicted in his prophecy of the prophet like himself.

Notice themes that occur again and again in the sermons of Acts: the resurrection and exaltation of Christ, the cross, the need for repentance, the fulfillment of the OT scriptures. This sermon is unique in the richness of its titles for Christ, several of which were unknown or unused by the Gentile churches, and the unique phrases "times of refreshing" and "restoration of all things" which we believe to refer to the fulfillment of prophecy and the blessings accompanying the return of Christ. This sermon, like the sermon of Acts 2, is very Jewish, and it is a direct appeal for them to repent of their crime of crucifying their Messiah.

Lessons for Life

1. The lame man is a picture of the misery and helplessness of mankind in the natural state. The healing of the lame man so he could walk and leap is a picture of the power and joy of salvation.
2. When God uses us or works through us, we must be careful that people know that it was **God** who does it, not we ourselves.
3. God fulfilled the prophecies of the sufferings of Messiah. He will just as surely fulfill the prophecies of his return and "the times of refreshing" and "the restoration of all things."
4. Jesus is unique. We cannot compromise with the universalism and syncretism which is so prevalent today.
5. It is a fearful thing to reject God's Messiah.
6. When the Jews repent as a nation (Rom 11:26; Zech 12:10-13:1), Messiah will come. God has a place for the Jews of our day, the descendants of Abraham through whom "all the families of the earth will be blessed," in bringing in the restoration of all things. We must be careful, however, of being so pro-Israel that we become anti-Arab or anti-Palestinian.

ACTS 4

THE ARREST AND INTERROGATION OF PETER AND JOHN

The events of Acts 4 follow immediately those of Acts 3 and are part of one uninterrupted story from Acts 3:1 through the end of Acts 5. This section describes the gathering storm of opposition and persecution that will reach its climax in the stoning of Stephen in chapter 7.

How will the infant Jesus movement respond to opposition? Will it be strong enough to survive? It must be remembered that the number of disciples of Jesus among the Jews, despite the rapid increase of believers to over 5,000 (4:4), it is still a small fragile minority.

ৎ৶৶

Acts 4:1-7

The Arrest

1 And as they were speaking to the people, the priests and the captain of the temple and the Sadducees came upon them, 2 greatly annoyed because they were teaching the people and proclaiming in Jesus the resurrection from the dead. 3 And they arrested them and put them in custody until the next day,

for it was already evening. 4 But many of those who had heard the word
believed, and the number of the men came to about five thousand.

5 On the next day their rulers and elders and scribes gathered together
in Jerusalem, 6 with Annas the high priest and Caiaphas and John and
Alexander, and all who were of the high-priestly family. 7 And when they
had set them in the midst, they inquired, "By what power or by what name
did you do this?"

4:1-3 Peter and John were suddenly arrested while they were speaking. We
have Peter's speech in chapter 3 but the word *they* shows that John also spoke.

By *the priests* "the chief priests" is no doubt meant; "the priests in authority,"
probably the same who are named in verse 6. *The captain of the temple* was next
in power to the high priest. The Sadducees were the dominant party politically
even though the Pharisees probably outnumbered them. In some ways they
were the "conservative" party; they refused the oral tradition of the Pharisees
which later grew into the Talmud. They denied some doctrines of Judaism
which were largely intertestamental developments such the resurrection
of the dead. In some ways they were rationalist. They denied the need for
miraculous interventions by God and they believed that the Macabbees had
begun the messianic age and so they denied any future (or present) appearance
of Messiah. Politically they were pragmatic and did not want to antagonize
Roman rule in any way. All this makes it very understandable that they were
"exasperated" (*greatly annoyed*) at the preaching about Jesus, whom they
regarded as a false Messiah, and the preaching of his resurrection, because they
knew such a thing was impossible.

So they seized Peter and John with the same temple police force that had
arrested Jesus. They were kept in custody overnight because there was no such
thing as bail in those days. Incarceration was the only way to keep a suspect
for trial. The arrest and interrogation of Peter and John is ominously similar
to the arrest and interrogation of Jesus before the Sanhedrin. Peter and John
and the believers must have wondered that night if these two would be jailed
indefinitely, or even executed. Were their hearts fortified by recalling that their
Master had warned them about this very thing: *When they bring you before*
the synagogues, and the rulers, and the authorities, do be anxious about how you
should defend yourself or what you should say, for the Holy Spirit will teach in that
very hour what you ought to say (Luke 12:11-12)?

4:4 Verse 4 is not chronologically out of place. After the arrest of the preachers, at least 2,000 more conversions take place, though there may have been some converts between chapters 2 and 3. Other apostles and believers must have been busy counseling inquirers. It is remarkable that the arrest of Peter and John did not frighten inquirers away. It is as if Billy Graham were arrested during an evangelistic rally and the meeting continued anyway!

4:5-7 The priests wasted no time in interrogating Peter and John before the Sanhedrin (v. 15). This new movement was perceived as a dangerous threat to the stability of the nation. Verse 5 seems to indicate that some of those who hastily gathered came from outside Jerusalem. The rulers (the high priests mentioned by name in verse 6), the elders, and the *grammateis* (scribes or teachers of the law) are the three bodies composing the 70-member Sanhedrin. It was of course the very same body that had condemned Jesus not many weeks earlier.

As in the trial of Jesus, Caiaphas was still presiding as high priest. Annas, the same Annas of John 18:13, had been high priest from A.D. 6-15 but just as former U.S. presidents still retain the title of "president" after leaving office, so Annas still had the title "high priest." There is no mention of John and Alexander anywhere else, though the Western text (D)[1] makes "John" "Jonathan" and if that is correct, he could be the man who replaced Caiaphas in A.D. 36. There were also others *of the high-priestly family.*

The line-up of power against two nobody disciples of Jesus was quite formidable. Every person of power past or present is around them in a semi-circle, glaring at them. No allies, such as Nicodemus or Joseph of Arimathea, are mentioned. The net effect must have been overwhelmingly intimidating. This makes the boldness of Peter's answer all the more remarkable.

The Sanhedrin wastes no time on preliminaries or establishing the identity of Peter and John. They get right to the point and demand to know *By what power or by what name did you do this?* Notice they do not say "this miracle of healing" but a derisive *this.* They cannot say "this crime" for no law has been broken.

---

1   The Western text, designated "D," is the New Testament text behind the Old Latin and Syriac translations from the Greek and is quoted by second and third century Christian Fathers Cyprian, Tertullian, and Irenaeus. It is noted for plausible additions to the "mainline" texts, especially in Acts.

Any reader of Luke's first volume will recall that Jesus had been challenged with almost the same question. *Tell us by what authority are you doing these things?* (Luke 20:2). *In what name* means "by whose authority." The implication, as it had been with Jesus, was that they were using the power of Satan.

∽∼∽

Acts 4:8-12

Peter's Answer

8 *Then Peter, filled with the Holy Spirit, said to them, "Rulers of the people and elders,* **9** *if we are being examined today concerning a good deed done to a crippled man, by what means this man has been healed,* **10** *let it be known to all of you and to all the people of Israel that by the name of Jesus Christ of Nazareth, whom you crucified, whom God raised from the dead—by him this man is standing before you well.* **11** *This Jesus is the stone that was rejected by you, the builders, which has become the cornerstone.* **12** *And there is salvation in no one else, for there is no other name under heaven given among men by which we must be saved."*

4:8 Peter did not hesitate, dumb and shaking with fear. He did not try to evade or prevaricate or defend himself. He did not start with a long explanation of the circumstances. When interrogated it is always wise to answer the question concisely, boldly, and clearly.

The secret of course, is that he was *filled with the Holy Spirit.* The Holy Spirit was giving him what to say and the boldness to say it. Every time the phrase "filled with the Holy Spirit" occurs in Acts, it is immediately followed with an act of speech boldly proclaiming Christ and his salvation.[2] Peter was filled before (2:4), but now at the crucial moment, he is filled again. He observes the necessary formalities by recognizing their authority as *rulers of the*

---

2   Acts 2:4; 4:8, 31; 13:9. "One baptism, many fillings."

people and elders. One wonders how John the Baptist might have addressed them (*generation of vipers?*)

4:9 Since no specific charge has been made, Peter rightly assumes that the vague *this* of the question is the *good deed done to a crippled man* yesterday. The implication is quiet but powerful: "How can you accuse us of doing something bad? It was an act of kindness to a poor crippled man." "You want to know **how** he has been healed (literally 'saved' in the Greek)"?

4:10 Their question has given him a perfect opening, but he must boldly seize it. "You as the representative rulers of the nation and all the people of Israel must know that this is a gracious "one more chance" appeal by God to believe in Jesus of Nazareth. You ask his name; his name is Jesus Christ of Nazareth, and it is in his power that this man stands before you healthy." The man had also been dragged before the court; perhaps not a wise move on the part of the prosecutors to bring "Exhibit A" for the defense into the courtroom. Again Peter presses on them the title *Christos* (Messiah) as he did in 2:31 and 38 and 3:6. That is the point at issue and Peter does not flinch.

That would have been enough, but Peter makes his situation worse! For the third time he accuses them, this time to their faces, by reminding them that they were responsible for crucifying God's Messiah! *Whom **you** crucified!* The *you* is emphatic.

But God *raised him from the dead.* The resurrection is the proof that Jesus of Nazareth really is the Messiah. God fixed what you destroyed. This healing of the crippled man is yet another sign that God can restore that which is dead. The resurrected one is his Messiah. If you will repent God can restore you to spiritual health as he has restored this man to physical health.

There is no doubt that this is again an appeal, the third appeal, to the leaders of the nation of Israel to acknowledge Jesus as Messiah. The grace of God in giving Israel so many opportunities to repent and believe is remarkable.

4:11 No testimony to Israel is complete without a proof from Scripture. The biggest obstacle ("stumbling block") for Jews of that day (and even to this day) was that Jesus had been crucified. How then could he be the Messiah? The answer is that his rejection was prophesied in Scripture and Psa 118:22 is one of the key proof texts. Psalm 118:22 was one of the favorites used by Jesus himself (Matt 21:42 [parallel to Mark 12:10-11 and Luke 20:17]) and the early church (here and 1 Pet 2:7). Here is another sword thrust to pierce the consciences of the Sanhedrin. *The stone you builders rejected has become the keystone.* The word *builders* was used as a figure of speech in rabbinical literature for teachers and students of the law and in the Qumran community for leaders of a religious community.[3]

The cornerstone was the large rectangular stone which set the exact location and direction of the whole foundation. (We should not imagine our modern cornerstones which are often not in the corner and whose chief function is to bear an inscription of the date of construction.) The cornerstone is the most important stone in the building. It has been carefully measured and precisely prepared at the stone quarry by expert craftsmen, but the builders on-site rejected it out of hand. The teachers and scribes have rejected Messiah but God will now make him the cornerstone of a new building, the temple which is his body, the Church.

4:12 Peter now shuts the door to other Messiahs. "There is no other Stone that fits, and you have rejected him. Now you must repent and accept God's only Messiah. Do not expect another Messiah. Salvation is found in no one else." Some have suggested the possibility that people of other religions call on Christ unknowingly under other names. Could we not concede that a Jōdō Shinshū (Buddhist) believer in Japan, for example, who calls on the name of Amida for salvation might in the end turn out to be calling upon the name of Jesus? In our day, theologies of a "wider hope" are being floated which suggest that some worship the true God or find salvation in Christ even within non-Christian religions.

But the Spirit says here through Peter that, not only is there no other savior, there is **no other name** guaranteeing (*must be saved*) salvation. The pressure for "tolerance" is powerful and growing; today the only heresy is to claim absolute truth (of any kind) and especially to claim an exclusive savior. Peter could not have consciously anticipated our modern era, but under the inspiration of the Spirit, his statement here in Acts 4:12, along with Jesus' own exclusive claim in John 14:6, rebuts the challenge of modern "tolerance." To compromise on this point is to betray the only true Savior and the only gospel that truly saves.

---

3   Bruce, 152.

Acts 4:13-22

The Decision of the Sanhedrin

13 Now when they saw the boldness of Peter and John, and perceived that they were uneducated, common men, they were astonished. And they recognized that they had been with Jesus. 14 But seeing the man who was healed standing beside them, they had nothing to say in opposition. 15 But when they had commanded them to leave the council, they conferred with one another, 16 saying, "What shall we do with these men? For that a notable sign has been performed through them is evident to all the inhabitants of Jerusalem, and we cannot deny it. 17 But in order that it may spread no further among the people, let us warn them to speak no more to anyone in this name." 18 So they called them and charged them not to speak or teach at all in the name of Jesus. 19 But Peter and John answered them, "Whether it is right in the sight of God to listen to you rather than to God, you must judge, 20 for we cannot but speak of what we have seen and heard." 21 And when they had further threatened them, they let them go, finding no way to punish them, because of the people, for all were praising God for what had happened. 22 For the man on whom this sign of healing was performed was more than forty years old.

4:13 When the Sanhedrin saw the boldness (Greek *parrēsia*, one of the key words of Acts) of Peter and John they were astonished (again one of Luke's key words). May the world also be astonished at our boldness in the face of persecution of opposition! They were astonished, not only at their boldness, but also at the wisdom and perception with which these "laymen" answered. Quoting Scripture was **their** specialty, not to be expected from untaught fishermen from Galilee! *Uneducated* does not mean that they could not read or write; even working men among the Jews of that day had some education.[4] What it means is that they were not trained in the rabbinic schools. The rulers

---

4   It must be admitted that the literal meaning of *agrammatos* and the meaning of the word outside the NT was "illiterate," "unable to write." See BAGD and Moulton and Milligan. This then may have been either a misconception on the part of the Sanhedrin, or, more likely, a deliberate insult. See John 7:15 for a very similar expression applied to Jesus.

correctly guessed that they must have learned from Jesus, whose knowledge of Scripture they had several times experienced in sharp debate.

From this passage we learn two lessons: First layman informally taught in the Bible and filled with the Spirit, are able to wield the sword of the Spirit. Knowledgeable laymen should be entrusted with ministry. Second knowledge of the Scripture is essential.

4:14-16 The smartest, most powerful men in all Israel are stumped by the bold simple answers of "ignorant" powerless Peter. And it was impossible to deny that a miracle had been done because it was standing right before them! So they dismissed the three defendants and held a consultation. The Sanhedrin was powerful, but they still feared public opinion, just as was the case with the popular Jesus whom they had arrested and tried secretly. That the Sadducees, who denied miracles, could not deny this miracle, is ironic.

4:17 The Sanhedrin's chief concern was not to determine the truth but to maintain the status quo; they do not want this movement to spread among the people and threaten their position and authority. It also seems very likely that they feared the spread of this sect might cause them to be charged with the blood of Jesus. So it is with the men of this world; they will do anything to save their own skins.

4:18 Since no law had been broken, the only thing they could do was attempt to intimidate the apostles. Though they had no legal ground to do so, they commanded the apostles not to speak or teach in the name of Jesus.

Now the apostles face a dilemma. In general, the rule of Jesus is that his followers must obey the law and the authorities. Jesus refused all temptations to rebel against the state. He paid his taxes (Matt 17:24-27) and told others to do the same (Mark 12:13-17 and parallels). He was not a political revolutionary.

4:19-20 Peter and John's reply provides a classic answer: "When the demands of the state conflict with the commands of God, the Christian must obey God as the higher authority." *Whether it is right in the sight of God to listen to you rather than to God, you must judge.* The Sanhedrin itself invoked the same principle numerous times in protecting their religion and law against the Roman state and had been granted a surprising amount of autonomy in the religious sphere. Pilate had, in the very beginning of his rule, been forced to back down when he attempted to bring in figures of the emperor on the Roman standards into Jerusalem. The Jews sent a delegation to Caesarea who pleaded for five days for the removal of the standards. Pilate ordered a detachment of soldiers to disperse among the crowds who at a given signal drew their swords. The Jewish delegation then all bared their necks and declared they would rather die than tolerate idolatrous images in Jerusalem. Pilate backed down (Josephus, *Jewish Wars* 2.9.2-3).

Furthermore, how can you prohibit talk about current events? *We cannot but speak* (the ordinary word for speaking; not the word for public speeches used in verse 18) *of what we have seen and heard.* It is always wise for Christ's witnesses to avoid theoretical claims and rather emphasize what actually happened. No one can dispute what Christ has done in lives. For us today, the official record of these events (*what we have seen and heard)* is in the Bible. That is the primary testimony. The secondary testimony is what Christ has done in our own lives.

4:21-22 The Sanhedrin is powerless. All they can do is threaten and bluster. They let the apostles go because they could not decide how to punish them. That might have been no problem if it had not been for the delight and favor of the crowd who had known this healed man as a beggar at the temple for most of forty years. The Sanhedrin thought they had gotten rid of this pest Jesus once and for all, but now the risen Christ, incarnate in his followers, continues to vex them.

∞

Acts 4:23-31

The Praise and Prayer of the Believers

23 When they were released, they went to their friends and reported what the chief priests and the elders had said to them. 24 And when they heard it, they lifted their voices together to God and said, "Sovereign Lord, who

*made the heaven and the earth and the sea and everything in them, 25
who through the mouth of our father David, your servant, said by the
Holy Spirit,*

*"'Why did the Gentiles rage, and the peoples plot in vain? 26 The kings
of the earth set themselves, and the rulers were gathered together, against
the Lord and against his Anointed'—*

*27 for truly in this city there were gathered together against your holy
servant Jesus, whom you anointed, both Herod and Pontius Pilate, along
with the Gentiles and the peoples of Israel, 28 to do whatever your hand
and your plan had predestined to take place. 29 And now, Lord, look upon
their threats and grant to your servants to continue to speak your word
with all boldness, 30 while you stretch out your hand to heal, and signs
and wonders are performed through the name of your holy servant Jesus."
31 And when they had prayed, the place in which they were gathered
together was shaken, and they were all filled with the Holy Spirit and
continued to speak the word of God with boldness.*

4:23 Peter and John went to their own (*tous idious*). This phrase usually refers
to one's own family or people. Its use here shows that the believers in Jesus
considered themselves one family. They did not need to be summoned; they
had no doubt already gathered to pray for Peter and John. When they reported
all that had happened the group burst into spontaneous praise.

4:24 The rest of the passage records at least one of their prayers. It forms a
model for our corporate prayer, especially in times of crisis. *They lifted their
voices together to God.* The Greek word for *together, homothumadon,* literally
means "with (the) same passion." Where is the passion in our corporate
prayer? It is not likely they all spontaneously recited this prayer in unison nor
that this was the only prayer. Perhaps many led in prayers to which there were
many fervent "amens."

First there is an invocation, then a citation of Scripture, then an
application of that Scripture to their immediate situation, and finally three
requests. The current ultra-informal style is to rush into the presence of God
with little pause, but these believers stopped to remember to Whom they were
speaking, the Sovereign and Creator of the universe. *Sovereign Lord* renders the
Greek *despotēs,* which at that time simply meant "master" or "lord" without
any of the negative connotation of the English word "despot."

Who made the heaven and earth and sea and everything in them is reminiscent of many OT prayers such as Psa 146:6. Hezekiah, in a time of crisis, prayed a similar prayer (2 Kings 19:15-19). Anything that weakens our perception of God as sovereign creator undercuts our faith for prayer.

4:25-26 This is a quotation of the opening verses of Psalm 2. Some Jews recognized this psalm as messianic before Christ came.[5] Jesus Himself may have taught them the messianic meaning of Psalm 2 (Luke 24:27). *The kings of the earth* (Gentiles) and *the rulers* (of the Jews) have united *against the Lord* (God the Father) and *his Anointed* (Christ).

4:27 The early believers now claim the fulfillment of these verses in Psalm 2. Herod was Herod Antipas who ruled Galilee under Rome from 4 BC to 39 AD. This Herod refused to take up Jesus' case (Luke 23:6-12). When Jesus was silent *Herod with his soldiers treated him with contempt and mocked him and dressed him in an elegant robe. That day Herod and Pilate became friends.* They hated each other but were united in their hatred of Jesus.[6] So it still often is in this world where unnatural allies combine to persecute the church of Christ.

Gentiles, that is, the Roman soldiers and *peoples of Israel,*[7] was another unnatural and demonic alliance. Who was responsible for the death of Christ? This verse makes it very clear that at least two Gentile rulers (though Herod was really half Jewish) and the Gentiles and certain *peoples* of the Jews shared the blame equally. But verse 28 makes clear that ultimately God himself was also responsible because the cross was his predestined plan.

4:28 "Man (even the worst of men) rules but God overrules." The crucifixion of Messiah, still a stumbling block to the Jews (and later the Muslims), was not an unfortunate accident but wholly in the sovereign plan and purpose of God.

---

5   Psalm of Solomon 17:22-23 (70-40 BC) and the Dead Sea Scrolls document 4Qflorilegum (first century).

6   According to Philo, Herod reported to Rome that Pilate had caused a riot at the Feast of Tabernacles in the year 32 (*Leg. Gai.* 299-305). This had caused enmity between Pilate and Herod. Cited from H. W. Hoehner, "Chronology" in *Dictionary of Jesus and the Apostles* (IVP, 1992), 121.

7   Luke may have used the plural *peoples* to indicate the various factions of Judaism (the Pharisees, Sadducees, the Zealots, and the Essenes), who quarreled bitterly among themselves but united in crucifying their Messiah.

This is a repetition of the theme of Acts 2:23. The same truth is stated in Rev 13:8 *the lamb slain from the foundation of the world.*

4:29-30 Lastly we have the petitions which are three: 1) That God may *look upon* the threats of the rulers 2) That they may speak the word with boldness and that 3), there might be more signs and wonders. It is remarkable that they do not ask for relief from the opposition or protection from persecution. That is the first thing most of us would ask for! In the request that God *look upon* the danger, they commit just how he handles the problem completely to him. Again we have that key word of Acts: boldness (*parrēsia*). It first means clarity of speech and secondarily boldness of speech, especially in the presence of superiors. How much we need clarity and boldness of testimony and evangelism throughout the world today! And the more dangerous the circumstances, the more we need *parrēsia*!

Your holy servant (pais) is a title used only in the earliest Jewish church (Acts 3:13; 26; 4:27; 30). As such it is evidence of the early date of this record. It seems to have been replaced by the title "Son of God" in the Hellenistic and Gentile churches. It is translated "servant" in most Bibles (except the KJV), but the original meaning of the word was "child." By extension it later also included servants or slaves in the household. It is a hard choice whether to translate it "servant" or "child" here. Either way, Jesus was both the servant of Jehovah and the Son of God and perhaps this ancient title combines both meanings.

Should we ask for *signs and wonders* today? The church today is divided (often rather sharply) between those who think that miracles of healing ceased with the Apostolic Age and those who think that the "full gospel" must include signs and wonders. My bias is toward the former, but I always told my students this: God can do miracles anytime and any place He wants to. There are many reports of signs and wonders in the underground churches of China. Second, always demand the real thing. Healing a headache or backache in a phony "healing meeting" is not the real thing. How about healing terminal cancer or Alzheimer's disease? Phony healers sometimes cruelly raise false hopes for the most desperate and then blame them for their lack of faith when there is no healing.

4:31 God acknowledged their prayers by shaking the place! This is not necessarily an earthquake. Such a shaking was a sign of the presence of God, as Sinai *trembled greatly* when the Lord descended (Ex 19:18). Despite many other miracles in the book of Acts, this event was unique. God does not always work in the same way.

Again they were all filled with the Holy Spirit. One baptism, many fillings. Nine times the filling with the Spirit is mentioned in Luke-Acts.[8] This is the third time in Acts. In each case the filling is to enable speaking for God. Here they *continued to speak the word of God (the message of Jesus) with parreisia (boldness).*

⌒⌒

Acts 4:32-37

The Sharing Church

32 Now the full number of those who believed were of one heart and soul, and no one said that any of the things that belonged to him was his own, but they had everything in common. 33 And with great power the apostles were giving their testimony to the resurrection of the Lord Jesus, and great grace was upon them all. 34 There was not a needy person among them, for as many as were owners of lands or houses sold them and brought the proceeds of what was sold 35 and laid it at the apostles' feet, and it was distributed to each as any had need. 36 Thus Joseph, who was also called by the apostles Barnabas (which means son of encouragement), a Levite, a native of Cyprus, 37 sold a field that belonged to him and brought the money and laid it at the apostles' feet.

This section forms an interlude between the events of the founding of the Jerusalem church to make a general statement of how the early church shared wealth and possessions. The Spirit filled church is a generous, giving church that takes care of its own. This generosity has a direct connection with testimony (v. 33). In verses 36 and 37 Luke gives a specific instance of the

---

8   Luke 1:15, 41, 67; Acts 2:4; 4:8, 31; 9:17; 13:9, 52.

generosity of Barnabas, which also serves to introduce Barnabas, who later becomes the man who brought Paul into ministry in the Antioch church.

4:32 The word *full number,* which translates the Greek *plēthos,* is here used to mean "congregation." [9]They were *of one heart and soul,* a result of being filled with the same Spirit. The infant church is still in a new-born ideal state which will be tested in chapter 5. As a specific concrete example of this spiritual unity, none claimed that what he possessed was his own exclusive possession, but was at the disposal of anyone in need.

As the following verses make clear, this does not mean that everyone sold everything and lived in a separate community or monastery like the Qumran community or the present-day Hutterites of North America. The phrase describes an attitude rather than a literal commune. This passage repeats the description of the church just after the Day of Pentecost (2:44-46) and must have been very important to Luke, whose gospel shows a special concern for the poor and needy.

4:33 There is a cause/effect relationship between verses 32 and 33. Sharing of material items led to greater power in testimony, specifically testimony about the resurrection of Jesus, which was always the heart of evangelism in the Apostolic Age. *Great grace was upon them all.* The grace of God appeared in supplying material needs as well as spiritual fruit and joy. Such unselfishness in attitude and action must have amazed the world around them and must have impressed the unbelieving Jews with an actual demonstration of the word in their Torah *There shall be no poor among you* (Deut 15:4).

4:34-35 These verses resume a concrete description of the *all things in common* attitude. No one lacked because the wealthy would *from time to time*[10] sell real estate and put it at the disposal of the apostles for distribution to the needy. One is surprised that the poverty of the needy was so serious that it called for the drastic measure of selling real estate. Not only that, but that wealthy believers were so strong in their faith that they could do such a radical thing.

---

9   Luke uses this word *plēthos* similarly to denote a body of believers in Acts 6;2, 5; 15:12, 30.

10   *From time to time* in the NIV accurately portrays the sense of the Greek imperfect tense, which here shows repeated acts in the past.

This incident no doubt reflects a sharp division of Jerusalem society into rich and poor, have and have-nots. In the time of Jesus there was no "middle class." One was either rich (owned land) or was poor and survived as a day laborer or a worker on rich men's estates. There was no government that provided hospitals, unemployment compensation, orphanages, old folks' homes, and all the largess of the modern welfare state.

Why did Jerusalem have such especially severe poverty even into the time of Paul, who was often preoccupied with the collection for the poor saints in Jerusalem? One scholar points to famine and political unrest and lack of employment among large numbers who flocked there from the countryside.[11] There may well have been another factor, and that is that many believers in the "false" Messiah Jesus may have lost their jobs.

Those who sold their lands were obeying literally the "hard word" of their Lord, who twice told his would-be followers to sell their lands and give to the poor.[12] We who live in rich modern capitalistic societies where most Christians own their own houses and own at least one car and often two or more, have a tough time with this command, usually watering it down to mean something like "Be willing to sell." Yes, the welfare state government takes care of the poor, and yes, in some countries it is hard to find truly starving indigent, but there is so much poverty in other parts of the world that we need to do some serious soul searching as to how much we keep for ourselves. In countries where real poverty prevails, the poor are constantly "one inch in front of our nose" (Japanese expression). In such cases, Acts 2 and 4 teach us that we must first take care of our own, that is, the household of faith, and then be generous with others as well. That the wealthy in the Jerusalem church were willing to share their homes for meetings, or sell them for the needy in their midst, was a potent witness to a Power that wipes out disparities of social class, prestige, and wealth. Without the same radical commitment, it is not surprising that we do not see the same radical results.

4:36-37 These verses illustrate a movement from the general (verses 32-35) to the particular. As one notable example of those who sold land, Joseph, whose

---

11   Joachim Jeremias, *Jerusalem in the Time of Jesus*. Philadelphia, Fortress, 1969, 121-122, cited by Longenecker, 310.

12   Once to the rich young ruler (Matt 19:21; Mark 10:21; and Luke 18:22), and once to his disciples (Luke 12:33). It is interesting that only Luke records the latter. Luke has a special interest in the poor.

nickname was *Son of Encouragement,* is mentioned.[13] He may not have given more than others (only one field!) but Luke introduces him here because he will play a key role in bridging gaps—the gap between Hebraic churches and Hellenistic churches and the gap between new convert Paul and the churches which were highly suspicious of persecutor Saul. Being a Levite he had status in the Jewish community; because he was from Cyprus, he understood the Jewish diaspora community. A study of the references to Barnabas in the NT is very rewarding.

Lessons for Life

1. Success in evangelism will often be followed by persecution. Expect it.
2. The secret of boldness in witness is being filled with the Holy Spirit.
3. There is only one way of salvation and only one Savior, and his name is Jesus.
4. Always obey the laws of men unless the command of God conflicts with the commands of men; then obey God.
5. Don't ask for persecution to be removed; pray for boldness to speak God's word anyway.
6. Spirit filled people are generous people who meet the needs of their brethren in Christ even if radical sharing is necessary.

---

13   The verb *parakaleō* and the noun *paraklēsis* are always fascinatingly ambiguous for they can mean 1) to exhort, exhortation, 2) to comfort, and 3) to encourage.

ACTS 5

ANANIAS AND SAPPHIRA
AND THE ARREST OF
THE APOSTLES

Acts 5:1-11

The Internal Attack: Ananias and Sapphira

1 But a man named Ananias, with his wife Sapphira, sold a piece of property, 2 and with his wife's knowledge he kept back for himself some of the proceeds and brought only a part of it and laid it at the apostles' feet. 3 But Peter said, "Ananias, why has Satan filled your heart to lie to the Holy Spirit and to keep back for yourself part of the proceeds of the land? 4 While it remained unsold, did it not remain your own? And after it was sold, was it not at your disposal? Why is it that you have contrived this deed in your heart? You have not lied to man but to God." 5 When Ananias heard these words, he fell down and breathed his last. And great fear came upon all who heard of it. 6 The young men rose and wrapped him up and carried him out and buried him.

7 After an interval of about three hours his wife came in, not knowing what had happened. 8 And Peter said to her, "Tell me whether you sold the land for so much." And she said, "Yes, for so much." 9 But Peter said to her, "How is it that you have agreed together to test the Spirit of the Lord? Behold, the feet of those who have buried your husband are at the door, and they will carry you out." 10 Immediately she fell down at his feet and breathed her last. When the young men came in they found her dead, and

*they carried her out and buried her beside her husband. 11 And great fear
came upon the whole church and upon all who heard of these things.*

For the time being, external opposition has failed and the baby Church is
victorious. But now, out of the blue, there is a Satanic attack from **within**, and
two believers fail badly. The pristine loveliness and holiness of the newborn
church is abruptly disfigured.

5:1-2 The deceit of Ananias and Sapphira. At first it seems that they are
following the illustrious example of Barnabas. But whereas Barnabas gave the
whole portion of the sale, this couple withheld a portion for themselves. The
word used (*nophizomai,* also in verse 3) is the same word used of Aachan in the
Greek OT (Josh 7:1) when he held back a portion of the loot that had been
dedicated to God. It is used only one other time in the NT (Tit 2:10), and
there it is translated "pilfer."

5:3-6 The Denunciation by Peter and the Death of Ananias. Peter, because
of special insight the Holy Spirit had given him, immediately challenges the
deceit of Ananias. In this Peter was like his Lord, who "knew what was in the
hearts of men." *Why has Satan filled your heart to lie to the Holy Spirit and to
keep back for yourself part of the proceeds of the land?* Behind the duplicity of
Ananias was the temptation of Satan. The ironic horror was that whereas the
hearts of the others were filled with the Holy Spirit, Ananias had allowed his
heart to be filled with the Dark Spirit, and the result was that he attempted to
deceive the Holy Spirit. *You have not lied to man but to God.* (Note here the
assumption of both the personality and the deity of the Holy Spirit.)

Peter's next words make it clear that the sin was not refusing to sell the
land (no one was being forced to sell) but in the **hypocrisy** of making a show
of donating the whole while withholding a part.

When Ananias heard these words, he fell down dead. He was struck
dead by God, not by Peter, just as Aachan (Josh 7) and Uzzah (2 Sam 6:7) in
the Old Testament, and the result was that *great fear* fell upon not only the
church, but also on all the non-believers who heard about it.

There is considerable resistance and aversion in the heart of present-day
believers (and contempt in the hearts of unbelievers) to the phrase "fear of
God." Usually we pass it off by saying, "Oh, that means 'trust in God; to fear
God is to trust God or to respect God.'" There is a large element of truth in
that explanation, but a passage like this is a healthy reminder that there is

such a thing as real fear in the Presence of God. The chief reason that we do not see revival in the church and conversions from the world is that today there is little fear of the judgment of God. Many believers are complacent and presumptuous because they "are saved" and many unbelievers seek God only when they get in trouble, not because they will someday stand before the Great White Throne (Rev 20:11-15).

5:7-11 The Judgment on Sapphira. An almost identical scene is played out three hours later when Ananias' wife comes in, perhaps for a prayer meeting, expecting praise and commendation for their generous contribution. She probably had every expectation of meeting her husband there. It does seem harsh that she had not been immediately notified of the death of her husband, and that indeed she had not even been invited to his funeral![1] But the conspiracy must be rooted out to cleanse the infant church. Peter gives her a chance to tell the truth, but she repeats the lie they had agreed upon. Peter pronounces sentence upon her with the prescience of an OT prophet and she is soon buried with her husband.

We must face squarely the question that occurs to anyone who reads this story, "Why were Ananias and Sapphira judged so harshly"? God is compassionate and forgiving, and if he treated us all so severely, no one in the church would be left alive, because we are all guilty of hypocrisy from time to time, even if not such a blatant deception. Three things can be said by way of understanding the severity of God in this case.

First, God the Spirit was present and openly active in a way that made this period very special. Miracles were occurring daily; the power of God was daily manifest to all. To try God in the white light of his manifest power made the offence much more serious. We see this in the harshness of punishments that God struck upon the Israelites among those who had seen the miraculous deliverance from Egypt and his daily provision in the wilderness. Later generations were given more leniency.

Second, we find that **the first time** a sin occurs in a new juncture in the economy of God, it is severely judged. Eve's sin in eating the forbidden fruit. The rebellion of the Israelites against Moses at the first giving of the Law

---

1   I am inclined to believe that J. D. M. Derrett "Ananias, Sapphira, and the Right of Property," *Studies in the New Testament Volume 1*, 193-201, cited by Witherington, 217) may be right in his opinion that proper mourning and burial, so important to the Jews, was denied to those, who like Nadab and Abihu in Lev 10:1-5, were struck down by God.

(Exod 32:35). The first time a man breaks the law of the Sabbath, he is put to death at God's command (Num 15:32-36), but this is the first and only time such severity is required. Aachan was the first to break the command about dedicating all of the spoils to God (Josh 7). We call this the **"law of first transgression."** The first time a commandment is broken, it is punished very severely, but then it is not punished so severely afterward. The case of Ananias and Sapphira fits this pattern.

Third, death for a believer, though drastic, is not to be cursed from the presence of God but to be sent home into the presence of God. I assume that Ananias and Sapphira, unlike Simon the Sorcerer of Acts 8, were true believers. At least Peter does not say they were false believers. Among the Corinthians, there were those who "slept" (died) because they had defiled the Lord's Table (1 Cor 11:30).

∽

Acts 5:12-16

Signs and Wonders Among the People

12 Now many signs and wonders were regularly done among the people by the hands of the apostles. And they were all together in Solomon's Portico. 13 None of the rest dared join them, but the people held them in high esteem. 14 And more than ever believers were added to the Lord, multitudes of both men and women, 15 so that they even carried out the sick into the streets and laid them on cots and mats, that as Peter came by at least his shadow might fall on some of them. 16 The people also gathered from the towns around Jerusalem, bringing the sick and those afflicted with unclean spirits, and they were all healed.

This paragraph is the third summary section in Acts (after 2:42-47 and 4:32-35) and like the first two, it highlights the victorious progress of the church. Themes common to all three include 1) Miracles done by the apostles. 2) The unity and solidarity of the believers. 3) The favor of the people. 4) Growth in membership. One theme that is absent in this summary is communal sharing of goods. On the other hand, there is much more emphasis on miraculous healings. Until now, besides the miraculous events of the Day of Pentecost, there has been only one specific miracle: the healing of the lame man in chapter 3. Now there is an outburst of miracles, just as the believers had prayed (4:30). The church has not lost its momentum or its power despite the tragedy of Ananias and Sapphira. Discipline in the church can work out for renewed zeal and the furtherance of the gospel.[2] The paragraph also explains the jealousy of the high priest in the following section.

So far only the apostles do miracles. Miracles served to authenticate the apostles as the foundation (Eph 2:20) of the church and as the true representatives of the Lord Jesus. None of the apostles are here mentioned by name, but we are confident that all twelve, including newly appointed Matthias (1:26), were active in the healing ministry.

The *they all* of verse 12 *they were all together in Solomon's portico* would of course include more than the apostles. Perhaps all 5,000 occasionally gathered at one time in the portico. This occupation of a section of the temple precincts would not have brought joy to the hearts of high priests and the Sanhedrin.

5:13 *None of the rest dared join them, but the people held them in high esteem.* Some commentators see three groups here: the believers in Jesus, *the rest* (*hoi loipoi*), and *the people.* The phrase *hoi loipoi* (*the rest*), without any qualifying phrase, usually refers to unbelievers.[3] Both *the rest* and *the people* are most likely the same group of not-yet-believing Jews. They were afraid to join the believers in Jesus of Nazareth, partly because of fear of the authorities, partly because of the fate of Ananias and Sapphira, and partly because in any group many fear change and wait on the sidelines to see what happens. Is not this still true today! Even in the presence of so many miracles! Fear is the chief barrier to commitment and faith.

5:14 *And more than ever (or from time to time) believers were added to the Lord, multitudes of both men and women* seems to contradict verse 13. Verse 13 gives the general picture of prevailing unbelief. But this is followed by a correction or qualification that many men (and women!) were believing.[4] Faith in Jesus

---

2   As in 2 Cor 7:11

3   Matt 25:11; Luke 8:10; Rom 11:7; 1 Thess 4:13; 5:6; Rev 20:5.

4   My rendering "from time to time" is an attempt to show the force of the Greek imperfect tense.

results in being *added to the Lord*. Yes, added to the church, but also added to the Lord.

5:15-16 *so that they even carried out the sick into the streets and laid them on cots and mats, that as Peter came by at least his shadow might fall on some of them. The people also gathered from the towns around Jerusalem, bringing the sick and those afflicted with unclean spirits, and they were all healed.*

So that seems to refer to the statement of verse 12 that *the apostles were performing many miraculous signs and wonders among the people* (NIV).

What are we to make of healings by Peter's shadow? Notice that the text does not actually say these people were healed by contact with Peter's shadow; though that is possible, as people were healed by Paul's handkerchiefs and aprons in Acts 19:12. People in ancient times were superstitious about shadows cast by persons and believed that the shadow "was seen as an extension of the person or personality, perhaps even in some contexts a manifestation of the soul or spiritual life force of a person."[5] In modern India, upper caste people fear lest the shadow of a lower caste fall upon them. But this is just the opposite: Peter's shadow was deemed a blessing, not a curse, and caused much popular excitement! Often revivals or healing movements, even today, are accompanied by gullibility and superstition. But God can overlook such human weakness and he honors the simple faith of the less sophisticated as he did for the woman who touched Jesus' robe (Mark 5:26-30) and for the crowds who lined the streets to *touch his garment* (Mark 6:56). What Jesus did on earth he is now doing from heaven by giving Peter the ability to do the same things he did on earth.

In verse 16 we are informed for the first time of the spread of the gospel beyond Jerusalem into nearby towns of Judea (Acts 1:8). No matter what the disease, *they were all healed*, whether cases of illness or demon possession. One wishes that *all were healed* would also be true of many present-day healing meetings, from which so many turn away cruelly disappointed.

---

5   Witherington, 227, footnote 128.

Acts 5:17-42

Before the Sanhedrin Again

17 But the high priest rose up, and all who were with him (that is, the party of the Sadducees), and filled with jealousy **18** they arrested the apostles and put them in the public prison. **19** But during the night an angel of the Lord opened the prison doors and brought them out, and said, **20** "Go and stand in the temple and speak to the people all the words of this Life." **21** And when they heard this, they entered the temple at daybreak and began to teach.

Now when the high priest came, and those who were with him, they called together the council, all the senate of the people of Israel, and sent to the prison to have them brought. **22** But when the officers came, they did not find them in the prison, so they returned and reported, **23** "We found the prison securely locked and the guards standing at the doors, but when we opened them we found no one inside." **24** Now when the captain of the temple and the chief priests heard these words, they were greatly perplexed about them, wondering what this would come to. **25** And someone came and told them, "Look! The men whom you put in prison are standing in the temple and teaching the people." **26** Then the captain with the officers went and brought them, but not by force, for they were afraid of being stoned by the people.

27 And when they had brought them, they set them before the council. And the high priest questioned them, **28** saying, "We strictly charged you not to teach in this name, yet here you have filled Jerusalem with your teaching, and you intend to bring this man's blood upon us." **29** But Peter and the apostles answered, "We must obey God rather than men. **30** The God of our fathers raised Jesus, whom you killed by hanging him on a tree. **31** God exalted him at his right hand as Leader and Savior, to give repentance to Israel and forgiveness of sins. **32** And we are witnesses to these things, and so is the Holy Spirit, whom God has given to those who obey him."

33 When they heard this, they were enraged and wanted to kill them. **34** But a Pharisee in the council named Gamaliel, a teacher of the law held in honor by all the people, stood up and gave orders to put the men *outside for a little while. 35 And he said to them, "Men of Israel, take care what you are about to do with these men. 36 For before these days Theudas rose up, claiming to be somebody, and a number of men, about four hundred, joined him. He was killed, and all who followed him were dispersed and came to nothing. 37 After him Judas the Galilean rose up in the days of the census and drew away some of the people after him. He too perished, and all who followed him were scattered. 38 So in the present case I tell you, keep away from these men and let them alone, for if this plan or this undertaking is of man, it will fail; 39 but if it is of God, you will not be able to overthrow them. You might even be found opposing God!" So they took his advice, 40 and when they had called in the apostles, they beat them and charged them not to speak in the name of Jesus, and let them go. 41 Then they left the presence of the council, rejoicing that they were counted worthy to suffer dishonor for the name. 42 And every day, in the temple and from house to house, they did not cease teaching and preaching that the Christ is Jesus.*

This section has two parts: 5:17-26, The Arrest of the Apostles; and 5:28-42, The Trial and the Release of the Apostles. The second part can be divided into two: 5:28-33, The Interrogation of the Apostles and 5:34-43, The Advice of Gamaliel and the Decision to Release the Apostles.

We have here the second of three cycles of arrest, inquisition, and sentence before the Sanhedrin. The first two (4:1-23 and 5:17-42) are very similar. Both arrests are a direct result of preaching Jesus in the temple. In both, apostles are examined before the Sanhedrin. In both, Peter gives a brief defense and accuses them of killing their Messiah and appeals for their repentance. Both describe the helplessness and frustration of the Sanhedrin. In both the apostles are commanded not speak any more in the name of Jesus and are released. In both, the disciples rejoice and defy the ban by continuing to preach Jesus. The third cycle is the arrest and conviction of Stephen (chapters 6 and 7).

But the stakes are here much higher and the tension much greater than in chapter 4. Not just Peter and John but all the apostles are arrested. Before the Council was *astonished* (4:13) but here they are *enraged* (5:33). The story is building up to the climax of persecution that will break out in 6:9 and end with the death of Stephen and *a great persecution against the church* (8:1).

Throughout, the main emphasis of the story is: 1) The power of God to deliver. 2) The impotence of the most powerful forces in the land against the power of God. 3) The persistence of the apostles in standing fast before the Sanhedrin, boldly urging them to repent and in preaching Jesus despite threats. God through the apostles is making a final direct appeal to the nation of Israel to repent of their sin of crucifying God's Messiah.

The words of 5:17-18 reflect 4:3. Again the Sadducees arrest them and throw them in jail. This time, though, they are *filled with jealousy*. They are more concerned with their own position and power than they are about the truth or falsity of the claims being made about Jesus of Nazareth.

5:19-20 *But during the night an angel of the Lord opened the prison doors and brought them out, and said,* **20** *"Go and stand in the temple and speak to the people all the words of this Life."*

This is the first of three miraculous "jail breaks" in Acts (see also the escape of Peter in chapter 12 and the escape of Paul and Silas in chapter 16). There is a possibility that the angel was not just any angel, but the angel of the LORD that appeared as a divine theophany in the OT (Genesis 16 and 22; Exod 3:2; and Judges 6 and 13). Is this Christ himself intervening on behalf of his own?

Why was this miraculous deliverance necessary? Could they not simply be escorted from prison to face the Council as in chapter 4? The miraculous escape was a potent testimony to the power of God and the futility of resisting him. It also underscores the divine imperative of seizing as much time as possible for preaching the risen Christ.

5:21-26 *Now when the high priest came, and those who were with him, they called together the council, all the senate of the people of Israel, and sent to the prison to have them brought.* **22** *But when the officers came, they did not find them in the prison, so they returned and reported,* **23** *"We found the prison securely locked and the guards standing at the doors, but when we opened them we found no one inside."*

Business got started early in the temple; the Sanhedrin, *all the senate of the people of Israel* gathered just as they had gathered at dawn to condemn Jesus of Nazareth. The apostles, meanwhile, were teaching the people about Jesus. The reader must smile at the irony of the situation.

5:24-26 *Now when the captain of the temple and the chief priests heard these words, they were greatly perplexed about them, wondering what this would come* *to. And someone came and told them, "Look! The men whom you put in prison are standing in the temple and teaching the people." Then the captain with the officers went and brought them, but not by force, for they were afraid of being stoned by the people.*

The prison doors were locked and the guards were awake and on post, completely unaware that some of the cells were empty. Imagine the perplexity and anxiety of the captain of the temple guard and the chief priests! "What do you mean, they are not there?" One would think the high priest would put two and two together and realize that the hand of God was at work. But no, they thrust aside the plain evidence and plunge ahead blindly.

Not by force, for they were afraid of being stoned by the people. "Excuse me gentlemen, but the Sanhedrin would like to have a word with you." Just as in the case of Jesus' arrest and trial the chief priests *feared the people* (Mark 12:12; Luke 20:19; 22:2). We see the importance of the fact that the believers in Jesus still had the favor of the people (2:47; 5:13).

5:27-33 The Interrogation of the Apostles. *And when they had brought them, they set them before the council. And the high priest questioned them, saying, "We strictly charged you not to teach in this name, yet here you have filled Jerusalem with your teaching, and you intend to bring this man's blood upon us."*

The high priest is that same Caiaphas who had recently condemned Jesus. Previously there was no legal accusation against the apostles; now they had disobeyed a direct order. The situation is very ominous; the apostles are in danger of their lives and the newborn church is in danger of total extirpation. Judaism, even then, tolerated a broad spectrum of religious views and a variety of sects. But the priests hated Jesus of Nazareth because he threatened the very foundations of their power. They feared this new teaching because the guilt of the blood of Jesus was on their heads. Notice that they cannot even bring themselves to pronounce Jesus' name; it is a put-down snarl, *this name.*

5:29-32 The Apostles' Answer. *But Peter and the apostles answered, "We must obey God rather than men. The God of our fathers raised Jesus, whom you killed by hanging him on a tree. God exalted him at his right hand as Leader and Savior, to give repentance to Israel and forgiveness of sins. And we are witnesses to these things, and so is the Holy Spirit, whom God has given to those who obey him."*

There is not one word of apology or flattery. This is again an unbelievably bold head-on confrontation. The words are an even more terse repetition of what Peter had said in 4:8-12. First, as to the charge of disobedience, as we said before (4:19), we must obey God rather than men. Second, God raised up Jesus, whom **you** crucified (the third time for this accusation). Third, God exalted him and now he is Prince (*Archēgos*, that same title given Jesus in 3:15) and Savior. Fourth, he is still offering repentance and forgiveness of sins to you and to all Israel. Fifth, we, along with the Spirit of God himself, are the official witnesses of these facts; we are bound with a holy obligation and cannot obey your commands to cease our testimony.

For the first time, the title *Savior* is used in Acts (The only other place is Acts 13:23). The title *Archēgos*,[6] having little meaning among the Gentiles, soon dropped out and the title *Sōter* (Savior) became more popular. As *Archēgos* Jesus demands and grants repentance; as *Sōter* he provides forgiveness. Even this appalling sin can be forgiven; it is not yet too late.

Repentance is still being offered to and demanded of Israel. Though several thousands of Jews have repented and believed, the nation as a whole has not, and is tragically close to spurning the gift of God again. Repentance here, as in Acts 11:18; Rom 2:4; and 2 Tim 2:25, is a gift of God. At the same time it is the responsibility of man.

Still today, two thousand years later, all people everywhere are responsible before the God who raised Jesus from the dead to repent and believe the testimony that the apostles gave. And all believers are responsible before their Lord and Savior to continue the witness the apostles began. Those who repent and believe are those who obey the testimony of the Spirit and so receive the gift of the Spirit.

5:33 *When they heard this, they were enraged and wanted to kill them.* The Greek word for *enraged* is literally "sawn through." The Greek indicates that they not only *wanted* to put them to death, they started planning to kill them. Instead of acknowledging their sin, they erupt in fury against those who point out their sin. Such is human nature the world over, and all the more so for those who sit in the seat of pride and power. Peter has gone too far, said too much, and now he will be to blame for the deaths of all of them.

---

6 What would this word, not followed by the words *of life* as in 3:15, mean to the Sanhedrin? *Archēgos* was used in the Greek OT (LXX) 28 times and meant "leader" or "head" and most often "military captain or leader." It is not unlikely that to the first century Jews, the term in the singular referred to the Messiah who would triumph over the ungodly nations (Psa Sol 17:23-27, Sibylline Oracles 3.652-56).

5:34-42 The Counsel of Gamaliel and the Release of the Apostles. No one could have predicted this. Help rises from within the ranks of the enemy! The story begins with a miraculous deliverance. It concludes with a providential deliverance. Perhaps the latter is more remarkable.

Who was Gamaliel? This is Gamaliel the First (the elder), not to be confused with Gamaliel II (who lived about 100 AD). Gamaliel I was of the moderate school of Hillel, the grandson of Hillel, the president of the Pharisees' tribunal *Beth Din*, one of the most revered rabbis of his time, and the mentor of Saul of Tarsus (Acts 22:3). "When Rabban ('our Master') Gamaliel the elder died the glory of the Torah ceased, and purity and separateness died."[7] His irenic nature and moderate views were a godsend to the nascent Christian movement at a most critical stage. He takes charge of the proceedings and commands that the defendants be dismissed while he delivers his speech.

5:35-37 *And he said to them, "Men of Israel, take care what you are about to do with these men. For before these days Theudas rose up, claiming to be somebody, and a number of men, about four hundred, joined him. He was killed, and all who followed him were dispersed and came to nothing. After him Judas the Galilean rose up in the days of the census and drew away some of the people after him. He too perished, and all who followed him were scattered.*

Gamaliel defuses the explosive atmosphere by bringing up two cases of false Messiahs whose movements came to nothing. False Messiahs were not uncommon in the tumultuous period of Roman rule from Hezekiah the "robber-chief" in the time of Herod the Great to Simon Bar Kochba who led the last Jewish rebellion in 135 AD. There were at least six false Messiahs that we know about, and probably others of whom we have no record.[8]

Theudas claimed to be *somebody*, probably Messiah, and attracted 400 fanatic followers, but he was killed and his followers dispersed and the movement disappeared. Critics have pounced on verse 36 as one of Luke's most glaring historical blunders. Josephus mentions a Theudas (*Antiquities*, 20.97ff)

> "a certain magician, who persuaded a great part of the people to take their effects with them, and follow him to the river Jordan; for he told

---

7   MSotah 9.15 as cited by Bruce, 175, and many other commentators.

8   Sigmund Mowinkel, *He that Cometh*, Abingdon Press, 1954, 284.

them that he was a prophet, and that he would . . . divide the river
. . . and many were deluded by his words."

The governor of Judea, Cuspius Fadus, sent the cavalry after them. Many were killed or captured and Theudas was decapitated. But Cuspius Fadus did not become prefect until AD 44, at least ten years **after** the events of Acts 1-5.

There are three possibilities. 1) Josephus was correct and Luke is in error. 2) Luke was correct and Josephus is in error. 3) There was another rebel named Theudas, unrecorded by secular history, who rebelled **before** the year AD 6. Although Josephus was capable of error and it can be shown that some of his statements are incorrect (see Witherington's detailed discussion, *Acts*, 238-240), it is hard to imagine either of these careful historians off by some forty years. It is best to take option 3: The name Theudas, like Judas and Jesus and Simon, was very common. The Western text of Acts tells us that the Theudas mentioned here committed suicide, whereas the Theudas Josephus mentions was captured alive and beheaded.

There is no problem with Gamaliel's mention of Judas the Galilean. Josephus mentions the same rebel Judas: "While Quirinius was taking the census of Judea, he (Judas the Galilean) drew the people into revolt against the Romans." (*Antiquities* 20.5.2).

Gamaliel's point is clear. **Both of these movements were obviously not of God because they came to nothing.** If this movement of the Nazarenes is not of God it too will be destroyed by the providence of God. We do not need to destroy it (and assume the risk of punishment by the Romans).

Let them alone, for if this plan or this undertaking is of man, it will fail; but if it is of God, you will not be able to overthrow them.

Did Gamaliel think of 2 Chron 13:12 *Men of Israel, do not fight against the LORD, the God of your fathers, for you will not succeed?*

Gamaliel's advice is in line with that of our Lord himself: *Every plant, which my heavenly Father has not planted will be rooted up. Let them alone!* (Matt 15:13).

How many well-meaning governments, many of them "Christian," have ignored this advice in attempts to eradicate "false religion" and "heresy." The religious persecution we see throughout the world today would cease if the perpetrators practiced this principle.

5:40-42 The Release of the Apostles. Amazingly, Gamaliel's advice won the day. But the Nazarenes had insolently disobeyed a direct order, and they cannot go unpunished, so they were beaten before they were released. The word of Jesus was fulfilled: *they will hand you over to the local councils and flog you in their synagogues* (Matt 10:17).

Luke concludes the section of confrontation with the Sanhedrin (3:1 to 5:40) by emphasizing two things: the joy of the believers, and the fact that the gospel proclamation is completely unhindered and even strengthened. Joy is a favorite theme in Luke's writings, especially rejoicing in the face of persecution. Indeed, they count it an honor to suffer shame for the Name, the only Name by which one can be saved (4:12). They did not flinch or retreat one inch. They continued to evangelize and preach Jesus as Messiah not only in the temple but now also *from house to house*. Their antagonists are helpless to stop them.

Lessons for Life

1.   The wrong use of wealth is a serious sin.
2.   Hypocrisy and lying are serious sins.
3.   There is such a thing as a healthy fear of God.
4.   When the commands of man conflict with the commands of God, obey God rather than man.
5.   God is able to deliver us from danger, whether directly through miracle, or indirectly through his remarkable providence.
6.   Nothing can quench the evangelistic zeal of the Spirit filled.

ACTS 6-8

THE TRANSITION THROUGH "HALF-JEWS"

Three groups of people now become prominent in the spreading of the gospel. In Acts 6 we are introduced to the "Hellenists," who were Greek-speaking Jews. Many of them became converts to Jesus of Nazareth. Second there were the Samaritans of Acts 8. Lastly, proselytes to Judaism are represented by the Ethiopian eunuch of the latter half of Acts 8. These three groups might be thought of as quasi-Jews or Jews with some Gentile characteristics. They were the first "bridges of God" to enable the gospel to cross linguistic and cultural barriers.

ACTS 6

THE APPOINTMENT OF SEVEN DEACONS AND THE ARREST OF STEPHEN

Acts 6:1-6

The Appointment of Seven Deacons

1 Now in these days when the disciples were increasing in number, a complaint by the Hellenists arose against the Hebrews because their widows were being neglected in the daily distribution. . . . 5 And what they said pleased the whole gathering, and they chose Stephen, a man full of faith and of the Holy Spirit, and Philip, and Prochorus, and Nicanor, and Timon, and Parmenas, and Nicolaus, a proselyte of Antioch. 6 These they set before the apostles, and they prayed and laid their hands on them.

With the phrase *in these days* Luke pauses from the main flow of narrative to give background information. Notice that the problem (a bad thing) comes in because of a good thing (the church was growing). Church growth always brings new problems. That is why some shrink back from growth; "if the church is large enough to support the pastor, why multiply problems by growing?" is the unspoken thought of some.

The particular problem in this case grew out of the church's charity towards the widows. In societies before the modern welfare state, the sick, the disabled, and the widows were taken care of by their families or they became beggars. There may have been a number of widows because, even to this day, many Jews spend their last days in Jerusalem in hopes of being buried in the Holy City. Much of the valley slopes between the Mount of Olives and the old city of Jerusalem are today taken up with Jewish tombs. If their husbands died first, and if they had no one to take care of them, they would have been left destitute. This would have been particularly true of the Hellenist widows.

Who were **the Hellenists**? The word occurs only in the New Testament and in a few places in early Christian literature. The most significant of these are in two sermons by the great Greek preacher John Chrysostom (fourth century) who in commenting on Acts 6:1 and 9:29 defines the word to mean "Greek speaking Jews."[1] In the Macedonian Empire established following the conquests of Alexander the Great (died 323 BC), from Athens to India, from Egypt to Macedonia, the common language was Greek and the dominant culture was Greek. This was true of the Jews as well, especially of those of the diaspora (see Acts 2:8-11). If a Jew from Rome, whose native language was Latin, wanted to speak to a Jew from Egypt he used the common language which was Greek; just as an Indian from Delhi and an Indian from Madras use their common language English. Of course a certain amount of culture and worldview accompanies language and this may have caused some tension with the *Hebraioi,* who spoke not Hebrew, but its contemporary form Aramaic. The Aramaic-speaking Jews of Palestine read the Scriptures in Hebrew and conducted their synagogue services in Aramaic and Hebrew, though they too knew some Greek for business in the outside world. On the other hand, the Hellenists read the Scripture in Greek (the Septuagint) and worshipped in Greek in separate synagogues (6:9). Contrary to the ideas of nineteenth century German scholarship, the Hellenist Jews were not more "liberal" doctrinally than the "Hebraists." It was Hellenists, who in their zeal for the Torah of Moses and the temple, attacked Stephen.

Whatever the system for distributing the rations of charity in the Jerusalem church, it was not working properly. The Hellenist widows were being neglected and this caused *goggusmos, grumbling.* Why should they care about food when so many marvelous things were occurring and so many converts were being added to the church daily? Alas, even pious widows must

---

1   Homily 14 on Acts 6:1 and Homily 21 on Acts 9:29.

eat. Even an ideal church has mundane problems and Christians of any age, and any land can nod their heads from personal experience.

6:2-4 When problems arise in the church, it is not unusual for leadership to 1) ignore the problem, 2) minimize the problem, 3) wait to see if the problem goes away or solves itself, or 4) do the work themselves so that it will be done properly. The Twelve Apostles, the God-ordained leadership, did none of these. They immediately called a meeting, not just of the Twelve, but also of all the believers. Here, as elsewhere in Acts, the word *disciple* simply means "believer." Instead of solving the problem themselves they asked the body to help solve the problem. The whole church had to be responsible or "take ownership" for the problem and its solution. The Apostles had the primary task of two ministries (*diakonia*), the ministry of the Word and the ministry of prayer (literally *the* prayer). The former was the preaching of the message about Jesus to the world and teaching its implications to the believers, and the latter the conducting of joint prayer meetings (worship meetings?) among the believers. Preaching and prayer were the chief content of their meetings. Since the beginning of the Pietist movement in the eighteenth century, evangelical believers have tended to place more emphasis on private prayer than on corporate prayer. In Acts, the emphasis is the opposite. Though the Apostles probably spent time in private prayer, it is most likely that the prayer mentioned here was prayer together with other believers such as we saw in the beginning of Acts 2 and the end of Acts 4. They were uniquely gifted and called to these ministries and they could not neglect them to get bogged down in an administrative function. It was not that *serving tables* was too menial for them or beneath their status; it was a question of different gifts and calling. Pastors! Do not let any good thing distract you from your chief calling and duty, the preaching of the Word and prayer!

It is probably impossible to form a complete theology of church government by studying the book of Acts, but we do see here a fine balance between authoritarian concepts and congregational (or democratic) concepts of how to govern the church. As for the former, the apostles are clearly in charge, ordained of God, and move first to solve the problem. They set the qualifications: *of good repute, full of the Spirit and of wisdom.* The apostles *laid their hands* on the selected candidates, which made their selection official. But in between these two apostolic actions the body of believers as a whole selected the first "deacons."[2] Whether this was done by nomination and voting or by informal discussion and consensus is impossible to tell. One suspects the latter. In any case, without congregational participation in the decision, the *grumbling* probably would have continued.

The people they chose were all men and all Hellenists.[3] Was male leadership a concession to the social realities of those times, or was it a permanent principle? Today the issue of women in ministry is a hot topic, which is dividing many churches and denominations. It is perhaps more remarkable that they were all Greek-speaking Jews. The "Hebrews," who were most likely the majority, showed grace and wisdom and trust in selecting only Greeks; grace in yielding leadership to the other side; wisdom in selecting those best qualified to minister to the Greek speakers (though they were in charge of the whole distribution, not just that distribution to their own people); and trust in that they did not insist on one of their own to "check up on" the other side. What a wonderful example for church disputes in our day!

6:7 A Summary Verse. *7 And the word of God continued to increase, and the number of the disciples multiplied greatly in Jerusalem, and a great many of the priests became obedient to the faith.*

Every once in a while Luke pauses and gives a summary statement or "progress report" (6:7; 9:31; 12:24; 16:5; 19:20; and 28:31). Longenecker sees these summaries as the markers of the main structural divisions of Acts which divide it into six "panels."[4] Some of them, as here, seem to divide the flow of a particular story. All of the progress reports show the growth and unity of the church soon after a crisis. "Problem solved, church still growing victoriously." We need to see church problems not as stumbling stones, but as stepping-stones.

It is most interesting that *a great many of the priests became* (better: *were becoming*) *obedient to the faith.* According to Josephus, there were 20,000 priests, and 5,000 of them on duty at one time. During the "off times" they had to eke out a living from a secular trade. We do not read of the conversion of any chief priests. But many from the ordinary priests, men like Zacharias

---

2   The Greek word used here, *diakoeō*, originally meant "to serve tables." It was not until later that the churches instituted **the office** of deacons, but it is not objectionable to call these seven "the first deacons."

3   The names are all male and all Greek.

4   Longenecker, 234. The term "progress report" is Longenecker's phrase.

in Luke 1, believed in Jesus of Nazareth as Messiah. To believe is to obey. Too often the gospel is presented as a personal choice, a mere preference, for those who might need it to solve their problems. We must also present it as an act of obedience demanded by God of all men (Acts 5:32; 17:30; Rom 1:5; 15:18; 2 Thess 1:8; 1 Pet 1:2; 22; 4:17).

For the first time the word faith is used as "the body of truth concerning Jesus the Christ and his salvation" (Gal 1:23; Jude 3; and many passages in the Pastoral epistles such as 1 Tim 5:8). It bears an exclusive claim; there is no other true faith; it is **the** faith.

∽⁀∿

Acts 6:8-15

The Charge of Blasphemy Against Stephen

One of the purposes of 6:1-6 is to introduce Philip, who will appear in chapter 8, and Stephen, who gives a stirring defense of the faith in chapter 7. This paragraph is really the introduction to chapter 7 and is one piece with it.

> **8** And Stephen, full of grace and power, was doing great wonders and signs among the people. **9** Then some of those who belonged to the synagogue of the Freedmen (as it was called), and of the Cyrenians, and of the Alexandrians, and of those from Cilicia and Asia, rose up and disputed with Stephen. **10** But they could not withstand the wisdom and the Spirit with which he was speaking. **11** Then they secretly instigated men who said, "We have heard him speak blasphemous words against Moses and God." **12** And they stirred up the people and the elders and the scribes, and they came upon him and seized him and brought him before the council, **13** and they set up false witnesses who said, "This man never ceases to speak words against this holy place and the law, **14** for we have heard him say that this Jesus of Nazareth will destroy this place and will change the customs that Moses delivered to us." **15** And gazing at him, all who sat in the council saw that his face was like the face of an angel.

Stephen, though just a "layman," and just an administrator of the food distribution had unusual powers of doing miracles. This was because of the sovereign grace and power of God. We do not read that the other six deacons could do these miracles. Apparently Stephen was also proclaiming the gospel and debating as well, because the Hellenists of the Freedmen Synagogue lost arguments with him. This is the first time we read of opposition from among ordinary Jews, and they are "foreign" Jews. They are zealous for the old ways, as was Saul of Tarsus. Saul may have attended that synagogue *(those from Cilicia)* and known these zealots well. The words of Jesus are being fulfilled: *if they persecuted me they will persecute you too* (John 15:20). *For I will give you words and wisdom that none of your adversaries will be able to resist or contradict* (Luke 21:15 NIV).

6:8-15 The charge is blasphemy *against Moses and against God* and, in v. 13, against the Temple (*this holy place*). Some have assumed that there is some substance to the charge and that Stephen, even if he was misunderstood, was a "liberal" Hellenist who really did say things that could be construed as anti-Torah or anti-Temple. But the text says twice that they set up false witnesses who made such a claim. If Stephen had clearly spoken against the Law or the Temple, they would not have needed false witnesses. On the other hand, just as in the case of Jesus (Mark 7:1-15), his accusers may have been reacting against criticism of the oral tradition, which for them had just as much force as the words of Moses himself. Much of the opposition to the gospel then and now is a paranoid reaction against any change in the customs handed down from the forefathers.

One is reminded of hard-core Islamists who insist on the Law of Sharia and trump up false charges against Christians. Some have been put to death in the name of fanatic religion.

Stephen is dragged before the Sanhedrin. Did the Christians think "No problem. God will save him like he did the apostles"! But this time *the people*, previously favorable to the Nazarenes, are now stirred up against them. This time there is no Gamaliel to intervene.

6:15 *And gazing at him, all who sat in the council saw that his face was like the face of an angel.*

Luke uses one his favorite words, *atenizo*, "to gaze at intently," to heighten the dramatic tension. Far from looking like a wicked apostate or cringing reprobate, Stephen glowed like an angel. He was so full of the Spirit that he could not be filled with fear.

Lessons for Life

1. Growth of the church always brings new problems. But that is no reason to resist or resent growth.
2. Stumbling blocks in life and in the church can, by the grace of God, become stepping-stones.
3. Those gifted in the ministry of the Word must not be distracted from that ministry. Concentrate on the main thing!
4. In Christ, there is power to overcome barriers of language and culture.
5. There needs to be a good balance of authority and "democracy" in the church.
6. If you are faithful to Christ and filled by the Spirit, there will be, sooner or later, opposition from the world.

ACTS 7

STEPHEN'S INDICTMENT OF THE SANHEDRIN[1]

We must ask the question at the outset: why is this speech so long? Luke is not one to waste words; indeed, he is capable of severe abbreviation. Why does he consider this speech by a minor character so important? If he only wanted to relate the martyrdom of Stephen, he could have skipped verses 2-50 entirely. The famous skeptical playwright George Bernard Shaw called Stephen "a tactless and conceited bore." He "inflicted on them a tedious sketch of the history of Israel, with which they were presumably as well acquainted as he."[2] Famous German critic Dibelius also dismissed this speech as "irrelevant."[3]

Both critics fail to understand the place of the recitation of national history in ancient argumentation, especially among the Jews, but also among Greek historians like Herodotus and Thucydides. There is Jewish precedent for reciting the history of the nation as a persuasive technique in passages like Joshua 24, Neh 9:7-27, Ezek 20:5-44, and Psalms 78 and 105. First century Jewish historian Josephus uses this technique to try to persuade the Jews that war against the Romans is futile (*Jewish Wars* 5.376-419). The point of such narrations is not to provide new information but to make points of persuasion by either including or excluding points of the common history.

---

1   We depart from our usual format in this chapter. We have omitted the Bible text and discuss Stephen's speech as a whole and reserve comments on exegetical points for notes at the end of the chapter.

2   Cited by John Stott, 129.

3   Dibelius, Martin, *Studies in the Acts of the Apostles*, New York: Scribner, 1956, 167.

A second question we might ask is "What is the point"? Stephen is accused of 1) Speaking against the temple and 2) That Jesus will change the Law of Moses (6:13-14). How does his speech answer these charges, if it does at all? Stephen never does give a direct answer to the simple question the high priest asks, *Are these things so?* (7:1).

The speech is often called an *apologia*, a defense. There are subtle answers to the charges, but it is really more an accusation than a defense. This can be seen most clearly in the emotional outburst of verses 51-53.

The speech is easily divided into the following sections:
1. Address and appeal for a hearing 7:2b.
2. God appeared to Abraham 7:2c-8; seven verses.
3. The selling and preservation of Joseph 7:9-16; eight verses.
4. God appeared to Moses and was rejected by our fathers 7:17-43; twenty-six verses.
5. God directed the making of the tabernacle and the temple, but they do not contain Him 7:44-50; seven verses.
6. The accusation of resisting the Holy Spirit and of murdering the Messiah 7:51-53; three verses, interrupted by a lynching.

Why does Stephen take so long to get to the climax? Indeed, why does the high priest allow him to go on at such length with no direct answer to his question? Why is the beginning of the speech so bland and neutral and the ending so confrontational?

Recent research into the relationship between the ancient Greek art of rhetoric (formal rules for making persuasive speeches) and the New Testament sheds much light on Stephen's speech. In a 1985 article, Belgian scholar J. DuPont suggested that Stephen's speech is really a good example of ancient rhetoric.[4] DuPont analyzed the speech rhetorically as follows: *Exordium* (Address) 7:2a, *Narratio* (Narration of background) 7:2b-34. The purpose of *narratio* was to establish rapport by means of a recitation of commonly agreed upon facts with which the hearers could hardly disagree. At the same time it probably contained hints of the main theme, which would be coming. The narratio was to be followed by the main theme, the *argumentatio*, in this

---

4   J. DuPont, "La structure oratoire du discours d'Etienne (Actes 7)," *Biblia* 66 (1985), 153-167.

speech 7:35-50. The speech was to finish with an appeal of some intensity and emotion summing up the argument (*peroratio*) 7:51-53.[5]

Stephen, who was a Hellenist, could have been trained in rhetoric. He was probably speaking Greek, since he quotes the Greek OT. If this analysis is true, it explains why Stephen took so much time to build to his climax. It would explain why the high priest let him go on and on. And it would also explain why the first section of the speech (up to v. 35) is so neutral.

Narratio 7:2b-34. *The God of glory appeared to our father Abraham.* The story of the chosen nation begins with the **God of glory** who appeared to Abraham and commanded him to leave his father's house and journey to a land he would show him afterward. The chapter begins with Abraham seeing the God of glory and ends with Stephen seeing the glory of both God and Jesus. And in the middle Moses sees the glory of God in the burning bush.

There is a problem as to just when this call of Abraham occurred. Acts 7:2 says quite specifically that God called Abraham while he was living in Mesopotamia **before** the move to Haran. On the other hand, in Genesis the call seems to come **after** the move to Haran (Gen 11:31-32; 12:1). The KJV and NIV solve the problem by translating the Hebrew *wayomer* of Gen 12:1 with the English pluperfect tense *God **had** said.* Though in most contexts the usual translation is simply *and God said,* Kidner quotes an authority on Hebrew tenses, S. R. Driver, that this tense can be "amplifying the preceding narrative regarded as a whole, and not meant merely to be the continuation, chronologically, of its concluding stage."[6] Bruce also points out that Gen 15:7 and Neh 9:7 say that God brought Abraham *out of Ur of the Chaldees,* hinting that the call of God to leave his homeland may have been earlier.[7]

One point that many commentators see coming through in the bland recitation of the story of Abraham and the patriarchs is that in all these hundreds of years there was neither Law nor Temple. There is a hint here that the faith will henceforth be confined to neither as it leaves the land of its origin and goes out into the world.

The *narratio* continues into the Joseph story. One might ask why this is important. For the first time there is a mention of ill treatment of one who

---

5   Summarized in English in Witherington, 260-261.

6   Derek Kidner, *Genesis*, London: Tyndale Press, 1967, 113, n. 1.

7   Bruce, 192.

later became ruler. Though there is no direct warrant in the NT, I believe that **Joseph is a type of Christ.**[8] Joseph was sold into slavery by his brothers; Jesus was betrayed by his own people and crucified. Joseph was rescued by the providence of God; Jesus was rescued from death by resurrection. The brothers of Joseph bowed before him; Bible prophecy says that someday every knee shall bow to Christ the Lord (Phil 2:10) and that specifically *they will look upon him whom they have pierced* and will repent (Zech 12:10f; Rev 1:7). And just as there was forgiveness for Joseph's brothers, so there will be forgiveness for Jews who turn to Jesus (Zech 13:1).

Stephen brings the *narratio* further into the life of Moses, to whom he devotes most of his time, as the centerpiece of his accusation (verses 17-43). Within the Moses story, there are two occasions of visiting his brother Hebrews. In the first he kills an Egyptian who was beating a Hebrew, but instead of gratitude from the Hebrews, he is challenged and insulted (verses 23-29). Forty years later, after the seminal events of the faith of the Jewish nation, the appearance to Moses in the burning bush and the giving of the Law, Moses is again repudiated by the rebellious Israelites (verses 39-43).

DuPont chose verse 35 as the point where the speech passes from *narratio* to *argumentatio*. There is a break in the recitation of the history to incisive interpretation of that history marked by five references to Moses with the Greek word for *this* (*houtos/touton*) beginning with *this Moses* in verse 35. *This is the same Moses whom they had rejected with the words, 'Who made you ruler and judge?' He was sent to be their ruler and deliverer by God himself* (NIV). This Moses was the one who did *wonders and signs* (36), who predicted the coming of one who would be a prophet like himself (v. 37 quoting Deut 18:15; also cited in Acts 3:22-23), and the one who received the Law on Sinai (38). If the people did not listen to this prophet, they would be judged severely (Deut 18:19; Acts 3:23). This Moses our fathers *refused to obey and in their hearts turned to Egypt* (39), and just at the time of receiving the Law were breaking its first commandment by making a golden calf (40-41).

Stephen has yet to say, "You have rejected God's ruler Jesus of Nazareth the same way your fathers rejected Moses," but the argument is slowly becoming clear. There has been a dramatic increase in intensity beginning with verse 35. **Moses is another type of Christ**. Both were in Egypt in infancy. Moses

---

8   Schnabel agrees that Joseph is a type of Christ, 371.

delivered the people from Egypt; Christ saves his people from the bondage of sin. Both did signs and wonders. Both were prophets and mediators of a new law. Both were chosen by God as *ruler and redeemer*. Moses was rejected by his people when he tried to help them; Christ was rejected by his people and crucified. Moses was gone for a long time and returned to lead his people out of Egypt; Christ is gone for a long time in heaven and will come again to take his people to heaven.

Verses 42 and 43 sound the note of judgment: God abandoned them to their idolatry (see Rom 1:24, 26, 28), specifically worship of the heavenly bodies. The first mention of worship of the heavenly bodies by the Israelites was in the reign of Manasseh (2 Kings 21:5; 2 Chron 33:3), and though these altars were removed by Josiah (2 Kings 23:4), Jeremiah and Zephaniah later indict the people for star worship (Jer 19:13; Zeph 1:5). However, Stephen's citation of Amos 5:25-26 shows that the idolatrous worship of stars started in the forty-year period in the wilderness. Stephen is quoting his Bible, the Septuagint; and that translation seems to be based on a different pointing of the Hebrew vowels than the Hebrew text. So what in the Masoretic text (and in modern versions like the RSV) reads *Sakkuth* (the Akkadian god of the planet Saturn) *your king* and *Kaiwan* (another name for Saturn), *your star-god* becomes in the Septuagint *the tabernacle of Molech and the star of your god Raiphan.*[9]

Stephen's argument is that their ancestors rebelled against and rejected God's appointed ruler, Moses, and from the earliest days were guilty of breaking the first two of the ten commandments.

Some have tried to make Stephen into an anti-temple agitator and cite these verses 44-50 as evidence. But on the contrary, Stephen presents the tabernacle and its successor the temple as God ordained and built under the godly impulses and faith of the two greatest kings of Israel, David and Solomon. He is not anti-temple. But he does point out its limitations; that according to Isa 66:1-2, the dwelling place of God is not the temple, but the *heaven of heavens*. The temple cannot contain all of God, so in that sense it is not absolute. Though Stephen is not, as charged, anti-temple, it is true that

---

9   It is not known how "Kaiwan" became "Raiphan," though I like the suggestion of Bruce that it is close to "Repa," another name for Seb, the Egyptian god of the planet Saturn. Since the Septuagint was made in Egypt, this suggestion is particularly apt. See Bruce, 204.

his Spirit-given speech does anticipate a day when the temple of God will be the new people of God.

> *51 "You stiff-necked people, uncircumcised in heart and ears, you always resist the Holy Spirit. As your fathers did, so do you. 52 Which of the prophets did your fathers not persecute? And they killed those who announced beforehand the coming of the Righteous One, whom you have now betrayed and murdered, 53 you who received the law as delivered by angels and did not keep it."*

Abruptly Stephen switches to *peroratio*, a scathing accusation of the Sanhedrin. He whacks the bear with a stick and dares him to attack. They are stiff-necked like their (notice the change in pronoun from *our* to *your*) ancestors, circumcised in body, but not where it really counts, in heart and ears. Their hearts and ears are blocked. They, like their fathers, always resist the Spirit of God who is trying to persuade them to repent. They are like the murderers of the prophets in that they have murdered the Righteous One (a Jewish title for Messiah as in Acts 3:14 and 22:14). This is the fifth time the people or the Sanhedrin is accused of Messiacide in the book of Acts (2:23; 3:15; 4:10; 5:30). The final thrust is that they, who pride themselves on meticulously keeping the Law and enforcing it on others, have not kept it themselves.

If Stephen were not filled with the Spirit (v. 55), we would have to conclude that he is deliberately courting death and foolishly endangering the new faith. The Sanhedrin's reaction is not surprising. Yet it could have been the other way. A stunned silence, a dismissal of Stephen, a serious discussion as to whether Jesus could indeed be the Messiah; this was what God desired. God was appealing to the leaders of the nation one more time. The appeal of God through his spokesmen was gentle at first but has now reached a screaming crescendo! He can say no more. He has been gracious to say this much!

Stephen has been God's witness; now God himself and Jesus himself appear as Stephen's witnesses, not to the eyes of unbelief, but to their martyr ("witness") Stephen.

> *54 Now when they heard these things they were enraged, and they ground their teeth at him. 55 But he, full of the Holy Spirit, gazed into heaven and saw the glory of God, and Jesus standing at the right hand of God.*

56 And he said, "Behold, I see the heavens opened, and the Son of Man standing at the right hand of God." 57 But they cried out with a loud voice and stopped their ears and rushed together at him. 58 Then they cast him out of the city and stoned him. And the witnesses laid down their garments at the feet of a young man named Saul.

Stephen is so taken up with the vision of the glory of God and the sight of Jesus that he seems oblivious to his fate. Stephen experiences the Beatific Vision, the sight of the glorified face of Jesus. Jesus would ordinarily be seated, but He is standing to welcome His faithful witness. "Jesus is seen as an advocate for Stephen, a vindicator of his claims" (Bock, 312).

The Sanhedrin can take no more. In complete disregard for their own rules of legal procedure and their own dignity as the senators of Israel, and in complete disregard of the fact that the Romans had denied the power of the death penalty to them, they bellow like bulls, cover their ears, and rush upon Stephen like a stampede of cattle. They take him out of the city, lest they defile the holy place, and stone him.

59 And as they were stoning Stephen, he called out, "Lord Jesus, receive my spirit." 60 And falling to his knees he cried out with a loud voice, "Lord, do not hold this sin against them." And when he had said this, he fell asleep.

Stephen is, like any believer should be, a "little Christ," a small embodiment of the Christ to represent him in this world. Like his Savior, he prays *that this sin not be held against them* (Luke 23:34) and like Christ *receive my spirit* (Luke 23:46). One cannot imitate Christ by sheer self-effort and determination. These words are Spirit-inspired.

Why does the Spirit through Luke include Stephen's long speech? We must remember the great unexpressed doubt that would be in the minds of Gentile readers of the gospels and Acts. It is this: If Jesus was really the Messiah, why did his own people, and especially the religious experts, reject him? The answer is that though they were exposed to miracle after miracle, and the plainest proofs from Scripture, and the miracle of the resurrection, and repeated earnest appeals by both Jesus and his Spirit-filled representatives; they shut their eyes, stopped up their ears, and stubbornly refused the Truth. In the end **they had no rebuttal but the lynch mob.** This long speech is the Father's final official appeal to the murderers of his Son. But He will wait almost forty years until the year 70 AD to completely destroy them and their temple.

Notes

7:6. *who would enslave them and afflict them four hundred years.* According to Exod 12:40 the time in Egypt was 430 years. Stephen may have been using round numbers. We should not expect mathematical precision from an impromptu speech.

7:16 *and they were carried back to Shechem and laid in the tomb that Abraham had bought for a sum of silver from the sones of Hamor in Shechem.* Stephen telescopes two purchases of burial plots and several burials. Abraham bought a burial cave from Ephron the Hittite near Hebron (Gen 23:16-20). Strictly speaking, Jacob was buried at Hebron, the place of the burial of Abraham and Sarah and Isaac and Rebekah and Leah (Gen 49:29-32; 50:13). Only Joseph was buried at Shechem (Josh 24:32). The OT does not tell us where the eleven tribal fathers were buried, but Josephus records that they were buried at Hebron (*Antiquities*, 2.199). This seems to conflict with Acts 7:16 which says that they were buried with Joseph at Shechem. Even today the Jews are very particular about the final disposition of the deceased.

7:23 *When Moses was forty years old, he decided to visit his fellow Israelites.* Luke here tells us what the OT does not: the age of Moses when he fled from Egypt.

7:25 *He (Moses) supposed that his brothers would understand that God was giving them salvation by his hand, but they did not understand.* This too is not in the OT record, but is Stephen's interpretation of what Moses was undoubtedly thinking. This verse serves to set up the comparison with Jesus who came to save his people.

7:30 *an angel appeared to him . . . in a flame of fire in a bush.* In Exodus (2:2) it is *the angel of the LORD*, who is understood to be God himself.

7:35 *This Moses, whom they rejected, saying, 'Who made you a ruler and a judge?' this man God sent as both ruler and redeemer . . .* Notice the sharpness of contrast. The Hebrew slaves rejected Moses as their ruler and judge, but God sent Moses as not only ruler (the same word, *archōn*) but also as deliverer (*lytrōtēs*, also translatable as "redeemer"). The latter word, used only here in the NT, is used for God as Redeemer in the Greek OT of Psalm 78:35.

7:38 *This is the one who was in the congregation in the wilderness . . .* The word *congregation* is *ekklēsia*, elsewhere in the NT translated "church." In the OT it was used for the Hebrew *qahal* (assembly, congregation).

7:38 *He received living oracles to give to us.* This is a reference to the Law of Moses. The word of God is seen as both alive and imparting life (compare Heb 4:15 and 1 Pet 1:23). Again, as in verses 30, 38 and 53, the mediating angel is very prominent. The mediation of the Law by angels is one key point of Paul's argument in Gal 3:19.

7:42 *written in the book of the prophets . . .* that is, in the book of the Twelve Prophets, which were regarded as one book of the Hebrew Bible. The quotation is from Amos 5:25-27.

7:44 *the tent of witness . . .* The tabernacle is called the tabernacle of witness because its most precious object was the *ark of the testimony* (Ex 25:22 and twelve other references) containing the two tablets of stone on which were inscribed the Ten Commandments.

7:52 *Which of the prophets did your fathers not persecute? And they killed those who announced beforehand the coming of the Righteous One.* This echoes Jesus' words in Matt 23:29-37 and the accusation of Nehemiah (Neh 9:26). Jezebel killed fifty prophets of Yahweh (1 Kings 18:4). The prophet Uriah the son of Shemaiah was killed by King Jehoiakim (Jer 26:20-23). Ahikam (Jer 26:24) and Zechariah son of Jehoiada the priest (2 Chron 24:21) were both killed. There is no record in the OT of the deaths of writing prophets. However, the apocryphal *Martyrdom of Isaiah* records that Isaiah, the pre-eminent prophet of Messiah, was sawn in two by Manasseh; and Tertullian and Jerome both report traditions that Jeremiah was stoned to death by Jews who took him to Egypt.

7:54 *they were enraged* . . . the word in Greek originally meant "being sawed through." They could stand no more. The word appears also in Acts 5:33.

7:56 *the Son of Man* . . . Here is the only instance of this phrase in the NT outside the gospels. In the gospels it is used only by Jesus and only about himself. Scholars have debated the origin and meaning of this term, but it is most likely that Jesus consciously referred to the Son of Man vision in Dan 7:13 and following. He comes with the clouds of heaven to receive universal dominion. It would then be equivalent to "Messiah." Here Stephen calls Jesus *the Son of Man*, but in verse 59, when he addresses him directly, he calls him *Lord Jesus*. "When Stephen declares that he sees the Son of Man standing at the right hand of God, he is stoned for blasphemy because, in the view of these Jews, no one has the right to be at the side of God's heavenly presence" (Bock, 312).

7:58 If they were self-possessed enough to follow proper procedure, they did not just start throwing stones but executed the stipulations of the Talmud (m*Sanhedrin* 6.3f):

> "Four cubits from the place of stoning the criminal is stripped . . . The drop from the place of stoning was twice the height of a man. One of the witnesses pushes the criminal from behind, so that he falls face downward. He is then turned over on his back. If he dies from this fall, that is sufficient. If not, the second witness takes the stone and drops it on his heart. If this causes death, that is sufficient. If not, he is stoned by all the congregation of Israel, as it is written (Deut 17:7): 'the hand of the witnesses shall be first against him to put him to death, and afterward the hand of all the people." (Cited from Bruce, *Acts*, 212)

7:60 *He fell asleep.* Even in the midst of horrific violence, for the believer, death is *falling asleep*, the phrase used for the death of believers throughout the NT (for example 1 Thess 4:13).

Lessons for Life

1. God miraculously preserved Peter and the apostles but he did not intervene to save Stephen. We must be ready, if necessary, to die for the Lord Jesus.
2. Our defense against those who accuse us and persecute us for our faith is first to be filled with the Spirit. Then he will give us what to say to our accusers (Luke 12:12).
3. Every Christian is a "little Christ," and as such he or she will suffer as Jesus did and be enabled to bear suffering as Jesus did.
4. Loving one's enemies may sometimes include confronting them boldly head-on. Silence is often simply cowardice.

ACTS 8

PHILIP'S MISSION IN SAMARIA AND THE ETHIOPIAN EUNUCH

It is clear that Luke intends this chapter to illustrate the witness of the gospel to the second of the three locations given by Jesus himself in Acts 1:8: *you will be my witnesses in Jerusalem, **and in all Judea and Samaria**, and to the ends of the earth.* For the second time the witness of a non-apostle, Philip, later called "Philip the Evangelist," is highlighted. Both Stephen and Philip were Hellenists who had been selected as deacons. It was the death of Stephen which initiated a chain reaction: the martyrdom of Stephen triggered an outbreak of persecution of the Jerusalem church (8:1a); the persecution caused a scattering to country regions of Judea and Samaria (8:1b); and the scattering led to the evangelization of new regions. From verses 5-25 the story moves from the general statement of verse 4 to a most striking example of that evangelism, the remarkable success of the preaching of Philip in a city of Samaria and the satanic opposition to that success in the person of Simon the sorcerer. The chapter then concludes with an abrupt change to the evangelization of a very serious inquirer into Judaism, a high official from black Africa on the outer edge of the huge unknown continent to the south.

ᗡᏋᗞ

Acts 8:1-25

Philip's Remarkable Mission in Samaria

8:1-3 Persecution Breaks Out

1 And Saul approved of his execution. And there arose on that day a great persecution against the church in Jerusalem, and they were all scattered throughout the regions of Judea and Samaria, except the apostles. 2 Devout men buried Stephen and made great lamentation over him. 3 But Saul was ravaging the church, and entering house after house, he dragged off men and women and committed them to prison.

The first sentence about Saul is rightly printed as the last sentence of the final paragraph of chapter 7 in many Bibles. Saul is not mentioned again in chapter 8, but the story of his conversion will be taken up in chapter 9.

Why did the martyrdom of Stephen trigger a general persecution? And who were the persecutors? Was it only the Jewish leadership or did the general population turn against the new messianic movement? How bad was the persecution? Were some killed? Luke is not concerned to give us all the details. His main concern was the spread of the gospel. We may however speculate about some of the answers to these questions.

Since the main antagonist in chapters 3 through 7 has been the Jewish Sanhedrin, the main impulse and directive for persecution came from them. Saul (see 9:1) was one of their most eager agents of persecution. It is impossible to say how much the general Jewish populace was involved. Until now Luke has pointed out in two places that the new sect had *favor with all the people* (2:47; 5:13), but from now on there is no more mention of the favor of the general population. The Christian church was at first simply a sect of Judaism, but this persecution was the first major rupture in a long process of separation from Judaism which culminated in the rabbinic Council of Jamnia in AD 92.

As for the severity of the persecution, we see in 8:3 that Saul, the chief inquisitor, imprisoned *both men and women*, and Acts 9:21 and Gal 1:13 say that Saul tried to *destroy* the church.[1]

In the midst of this storm of persecution two things are remarkable. First, that the apostles did not flee the city, and second that some *godly men* took the time to bury Stephen. Bruce points out that, though the burial of executed criminals was required by the Law (Deut 21:22f), it was forbidden to make public mourning for them.[2] As leaders of the sect of the Nazarenes, the apostles would be in most danger and would be expected to be the first to flee. They may have realized that if the center of the church were scattered, the fragile new movement would have disintegrated. Because of the miraculous preservations in Chapters 4 and 5, the Sanhedrin may have been afraid to lay hands on them again, and so they may have had the courage to stay where they were.

When persecution or danger breaks out on the mission field today, it is always a tough decision for the leadership whether to order evacuation or not. When the Communists overran China in 1949, many missionaries wanted to stay so as not to desert the churches. However, they were urged by the church people to leave, as their presence would make the situation that much more difficult for the Chinese believers. Every situation must be evaluated separately between the extremes of "stay no matter what" and "flee at the first scent of danger." Certainly in this passage there is both warrant for judicious retreat (which worked out to the furtherance of the gospel), and staying at one's post and entrusting the outcome to God. The latter may result in martyrdom. James would not have died if he had fled Jerusalem (Acts 12:1-2).

8:4-8 The Samaritan Pentecost

4 Now those who were scattered went about preaching the word. 5 Philip went down to the city of Samaria and proclaimed to them the Christ. 6 And the crowds with one accord paid attention to what was being said by Philip, when they heard him and saw the signs that he did. 7 For unclean spirits, crying out with a loud voice, came out of many who had them, and

---

1   The Greek verb *portheō*, used in both verses, means "to attack and cause complete destruction, pillage, make havoc of, destroy, annihilate" (BAGD, 853).

2   Bruce, 215.

many who were paralyzed or lame were healed. 8 So there was much joy in that city.

It has often been pointed out that those who *preached the word* (literally "evangelized") were the laymen, as the "clergy" (the apostles) stayed in Jerusalem. Some of these lay evangelists may have attracted crowds in the marketplaces, but probably most of them simply gossiped the gospel wherever they could find work or a place to live. It seems they were more concerned about spreading the good news than they were about their personal livelihoods or security.

Luke does not seem to be interested in which city of Samaria the revival occurred. The NIV says *a city of Samaria* but many of the better texts have the definite article: *the city of Samaria*. Even if the latter is correct, we do not know which city of Samaria. It could have been Sebaste, the current Roman name for the ancient capital Samaria (Shechem), or it could have been Neapolis (present day Nablus). All we can say is that it was a *polis* ("city"), not a village.

The Samaritans were a sect of Judaism despised by mainstream Jews. Any Bible dictionary will detail the hundreds of years of animosity and hatred between the Jews and the Samaritans. In 129 BC John Hyrcanus, the Macabbean king of Israel, destroyed the Samaritan temple on Mount Gerizim. In 6 AD some Samaritans defiled the Jewish temple in Jerusalem by scattering human bones in the holy precincts. Jesus' family, when he was a boy, as did most Jews in Galilee, made the annual pilgrimage to Jerusalem by a long detour east of the Jordan River so that they would not have to pass through Samaria. For a Jew to call someone "a Samaritan" was a curse (John 8:48). John sums it up with an understatement: *The Jews have no dealings with the Samaritans* (John 4:9). But the gospel of reconciliation worked to heal this breach as we see in the story of Jesus' encounter with the Samaritan woman (John 4) and the parable of the Good Samaritan (Luke 10:25-37). This story in Acts 8 is the next episode in the healing of this ancient hatred.

The ESV is correct in translating *the Christ* instead of simply *Christ* (as in the KJV). The Samaritans were indeed looking for the Messiah, the prophet of Deuteronomy 18 whom they called the *Taheb* ("the Returning One"). Josephus indirectly testifies to the messianic expectation of the Samaritans during this time. He records that near the end of Pontius Pilate's ten-year service as prefect (about 36 AD), that Pilate slaughtered thousands of Samaritans who had gathered on Mount Gerizim around a messianic pretender (*Antiquities* 18:85-87).

The text of Acts 8 explains the keen attention and receptivity of these Samaritans because of the sensational miracles of healing and exorcism which Philip performed. Philip was a "little Christ" who did some of the same things Jesus had done and proclaimed forgiveness of sins in his name. No wonder there was *great joy* in that city! Luke never fails to mention the joy of salvation.

8:9-13 The Conversion of Simon the Sorcerer

> *9 But there was a man named Simon, who had previously practiced magic in the city and amazed the people of Samaria, saying that he himself was somebody great. 10 They all paid attention to him, from the least to the greatest, saying, "This man is the power of God that is called Great." 11 And they paid attention to him because for a long time he had amazed them with his magic. 12 But when they believed Philip as he preached good news about the kingdom of God and the name of Jesus Christ, they were baptized, both men and women. 13 Even Simon himself believed, and after being baptized he continued with Philip. And seeing signs and great miracles performed, he was amazed.*

Philip had unwittingly upstaged the local magician, Simon, who was revered throughout Samaria as a wonder worker. We do not know if Simon was simply a clever trickster or whether he could actually perform demonic miracles, as did the magicians of Pharaoh in Exodus, or whether there was a combination of both. At any rate the Samaritans were very impressed, and they practically deified him as *the power of God that is called Great.*[3]

We have here what is in today's missiology called a "power encounter." The miracles and the gospel of Christ were more impressive than the tricks of the magician. Simon was clever enough not oppose a popular miracle worker. What he wanted to know was the secret of how it was done! The Samaritans were believing and being baptized. Baptism in Acts always closely follows profession of faith. In fact, baptism seems to have been the outward profession

---

3   According to many references cited by Bruce, Acts 217-219, probably a reference to deity. It may be that the Samaritans thought Simon was a spokesman for God. It certainly fits with their gullibility in believing the pretender mentioned by Josephus.

of faith, for which we have today substituted decision cards, "going forward," and the "sinner's prayer." (We do not oppose these things; we simply point out that they were unknown in NT times and that the normal expression of faith in those times was baptism.) Simon too professed faith and was baptized and followed Philip everywhere. It would have made a wonderful story for a prayer letter!

8:14-24 Peter and John Expose the Hypocrisy of Simon

14 Now when the apostles at Jerusalem heard that Samaria had received the word of God, they sent to them Peter and John, 15 who came down and prayed for them that they might receive the Holy Spirit, 16 for he had not yet fallen on any of them, but they had only been baptized in the name of the Lord Jesus. 17 Then they laid their hands on them and they received the Holy Spirit. 18 Now when Simon saw that the Spirit was given through the laying on of the apostles' hands, he offered them money, 19 saying, "Give me this power also, so that anyone on whom I lay my hands may receive the Holy Spirit." 20 But Peter said to him, "May your silver perish with you, because you thought you could obtain the gift of God with money! 21 You have neither part nor lot in this matter, for your heart is not right before God. 22 Repent, therefore, of this wickedness of yours, and pray to the Lord that, if possible, the intent of your heart may be forgiven you. 23 For I see that you are in the gall of bitterness and in the bond of iniquity." 24 And Simon answered, "Pray for me to the Lord, that nothing of what you have said may come upon me."

Notice that Peter does not decide to go on his own; he is sent by the body of the apostles in Jerusalem. When Peter and John prayed for the converts and laid their hands on them, they received the Holy Spirit. This raises two problems. First, how did the two apostles know that the Samaritan believers had not received the Holy Spirit? One explanation is that there were no external manifestations of the Spirit such as speaking in tongues or prophecy.

Second, in other passages in Acts the reception of the Spirit is simultaneous with baptism (2:38), or even **before** baptism (10:44-47). Neither case mentions the laying on of hands. Saul seems to have received the Spirit by the laying on of hands of Ananias (9:17) **before** he was baptized and the disciples of John the Baptist in Ephesus **after** baptism and the laying on of hands by Paul (19:1-7). It is not possible to build a doctrine of conveying the Spirit by laying on of hands from this passage alone. One must consider all the passages as well as the teachings of passages like Romans 8:11 which show that all true believers have the indwelling Spirit.

A plausible explanation for the three cases where the Holy Spirit is received by the laying on of hands is that all three involved persons under suspicion, perceived either as enemies or as rivals of the church. Believers in other churches would not believe that God would save Saul or Samaritans. Even "believers" who were disciples of John the Baptist might have been suspect (19:1-7). The fact that the apostles, or a divinely sent agent like Ananias, mediated the giving of the Spirit united these suspicious converts into the true church without further suspicion. This action preserved the unity of the church by forestalling divisions. The Samaritan believers received the blessing of the apostles, the highest authorities in the church.

Simon was even more impressed with the power of Peter and John to bestow the Spirit. There must have been some outward manifestation of Spirit filling that impressed Simon. So, like one magician to another, he offered them money to learn "the secret."

This brazen request earns him the thundering denunciation of Peter (again the chief mouthpiece of God). Simon has "believed" and even undergone the rite of baptism, but he was not a true believer at all. "You cannot buy the gift of God with money! Your heart is still corrupt. You are still a captive of sin. You must repent and maybe the Lord (Jesus) will forgive you and save you."[4]

I was once reproached (gently I might say) by the Japanese pastor who succeeded me for baptizing a young man with emotional problems who later showed no signs of faith and caused problems in the church. My defense was that even Philip could make such a mistake!

Baptism does not guarantee salvation. Unless God does a thorough work of conversion in the heart, there is no conversion at all. Simon's response, *Pray for me to the Lord, that nothing of what you have said may come upon me*, does not qualify as repentance. He does not admit that his heart is wrong, he only wants to escape the punishment of his sins; remorse but not true repentance.

---

4   Some of the third century church fathers said that Simon was the originator of
      Gnosticism.

Lessons for Life

1. Persecution is usually an opportunity for witness and extension of the gospel.
2. Evangelism is the responsibility of every Christian, not just the clergy.
3. The message of the gospel breaks through ethnic, racial, and tribal barriers, hatreds, and rivalries. *God so loved the world . . .*
4. Believers must beware of magnetic popular but false gurus.
5. Influence and power in the church are not for sale.

⊘‍ℯ‍⊘

Acts 8:26-40

Philip and the Conversion of an Ethiopian

Philip's encounter with the Ethiopian official is one of the most interesting stories in the book of Acts. It comes out of nowhere and leads to nowhere as this man disappears from the narrative after Philip was snatched away from him. It does, however, fit the pattern Luke is developing in the book of Acts; first the gospel goes to the Jews in Jerusalem, then to Judea and the fringe Jews of Samaria, then to one on the edge of Judaism, a God-fearer from the ends of the earth, deep in the vast mysterious continent of Africa.

8:26-30 The Divine Guidance to the Ethiopian

26 Now an angel of the Lord said to Philip, "Rise and go toward the south to the road that goes down from Jerusalem to Gaza." This is a desert place. 27 And he rose and went. And there was an Ethiopian, a eunuch, a court official of Candace, queen of the Ethiopians, who was in charge of all her treasure. He had come to Jerusalem to worship 28 and was returning, seated in his chariot, and he was reading the prophet Isaiah. 29 And the Spirit said to Philip, "Go over and join this chariot." 30 So Philip ran to him and heard him reading Isaiah the prophet and asked, "Do you understand what you are reading?"

The direct intervention of angels is very prominent in the first half of the book of Acts. An angel of the Lord frees the apostles from prison (5:19). An angel of God appears in a dream to Cornelius (10:3). An angel of the Lord frees Peter from prison (12:7). An angel of the Lord strikes down Herod Agrippa I (12:23).

The apostles did not have a strategy session on how they were going to reach Ethiopia. God intervened directly and started the mission to Ethiopia in a most unusual and striking way. It took a direct command from God through an angel to move Philip away from a very successful evangelistic campaign with crowds of Samaritans to go to one Gentile foreigner in a remote place.

Philip receives very explicit instructions: he is to go to the Jerusalem-Gaza road (about two days journey) that took off from the main north-south trunk road along the highlands to the southwest. He is not told why or who or what for. But he obeys. It is not clear at what point on this road of some 44 miles that Philip met the Ethiopian. The precise location is not important to Luke.

They met in *a desert place*. The word *desert* here means "uninhabited." There is only one town at less than half-way, the inn town of Betogabris. Gaza was a two-day journey from Jerusalem. At Gaza the Ethiopian would join the main coastal road to Egypt. He was returning from Jerusalem where he had gone to worship at the temple in Jerusalem. This was an incredible, maybe once in a lifetime, journey of some 1,240 miles one way.

Who was this man? The text tells us that he was the official in charge of the treasury of Candace, queen of the Ethiopians. *Candace* is not a name but a title for the queen mother, just as "Pharoah" was not a name but a title for the kings of Egypt.[5] Her son was deemed to be a god but the queen mother held the real power. "Ethiopia" at that time could refer to any part of a vast region of many different peoples covering parts of southern Egypt, modern Sudan, and Abyssinia (modern Ethiopia). We do know that the queens called Candace ruled in the city of Meroe between the third and fourth cataract on

---

5   In Greek Candace was pronounced "Kān-**dā**-kay," with the a's long as in "father."

the Nile and that they were a Nilotic Negroid people with close cultural and trade ties with ancient Egypt. They built small pyramids and made wonderful items of gold and precious stones.

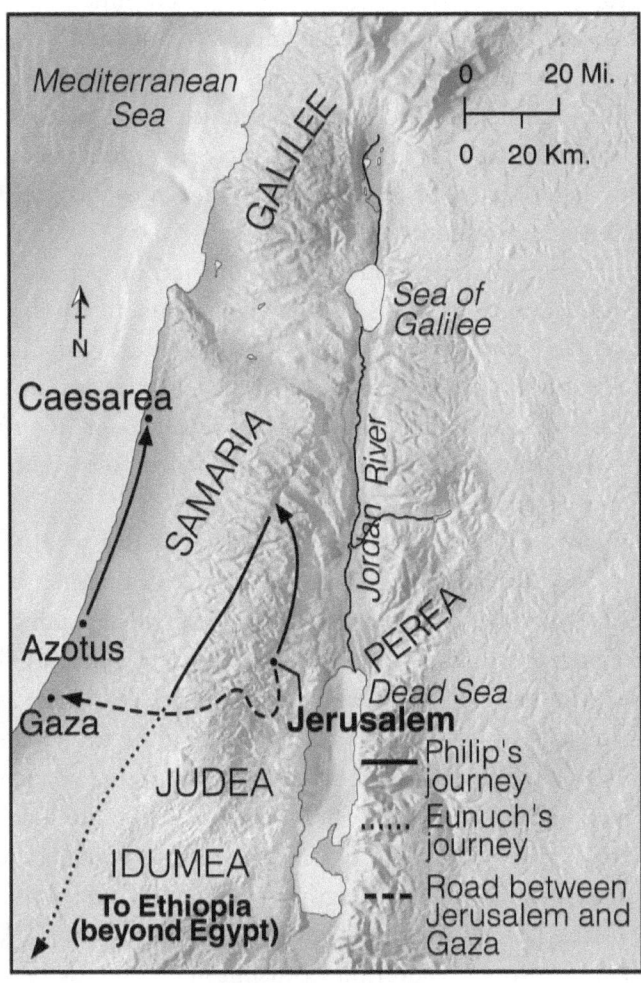

Philip's Ministry

This man is called a *eunuch*, which means a castrated male. It is not certain that this was literally the case with this man; the word could simply mean an official who was not castrated. For example, the word "eunuch" is used in the Greek OT (Septuagint) for Potiphar the servant of Pharoah (Gen 39:1) who was a married man. Though the word is very frequent in the OT

(38 times), it occurs in the NT only in our Lord's saying in Matt 19:12 and in this passage. I am inclined to think that he was a literal eunuch.

He seems to have been what the NT calls a *God-fearer* (*phoboumenos ton theon* (Acts 10:2, 22; 13:26, 50; 17:4, 17). This was a technical term to denote Gentiles who were inquirers of Judaism and often attended the synagogue. They had not yet taken the step of circumcision and baptism, which would have made them full-fledged Jewish converts called proselytes. He possessed a copy of a scroll of Isaiah (in Greek), which says something about both his piety and his wealth. Luke is often interested to show how the gospel appealed to people in important positions.

How did this man know about the God of Israel in such a distant land? A strong Jewish community flourished in Syene (modern Aswan) in Upper Egypt from as early as the sixth century BC. In the OT Ethiopia is called "Cush" and there was much contact between the Cushites and ancient Israel. The prophet Jeremiah tells of *Ebed-melech the Ethiopian, a eunuch who was in the king's house* who appealed to King Zedekiah to allow him to rescue Jeremiah from a cistern (Jer 38:7-13).

We wish that all our seekers were as zealous as this man! In order to find the true God, he had to overcome the barrier of distance (2,500 mile round trip), the barrier of a foreign religion, the barrier of reading about the religion in a different language (Greek), the barrier of a difficult religion (the numerous detailed prescriptions of the Mosaic Law), the barrier of a dishonest hypocritical religion (think of Jesus' sharp critiques of the Judaism of his time), and finally the barrier of personal disfigurement. As a eunuch he could never be circumcised or be allowed to become a true convert to Judaism (Deut 23:1). And yet **in spite** of all these barriers, he went to Jerusalem to worship the God of Israel. He went to great lengths to find God; God rewarded him by going to great lengths to give him the gospel of Christ's salvation. We will see a similar case in the Roman centurion Cornelius in chapter 10.

8:28-35 The Conversation Between Philip and the Ethiopian

28 He was returning, seated in his chariot, and he was reading the prophet Isaiah. 29 And the Spirit said to Philip, "Go over and join this chariot." 30 So Philip ran to him and heard him reading Isaiah the prophet and asked, "Do you understand what you are reading?" 31 And he said, "How can I, unless someone guides me?" And he invited Philip to come up and sit with him. **32** *Now the passage of the Scripture that he was reading was this:*

"Like a sheep he was led to the slaughter and like a lamb before its shearer is silent, so he opens not his mouth. **33** *In his humiliation justice was denied him. Who can describe his generation? For his life is taken away from the earth."*

34 *And the eunuch said to Philip, "About whom, I ask you, does the prophet say this, about himself or about someone else?"* **35** *Then Philip opened his mouth, and beginning with this Scripture he told him the good news about Jesus.*

Philip heard the man reading because in ancient times people seldom read silently; they sounded out each word vocally. *Chariot* might better be translated *carriage.* No doubt it had a driver and there must have been bodyguards for a person of such high rank. Whether the carriage was moving or not, the text does not tell us; I prefer to think that they were stopped for a rest and the Ethiopian was so anxious to read his (newly acquired in Jerusalem?) precious scroll that he used any opportunity to read it.

Now it just so "happened" that at that moment he was reading the most evangelistically important passage in all the Old Testament, Isaiah 53. This whole chapter, beginning with 52:13, is a remarkably detailed description of the Messiah, the suffering servant of Yahweh, and contains a more explicit explanation of the meaning of his suffering (the atonement) than any NT passage! Parts of this passage are quoted seven times in the NT (Rom 15:21; John 12:38; Rom 10:16; Matt 8:17; this passage; 1 Pet 2:22, and Luke 22:37). Only 53:7-8 are quoted here, but Philip no doubt used the whole passage to explain the identity of the Messiah and the meaning of the cross. We have the essential elements of the gospel in Isaiah 53:6: The reality of universal sin is expressed in verse 6a: *All we like sheep have gone astray; each of us has turned to his own way.* That is a perfect explanation of what sin is. The solution for human sin is given in the very next line: *but the Lord has laid on him the iniquity of us all.* Also: He was *like a lamb that is led to the slaughter.* There is even a hint of Messiah's resurrection in verse 11: *Out of the anguish of his soul he shall see and be satisfied . . . therefore I will divide him a portion with the many and he shall divide the spoil with the strong.*

One understands the meaning of this prophecy only after the fulfillment. Even Philip would not have known the full meaning before the Cross. He probably learned the full explanation from the apostles who used certain key OT Scriptures as their evangelistic *testimonia*. They in turn no doubt learned these Scriptures from Jesus himself during his forty days of post-resurrection ministry (see Luke 24:25-27).

This was not the only Scripture. Notice in v. 35 that Philip **began** with that passage. He very likely went on to quote many others and explain to this man the meaning of the life and death of Jesus. It might have taken many hours. Sometimes our modern methods of witness, following a simple plan or outline developed in America for Americans of a generation who at that time had a general cultural knowledge of the life and death of Christ, are applied too briefly and too mechanically in cultures where much more explanation is necessary.

The King James says in v. 35 *he preached to him Jesus*. There is a slight emphasis in the original text on the word *Jesus*. It is easy to lose this emphasis in our evangelism and preaching. Do not preach Christianity. Preach **Christ**! We find in many countries that Christianity has a bad reputation. It carries the baggage of two thousand years of checkered history, bright here and soiled there, true here and phony there, and "Christianity" is seen as a rival to the national or ethnic religions of Buddhism, Islam, and Hinduism. In Japanese and Chinese, the names of religions end in the character "teaching" (*kyō*). Invariably our hearer will want to pit his religion (kyō) against our "kyō," (Christianity). We can escape this futility only by constantly referring the inquirer to Christ himself: his life, his character, his sayings, his cross and resurrection.

One could wish that we all had such golden opportunities! Ponder the marvel of the providence of God in joining these two men in a desert place at just the right time. This timing of providence is more remarkable than the appearance of an angel. God must have a person whom he can trust to be absolutely obedient to divine direction. Is it possible that we have few opportunities to witness because we have neglected too many opportunities we have already been given?

Philip asked the man if he understood what he was reading. The man said, *How can I, unless someone guides me?* Some people come to Christ alone, reading the Bible with no one to explain it to them. But these are exceptions. God usually sends a human being, filled with the Spirit, to explain salvation in Christ from the Scriptures. This is why translation of the Bible alone and distribution of the Bible alone, or even evangelistic literature alone, is not enough. God usually sends someone to explain it in person, sometimes in mass meetings, as in the first half of chapter 8, and sometimes in one-on-one encounters, as in this story.

8:36-40 The Baptism of the Ethiopian

> *36 And as they were going along the road they came to some water, and the eunuch said, "See, here is water! What prevents me from being baptized?" 38 And he commanded the chariot to stop, and they both went down into the water, Philip and the eunuch, and he baptized him. 39 And when they came up out of the water, the Spirit of the Lord carried Philip away, and the eunuch saw him no more, and went on his way rejoicing. 40 But Philip found himself at Azotus, and as he passed through he preached the gospel to all the towns until he came to Caesarea.*

As they were traveling, they came to some water. The Ethiopian must have seen many Jewish *mikvoth* or ritual bathing pools[6] outside the temple in Jerusalem supplied by the aqueduct that Herod had built. We may want to know where this water was, how deep it was, and whether it was a river or a pond. In that dry country water was not plentiful. But Luke is not interested in the details that interest us. The Ethiopian is ready to make his decision. He wants to be baptized. Again, an ideal inquirer! Would that all seekers made the best decision in life so quickly!

Two errors beset the practice of baptism. One is baptismal regeneration; that is the teaching that one is born again by being baptized and cannot be truly saved without being baptized. Though there are Scriptures that seem to support this teaching such as Acts 2:38 and Mark 16:16, most of the Protestant church has rightly rejected this idea as inconsistent with the tenor of the whole doctrine of salvation.

The second error is more common in present day churches and that is that baptism does not matter all that much and can be indefinitely postponed without harm. And even among those who urge new converts to be baptized, many modern pastors would have answered the Ethiopian, "Wait a minute. Our policy requires three months of baptismal preparation classes and examination by the board of the church." The purpose is to make sure we are

---

6   See a picture in Peter Connolly, *Living in the Time of Jesus of Nazareth*, Jerusalem: STEIMATSKY LTD (Originally published by Oxford University Press), 1999, 53.

baptizing a true believer, not a Simon Magus.

Our suggestion is that we baptize sooner rather than later, with preparation covering only the minimum necessary to know whether the candidate is a genuine believer. (Even if the preparation time is longer, we will probably make mistakes.) Instruction in the basics of the Christian life and the policies and expectations of church members should be a required **post** baptism course. I always told our Japanese candidates that baptism is not a *sotsugyōshiki* (graduation ceremony) but a *nyūgakushiki* (school entrance ceremony).

As to the mode of baptism, a dividing point among Protestant denominations, this passage does not answer that question, but it does make clear that they both went down into the water and came up out of the water. That would permit immersion, and maybe even suggest it, but not require it. The earliest Christian baptistry we have in the archaeological record is a very shallow pool in which the candidates seem to have been baptized by pouring. However, if Philip only sprinkled the Ethiopian, why did they enter the water?

When they came up out of the water, the Spirit of God suddenly raptured Philip away and deposited him in Azotus, a town on the Mediterranean coast.[7] This is in some ways an unsatisfying conclusion. What happened to the Ethiopian when he finally returned to Meroe? Did he start the church in Ethiopia?[8]

And what about the miraculous snatching away of Philip? Can we seriously believe such a thing? We can believe it if we can believe that Enoch was transported to heaven (Gen 5:24) or that Elijah was taken up into heaven (2 Kings 2:11) or that Paul was caught up to the third heaven (2 Cor 12:1-4) or that we ourselves who believe will be caught up into heaven at the return of Christ (1 Thess 4:17). If we can believe the resurrection, we can believe in rapture (the Greek word in all three NT passages is *harpazō,* to snatch away forcefully).

Why was this miracle necessary? There is "an economy of miracle" in the gospels and Acts. If Philip walked to get on the Gaza Road, could he not walk back? Our only answer is that God, who spends miracles very frugally, spent

---

7   The Western text has a longer version of v. 39: *the Holy Spirit fell on the eunuch, and an angel of the Lord caught up Philip.* Omission of one line by a copyist could explain the absence of the phrase from most texts. This reading is not improbable, and would continue the emphasis on the Holy Spirit possessing new converts.

8   Irenaeus says (*Haereseis 3.12.10)* that the new convert "was sent to the regions of Ethiopia to proclaim the message which he had believed" (Cited from Bruce, 230).

many of them to launch the church on her worldwide mission. No doubt it made an unforgettable impression on the suddenly deserted Ethiopian convert who *went on his way rejoicing.*

Meanwhile Philip must begin an important preaching tour up the Mediterranean coast of Judea, which might have included the cities of Azotus (OT Ashdod), Jamnia, Lydda, Joppa, and Caesarea. It is in Caesarea where Paul and his party returning from the third missionary journey find "Philip the Evangelist" and his four daughters who were prophetesses in Acts 21:8-9.

Lessons for Life

1.   A good witness must be sensitive to the promptings of the Holy Spirit.
2.   One-on-one evangelism is just as important as mass evangelism.
3.   God rewards those who seek him with all their hearts.
4.   Preach Christ, not Christianity.
5.   Evangelize from the Scriptures. To do that you must know the Scriptures.
6.   Baptism is not a means of salvation, but is like a signature showing one's commitment. It is not an optional after-thought, but the norm for those who profess faith in Christ.

ACTS 9

THE CONVERSION OF SAUL OF TARSUS AND PETER'S MIRACLES OF HEALING

Acts 9:1-31

The Conversion of Saul of Tarsus

In Acts 8, 9, and 10 we have three remarkable conversion stories: an unnamed African on the edge of Judaism, Saul the chief inquisitor and persecutor of the infant church, and Cornelius, the first Roman convert. Any conversion is the work of God, but in these three conversions the work of God is so unmistakably and visibly manifest that there is no doubt that God himself is at work launching his church. As such, these accounts have high apologetic value. This religion is true because God himself is causing it to grow.

Perhaps we do not fully understand the importance of the conversion of Saul. It is not an accident that portions of his conversion story are repeated in his own words in chapters 22 and 26. Together these three accounts are 74 verses in length, which is 7.4% of the entire book of Acts. Luke, inspired by the Spirit, is establishing the credibility of the hero of the book of Acts: Paul the Apostle. The entire second half of the book, chapters 13 to 28, is devoted to the mission and sufferings of the Apostle Paul. Paul is not only the hero of Acts, he is also the human author of about one third of the New Testament. Through him God revealed distinctive doctrines which are not as fully developed in the teachings of Jesus or the other apostles: justification by

124

faith; the role of the law of Moses; the identity of the believer with Christ in death, burial, and resurrection; the doctrine of sanctification; the church as the body of Christ; and extensive teaching on the resurrection of the believer and the rapture of the church.

Paul has been rightly revered throughout most of church history, but we forget that neither he nor his teachings were enthusiastically received by many of the earliest Christians. He defended his legitimacy as an apostle in his epistles against his many detractors (Galatians 1 and 2; 1 Cor 9:1-18; 2 Cor 10-13). In nine of his thirteen epistles he emphatically refers to himself as "Paul an apostle" in the opening greetings.[1] His detractors and doubters may have said, "He is not one of the Twelve who walked with Jesus and heard his teachings." "His teachings are different from the Lord Jesus." "He preaches that converts do not need to obey the Torah." Many if not most modern liberal scholars distinguish between "the religion of Jesus and the religion of Paul," as if Paul's ideas were purely his own, superfluous embellishments on the simple teachings of Jesus.

To counter the detractors and doubters of the Apostle Paul, Luke records the story of Paul's miraculous conversion three times and, as we shall see later, parallels the miracles of Paul with those of Peter. Paul is one of the most important of those through whom Jesus **continued** *to do and to teach* (Acts 1:1). For Luke, Paul's teaching is authoritative because it was the teaching of the risen Lord through Paul.

The conversion of Saul of Tarsus was not only an apologetic for Paul as a legitimate apostle, but also an important defense of the faith he preached. James Boice tells the story of two eighteenth century English lawyers who were skeptical about the veracity of Christianity, but were open minded enough to examine carefully what they thought were its two main pillars, the resurrection of Christ, and the conversion of Paul. Gilbert West came to the conclusion that it was easier to believe the resurrection of Jesus than to accept any alternative explanation. Lord Lyttleton similarly found no rational non-miraculous explanation for the radical change in Saul the persecutor other than that recorded in Acts.[2]

---

1   The exceptions are Philippians, 1st and 2nd Thessalonians, and Philemon. Paul had the least opposition in these churches.

2   James M. Boice, Acts: an Expositional Commentary, 148. Lord Lyttleton on the Conversion of St. Paul and Gilbert West on the Resurrection of Jesus Christ, New York: The American Tract Society, 1929.

9:1-9 The Light from Heaven

1 But Saul, still breathing threats and murder against the disciples of the Lord, went to the high priest 2 and asked him for letters to the synagogues at Damascus, so that if he found any belonging to the Way, men or women, he might bring them bound to Jerusalem.

3 Now as he went on his way, he approached Damascus, and suddenly a light from heaven shone around him. 4 And falling to the ground, he heard a voice saying to him, "Saul, Saul, why are you persecuting me?" 5 And he said, "Who are you, Lord?" And he said, "I am Jesus, whom you are persecuting. 6 But rise and enter the city, and you will be told what you are to do." 7 The men who were traveling with him stood speechless, hearing the voice but seeing no one. 8 Saul rose from the ground, and although his eyes were opened, he saw nothing. So they led him by the hand and brought him into Damascus. 9 And for three days he was without sight, and neither ate nor drank.

Saul is again pictured as a wild animal roaring against the church. He was a zealous Pharisee, unwilling to ignore the danger of a rapidly growing heresy of a false messiah. Most of the heretics had fled Jerusalem and scattered but he heard that there were a number of them taking refuge in the synagogues in Damascus, 183 miles distant, a six-day journey to the north and east. Note that the Jewish believers in Jesus still seem to be attached to the regular Jewish synagogues. Josephus says that there were 10,500 Jews in Damascus,[3] so that there must have been dozens of synagogues. Damascus is one of the oldest continuously inhabited cities in the world, old even in the time of Abraham. In Acts 8, the gospel makes a big leap to the south; here it jumps to the north.

The high priest was still Caiaphas, the man responsible for condemning Jesus. The year is roughly 32-33 AD, perhaps two or three years after the crucifixion of Jesus.[4] It is surprising that Saul can be given authority to arrest

---

3   *Jewish Wars* 2.561. He claims the number to be 18,000 in 7.368.

4   The precise date of both Jesus' crucifixion and the conversion of Paul are still unclear. Some place the crucifixion in April 30 AD and some April 33 AD. The above dates are suggested by Colin Hemer, who has written in detail on the chronology of the life of Paul in *The Book of Acts in the Setting of Hellenistic History*, chapter 6. John McRay opts for the crucifixion of Jesus in 30 AD and the conversion of Saul in 34 AD (*Paul: His Life and Teaching*, chapter 3).

Jews in a foreign land, but Bruce makes it clear (p. 233) that the Romans had given rights of extradition to the Jewish high priest as early as 138 BC. After five weary days, Saul's journey is almost over, and the wolf presses on, hungry for lunch, eager to lay hands on his prey. It was noon (22:6; 26:13), and he could see the city in the distance. That was the last thing he saw for a while.

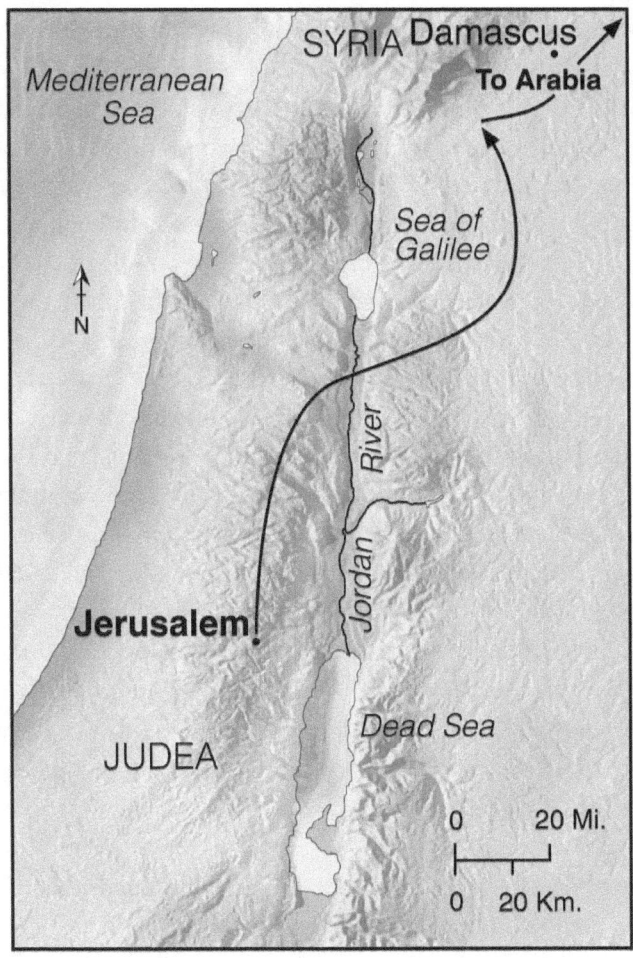

Saul Travels to Damascus

Suddenly there is a blinding light *brighter than the sun* (26:13) from above spotlighting Saul. It knocks him off his mount (surely such an important official would not have to walk!). Terrified and confused, he hears a voice from above clear, calm, and overwhelming, speaking in his native tongue: *Saul, Saul, why are you persecuting me?* Saul knows that this is the voice of God. He knows that it is the Lord. It is possible to translate the Greek word *kurie* simply as "sir" or "mister," but Saul knows it is not the voice of man. *Kurie* then must refer to deity. And then came a shock that dumbfounded him: *I am Jesus, whom you are persecuting.* Saul learns by stunning personal experience three instant theology lessons. First was that **Jesus of Nazareth**, whose followers he was seeking to destroy, was indeed risen and was indeed **Lord**. He was soon proclaiming in the synagogues that Jesus, who he had been absolutely sure was an imposter, is really *the Son of God* (9:20). Second was what he later taught as the doctrine of the Body of Christ: to touch a believer in Jesus is to touch Jesus himself. The third theological lesson was overwhelming grace. You don't bargain with your enemies; you imprison them, you kill them. Saul should have been dead. He never recovered from this amazing grace. It gripped him and compelled him for the rest of his life, and he never tired of referring to it.

But rise and enter the city, and you will be told what you are to do. Saul is not ready for God's full agenda. His life is suddenly changed forever. The old Saul is dead; the one out to capture believers in Jesus is now a captive of Jesus. Blind, perhaps for life, absolutely helpless, he is led on shaky feet into the city. His subordinates are speechless with fright and amazement; they had heard a voice, but did not understand it (compare John 12:28-29), and had seen nothing.

Saul had been hungry but now he has lost his appetite. More important things than lunch swirl in his mind. As a sign of repentance, he fasts for three days. Maybe God will give him back his sight. He needs time to absorb the enormity of his guilt and to process this experience. Neither did he touch wine or any other beverage; we can presume that he drank water or he would have fainted with dehydration.

We are told in verse 11 that Saul prayed. He thought back on his life. His early training in Tarsus. His training under Gamaliel in Jerusalem. The reports that he had heard of Jesus. Maybe even of a time when he had seen Jesus teaching in the temple, surrounded by large crowds. Oh, that he would have followed his mentor's advice (5:38-39) and left these Nazarenes alone! He thought of the way Stephen had died and how he had assisted the killers. He thought of the faces of men and women whom he had voted to put to death. He confessed each crime against Jesus the Lord again and again. His mind went over some of the Scriptures and he saw how the Rabbis should have known that this man Jesus really was the Christ. He had a vision of a man named Ananias who would come to give him back his sight. At times he sank into an exhausted sleep only to wake at odd hours and continue his prayer and meditation. He was oblivious to time, barely conscious whether it was day or night.

9:10-19a Baptized by Ananias

10 Now there was a disciple at Damascus named Ananias. The Lord said to him in a vision, "Ananias." And he said, "Here I am, Lord." 11 And the Lord said to him, "Rise and go to the street called Straight, and at the house of Judas look for a man of Tarsus named Saul, for behold, he is praying, 12 and he has seen in a vision a man named Ananias come in and lay his hands on him so that he might regain his sight." 13 But Ananias answered, "Lord, I have heard from many about this man, how much evil he has done to your saints at Jerusalem. 14 And here he has authority from the chief priests to bind all who call on your name." 15 But the Lord said to him, "Go, for he is a chosen instrument of mine to carry my name before the Gentiles and kings and the children of Israel. 16 For I will show him how much he must suffer for the sake of my name."17 So Ananias departed and entered the house. And laying his hands on him he said, "Brother Saul, the Lord Jesus who appeared to you on the road by which you came has sent me so that you may regain your sight and be filled with the Holy Spirit." 18 And immediately something like scales fell from his eyes, and he regained his sight. Then he rose and was baptized; 19 and taking food, he was strengthened.

God prefers to work through human agents. In this case a "disciple," that is, a believer in Jesus, is sent on a mission to the devil himself. No apostles are available. We do not even know that Ananias (a good Jewish name, Hananiah) was a leader among the Nazarenes. He has a vision, that is, a dream while awake, and the Lord Jesus tells him to look for Saul of Tarsus. "Excuse me, Lord; I think there must be some mistake. Are you trying to get me arrested and maybe killed"? But the Lord replies, "He is no longer Saul the Persecutor. He is now Saul my Chosen Instrument to bear my name and the message he despised to the Gentiles, and to kings, and to the children of Israel." He also has a mission of suffering: *I will show him how much he must suffer for the sake of my name.* He has caused much suffering to my people, so now he will suffer for my sake. We believe that verses 15 and 16, as we will comment later, are the key to understanding Acts 13-28.

Ananias went to the street called "Straight," which is still a major east-west street in Damascus, and started inquiring where he might find "Saul of Tarsus." No street addresses or mobile phones in those days! Eventually Ananias locates the house and enters hesitantly. Then, gathering courage, he finds a man praying. Without greeting or explanation or even asking, "Are you Saul of Tarsus? My name is Ananias," he first places his hands on Saul's head and says *Brother Saul.* Not a hated enemy, but one of the family of the believers in Jesus of Nazareth, a **brother,** accepted in the Beloved. This must have been a beautiful word to Saul. For these three days Saul was isolated between two groups of people who hated him, the Orthodox Jews and the Nazarene Jews. As far as he knew, he had no friends in all the world. *"Brother Saul, the Lord Jesus who appeared to you on the road by which you came has sent me so that you may regain your sight and be filled with the Holy Spirit."* The Lord could have healed Saul's blindness and filled him with the Spirit without human assistance. But these graces are mediated through a human instrument to make Saul a member, not only of the heavenly Body, but also the earthly community of saints. This is the second time the Spirit is given by the laying on of hands.[5]

The visible sign of the Spirit's coming does not seem here to be tongues but the healing of his blindness. "Scales" fell from his eyes. And, after only three days of baptismal instruction, Saul received baptism, not in a synagogue service, but in a private ceremony attended only by two. Suddenly he was very hungry and broke his fast with great joy.

9:19b-25 Dangerous Days in Damascus

For some days he was with the disciples at Damascus. **20** *And immediately he proclaimed Jesus in the synagogues, saying, "He is the Son of God."* **21** *And all who heard him were amazed and said, "Is not this the man who made havoc in Jerusalem of those who called upon this name? And has*

---

5   Acts 8:18, 19 when the Samaritan believers received the Holy Spirit was the first.

*he not come here for this purpose, to bring them bound before the chief priests?" **22** But Saul increased all the more in strength, and confounded the Jews who lived in Damascus by proving that Jesus was the Christ.*

*   **23** When many days had passed, the Jews plotted to kill him, **24** but their plot became known to Saul. They were watching the gates day and night in order to kill him, **25** but his disciples took him by night and let him down through an opening in the wall, lowering him in a basket.*

Saul very quickly began testifying in the many synagogues to his new faith, summed up in one phrase, ***This one*** (literal Greek) *is the Son of God.* This is the only occurrence of the phrase "Son of God" in Acts. To his Jewish audiences, that would at least mean, "Jesus is the true Messiah."[6] To Saul, "Son of God" meant at very least the Lord who had appeared to him. Later he will expound Jesus as the Lord of Philippians 2:5-9 and the co-Creator of Colossians 1:15-17.

Saul's preaching caused a sensation in every synagogue, perhaps more among the unbelieving Jews than the believing. "Isn't this the chief inquisitor?" But Saul was not daunted by their reaction and testified more boldly. No doubt he told them again and again of the light from heaven. He appeals to the minds of the hearers as is shown by the word *proving* that Jesus is the Messiah. *Sumbibazō* means "to bring up together," and in this case "to prove logically by bringing up many lines of argument." At this point, how much did Saul understand? What Scriptures or lines of argument did he use? This style of persuasion would characterize his entire ministry. The Western text adds *in the Word* after *grew more and more powerful.* There is development in his understanding of his new Lord.

It was probably during the period of *when many days had passed* of verse 23 that Paul went to Arabia, the Nabatean Kingdom whose capital was Petra. The Jews regarded the Nabateans as descendants of Ishmael and thus as a kindred tribe. He spent three years there (Gal 1:17-18), and it was during those three years that he seems to have incurred the wrath of King Aretas of Nabatea (2 Cor 11:32, 33), perhaps by aggressive evangelism. He then returned (fled?) to Damascus where Luke resumes his telescoped narrative in verse 23.

---

6   Bruce cites Mark 14:61; Acts 4:25; 13:33; 1 Enoch 105:2; 4 Ezra 7:28ff; 13:32, 37, 52; 14:9 in favor of this understanding "Son of God" as Messiah (p. 240).

The unbelieving Jews could not refute Saul, so they plotted to kill him,[7] not in the synagogue or the city, but they watched the gates to kill him when he left town. One is reminded of Islamist extremists in our day who are slaughtering infidels and the Muslims who cooperate with them. There was a special hatred for Saul, of course, because he was a turncoat and a traitor.

The one who was miraculously converted has no miraculous escape. He sneaks out of town secretly at night by being lowered ignominiously from an opening in the wall in a basket. No matter, an escape is an escape, and God has his hand on his new apostle. "We are immortal until our work is done."

9:26-31 Danger in Jerusalem

26 And when he had come to Jerusalem, he attempted to join the disciples. And they were all afraid of him, for they did not believe that he was a disciple. 27 But Barnabas took him and brought him to the apostles and declared to them how on the road he had seen the Lord, who spoke to him, and how at Damascus he had preached boldly in the name of Jesus. 28 So he went in and out among them at Jerusalem, preaching boldly in the name of the Lord. 29 And he spoke and disputed against the Hellenists. But they were seeking to kill him. 30 And when the brothers learned this, they brought him down to Caesarea and sent him off to Tarsus.

Why did Saul return to the most dangerous place he could have gone? He probably felt a great need to connect with the leaders of the church so that there would be one church and not two: a Jerusalem Church and a Pauline Church. In Galatians 1:18 Paul says that he went to Jerusalem specifically to consult with Peter and had fifteen days with him. On the other hand, Galatians makes clear that he was anxious to maintain a degree of independence from the other apostles.

The visit to Jerusalem has a number of parallels to the time in Damascus. There was hesitation to believe in the genuineness of Saul's conversion in both 9:13-14 and 9:26. There was reassurance from the Lord himself in 9:15-16 and reassurance from Barnabas in 9:27. Saul's meeting with the disciples in Damascus (9:19b) is parallel to 9:28a. Saul is bold to preach and testify in

---

7   Paul tells us in Gal 1:17 that he went into Arabia and then returned to Damascus.

both cities (9:20-22 and 9:28-29). There is a plot to kill Saul in both cities and he successfully escapes with the help of friends.[8]

Barnabas, one of the unsung heroes of Acts, was the critical link to persuade the apostles that it was not a clever trick; Saul was truly converted. He told them the story of the light from heaven and how Saul had fearlessly preached Jesus as Messiah in Damascus. Saul again proves the genuineness of his conversion by preaching the same message in the most dangerous place he could possibly do it, the headquarter city of his enemies. Today, it would be like preaching Christ the Son of God in Mecca. The courage and spiritual insight of Barnabas are most noteworthy. If there had been no Barnabas, there might have been no Paul and none of his epistles.

It is not clear how Saul was able to go about freely and preach boldly without being arrested. If, according to the chronology we are assuming, this is about the year 37 AD, there would have been a change from Pilate to Marcellus as prefect of Judea. Caiaphas was deposed from the high priesthood in 36. The new rulers may not have been so zealous to kill the turncoat. However, Saul was not without deadly enemies; the Hellenist Jews hated his message and tried to kill him. Just because Hellenist Jews had much foreign influence and read the Torah in Greek, and just because Saul was a fellow Hellenist, does not mean that they were any less zealous to destroy the turncoat.

Again Saul escaped their plots. Somehow, in the providence of God, he heard about their plot and fled to Caesarea, the chief port. From there he boarded a ship for his native province of Cilicia and his hometown Tarsus. After a brilliant start, suddenly he is put on the shelf. His life is preserved but his career seems to be on indefinite hold. However, he may well have had a ministry *in the regions of Syria and Cilicia* (Gal 1:21). God had more preparation for "the apostle of the Gentiles."

9:31 A Pause to Reflect

So the church throughout all Judea and Galilee and Samaria had peace and was being built up. And walking in the fear of the Lord and in the comfort of the Holy Spirit, it multiplied.

---

8   From Fitzmyer, 438.

The church is now about seven years old. It had a wonderful start in Jerusalem but was scattered by persecution. Now it has taken root in many towns of the three main divisions of Palestine: Judea, Samaria, and Galilee. This is the only time churches are mentioned in Galilee, Jesus' home region. Who started them? How did they spread? We would like to know, but Acts is not a complete history of the earliest churches; it is very selective in its content.

Church is singular; there were many churches, but they were all one Church. Would that we had this unity today! The persecution had lost momentum and there was *peace*. This enabled the church, in the encouragement (*paraklēsis*) of the Holy Spirit, to grow in spiritual strength and in number. Persecution had stimulated the growth of the church, but now the church needed a time of peace to let down roots. The lives of these Jews were changed. They now lived before their neighbors *in the fear of the Lord*, the same *fear* they had in Acts 5:11 in Jerusalem. "Let us cultivate that holy filial fear of Jehovah that is the essence of all true religion---the fear that consists of reverence, of dread to offend, of anxiety to please, and of entire submission and obedience." "If we fear God we may dismiss all other fear."[9]

Lessons for Life

1. The conversion of Saul of Tarsus was an act of unilateral sovereign grace. So are all conversions.
2. If God could convert and save a zealous enemy like Saul of Tarsus, he can save anyone.
3. What we do to believers in Christ we do to Christ himself.
4. The Lord usually involves his human agents in the process of the salvation of souls.
5. Those who testify boldly for Christ will suffer opposition.
6. We need more spiritually sensitive bridge-builders like Barnabas.

ᐤᐤ

---

9   C. H. Spurgeon, *The Treasury of David*, commenting on Psalm 128. Arranged and edited by James M. Renihan, *Daily Treasure*, Darlington England and Auburn MA USA: Evangelical Press, 2000, 17 November.

Acts 9:32-12:23

The Acts of Peter

We now come to a series of three stories in which Peter is the main actor, the principle agent of the Acts of the Risen Christ. Of course Peter has been the hero and chief spokesman since chapter 1, but here Luke focuses on Peter especially before taking up the "Acts of Paul" in chapters 13-28. Now we have 1) two miracles of healing through Peter (9:32-41), 2) the conversion of Cornelius through Peter (10:1-11:18), and 3) Peter's escape from jail and God's judgment on his tormentor (12:1-23).

9:32-35 The Healing of Aeneas and the Raising of Dorcas

32 Now as Peter went here and there among them all, he came down also to the saints who lived at Lydda. 33 There he found a man named Aeneas, bedridden for eight years, who was paralyzed. 34 And Peter said to him, "Aeneas, Jesus Christ heals you; rise and make your bed." And immediately he rose. 35 And all the residents of Lydda and Sharon saw him, and they turned to the Lord.

We have not heard from Peter since he returned to Jerusalem from laying hands on the Samaritan converts of Philip and preaching in many of the villages of Samaria (8:25). Maybe the peaceful conditions described in 9:31 made the apostles feel free to leave Jerusalem and to do more evangelistic and pastoral tours.

Lydda was the current name of the OT city of Lod (1 Chron 8:12), 12 miles (17 km) inland from Joppa on the coast. Lydda in NT times was important politically as one of eleven regional capitals (*toparchies)* and commercially as the hub of seven roads, including the road from Jerusalem to Joppa. It had a mixed Gentile/Jewish population, including a number of Jewish Nazarenes, here called, as Paul in his epistles so often referred to them as "saints." The gospel is again seeping out into places that are not purely Jewish.

Aeneas (a Greek name recalling the founder of Rome) was probably a Jew and may or may not have been a convert to Jesus of Nazareth. We pass over the word *paralytic* but should pause to consider the helplessness of such a person, even in modern times, and the burden on the care-giving family. The Greek is ambiguous. He could have had the paralysis from age eight or for eight years. We knew such a person in Japan. He contracted a severe diarrhea and very high fever at age eight, which left him speechless and crippled from the neck down for life. Mizuno Genzō became a Christian through his misery and became famous for his wonderful poetry before being released to the freedom of heaven. How one wishes for the power of Christ Peter had here for such a person!

Peter has exactly the same healing power that Jesus demonstrated in Luke 5:24-26 in commanding a paralytic to *rise, take up your bed and walk.* In fact Luke seems to couch the story in much of the same vocabulary, except that Peter makes it clear that *Jesus Christ heals you* (the present tense could be understood "is about to heal you"). Aeneas had enough faith to get up immediately, using muscles that had not been used for eight years (the healing restored more than damaged muscles). The miracle caused such amazement that it led to the conversion of many of the people of Lydda (*all*, as in many places in the Bible, here means "a great many"). Lydda later became a bishopric and sent a representative to the Council of Nicea in 325 AD. There were many conversions from among the people scattered over the Sharon Plain (the coastal plain region from Lydda north to Dor, much of which was too marshy to inhabit).

9:36-43 Dorcas Restored to Life

36 Now there was in Joppa a disciple named Tabitha, which, translated, means Dorcas. She was full of good works and acts of charity. 37 In those days she became ill and died, and when they had washed her, they laid her in an upper room. 38 Since Lydda was near Joppa, the disciples, hearing that Peter was there, sent two men to him, urging him, "Please come to us without delay." 39 So Peter rose and went with them. And when he arrived, they took him to the upper room. All the widows stood beside him weeping and showing tunics and other garments that Dorcas made while she was with them. 40 But Peter put them all outside, and knelt down and *prayed; and turning to the body he said, "Tabitha, arise." And she opened her eyes, and when she saw Peter she sat up. **41** And he gave her his hand and raised her up. Then, calling the saints and widows, he presented her alive. **42** And it became known throughout all Joppa, and many believed in the Lord. **43** And he stayed in Joppa for many days with one Simon, a tanner.*

Joppa (present day Jaffa) was a pleasant town on the coast, one of the very few seaports available to the Jews. In OT times it was a Phoenician port; from here Jonah tried to escape to Tarshish. In Joppa there were disciples of Jesus, including **Tabitha,** who was *full of good works and acts of charity.* In Greek her name was Dorcas; both names mean "gazelle," recalling the grace and beauty of that animal. She may well have been a woman of some means to be able to do so many good works. Then tragedy struck. Tabitha died from an unnamed sickness. The believers must have prayed earnestly for her, but she died. The women began funeral preparations.

The believers heard that Peter was in nearby Lydda, so they asked him to come without delay. This was a tremendous act of faith on their part. It was already too late. Their beloved Tabitha was dead and laid out in an upper room. They may have thought that if Peter could raise a paralytic by the power of Jesus, maybe he could raise the dead by the power of Jesus.

When Peter arrived, he was escorted immediately to the upper room. All the widows whom Tabitha had helped were weeping and showed Peter the robes and other clothing Tabitha had made, maybe many of them being then worn by the women. Peter made them all leave the room, reminiscent of Jesus when he raised the daughter of Jairus (Matt 9:25; Mark 5:41). Perhaps the presence of a weeping, distraught crowd would have disturbed his concentration. Maybe he was not sure at first that his prayer would be answered. Peter must have recalled that incident and prayed earnestly that Jesus would do it again. He is given enough assurance so that he could say, in almost the same words Jesus used (*Talitha cum* Mark 5:41), *Tabitha cum.* And, like Jesus, Peter took her by the hand and helped her stand. The joy and astonishment of the widows and the other believers soon spread all over town, and the result was that *many believed in the Lord.*

The second healing story is a contrast to and an advance on the first. Aeneas was paralyzed; Tabitha was dead. About Aeneas we are told nothing;

Tabitha was a woman of wonderful Christian character. Aeneas was a helpless burden on his family and friends; Tabitha was very important in her community. Luke seems to feature godly women, both in his gospel and the book of Acts.[10]

Peter stayed in Joppa for many days with one tanner, Simon. Luke always skillfully anticipates the next scene, and this verse acts as a transition to the next story. Again, Peter is lodging in the fringes of acceptable Jewish society. Because they constantly dealt with dead animals, and because the business saturated both the tanner and the tannery with the unpleasant odor of dog dung and fermenting bran and vinegar, tanners were considered unclean by the orthodox Jews.[11] Though it does not say that Simon was a believer in Jesus, that would be the most natural assumption, as an ordinary Jew would not receive Peter gladly. He may have found an acceptance among the Nazarenes that he did not find among other Jews. Did Peter stay with him to encourage and disciple him?

Lessons for Life

1. We may not have the healing gift Peter had, but we should seek to heal the sick and pray for them as Christ himself would have done.
2. We should be women (and men!) who are less "full of good words" and more "full of good works."
3. Some believers are low status and stink. Love them especially.

---

10   We are indebted to Witherington (330-31) for these contrasts.

11   "Tanner," in the *International Bible Encyclopedia*. Those who dealt in animal hides were part of the outcaste "Eta" in old Japan.

Acts 10-11:18

The Gentile Pentecost

The conversion of Cornelius and his household marks the second time, after the Ethiopian eunuch, that a Gentile is converted. But here too, as in the case of the Ethiopian, Cornelius is not a typical pagan Gentile. He is said *to fear God with all his house.* Traditional scholarship since Kirsopp Lake has seen in the phrase *one who fears God* (ten times in the book of Acts) as a technical term for one who is attracted to Judaism, perhaps observes the Sabbath and attends the synagogue services, but has not received circumcision and baptism to become a full proselyte. Recent research has made this distinction less clearcut.[12] Nevertheless, it is clear, that like the Ethiopian, Cornelius is a "bridge" for the gospel between Judaism and paganism.

Luke considers this transition very important, for he spends a great deal of precious manuscript space on this incident and repeats the story of Peter's dream three times. Why is this story so important?

We in our day find it hard to comprehend the depth of the chasm between Jew and Gentile that prevailed in NT times. To enter the house of a Gentile left a Jew unclean until evening (John 18:28). No pious Jew could eat with a Gentile. If cooking utensils were bought from a Gentile, they had to be purified by fire, knives newly sharpened, spits made red hot before use. A Jewish woman could not help her Gentile neighbor in childbirth. And so on and so on.[13]

The OT Law does not stipulate that Jews could not associate with or eat with Gentiles.[14] But the Jewish oral tradition expanded the dietary laws of Leviticus 11 and the abhorrence of idolatry and intermarriage to the Canaanites (Deuteronomy 7) into a maze of rules that made ordinary association with Gentiles almost impossible. What is hard for us to grasp is

---

12   See the discussion in Witherington, 341-344.

13   These examples are a few of those given by Alfred Edersheim's *Sketches of Jewish Social Life in the Days of Christ,* London: James Clarke & Co., 1961, 26-29.

14   The book of Jubilees (from the intertestamental period) does say "Separate thyself from the Gentiles and do not eat with them" (22:16).

how deeply these customs gripped even the first Jewish Christians, including its top leadership. Their Lord had commanded them to take the gospel *into all the world* (Matt 28:18-20; Mark 16:15; Luke 24:47), but it was practically impossible until the dietary and social barriers were removed. Jesus had first taught an abrogation of the dietary laws in Mark 7:1-23. *Are you so dull?* he asked. *Don't you see that nothing that enters a man from the outside can make him 'unclean'? For it doesn't go into his heart but into his stomach, and then out of his body* (NIV). **In saying this, Jesus declared all foods 'clean'** (7:18-19). Now that lesson will be driven home forcefully.

The story unfolds in seven scenes, like the acts of a play. 1) Cornelius sees a vision (10:1-8); 2) Peter sees a vision (10:9-16); 3) Peter meets with the messengers from Cornelius and travels to Caesarea (10:17-23a); 4) Peter talks with Cornelius about the visions (10:23b-33); 5) Peter gives an evangelistic sermon (10:34-43); 6) The Spirit falls on Cornelius and his house (10:44-48); and 7) Peter tells the story to the church in Jerusalem (11:1-18).

10:1-8 An Angel Appears to Cornelius

1 At Caesarea there was a man named Cornelius, a centurion of what was known as the Italian Cohort, 2 a devout man who feared God with all his household, gave alms generously to the people, and prayed continually to God. 3 About the ninth hour of the day he saw clearly in a vision an angel of God come in and say to him, "Cornelius." 4 And he stared at him in terror and said, "What is it, Lord?" And he said to him, "Your prayers and your alms have ascended as a memorial before God. 5 And now send men to Joppa and bring one Simon who is called Peter. 6 He is lodging with one Simon, a tanner, whose house is by the sea." 7 When the angel who spoke to him had departed, he called two of his servants and a devout soldier from among those who attended him, 8 and having related everything to them, he sent them to Joppa.

Cornelius was probably a descendant of one of ten thousand slaves who had been freed by P. Cornelius Sulla in 82 BC, who took Sulla's second name (*gens*). A centurion was commander of 100 men, like a captain in charge of a company in a modern army. Dependable centurions were the backbone of the Roman army. Centurions are always mentioned favorably in the gospels and Acts and are often examples of faith and insight not found even among the

Jews (Luke 7:2-10; 23:47). It is remarkable that the key officers of the hated Roman occupiers are mentioned so often and so favorably in the NT.

We know that *The Italian Cohort* was present in Syria in 69 AD. The regiment may have been composed of Italians originally, but we know that between 6 and 66 AD there were no regular Roman legions in Judea; the military units were auxiliaries composed of men from various ethnic groups in the region. Their officers, however, may have been Romans.

Quite remarkable for a Roman officer, Cornelius is a very zealous God-fearer, who was generous in giving to the poor and prayed to God *continually.* These were prime marks of piety in Judaism. God rewarded his faithfulness by leading him to the Jewish Messiah (v. 4). Cornelius is an example of God rewarding pagans who live up to the light that they have. God then leads them to more light.

During one of his regular times of prayer at 3:00 PM (no story in the NT tells the time of day as much as this story), God gives Cornelius a vision of an angel. 3:00 PM was the hour of the evening sacrifice in the temple. It was no hazy dream; he saw the angel *clearly.* And just as clearly, he hears the angel's voice. *Cornelius!* Slightly differently than Saul in chapter 10, he asks not *Who are you, Lord?* but *What is it, Lord?* The angel assures the frightened officer by saying that God is rewarding his piety and prayers and now commands him to send men to Joppa to find one Simon Peter who is staying by the shore with one Simon the Tanner. The angel cannot save time by telling the gospel message to Cornelius by himself; it must come through the missionaries of the gospel, and in this watershed case, through the head apostle.

10:9-16 God Gives Peter "Food for thought"[15]

> *9 The next day, as they were on their journey and approaching the city, Peter went up on the housetop about the sixth hour to pray. 10 And he became hungry and wanted something to eat, but while they were preparing it, he fell into a trance 11 and saw the heavens opened and something like a great sheet descending, being let down by its four corners upon the earth. 12 In it were all kinds of animals and reptiles and birds of the air. 13 And there came a voice to him: "Rise, Peter; kill and eat." 14 But Peter said,*

---

15   This phrase is from Witherington, 349.

"By no means, Lord; for I have never eaten anything that is common or unclean." 15 And the voice came to him again a second time, "What God has made clean, do not call common." 16 This happened three times, and the thing was taken up at once to heaven.

Just as in the case of Saul, who was approaching Damascus about noon (Acts 22:6; 26:13), the two messengers and their bodyguard were approaching Joppa about noon, when God gave another vision, this time to Peter. The distance from Caesarea to Joppa was 34 miles (55 km) and would usually take 10-11 hours on foot. The fact that the messengers arrived about noon shows that they must have traveled most of the night. (No mention is made of horses, which would have made the journey faster.) Noon was not a set time for public prayer among the Jews, but those who prayed privately three times a day would have prayed at noon (Psa 55:17; Dan 6:10).

Peter's prayers were somewhat hindered by hunger pangs, and his thoughts may have drifted from spiritual things to food. This is one of Luke's many humorous touches in Acts and serves to add spice to the story. It is as if God is saying, "Are you hungry Peter? Let me give you something to eat!" Unlike the case of Cornelius, who was wide-awake when the angel appeared, Peter falls into a trance of a surreal dreamlike sight. Animals are descending from above contained in something like a large sheet or sail.[16] It contained all kinds of animals, wild and domestic, four-footed mammals, some of which would have been clean, and maybe pigs and rabbits and camels, which were unclean, as well as reptiles and shellfish and other disgusting things, which would have been unclean. There may have been unclean birds like ostriches, owls, and storks. All the creatures of the ark appear before Peter! Then Peter hears the voice of God, *Rise Peter! Kill and eat!* The response of Peter, the head apostle, is less noble than that of Cornelius, the Gentile seeker. In modern English it may be translated, "No way, Lord! For I have never eaten anything common ("defiled," perhaps by being offered to idols) or unclean (that which is clearly prohibited in the Torah).[17]

The Lord's (Jesus?) answer is *What God has made clean, do not call common.* How ironic! Peter is like a little boy smearing a muddy finger on his

---

16   The word *othunos* is sometimes used of sails.

17   The unclean creatures are listed in Leviticus 11 and Deuteronomy 14.

mother's clean laundry! He did not yet understand the lesson of Mark's gospel (which he later supervised) *This he (Jesus) said, making all things clean* (Mark 7:19).

No wonder Peter was shocked. Had not God given Israel an **everlasting** Law (Exod 12:14; Lev 16:34; 24:8; 1 Chron 16:17)? Nevertheless, even among the Jews, some said that when Messiah comes, all the animals in the world previously considered unclean would be declared clean (Midrash Ps. 146/4).[18]

There is great missiological significance to what people eat and do not eat. One people's feast can be taboo or disgusting to other peoples. The Japanese relish seaweed (really "weed" is a prejudicial term) and raw fish. Some Korean restaurants serve dog meat. The Chinese eat such strange things as bird's nests and shark fins. Hindus are vegetarian and consider the consumption of any flesh taboo. To Muslims, of course, pork is unclean. The missionary must learn to eat the food of the people to whom he is sent. He must lay his own deeply engrained cultural taboos and learn to eat what the people of his adopted country eat. In 34 years in Japan I was often asked, "Do you like Japanese food"? Fortunately, with a few exceptions, I could answer yes. What they were asking was, "Do you accept us and our ways?"

The gospel must now go out into the entire world. God is preparing for thousands of cross-cultural mission encounters by "making all foods clean." Unnecessary barriers to the gospel must be removed or it will never leave the confines of Judaism.

10:17-23a Peter Meets with the Messengers from Cornelius and Travels to Caesarea

17 Now while Peter was inwardly perplexed as to what the vision that he had seen might mean, behold, the men who were sent by Cornelius, having made inquiry for Simon's house, stood at the gate 18 and called out to ask whether Simon who was called Peter was lodging there. 19 And while Peter was pondering the vision, the Spirit said to him, "Behold, three men are looking for you. 20 Rise and go down and accompany them without hesitation, for I have sent them." 21 And Peter went down to the

---

18   Cited by Witherington, 350.

men and said, "I am the one you are looking for. What is the reason for
*your coming?" **22** And they said, "Cornelius, a centurion, an upright and*
God-fearing man, who is well spoken of by the whole Jewish nation, was
directed by a holy angel to send for you to come to his house and to hear
*what you have to say." **23** So he invited them in to be his guests.*

The Lord does not explain the vision or the bizarre command *Kill and*
eat; he leaves Peter to ponder the meaning. This is so like God's pedagogy. He
makes the student think about the problem before giving an answer. Luke's
first readers would also be puzzled. "What could this possibly mean?" A good
story does not reveal the end in the beginning. Much of the NT revelation is
given, not by logical discourse, but by narrative, or storytelling. Any people,
no matter how primitive or illiterate, can relate to stories. That is why so much
of the Bible is narrative. A good preacher knows how to tell stories effectively.

The first clue to the meaning of the vision is standing at the gate, calling
out and asking if this is the lodging of Simon Peter. A direct revelation of
the Spirit gives a second clue: "Even though these men are Gentiles, go with
them." But again, the Spirit does not give a complete explanation.

The two messengers explain their request. But at this point neither
Cornelius nor his messengers understand just why Peter must go so urgently
to the house of Cornelius.

Peter invites them in. This shows that he is learning the lesson of the
animals in the sheet. A good Jew like Peter should never invite Gentiles into
his lodging and certainly not eat with them. The Greek word for *to be his*
guests, xenizo, certainly included the serving of a meal. Is this the first time in
his life that Peter ate with Gentiles?

10:23b-33 Arrival at Caesarea and Peter's Conversation with Cornelius

23 *The next day he rose and went away with them, and some of the*
*brothers from Joppa accompanied him. **24** And on the following day they*
entered Caesarea. Cornelius was expecting them and had called together
*his relatives and close friends. **25** When Peter entered, Cornelius met him*
*and fell down at his feet and worshiped him. **26** But Peter lifted him up,*
*saying, "Stand up; I too am a man." **27** And as he talked with him, he*
*went in and found many persons gathered. **28** And he said to them, "You*

yourselves know how unlawful it is for a Jew to associate with or to visit anyone of another nation, but God has shown me that I should not call any person common or unclean. 29 So when I was sent for, I came without objection. I ask then why you sent for me."

30 And Cornelius said, "Four days ago, about this hour, I was praying in my house at the ninth hour, and behold, a man stood before me in bright clothing 31 and said, 'Cornelius, your prayer has been heard and your alms have been remembered before God. 32 Send therefore to Joppa and ask for Simon who is called Peter. He is lodging in the house of Simon, a tanner, by the sea.' 33 So I sent for you at once, and you have been kind enough to come. Now therefore we are all here in the presence of God to hear all that you have been commanded by the Lord.

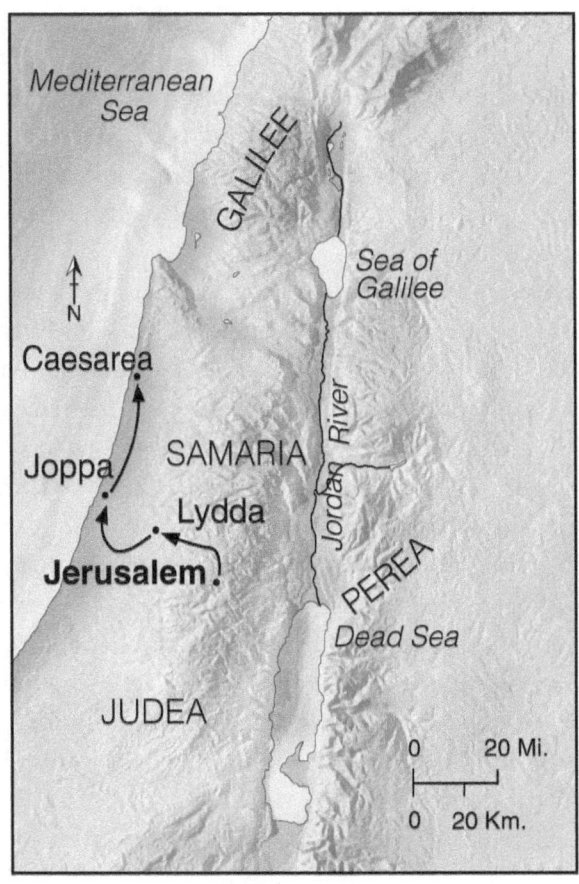

Peter's Ministry in Caesarea

By the time the guests had finished their noon meal, it was too late to travel so they rested and started out the next day with Peter and six brothers from Joppa (the number is given in 11:12). They are later necessary as witnesses to this dubious event.

Though many Jews lived in Caesarea, that Roman city was to a pious Jew the heart of darkness, the capital of the hated occupying power. Caesarea had been built by Herod the Great to provide a port on a smooth coastline with no natural harbors. It was a magnificent engineering achievement, complete with aqueduct (the remains of which can still be seen today), an amphitheater facing the sea, sumptuous palaces and public buildings, and a sewer system. But the greatest engineering feat was the construction of an artificial harbor. Huge stones (50 x 18 x 9 feet) were sunk in water 120 feet deep to form the foundation of a small harbor 200 feet across.

The pagan darkness had already been illuminated in Caesarea with the light of the gospel; this was the residence of Philip the Evangelist and his four daughters who prophesied (8:40; 21:8). Why didn't God send Philip, who was right in town (unless he was on an evangelistic trip), instead of Peter? It may be that this event was so important that no one less than Peter was sufficient for the task.

Cornelius was eagerly waiting for Peter and met him at the door and fell down on his knees at Peter's feet, as if greeting the emperor himself. What an astonishing spectacle, that a Roman officer should humble himself in such a way before a Jewish fisherman! Peter, no doubt a little embarrassed, told Cornelius, with a light humorous touch, *Stand up, I too am (only) a man!* The pagan Greeks invented democracy, but it was genuine Christianity that eventually leveled caste, rank, and privilege.

On entering the atrium, Peter and his friends were amazed to find a large group of expectant relatives and friends of Cornelius. Acutely aware of the anomaly of Jews appearing in the midst of so many Gentiles, Peter explained that though it was against Jewish custom to associate with *anyone of another nation,*[19] God had showed him that he could consider no human being "common or unclean." God had not said this in so many words, but Peter had

---

19   The phrase *unlawful (athemitos)* might be better rendered "against our custom." Peter
      knew that these taboos were not in the Torah of God but in manmade customs. The
      word translated *another nation* is *allofulos,* "foreigner."

correctly concluded that his dream about animals was about more than just food. The dream made a deeper impression than a direct command from God! But Peter still does not know exactly why he has been summoned so urgently.

Cornelius explains (verses 30-33) about the vision of an angel and how he was commanded to send for Peter. The story within the story now appears for the third time. The effect is to remove any possible doubt that this is the work of God. *Now therefore we are all here in the presence of God to hear all that you have been commanded by the Lord.*

Would that all missionaries met with such a prepared and eager audience! Would that all of Christ's witnesses were as prepared to give the gospel!

10:34-43 Peter's Evangelion

34 So Peter opened his mouth and said: "Truly I understand that God shows no partiality, 35 but in every nation anyone who fears him and does what is right is acceptable to him. 36 As for the word that he sent to Israel, preaching good news of peace through Jesus Christ (he is Lord of all), 37 you yourselves know what happened throughout all Judea, beginning from Galilee after the baptism that John proclaimed: 38 how God anointed Jesus of Nazareth with the Holy Spirit and with power. He went about doing good and healing all who were oppressed by the devil, for God was with him. 39 And we are witnesses of all that he did both in the country of the Jews and in Jerusalem. They put him to death by hanging him on a tree, 40 but God raised him on the third day and made him to appear, 41 not to all the people but to us who had been chosen by God as witnesses, who ate and drank with him after he rose from the dead. 42 And he commanded us to preach to the people and to testify that he is the one appointed by God to be judge of the living and the dead. 43 To him all the prophets bear witness that everyone who believes in him receives forgiveness of sins through his name."

Luke now gives a synopsis of Peter's speech. Peter begins with the lesson that has just been impressed upon him so powerfully. It is the "key center"[20]

---

20   Irving L. Jensen in his book *Independent Bible Study* (Chicago: Moody Press, 1963) encouraged his students to find a phrase or sentence in the text of a given section or paragraph of Scripture which summarizes the message of the whole section which he called "the key center."

of this passage: ***God is no respecter of persons*** (KJV).[21] Despite the fact that he had chosen Israel as the nation through whom salvation would come, Israel is not his special favorite, and he will accept those of any nation who seek him. They seek him by *fearing him* and *doing right*.

Some have wondered if Cornelius was already saved, as much as any OT believer could be saved, responding to the light that he had before the way of salvation was made explicitly clear. Some then go on to speculate that perhaps some "who never had opportunity to hear the gospel" could be saved on the same basis. We are in the realm of speculation here, but how can one *fear God* (the One and Only God) without the work of the Holy Spirit in his/her heart? At any rate, the message of this passage seems to be that to such people God will give the light of the gospel of Christ.

Peter then gives an outline of the standard evangelion (gospel content) which could furnish an outline for the gospel of Mark, of which Peter is said to be the real author. The grammar is rough, as if indeed this were not a polished sermon, but sermon notes. This sermon is like other evangelistic speeches in the book of Acts: 1) Who Jesus is and what he did. 2) He was killed by hanging on a tree (cross). 3) But God raised him from the dead and we are witnesses of these things. 4) If you believe in him your sins will be forgiven. Peter makes no quotations from the OT, and there is a little more detail on the life and ministry of Jesus. This nicely fits a Gentile audience.

In the *preaching good news of peace* in v. 36 we may have an echo of Luke's Christmas evangel *Glory to God in the highest, and on earth peace to men on whom his favor rests* (Luke 2:14). The peace is first peace **with** God, and then the peace **of** God, and then peace **between** men. Jesus Christ is *Lord of all*, that is all human beings and all nations.

Verse 37 intimates that this audience, because they were living in Palestine, probably had heard reports of Jesus of Nazareth. They were not entirely ignorant.

Verse 38 is a summary of Mark chapters 1 to 10. Deliverance from demon possession is especially prominent in the gospel of Mark. At this point Peter does not say with the gospel of John that "Jesus is God," but is content

---

21   The word in Greek is a noun, *prosōpolēmptēs,* and means literally "receiver of face," in other words one who responds to people by their reputation or rank. The word appears here for the first time in all Greek literature, and may have been coined by the Christians.

to lay that foundation with a simple "God was with him." He was Immanuel. In evangelistic work we do well not to dump the whole truth on strangers to the Bible in one truckload.

Verse 39 makes two points: the first that these claims are backed up by living witnesses, and the second that *they* (in Jerusalem), not specifying either Jews or Romans, killed Jesus by hanging him on a tree. "Hanging him on a tree" is also found in Acts 5:30. The reference to "hanging on a tree" (literally *on wood*) may have been a euphemism to avoid the stark and ugly word "cross" or "crucify." Crucifixion was a familiar horror to any resident of Palestine in those times; this is before the word "cross" became a precious symbol of the faith.[22]

The resurrection (verses 40-41) was an essential element of the early *kerygma* (content of the gospel preaching) and is never omitted in evangelistic messages in Acts. The risen Christ not only was visible, but also ate and drank with them. Only Luke mentions this particular detail (Luke 24:41-43; for him it was telling evidence that the risen Jesus was more than a spirit or apparition. It seems especially appropriate in a chapter whose chief sub-theme is eating and food.

The risen Christ commanded them to preach to *the people* (Greek *ho laos*). Usually that phrase in Luke/Acts refers to the Jewish people (as in 10:2). Actually, Jesus had said that they would be witnesses to the whole earth (1:8).

Jesus must be proclaimed as *the Judge of living and dead.* This element is missing in much of modern evangelism. But without the judgment of verse 42, the offer of forgiveness in verse 43 is unnecessary and meaningless. The reason so many people throughout the world are indifferent to the gospel is that they do not really know or believe that they will face any kind of judgment after death, let alone face Christ as their Judge.

As in 3:18, this forgiveness was prophesied by *all the prophets.* It would be an interesting exercise to go through the books of the prophets and mark all the references to forgiveness in general and to forgiveness in a coming Messiah in particular. The "proof from prophecy" was always a major element in apostolic preaching.

---

22   "Let the very name of the cross be far away not only from thy body of a Roman citizen, but even from his thoughts, his eyes, his ears" (Cicero, *ProRabirio*, 5). The book of Acts uses the word "crucify" only twice, both accusations of the Jewish leaders (2:36; 4:10). The word "cross" is not used at all in Acts. Interestingly enough, neither word is used in the book of Romans, except in Rom 6:10.

10:44-48 The Spirit Falls on Cornelius and His House

44 While Peter was still saying these things, the Holy Spirit fell on all who heard the word. 45 And the believers from among the circumcised who had come with Peter were amazed, because the gift of the Holy Spirit was poured out even on the Gentiles. 46 For they were hearing them speaking in tongues and extolling God. Then Peter declared, 47 "Can anyone withhold water for baptizing these people, who have received the Holy Spirit just as we have?" 48 And he commanded them to be baptized in the name of Jesus Christ. Then they asked him to remain for some days.

Preachers usually hate interruptions. But Peter, after some initial consternation, may have been delighted with this interruption. Literally the text says that *the Holy Spirit fell on all who were listening to the message.* Notice the connection between the preaching/hearing of the message of the gospel and the work of the Spirit. Even if much less spectacular, we need a similar work of the Spirit every time the message is preached.

God took over in an irresistible act of saving grace. It does not say that the Spirit came only on those who heard and believed, but that He came on everyone who was listening. Their listening did, however, show the desire of their hearts. The Jewish believers who had come with Peter knew of the outpouring of the Spirit because they heard the Gentile converts speaking in tongues and praising God. There is no good reason to believe that the speaking in tongues here is any different than what occurred to Jewish disciples of Jesus in chapter 2. Luke presumes his readers would assume it is the same phenomenon, that is the miraculous speaking of foreign languages, which the speakers did not know. Just as in Acts 2, the tongues speakers praised *the mighty works of God* (2:11), here they *were extolling God.*

Again, so characteristically of conversions in the book of Acts, the converts are baptized immediately. Baptism was the outward act of submission by the seekers that they were now believers in and followers of Jesus Christ. At the same time, it was a sign of the acceptance of the new believers by the church. An instant church was formed! Notice that baptism is not a pre-condition of receiving the Spirit, as in Acts 2, but rather that the Spirit fell **before** the water baptism.

Then they asked Peter to remain for some days. The baptismal preparation classes were given post baptism. In the latter years of our church planting ministry in Japan, we conducted baptismal preparation classes of six sessions as required by our denomination, but then continued with post-baptismal discipleship classes (often one-on-one) as long as the new Christian was willing to continue. We were concerned that the baptism be seen not as a "graduation ceremony," but as a "school entrance ceremony."

ACTS 11

THE GENTILE PENTECOST CONTINUED

Acts 11:1-18

Validation by the Jerusalem Church

1 Now the apostles and the brothers who were throughout Judea heard that the Gentiles also had received the word of God. 2 So when Peter went up to Jerusalem, the circumcision party criticized him, saying, 3 "You went to uncircumcised men and ate with them." 4 But Peter began and explained it to them in order: 5 "I was in the city of Joppa praying, and in a trance I saw a vision, something like a great sheet descending, being let down from heaven by its four corners, and it came down to me. 6 Looking at it closely, I observed animals and beasts of prey and reptiles and birds of the air. 7 And I heard a voice saying to me, 'Rise, Peter; kill and eat.' 8 But I said, 'By no means, Lord; for nothing common or unclean has ever entered my mouth.' 9 But the voice answered a second time from heaven, 'What God has made clean, do not call common.' 10 This happened three times, and all was drawn up again into heaven. 11 And behold, at that very moment three men arrived at the house in which we were, sent to me from Caesarea. 12 And the Spirit told me to go with them, making no distinction. These six brothers also accompanied me, and we entered the man's house. 13 And he told us how he had seen the angel stand in his house and say, 'Send to Joppa and bring Simon who is called Peter; 14 he will declare to you a message by which you will be saved, you and all your *household.' **15** As I began to speak, the Holy Spirit fell on them just as on us at the beginning. **16** And I remembered the word of the Lord, how he said, 'John baptized with water, but you will be baptized with the Holy Spirit.' **17** If then God gave the same gift to them as he gave to us when we believed in the Lord Jesus Christ, who was I that I could stand in God's way?" **18** When they heard these things they fell silent. And they glorified God, saying, "Then to the Gentiles also God has granted repentance that leads to life."*

Why is the story repeated? Very little new information is added. It serves to underline the epochal importance of the Cornelius event and to demonstrate vividly the reluctance the Jewish church had in accepting Gentiles. Every detail reinforces the fact that God is in control in both the abrogation of the dietary laws and the conversion of Gentiles. This time the story is told from the viewpoint of Peter.

The word of God in verse 1 is the "the gospel," "the message of Jesus and his salvation." The wording reminds us of how the apostles had heard that the Samaritans *had received the word of God* (8:14). The apostles are still in Jerusalem and some of the *brothers* have evidently returned from the scattering of 8:1. The phrase in verse 2 *the circumcision party* is literally "they of the circumcision."[1] This phrase usually means simply "Jews."[2] In Acts 10:45 it referred to "Jewish believers," and many presume that it means the same in 11:2. However, we are inclined to think this meaning does not fit 11:2 very well for the simple reason that all the brothers in Jerusalem at this point were Jewish, so to designate them all as *they of the circumcision* (= "Jewish") would be pointless. The phrase may sometimes, as it does in Titus 1:10 and Gal 2:12, denote a party within the Jewish believers in Jesus who were especially strict advocates that Gentile converts must practice the Jewish traditions. Notice it does not say that the apostles and the brothers challenged Peter's violation of the taboo against eating with Gentiles; it was *the circumcision party.*[3] These

---

1   *hoi ek peritomē*

2   As in Rom 3:30; 4:9; Gal 2:7-9; Col 3:11; and others.

3   Bruce thinks these people may have been the same party mentioned in Acts 15:5 (*some of the sect of the Pharisees*) and 21:20 (*myriads of Jews who have believed who are all zealous for the law*) (*Acts*, 267). Witherington also suggests the idea of a Judaizing party within Jewish Christianity (362).

Jewish believers may have feared another backlash from the Jewish community such as that which happened in the killing of Stephen. Nevertheless, their lack of enthusiasm for the conversion of the Gentiles is a serious defect. All they can do is focus myopically on the preservation of the "no eating with Gentiles" taboo. Sadly, we see the same attitude in churches today.

Verses 4 to 17 are Peter's defense against this charge. He explained what had happened step-by-step from the beginning. Like a good witness in court, he does not argue or give his opinion, or even assert his authority as the chief apostle, he simply tells what God did. In his version of what happened, a few new details emerge. In verse 6, there were also *beasts of prey* (*thēria*) in the dream, things like bears and lions and wolves. In verse 12 we learn that there were six Jewish men who went with Peter to Caesarea. Their witness is important to establish the facts of the case. Verse 14 is completely new: *He will declare to you a message by which you will be saved, you and all your household.* This anticipates a similar promise to the Philippian jailor (16:31) about household salvation.

Verses 15-17 give Peter's reasoning and conclusion: First the baptism of the Holy Spirit was the same thing that had happened to *us* (Jewish believers) on the Day of Pentecost. Second, this was a fulfillment of what the Lord had said to John the Baptist about the baptism of the Spirit. (Our Lord predicted this.) Third, if God gave them the Spirit, how could I resist God? ("You cannot fight against God. Accept the fact that they are a part of us.")

Verse 18 shows that Peter's argument was unanswerable. They *fell silent*, (indicating a hubbub of opposition) and glorified God and gladly admitted that God himself had done it; **God himself** *has granted repentance that leads to life*,[4] even to the Gentiles! Gentiles, and not just to these Gentiles only, but to Gentiles in general. To their credit they realized that the Gentile believers must be fully accepted. An epochal and essential change had occurred in the thinking of the church. From now on, the door to Gentile evangelism, which will be the theme of the rest of the book, is open.

---

4   This supports the Calvinist position that God must give repentance before a person can repent. See also Acts 5:11 and 2 Tim 2:25. But that does not relieve mankind of the responsibility to repent: Matt 3:2; Mark 6:12; Luke 13:3; Acts 2:38; 3:19; and especially 17:20.

Lessons for Life

1. "God is no respecter of persons." Are we?
2. God is sovereign in salvation. But those who seek him will find him.
3. God, however many visions or miracles he gives, uses human witnesses to convey his message.
4. God's pedagogy (method of teaching) is to give us the pieces and let us put the puzzle together.
5. The most powerful way of conveying truth is to tell a story.
6. In mission, we must be prepared for radical adjustments: new language, new food, new friends.
7. Tongues in Acts were real languages and powerful symbols showing that the gospel must go to all the languages of the earth. Tongues also symbolized the diversity and unity of the one Body.
8. Some in the church will not accept you if you violate one of their taboos or "Shibboleths" (11:2).

Acts 11:19-30

Antioch, the Church that Started by "Accident"

11:19-26 The Birth of the Church in Antioch

19 Now those who were scattered because of the persecution that arose over Stephen traveled as far as Phoenicia and Cyprus and Antioch, speaking the word to no one except Jews. 20 But there were some of them, men of Cyprus and Cyrene, who on coming to Antioch spoke to the Hellenists also, preaching the Lord Jesus. 21 And the hand of the Lord was with them, and a great number who believed turned to the Lord. 22 The report of this came to the ears of the church in Jerusalem, and they sent Barnabas to Antioch. 23 When he came and saw the grace of God, he was glad, and

he exhorted them all to remain faithful to the Lord with steadfast purpose,
24 for he was a good man, full of the Holy Spirit and of faith. And a great
many people were added to the Lord. 25 So Barnabas went to Tarsus to
look for Saul, 26 and when he had found him, he brought him to Antioch.
For a whole year they met with the church and taught a great many people.
And in Antioch the disciples were first called Christians.

Luke, as a good writer always does, carefully prepares his readers for the Gentile mission of chapters 13-19 by explaining the origin of the base of that mission, the church in Antioch. This did not happen by the means of the careful planning by the headquarters church in Jerusalem, but by the providence of God. Indeed, one of the mysteries of Acts continues: Why was the church in Jerusalem still so unresponsive to the Great Commission? The conversion of Gentiles happens in spite of the Apostles' lethargy toward evangelism of the Gentiles. Certain nameless Jewish converts to Jesus from Cyprus[5] and Cyrene, Hellenistic Jews, who had been scattered in the great persecution at the time of the martyrdom of Stephen (8:1), were the bridges of God to the conversion of *a great number* of Greeks[6] to the Lord Jesus. The word "Greeks" here refers, as it does in Rom 1:16 and John 7:35, to "non-Jewish persons of Greek culture," not to ethnic Greeks only.

Antioch was the capital of the Roman province of Syria, the third largest city in the Roman Empire after Rome and Alexandria. It had a population of 500,000.[7] (The present-day population of the Turkish city Antakya (Hatay) on the same location is 145,000.) On its coins was the inscription "Antioch, metropolis, sacred, and inviolable, and autonomous, and sovereign, and capital of the East."[8] It was called "Antioch of Syria" to distinguish it from the fifteen other cities that Seleucus I built and named after his father Antiochus.

Josephus tells us that there were many Jews and proselytes to Judaism in Antioch. It was the first cosmopolitan center for the new faith and the first

---

5   The eastern tip of Cyprus is only ninety miles away from the seaport of Antioch, Seleucia Peirea. Its mountains are visible from there on a clear day.

6   The best manuscripts are divided between the readings *Hellenas* (Greeks) and *Hellenistas*, ("Jewish speakers of Greek"). Since there is a pointed contrast here with *no one except Jews* in verse 19, the better choice is *Hellenas* (Greeks), that is Greco-Roman Gentiles. "The reading 'Greeks' . . . is probably the best reading" (Bock, 414).

7   Some sources report the population as 250,000.

8   Witherington, 366.

place where the believers in Jesus were called "Christians" (v. 26). Antioch was notorious for its moral decadence. Only five miles away in the suburb of Daphne was a famous temple of Apollo and Artemis filled with cult prostitutes. The Roman writer Juvenal lamented that "the Orontes (the river flowing through Antioch) is discharging its contents into the Tiber" (*Satires* 3.62).

After many centuries of neglecting the countryside and rural areas of the world, much mission work in the nineteenth and twentieth centuries turned away from relatively well-evangelized coastal cities to concentrate on the neglected interior of countries like China and continents like Africa. Today the small towns and villages of the interior are flowing into huge mega-cities on every continent, and it is these over-crowded cities with squalid slums and a hodge-podge of ethnic and class mixture and terrible pollution problems and flagrant immorality that are more neglected. May the Lord, as he did then, again send witnesses into the chaos and conflict of these mega-cities like Kolkata and Jakarta so that *a great number* of people might believe and turn to the Lord.

Again, as in Samaria (8:14), and the case of Cornelius (11:1-18), the first church of Jerusalem must investigate and approve this strange turn of events. "Raw pagans believing in our Messiah?! Are they really converted?" This time, instead of sending an apostle, they send Barnabas, "the son of consolation." They could not have made a better choice. When Barnabas saw the results of the grace of God in their lives, he had no doubts about the genuineness of their conversion and rejoiced. Luke never fails to mention the joy of conversion, both for the converts and for those who shepherd them. Barnabas (his name could also be translated "son of exhortation") exhorts them to *remain faithful to the Lord with steadfast purpose*. This is what every new convert needs. He must resolve to follow the Lord Jesus no matter what the opposition or temptation.

When a man is filled with goodness, faith, and the Holy Spirit like Barnabas, such an exhortation has tremendous power. May all of our pastors and leaders be like Barnabas! The result is a chain-reaction. Again a *great many* people are brought to the Lord Jesus. Notice *to the Lord.* People are brought to him, not to the church (although that also is true), or to Barnabas, or to Christianity, but to the **Lord** (the fifth time the word "Lord" occurs in this short passage).

If Barnabas were like many missionaries and pastors today, he would relish his prestige as the king of his little kingdom and put a big sign on the church: "Pastor: Barnabas of Cyprus." He would smile with pride when people called his church "Barnabas' Church." He certainly would not want any outsider interfering with "his" work. Fortunately, Barnabas did something we too seldom see today. He said to himself, "This church is too big for me to handle alone. (Three times *a great many* people are mentioned in this passage.) They need teaching and that is not my strongest gift. I know! I'll get Saul to help me out!"

So even at the risk that Saul would be more prominent in the church than himself, Barnabas rescued Saul of Tarsus from oblivion the second time. Tarsus was just around the northeast corner of the Mediterranean, 160 kilometers and five days' journey one way by foot. When Barnabas arrived in Tarsus, he had to hunt for Saul diligently (the same word is used for Joseph and Mary looking for their lost son in Luke 2:44-45). He finally found him[9] and persuaded him to take up a ministry of teaching in Antioch. Barnabas went to a great deal of trouble to find his co-worker.

So it was that the many new converts in Antioch were thoroughly grounded and discipled for one whole year by the first and greatest theologian and teacher of all time. Did they hear what later became the book of Romans, systematically expounded week after week? Did they learn the truth of the believer's identity with Christ and the great truths of resurrection and the coming again of the Lord Jesus? Were they schooled in stories of the life of Christ, which later became our gospels?

11:27-30 The Church in Antioch Sends Famine Relief

> **27** *Now in these days prophets came down from Jerusalem to Antioch.* **28** *And one of them named Agabus stood up and foretold by the Spirit that there would be a great famine over all the world (this took place in the days of Claudius).* **29** *So the disciples determined, everyone according to his ability, to send relief to the brothers living in Judea.* **30** *And they did so, sending it to the elders by the hand of Barnabas and Saul.*

The church of Antioch was a well-balanced church. It began with fervent lay **evangelism**. It grew with earnest **exhortation** from Barnabas. It was

---

9   Schnabel wonders if Saul was hard to find because he was out of town evangelizing
     (523).

grounded in the faith with the **teaching** of Saul of Tarsus. And now it is blessed with a ministry of **a charismatic gift**, the gift of prophecy. The result was not a seeking after the gift of prophecy, but a response of **compassionate giving** for emergency relief. We have such churches today, but they will be five different churches!

If this brief paragraph were missing, the flow of the book of Acts would still be smooth. The church of Antioch would still be established as the base for the Gentile mission of the latter half of the book. But the paragraph does serve some important purposes. First, it shows the reality of the gift of prophecy given by the Spirit in those days. Second, it shows that the fruit of true faith is good works. Third, it provides a link with a very prominent theme in Paul's epistles, the collection for famine relief.

In New Testament times, whatever else the gift of prophecy was, it included prediction of the future, as this passage clearly demonstrates (see also the appearance of this prophet Agabus in 21:10-11). Apparently, there were none yet with the gift of prophecy in the church of Antioch or there would have been no need for prophets to come down from Jerusalem.[10] The reason for having more than one prophet come is not clear.

The famine that Agabus predicted, and which occurred during the reign of Emperor Claudius (41-54 AD), has independent historical confirmation. There were at least four famines in various parts of the empire during the reign of Claudius. Josephus tells of a famine in Judea between the years 44 and 48 (Bruce, 276). Witherington points out that a famine affecting the whole empire would have been caused by a failure of crops in Egypt, the breadbasket of the empire (372-73). There was a super-flood of the Nile in 45, which destroyed crops and severely affected grain prices for several years.

Through prophecy God enabled the churches to prepare for the relief of a coming disaster. As this is being written in early January 2005 the world is shocked by the death of some 150,000 people in the Indian Ocean tsunami of December 26, 2004. If only the people had fifteen or twenty minutes of warning, many would still be alive. Desperate appeals for funds are being made and great amounts of aid are flowing in from all over the world, but the most effective work is done by organizations that have already stockpiled emergency supplies. These organizations need our contributions **before** the

---

10   Later there were *prophets and teachers* (13:1).

crisis strikes, yet the disaster must make TV news before most of us are moved to give. And when the immediate crisis is over and no longer in the news, the giving stops.

Second, the reality of the faith of the new disciples is demonstrated by their good works, who as they were able (always a good principle for giving), provided help for fellow believers in Judea. Apparently, the famine was worse in Judea than in Syria or the people of Antioch were in general wealthier than the people of Judea.

Notice that nothing is said about the famine collection coming at the instigation of either Saul or Barnabas. The decision to give seems to have arisen from within the church and the two "pastors" were commissioned to deliver the funds. There was no writing of checks or telegraphing money in those days. Only the top leadership could be entrusted with this task. Since his name is mentioned first, we surmise that Barnabas is still "senior pastor." This visit to Jerusalem is no doubt the same as that mentioned by Paul in Gal 2: 1-10, though some scholars dispute that.[11] The NIV correctly brings out the force of the Greek present tense in Gal 2:10: *They desired only that we continue to remember the poor.* The famine relief project could have been one of the reasons for Paul's visit to Jerusalem in Galatians 2.[12]

Lessons for Life

1. God is sovereign in the strategy of missions. The job of mission leadership is to catch up with what he is doing.
2. An ideal church has: a) spontaneous lay witness, b) exhortation to continue in the faith, c) solid grounding in doctrine, d) the free exercise of spiritual gifts, and e) compassion for the needy, especially needy believers.
3. Faith is loyalty to the Lord Jesus, not just Jesus. The word "Lord" is used liberally in the NT, but sparingly in our modern churches.

---

11   McRay dates this visit in 47 AD (McRay, 74).

12   Gal 2:11-14 adds interesting, though unflattering, incidents that happened in Antioch that Luke does not mention: the fact that Peter was there, the coming of "certain men from James," and the hypocrisy of Peter and Barnabas in separating themselves from Gentile believers during meal times.

4. Missions need to return to the great neglected cities of the world even if they are difficult anti-Christian places.
5. Pastors need the humility, faith, and spiritual insight of Barnabas and to be able to function in ministry teams. The pastorate is not a "one-man show."
6. We must prepare for disasters before they occur, and move expeditiously when they do occur.[13]

ⵐⵦⵠ

---

13 The churches of Japan were not quite ready for the Triple Disaster of the tsunami that killed twenty thousand people on March 11, 2011. But they scrambled and united to do a great work of relief that lasted for several years. Because of this experience they were better prepared for the Noto Peninsula earthquake of January 1, 2024.

ACTS 12

THE IMPRISONMENT OF PETER

Acts 12:1-19a

Peter's Escape

1 About that time Herod the king laid violent hands on some who belonged to the church. 2 He killed James the brother of John with the sword, 3 and when he saw that it pleased the Jews, he proceeded to arrest Peter also. This was during the days of Unleavened Bread. 4 And when he had seized him, he put him in prison, delivering him over to four squads of soldiers to guard him, intending after the Passover to bring him out to the people. 5 So Peter was kept in prison, but earnest prayer for him was made to God by the church.

6 Now when Herod was about to bring him out, on that very night, Peter was sleeping between two soldiers, bound with two chains, and sentries before the door were guarding the prison. 7 And behold, an angel of the Lord stood next to him, and a light shone in the cell. He struck Peter on the side and woke him, saying, "Get up quickly." And the chains fell off his hands. 8 And the angel said to him, "Dress yourself and put on your sandals." And he did so. And he said to him, "Wrap your cloak around you and follow me." 9 And he went out and followed him. He did not know that what was being done by the angel was real, but thought he was seeing a vision. 10 When they had passed the first and the second guard, they came to the iron gate leading into the city. It opened for them of its own

accord, and they went out and went along one street, and immediately the
angel left him. ***11*** *When Peter came to himself, he said, "Now I am sure*
that the Lord has sent his angel and rescued me from the hand of Herod
and from all that the Jewish people were expecting."

12 *When he realized this, he went to the house of Mary, the mother*
of John whose other name was Mark, where many were gathered together
and were praying. ***13*** *And when he knocked at the door of the gateway, a*
servant girl named Rhoda came to answer. ***14*** *Recognizing Peter's voice,*
in her joy she did not open the gate but ran in and reported that Peter was
standing at the gate. ***15*** *They said to her, "You are out of your mind." But*
she kept insisting that it was so, and they kept saying, "It is his angel!" ***16***
But Peter continued knocking, and when they opened, they saw him and
were amazed. ***17*** *But motioning to them with his hand to be silent, he*
described to them how the Lord had brought him out of the prison. And
he said, "Tell these things to James and to the brothers." Then he departed
and went to another place.

18 *Now when day came, there was no little disturbance among the*
soldiers over what had become of Peter. ***19*** *And after Herod searched for*
him and did not find him, he examined the sentries and ordered that they
should be put to death.

Why is this story necessary to the book of Acts? It seems irrelevant to the
movement toward the Gentile mission which begins in 13:1. We may suggest
a few answers. First, Luke's purpose is to demonstrate the truth of the gospel
by the power of God in protecting the infant church. Peter can do nothing to
escape; he is completely helpless. Second, it is a great story. It was not written,
much less invented, by Luke merely to entertain; nevertheless, it has its exciting
and amusing aspects. Third, Luke's plan for the book is to wrap up the story of
Peter and proceed to the story of Paul in chapters 13-28. Except for the brief but
important appearance of Peter in Acts 15, the story of Peter is finished.

About that time is vague. Luke is not concerned with precise chronology
such as we insist on for modern historical records. It was about the same time
as the events in Antioch recorded in chapter 11. The reign of King Herod
Agrippa I over all Judea from 41 to 44 AD furnishes a benchmark for dating
events in Acts; we know that he died in 44 AD.[1]

---

1   Dated precisely by Josephus in *Antiquities of the Jews* 19.350 as "the fifty-fourth year of
     his age, and in the seventh year of his reign."

This King Herod (Agrippa I) was the son of Aristobulus. When he was very young, his cruel grandfather, Herod the Great, killed his father. In 7 BC he was sent to Rome with his mother Bernice and raised in the imperial family. He was a boyhood friend of two future emperors, Claudius and Gaius Caligula.[2] From 23 to 36 AD Herod Agrippa I lived in Idumea on a pension from his uncle Herod Antipas. He returned to Rome in 36 but offended Emperor Tiberius, who threw him into prison. The following year Tiberius died and the new emperor, Gaius Caligula, remembering their childhood friendship, freed him from prison and gave him a gold chain the same weight as his iron chain and also gave him the title of king. Claudius later expanded his domain to include all Galilee, Samaria, and Judea, and so he had the same territory as his grandfather Herod the Great and had even more authority than the Roman governor. He was an astute politician; in Rome he enjoyed the favor of the emperors, and in Judea he was much loved by the Jews in general and by the Pharisees in particular.

It is not clear exactly why Agrippa suddenly killed the Apostle James. The sect of the Nazarenes was now viewed as a threat to stability and the favor of the Jewish people had disappeared since the persecution after Stephen's death.

It is a fruitful meditation on the providence of God as to why James, one of the inner circle of Jesus' disciples, was killed but Peter was miraculously rescued, and John seems to have died of old age in Ephesus. The martyrdom of James fulfilled his Lord's prediction in Mark 10:38-39. Why does one die of cancer and another is miraculously cured in answer to prayer? There is no answer on this side of the grave, and we must simply leave these things to the wise and good providence of God.

When Agrippa saw that the Jews[3] were pleased by the beheading of James, he arrested another prominent leader of the pestiferous sect, Peter. Agrippa would do anything to please his people, even if that required the

---

2   The fascinating television series by BBC "I Claudius" based on the book of the same title by Robert Graves vividly portrays the lives of the emperors Augustus, Tiberius, Gaius Caligula, and Claudius. Herod Agrippa's life was intimately intertwined with the last three emperors. According to Josephus, it was Agrippa who advised a reluctant Claudius to accept the position of emperor at the assassination of Caligula (*Ant.* 19.236-244).

3   "The Jews" since Acts 9:23 (see also 10:39) are now the enemy of the church and will continue as enemies and persecutors through the rest of the book of Acts.

death of another innocent man. Providentially for Peter, this incident occurred during the eight-day period from Nisan 14-21, which was the Passover or the Feast of Unleavened Bread. No trials or executions could be held during Passover. The Jews zealously cleansed their houses of every crumb of yeasted bread but failed to cleanse their hearts of murderous thoughts against the Nazarenes.

We know the end of the story and feel no alarm, but this was a major crisis for the infant church. If all the leadership had been snuffed out, the movement might have died.

Agrippa must have been aware of Peter's previous miraculous release from jail (chapter 5). Perhaps he was emboldened to challenge God because God did nothing to protect James. But he takes no chances; he puts Peter in maximum security, probably in the Fortress of Antonia on the north side of the temple courtyard. Peter was locked in a cell and chained to two soldiers while two more stood guard outside the cell. There were two other guard posts and a large gate of iron bars. Escape or rescue was absolutely impossible. Impossible, that is, except to God.

And except for the earnest prayers of his people. Notice the powerful **but** in verse 5 that completely changes the situation. The Christians may have been praying for days, and now they are praying especially hard the night before Peter's trial, probably in an all-night vigil. It was the kind of prayer that makes *iron gates yield* (Psa 107:16; Isa 45:2). We pray in crisis, but do we pray this urgently even then?

Peter must have spent a miserable Passover holiday. Why didn't God answer the prayers of his people and rescue him sooner? The astonishing thing is that Peter is sleeping and does not seem to be worried about his fate the next day. He is not praying earnestly for release or confessing his sins and steeling his mind for martyrdom. Maybe he was exhausted from previous sleepless nights but now he is sleeping like a log and having a strange dream!

In chapter 10 Peter was hungry and had a vision. Now he is sound asleep and thinks he is dreaming. Peter comes across in Scripture as a man of healthy appetites, not a delicate saint but a hearty, hard-working, plainspoken, earthy man.

In his dream, he feels a strong blow on his side and a loud voice sternly commands "Get up! Quick"! One of the guards must be taking him out. Angels often appeared in Scripture as ordinary men. Peter did not see an "angelic" figure in gleaming white and large wings. Note that the angel does for Peter what he cannot do; break his chains, but he does **not** do for him what he can do; get dressed. A strange light is shining. "Get dressed! Put on your sandals! Put on your cloak and follow me"! Why is he no longer chained? Why are the two guards he was chained to sound asleep and why do the guards outside the cell door not hear all this noise yet seem to look right through them?

The strange dream continues. The sentries at the two guard posts seem to see and hear nothing. Then they come to the iron bars of the main gate. The gates swing open automatically[4] as if Peter is exiting a modern supermarket. They walk together one block out to a main street and suddenly Peter's escort is gone! Peter *came to himself* in the night chill and realizes that this is not a dream! Just as in chapter 10, it takes Peter a while to put it all together and to realize that an angel of God has rescued him from Herod and the Jews.

We must comment here on Luke's use of subtle humor. While the Christians are praying earnestly Peter is sleeping soundly. He is not raptured from prison; he must be told to get dressed and led like a little child. He thinks it is a dream but it is real. We will see other places in Acts where subtle ironies and touches of humor enliven the account.

Peter went to the home of Mary the mother of John Mark. Apparently she was the head of the house, maybe widowed, and wealthy enough to have a large house with servants. Lights are on for the Christians are gathered, praying earnestly. Peter knocks for admission. But now he has a harder time getting into the house of his friends than he did in getting out of the prison of his enemies! A servant girl (the word *paidiskē* usually connotes a "slave girl") named Rhoda ("Rose") comes to the door and recognizes Peter's voice but in her joy and excitement forgets to open the door! How often this humorous incident must have been told and retold among the Christians, including the poor girl's name! Peter keeps on knocking patiently, or impatiently, looking over his shoulder for Herod's police, and fearful of waking the neighborhood.

Every commentator mentions another irony; the saints do not realize that the answer to their prayers is pounding on the door trying to get in. *It is his angel.* Jews in those days believed that every person had a guardian angel (Matt 18:10) who could appear as that person's "double." Finally Peter, his knuckles sore, is admitted and tells the story to the amazed and delighted

---

4   The Greek word for 'by itself' is *automatos* from which we get the word "automatic."

prayer meeting. He tells them to report these things to James. This James is the brother of Jesus and the head of the church in Jerusalem.

Peter does not presume upon the grace of God to rescue him again; he quietly leaves town *to another place*. It is as if Luke does not want to reveal the secret of Peter's location. It is very unlikely that he went to Rome this early. Sometime later he went to Antioch where he incurred the rebuke of Paul (Gal 2:11f). Except for his important contribution to the Jerusalem Council (15:7-11). Peter now disappears from the story of Acts.

Herod was not amused. He assumes that the guards have betrayed their trust and, as Roman law demanded, had them put to death. Now God has a score to settle with Herod Agrippa I.

~ⅇⅇ~

Acts 12:19b-25

God's Vengeance on Herod

19 Then he went down from Judea to Caesarea and spent time there. 20 Now Herod was angry with the people of Tyre and Sidon, and they came to him with one accord, and having persuaded Blastus, the king's chamberlain, they asked for peace, because their country depended on the king's country for food. 21 On an appointed day Herod put on his royal robes, took his seat upon the throne, and delivered an oration to them. 22 And the people were shouting, "The voice of a god, and not of a man!" 23 Immediately an angel of the Lord struck him down, because he did not give God the glory, and he was eaten by worms and breathed his last.

24 But the word of God increased and multiplied. 25 And Barnabas and Saul returned from Jerusalem when they had completed their service, bringing with them John, whose other name was Mark.

Caesarea was the principle Roman city in the land. While Herod was there some representatives from the two Phoenician coastal cities of Tyre and Sidon made an appeal to the king. They were trying to patch up a quarrel and appease the wrath of Herod because they were dependent on the country of Judah for their grain supply. They secured the help of Blastus, the king's personal aide, maybe through a bribe, to gain an audience with Herod.

On the appointed day, Herod, vain as a peacock, appeared before them. Josephus independently describes this event (*Ant.* 19:344 ff):

> On the second day (of a festival in honor of Caesar) he put on a garment made wholly of silver, and of a contexture truly wonderful, and came into the theatre early in the morning; at which time the silver of his garment being illuminated by the fresh reflection of the sun's rays upon it, shone out after a surprising manner, and was so resplendent as to spread a horror over those that looked intently upon him. Presently his flatterers cried out, one from one place, one from another . . . that he was a god; and they added 'Be thou merciful to us; for although we have hitherto reverenced thee only as a man, yet henceforth own thee as superior to mortal man. Upon this the king did neither rebuke them no reject their impious flattery. But as he presently afterwards looked up, he saw an owl sitting on a certain rope over his head, and immediately understood that this bird was a messenger of ill tidings . . . and fell into the deepest sorrow. A severe pain also arose in his belly, and began in a most violent manner. . . His pain became violent and he was carried away to his palace . . . And when he had been quite worn out by the pain in his belly for five days, he departed this life, being in the fifty-fourth year of his life, and in the seventh year of his reign.[5]

The ruins of the seaside theater where this incident occurred are in fairly good condition, and one can sit there and easily picture the scene with the audience facing the sea to the west and the rising sun behind them falling on Herod's silver robe. It is remarkable to have such a detailed confirmation of Acts from secular history.

Luke says that the severe stomach pain was caused by *worms*. There is an intestinal parasite *Ascaris lumbricoides*, 26-36 centimeters long. Sometimes they form a ball and obstruct the small intestine. The pain is excruciating, and the patient sometimes vomits up worms or parts of worms. The stench is so

---

5   *The Works of Josephus*, translated by William Whiston, updated edition published in 1987 by Hendrickson Publishers, p. 523-24.

bad that no doctor or relative can stand to be near. Herod challenged God and lost his life in a most horrible death.

> **24** *But the word of God continued to increase and spread. When Barnabas and Saul had finished their mission, they returned from Jerusalem, taking with them John also called Mark.*

Verse 24 is one of Luke's "summary verses" that mark major divisions in the book (see also 6:7, 9:31, 16:5, and 19:20). Despite severe opposition *the word of God,* that is, the gospel of the Risen Christ, continues to grow numerically and spread geographically. Verse 25 resumes the story of the famine relief mission of Barnabas and Saul, left off at 11:30. They might have been in Jerusalem during the crisis over James and Peter. They will be the chief actors in the drama of Panel 4, the first mission to the Gentile world.

Lessons for Life

1. God sometimes allows his servants to die or be killed as martyrs.
2. God protected Peter in a special way. We are immortal until our work is done.
3. Fervent prayer is a mighty force in times of crisis.
4. *Vengeance is mine. I will repay, says the Lord* (Rom 12:19; Deut 32:35). Challenging God can be dangerous to one's health.

ACTS 13

PREACHING IN ANTIOCH OF PISIDIA

Acts 13:1-3

The Commissioning of the Missionaries

1 Now there were in the church at Antioch prophets and teachers, Barnabas, Simeon who was called Niger, Lucius of Cyrene, Manaen a lifelong friend of Herod the tetrarch, and Saul. 2 While they were worshiping the Lord and fasting, the Holy Spirit said, "Set apart for me Barnabas and Saul for the work to which I have called them." 3 Then after fasting and praying they laid their hands on them and sent them off.

We have come to a momentous divide in the book of Acts. The story moves from Peter to Paul, from the mission to Jews and Jewish proselytes and God-fearers to the mission to the Gentile world, from Palestine to major cities on the way to Rome, from "Jerusalem, Judea, and Samaria" to "the uttermost parts of the earth." The church at Antioch was the launching base for the first "overseas" mission.

A close analysis of the Greek text shows that there were "churches" in Antioch. The word *church (ekklēsia)* is singular, but it is preceded by the preposition *kata*. In many other places this construction means "in each _____," and in this case "in each church."[1] Churches in the first century (and

---

1   *Kata* with the accusative is often 'distributive': *kata oikon* "in each house" (Acts 2:46b; 5:42. See also Acts 15:21; 20:23, and Tit 1:5 "in every town."

well into the second) did not have a large meeting place or church buildings; they were divided into "house churches," but the many house meetings in a given city constituted one church.

There were *a great number* of Christians in Antioch (11:21). This explains why they needed so many *prophets and teachers*. As yet there are no "pastors," one man in charge of a single flock. Prophets had a ministry of *edification, exhortation, and comfort* (1 Cor 14:3), as well as conveying fresh revelations from God (1 Cor 14:29-30). Whether the gift of prophecy is still alive in the church today is a matter of controversy. Our own opinion is that once the written prophecy was complete (the New Testament), there was no more need (or at least much less need) for revelation in the churches. Today the ideal sermon is a ministry of "edification, exhortation, and comfort" based on exposition of the official once-for-all revelation (the Bible).

Did each of these five gifted men have both gifts? We cannot tell for certain, but the little untranslatable conjunction *te* might indicate a division into two groups: Barnabas, Simeon, and Lucius the prophets, and Manaen and Saul the teachers.[2]

Barnabas is listed first which probably indicates that he is the senior person in this multiple-staff ministry. Saul is last, showing that he is the most junior partner. Of the other three we know only what is told us here. *Niger* means "black" in Latin, so this Simeon may have been an African. Skin color was not an issue in the church in the first century. Nor was it an insult to call one "Niger." Simeon Niger was not only a member of the church, he was a leader in the church. Some speculate that this is the same Simon who carried Jesus' cross (Matt 27:32 and parallels). Lucius was from Cyrene, the bump on the Mediterranean coast of Africa where Libya is today. Manaen is distinguished as part of the aristocracy; he was a close friend of Herod Antipas since they were together in Rome as children. Antipas, the one Jesus called "that fox," the one who killed John the Baptist, was raised in Rome with his half-brothers Archelaus and Philip; so that means that Manaen was raised in the midst of the vices of the Roman aristocracy. How his destiny diverged from that of his childhood friends would be a fascinating testimony of the grace of God to save and use one from the corrupt upper class.

---

2   Longenecker, 416.

The first foreign mission was the result of a diverse church with a diverse leadership. In the providence of God, Antioch was the ideal church to launch the mission to the diverse peoples of the world.

It was God the Holy Spirit who started the mission.[3] While they (either the five leaders or the whole church) were worshiping and fasting, the Spirit spoke through one of the prophets or several of them that they should reduce their pastoral staff by 40% and send two of them on a mission that the Spirit would later reveal. How many churches today would be willing to part with their senior pastor so easily? How many senior pastors would be willing to leave their prestigious positions and comfortable homes and go overseas for an undefined job?

The call is vague. It is not to a specific people or country or region, but first to God Himself, just as Abram was not told where God was sending him. The missionary call is not first to such and such a country, but first a call to leave one's work and residence for the leading of the Spirit. Barnabas and Saul were not called to Galatia, but to *the work* the Spirit would later reveal to them.

Verse 3 is the obedient response of the church. Again *they* is ambiguous but no doubt means the whole church, not just the three leaders. Fasting is not an end in itself but a means to spend more time in prayer. Today, our churches send out missionaries with a lot of *feasting* and a little prayer. The Scriptural pattern is that missionaries were first called by God to a special work and then sent out (the word is literally "released") **by the church**. "Sent out" implies financial support and accountability to the church. Today we have an intermediate body called a mission agency, which has sometimes lost sight of the fact that the local church must send out the missionary and be vitally involved in the whole process. On the other hand, we have local churches that do not completely "release" their missionaries but insist on controlling every detail of their ministry.

---

3   Notice here the personality and divinity and authority of the Holy Spirit. He is not just an impersonal force or influence as anti-trinitarian sects would have us believe.

Acts 13:4-12

A Preaching Tour in Cyprus

4 So, being sent out by the Holy Spirit, they went down to Seleucia, and from there they sailed to Cyprus. 5 When they arrived at Salamis, they proclaimed the word of God in the synagogues of the Jews. And they had John to assist them. 6 When they had gone through the whole island as far as Paphos, they came upon a certain magician, a Jewish false prophet named Bar-Jesus. 7 He was with the proconsul, Sergius Paulus, a man of intelligence, who summoned Barnabas and Saul and sought to hear the word of God.

8 But Elymas the magician (for that is the meaning of his name) opposed them, seeking to turn the proconsul away from the faith. 9 But Saul, who was also called Paul, filled with the Holy Spirit, looked intently at him 10 and said, "You son of the devil, you enemy of all righteousness, full of all deceit and villainy, will you not stop making crooked the straight paths of the Lord? 11 And now, behold, the hand of the Lord is upon you, and you will be blind and unable to see the sun for a time." Immediately mist and darkness fell upon him, and he went about seeking people to lead him by the hand. 12 Then the proconsul believed, when he saw what had occurred, for he was astonished at the teaching of the Lord.

Seleucia Pieria was the port for Antioch, sixteen miles distant. Little is left today except a few stones on the shoreline, all that remains of ancient quays. An impressive mountain, Samandag in Turkish, dominates the coast to the south. Turning to the southwest, one can see the distant mountainous tip of Cyprus on a clear day, 60 miles (100 km) distant.

Cyprus (Greek *cypros* "copper") had been exploited since prehistoric times in turn by Minoans, Hittites, Assyrians, Egyptians, Phoenicians, and Greeks for its riches in copper, silver, iron, and precious stones, but most of all for its extensive cypress forests. The Romans had taken over and Cyprus became a Roman province in 58 BC.

Why the two missionaries went there first is not stated except that they were under the guidance of the Holy Spirit (v. 4). Ship traffic between Salamis (near present day Famagusta), the port nestled in a hollow on the south side of the coast, and Seleucia must have been frequent. Barnabas was a native of Cyprus and there were many Jews and Jewish synagogues there. Some of the refugees from the persecution that broke out at the time of Stephen's martyrdom had gone to Cyprus and had spoken the word to Jews (11:19). Barnabas and Saul seem to have been directed to their own kin and Christian contacts as a bridge to other peoples.

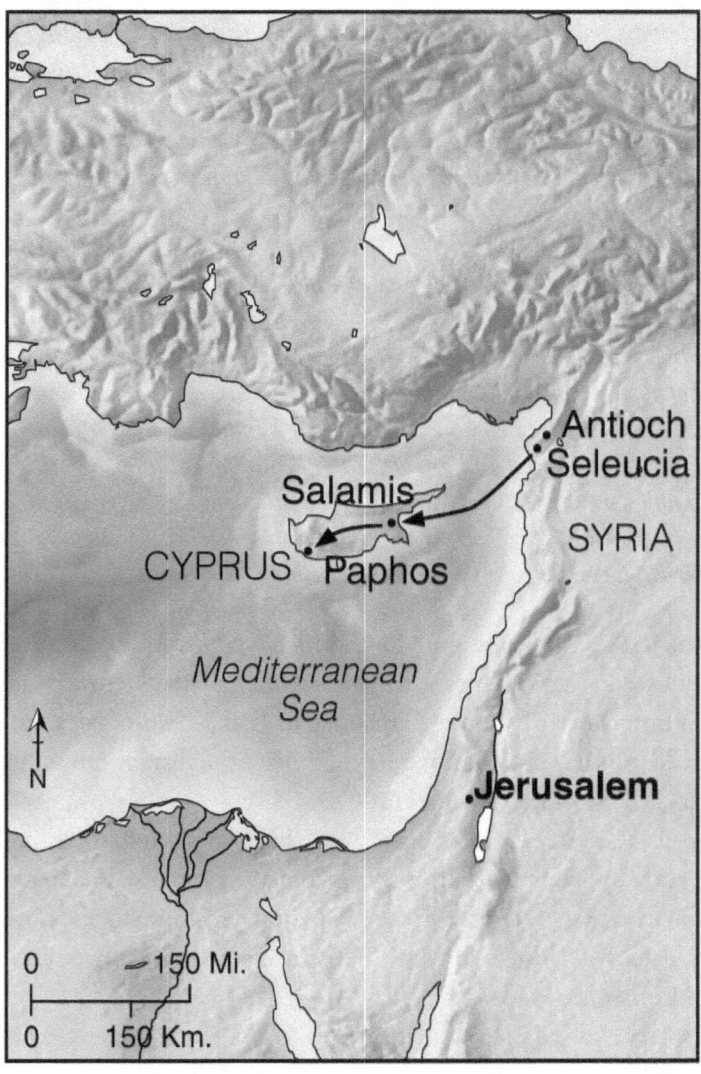

Ministry in Cyprus

Barnabas and Saul toured the synagogues of Salamis preaching the *word of God* (message about Jesus as the Messiah) without any reaction pro or con that Luke records. Perhaps it was this apathy that was the reason no churches are recorded as resulting from this itinerant preaching.

Almost as an afterthought, Luke adds that they had John Mark as their assistant. Whether he assisted only in menial matters like cooking and cleaning, or also in preaching, is not clear. Did Mark have a similar sense of calling or was he simply asked to help out?

The three traveled through the island, perhaps preaching in several towns of the interior or the south coast as they went until they came to Paphos, a harbor on the southwest bend of the island. This was really "New Paphos," a Roman city built by Augustus ten miles north of the original Paphos. It was the Roman capital of the province of Cyprus and had the usual temples, amphitheater, and baths.[4]

Their first evangelistic encounter was with a false prophet and sorcerer (*magos*) whose name was "Bar Jesus" ("son of Jesus") in Aramaic and Elymas in Greek. He seems to have been the personal fortuneteller of the proconsul Sergius Paulus. Here the missionaries are confronted by a direct challenge from an agent of Satan, just as Philip and Peter encountered false believer Simon Magus (8:9-24). This is the second of three encounters with apostate Jews who have occult powers (see also the seven sons of Sceva in Acts 19:13-16). This is what missiologists today call a "power encounter." The contest is for the faith of the highest official in the land, the Roman governor Sergius Paulus.[5] Demonic influence, scoffed at or unknown in most western sending countries, is a harsh reality in many countries today. In Luke's mind this is the most important incident of the tour of Cyprus.

Suddenly, filled with the Spirit, Saul glares at Elymas, denounces him as *You son of the devil, you enemy of all righteousness, full of all deceit and villainy,*

---

4   Schnabel, 557.

5   Two inscriptions with the names "Quintus Sergius Paullus" and a proconsul named "Paullus" have been found in Cyprus (Bruce, 297). Notice that Luke uses the correct title for the governor, *proconsul* (*anthupatos* in Greek), not "prefect" (*hēgemōn* in Greek). Administration of all Roman provinces was divided between the Senate and the Emperor. Generally the Emperor controlled the more rebellious provinces and the Senate the more stable. The governor for the former was called *proconsul*; the governor of the latter was called *praetor* or *procurator*. Pontius Pilate was the latter.

and pronounces God's curse upon him, temporary blindness. Just as he had once blinded Saul of Tarsus, God now blinds Elymas. It was a curse, but really a blessing to rebuke his error and lead him to repentance (Rom 2:4). The Spirit-filled boldness of Paul is amazing. Are we too timid today to confront unbelief and especially direct attacks of Satan? Today many missionaries say we must "preach a positive message," implying that there is never a place for criticism of opposing belief systems. Paul had apparently not heard of this taboo. Sometimes the most negative message gives the most positive results.

When the proconsul saw this miracle, he believed. It does not say "he was amazed at the power of Paul," but *he was astonished at the **teaching** of the Lord*. The miracle alone was not enough to bring conversion; its purpose was to corroborate the teaching of the gospel.

Commentators debate whether Sergius had a genuine conversion. Since baptism is not mentioned, some think this was merely the first step toward conversion. We think that the word "believe" would not have been used unless it were a true conversion. If so, the first convert on the first missionary tour was a very big fish indeed! Repeatedly Luke will tell how the Roman authorities were greatly impressed with Christ.

✐❧

Acts 13:13-15

The Opportunity in Antioch of Pisidia

13 Now Paul and his companions set sail from Paphos and came to Perga in Pamphylia. And John left them and returned to Jerusalem, 14 but they went on from Perga and came to Antioch in Pisidia. And on the Sabbath day they went into the synagogue and sat down. 15 After the reading from the Law and the Prophets, the rulers of the synagogue sent a message to them, saying, "Brothers, if you have any word of encouragement for the people, say it."

With the denunciation of Elymas, Saul has become Paul[6] and it is no longer "Barnabas and Paul" but "Paul and Barnabas." That Barnabas was now willing to play second fiddle is a testimony of his graciousness and humility.

John left them and returned to Jerusalem. There has been much speculation on the reason for John Mark's abrupt decision to quit the mission and go home. He may have lacked a clear sense of calling to the mission. Paul did not think highly of his departure; in 15:38 he calls it "desertion" (NRSV).[7] Mark's defection was the bone of contention that caused a split between Paul and Barnabas, who went their separate ways. By the grace of God, Mark was restored as a faithful co-worker of Paul (Col 4:10; 2 Tim 4:11) and was the writer of the gospel that bears his name.

Just exactly how they decided where to go is unknown. Why did they not stay on the coast and evangelize Perga and other important towns on the coast? Perga was the largest and most important city in western Pamphylia. Today there is an extensive area of fairly well-preserved ruins, including a stadium that held 13,000.

The theory of Witherington that Sergius Paulus had suggested that the evangelists visit his family in Antioch is very attractive.[8] On the other hand, the more traditional explanation that Paul went to Antioch of Pisidia because of an illness cannot be ignored. Galatians 4:14 says that *Even though my illness was a trial to you, you did not treat me with contempt or scorn. Instead, you welcomed me as if I were an angel of God, as if I were Christ Jesus himself* (NIV). William Ramsey made a strong case that Paul had malaria and that they went into the cooler Anatolian highlands to find relief.[9] A different case for their decision can be made geographically. The four churches addressed in the letter to the Galatians were all situated on the main east-west Roman road, the Via Sebastia. Churches planted in cities along the main highway would have great strategic influence.

---

6   His Hebrew name was Saul, but as a Roman citizen at birth he was given the Latin cognomen (third name) Paul at birth which means "Little One," probably a term of affection.

7   The Greek verb here, *aphistēmi,* can simply mean "leave," but often it connotes the more negative, "desert, commit apostasy."

8   The family of Sergius Paulus "land, power, and influence" in that city (Witherington, 403-404, citing R. L. Fox).

9   Ramsey, 91-92.

The journey from Perga to Antioch required a 130 mile (215 km) rough uphill climb through the rugged Taurus Range (altitude gain of 3,600 feet or 1,080 meters), a five or six day hike. The most direct route would have been to follow the gorge of the Cestris River, but there was no well-designed Roman road and no bridges, so the two missionaries would have had to ford an icy stream any number of times. Perhaps this is one place where Paul met *danger from rivers . . . danger from bandits* (2 Cor 11:26).

As the two lone missionaries toiled upslope day after day among towering mountains and immense lonely forests, one wonders if they were tempted to be discouraged at the immensity of the task and their own feebleness. Their Lord had said *Go into all the world and preach the gospel to the whole creation.* They did not know how vast that world was.

Pisidian Antioch (one of sixteen cities named "Antioch") was a Roman colony that served as the administrative center of the western portion of the Province of Galatia. It was located in a border region between the provinces of Asia and Galatia and the ethnic regions of Phrygia and Pisidia. The mix of ethnic groups on a main road in a borderland area made it a good choice strategically.

Luke passes over these details in silence. The important thing for him is that they received a warm welcome in the Jewish synagogue in Antioch. Paul's lifelong motto was *to the Jew first* (Rom 1:16) and this chapter introduces us to the pattern he followed in almost every place. He always went to the synagogue first. It was his desire that his countrymen believe in Jesus (Rom 9:1-3). The Jews as the heirs of the Word of God and the promise of Messiah must be told first. But apart from that personal burden, the most receptive Gentiles were the God-fearers in the Jewish synagogues.

Roman road with an arch on the Via Egnatia in Anatolia (now Turkey).
The Romans had built an empire-wide system of roads that in the
providence of God became "roads that carried the gospel."

Acts 13:16-41

The Pattern Synagogue Sermon

16 So Paul stood up, and motioning with his hand said:
"Men of Israel and you who fear God, listen. 17 The God of this people
Israel chose our fathers and made the people great during their stay in the
land of Egypt, and with uplifted arm he led them out of it. 18 And for
about forty years he put up with them in the wilderness. 19 And after
destroying seven nations in the land of Canaan, he gave them their land as
an inheritance. 20 All this took about 450 years. And after that he gave
them judges until Samuel the prophet. 21 Then they asked for a king, and

*God gave them Saul the son of Kish, a man of the tribe of Benjamin, for forty years. **22** And when he had removed him, he raised up David to be their king, of whom he testified and said, 'I have found in David the son of Jesse a man after my heart, who will do all my will.*

Paul unhesitatingly seizes the opportunity. Little did the rulers of the synagogue know what they were in for! He has a mixed audience of *men* (and no doubt women who were sitting in a separate section) *of Israel and you who fear God,* the technical term for Gentile inquirers who were attracted to the one true God of Israel.

He starts on common ground, first by mentioning *the God of our fathers* and then reciting some of their history. Before giving them startling new information, he must first establish rapport with his audience by reminding them of their common heritage. They did not complain, "We've heard that hundreds of times;" they were reassured by the recitation of their ancient history (recall our comments on Stephen's speech in Acts 7).

We wonder if missionaries today would do better by referring more often to the history of the people in their audience. Even in private conversation, the soul winner is wise to ask about a person's background first. No one tires of telling his own story.

The record we have is very likely not the text of the sermon but the sermon notes or outline of a message that must have taken much more time to deliver. Paul finishes a brief history of Israel focusing on obedient King David, the man after God's own heart. By contrast, there were those among their ancestors who were disobedient: those whom God *put up with*[10] forty years in the desert. God also put up with their demand for a king and gave them Saul, who was removed by God for disobedience. This is an appeal that his hearers must not follow the disobedient King Saul but the obedient King David.

---

10   There is a difficult textual problem in verse 18. The evidence is almost equally divided between *etropoforēsen* (he endured) and *etrofoforēsen* (he fed or nourished). The first verb is an allusion to Deut 1:31 where the Hebrew verb *nasah* has the same ambiguity; like the old English word "bear" it can mean either to "carry" or to "endure."

13:23-31 God has Brought to Israel Your Promised Savior, Jesus

23 Of this man's offspring God has brought to Israel a Savior, Jesus, as he promised. 24 Before his coming, John had proclaimed a baptism of repentance to all the people of Israel. 25 And as John was finishing his course, he said, 'What do you suppose that I am? I am not he. No, but behold, after me one is coming, the sandals of whose feet I am not worthy to untie.'

26 "Brothers, sons of the family of Abraham, and those among you who fear God, to us has been sent the message of this salvation. 27 For those who live in Jerusalem and their rulers, because they did not recognize him nor understand the utterances of the prophets, which are read every Sabbath, fulfilled them by condemning him. 28 And though they found in him no guilt worthy of death, they asked Pilate to have him executed. 29 And when they had carried out all that was written of him, they took him down from the tree and laid him in a tomb. 30 But God raised him from the dead, 31 and for many days he appeared to those who had come up with him from Galilee to Jerusalem, who are now his witnesses to the people.

God had promised some thousand years before to bring a Savior, the Messiah, to Israel from the descendants of David (2 Sam 7:12,13; Rom 1:3). The words *has brought to Israel a Savior, Jesus* in verse 23 must have startled the gathering. The mention of Messiah's forerunner, John the Baptist, may not seem so important to us, but the Jews knew of the prophecy that "my messenger" (Elijah) must come before the coming of Messiah (Mal 3:1 and 4:5). Jesus said that John the Baptist fulfilled this prophecy (Matt 17:11,12). The Baptist was so popular that he still had some disciples even in Asia Minor (Acts 19:1-7) and these Jews in Antioch must have known about him. In fact, considering the way Paul casually, and without explanation, introduces the name "Jesus" in verse 23, these Jews may have already heard of Jesus. Paul uses the teaching principle of establishing the known before proceeding to the unknown.

The repeated address *Brothers, sons of the family of Abraham, and those among you who fear God,* marks an important point: *To **us** has been sent the message of this salvation.* This is not just interesting historical information, this is your **salvation**. Do not make the same mistake as our leaders in Jerusalem, who fulfilled the prophecies of Messiah that they heard every week by asking Pilate to execute him. (Paul may have expanded at this point by quoting prophetic passages about Messiah from memory.) The terrible irony was that they heard these prophetic passages every Sabbath but fulfilled them by crucifying their Messiah.

They (*They* suddenly refers to a different group, the disciples of Jesus) *laid him a tomb **but God*** (compare 2:24; 3:15) *raised him from the dead!* If you doubt, then we have the testimony of those who saw him after his resurrection.

13:32-37 Scriptural Proof of the Resurrection

> ***32*** *And we bring you the good news that what God promised to the fathers,*
> ***33*** *this he has fulfilled to us their children by raising Jesus, as also it is written in the second Psalm,*
> > *"'You are my Son,*
> > *today I have begotten you.'*
> ***34*** *And as for the fact that he raised him from the dead, no more to return to corruption, he has spoken in this way,*
> > *"'I will give you the holy and sure blessings of David.'*
> ***35*** *Therefore he says also in another psalm,*
> > *"'You will not let your Holy One see corruption.'*
> ***36*** *For David, after he had served the purpose of God in his own generation, fell asleep and was laid with his fathers and saw corruption,* ***37*** *but he whom God raised up did not see corruption.*

Proof of the resurrection, the incredible claim, was not just a matter of living witnesses, as important as they were. The proof must be rooted in prophecy and now Paul puts together, in typical Jewish sermon style, a chain of three prophecies of Messiah's resurrection: Psalm 2:7, Isa 55:3, and Psalm 16:10. Psalm 16 had been used by Peter (Acts 2:25-31) to verify the resurrection of Messiah. Just as Peter had done, Paul shows that Psa 16:10 could not refer to David and therefore must refer to David's seed, the Messiah.

None of these verses mention the resurrection of Messiah directly, but take their fullest interpretation and ultimate referent from the undeniable physical evidence of Jesus' resurrection. Prophecy is fully understood only after its fulfillment.

Psa 2:7 *Today I have begotten you,* is interpreted here to mean not conception and birth, but a raising to new life. The psalm was originally used for the coronation of Israel's kings, the "begetting" referred, even in the original use of Psalm 2, not to birth but to exaltation to the throne. The extra-biblical book Psalms of Solomon (first century BC) alludes to this psalm as a reference to Messiah.[11]

The second reference, Isa 55:3, may seem obscure to us but Paul was using a Jewish sermonic technique called *gezerah shawah,* wherein the identical words in two passages (or more) were used to link the passages hermeneutically. The word that occurs in both Isa 55:3 and Psa 16:10 is *hosios,* in the former verse plural and translated *the holy* (blessings); and in Psa 16:10 is singular, holy one. Paul interpreted these two passages to mean that one of the holy blessings promised to David would be the resurrection of his descendant, the Messiah.

13:38-41 Application and Warning

> **38** Let it be known to you therefore, brothers, that through this man forgiveness of sins is proclaimed to you, **39** and by him everyone who believes is freed from everything from which you could not be freed by the law of Moses. **40** Beware, therefore, lest what is said in the Prophets should come about:
>
> **41** "'Look, you scoffers,
> be astounded and perish;
> for I am doing a work in your days,
> a work that you will not believe, even if one tells it to you.'"

Verse 38 is the climax of the sermon. It is underlined by the use of the word *Brothers* and *I want you to know* (this is the point). *Through this man (Jesus)* **forgiveness of sins** *is proclaimed to you,* Paul says nothing about the connection between the death of Jesus and forgiveness, what we call the

---

11   "See Lord, and raise up for them your king, the son of David, to rule over your servant Israel . . . to smash the arrogance of sinners like a potter's jar; to shatter all their substance with an iron rod." Psalm of Solomon 17:21 and 23. In verse 32 the author refers to "their king" as "the Lord Messiah" (*Christos kurios*).

doctrine of the atonement. That will come later in his extended doctrinal teaching as in the book of Romans. But the doctrine of justification, the heart of Romans, is clearly set forth here. The key word **"justified"** (*dikaioō*) is used twice in verses 38 and 39.[12] The Law of Moses could condemn, but it could not justify; but all who (simply) believe (in Jesus the Christ) *are being justified*.[13] Skeptics claim that the book of Acts is a work of fiction and that Luke "composed" this speech and put it in the mouth of the Apostle Paul. But the word "justify" is a genuine fingerprint of the Apostle Paul.

The one and only condition of receiving forgiveness and justification, is, precisely as in Paul's epistles, to **believe**, that is to put one's full confidence in Christ alone for salvation.[14] We cannot add to this one requirement any other requirement. Salvation is the free gift of God received by faith alone; and we cannot even pay the tip.

Just as Peter did (3:23), Paul ends his speech with a stiff warning. Paul quotes Hab 1:6. This may seem a bit harsh and provocative, since there is as yet no active opposition, but Paul has already experienced the unbelief and hostility of many of his countrymen. In fact many of them had tried to kill him. We must remember that among Jews, even today, sharp and vigorous debate is a cultural norm. This is quite different from many face-saving cultures. Nevertheless, we must be careful that our cultural sensitivity does not mask cowardice and "the fear of man." We need to recover something of the boldness of the apostles.

cee

---

12   Unfortunately, the ESV obscures the word "justified" by translating it "freed" and puts the translation "justified" in a footnote. The KJV and the NIV correctly translate the verb *dikaiountai* as "justify." The verb *dikaioō* does not mean "make righteous," but "pronounce" or "declare righteous."

13   The tense of the Greek verb is present, indicating continuous action.

14   Repentance is not mentioned here, though it is mentioned eleven times in Acts. It is not a separate requirement for salvation but the other side of the coin of faith.

Acts: 13:42-52

The Results of the Sermon

42 As they went out, the people begged that these things might be told them the next Sabbath. 43 And after the meeting of the synagogue broke up, many Jews and devout converts to Judaism followed Paul and Barnabas, who, as they spoke with them, urged them to continue in the grace of God.

44 The next Sabbath almost the whole city gathered to hear the word of the Lord. 45 But when the Jews saw the crowds, they were filled with jealousy and began to contradict what was spoken by Paul, reviling him. 46 And Paul and Barnabas spoke out boldly, saying, "It was necessary that the word of God be spoken first to you. Since you thrust it aside and judge yourselves unworthy of eternal life, behold, we are turning to the Gentiles. 47 For so the Lord has commanded us, saying,

"'I have made you a light for the Gentiles,
that you may bring salvation to the ends of the earth.'"

48 And when the Gentiles heard this, they began rejoicing and glorifying the word of the Lord, and as many as were appointed to eternal life believed. 49 And the word of the Lord was spreading throughout the whole region. 50 But the Jews incited the devout women of high standing and the leading men of the city, stirred up persecution against Paul and Barnabas, and drove them out of their district. 51 But they shook off the dust from their feet against them and went to Iconium. 52 And the disciples were filled with joy and with the Holy Spirit.

The initial reaction to the message was overwhelmingly positive. Verse 42 says *As they went out, the people begged that these things might be told them the next Sabbath.* Not only that, but many of the Jews and proselytes followed the two missionaries. There must have been many private conversations that week, and many must have believed in Jesus, because of the next words *they were urging them to continue in the grace of God.* They had received the grace of God in salvation; now they must continue in that same grace to live the life of faith.

These new believers must have "gossiped the gospel" among their friends and acquaintances, because the next Sabbath there was standing room only and people crowded around the synagogue windows trying to hear. If *almost the whole city* is to be taken literally, and not just hyperbole, a very large crowd would not have fit in the synagogue. Maybe they met in the theater or some other place.[15] Instead of rejoicing at the large crowd, *the Jews*, that is the unbelieving Jews, *were filled with jealousy* and *began to contradict* Paul by reviling him. Paul had evidently started to speak but was rudely interrupted. If they had reasonable objections, these are not recorded. Instead, they are moved by jealousy. The synagogue leaders were not satisfied with the many proselytes they had won; when Paul attracts more, they are jealous. How typical this is of clergymen even today. The chief sin of clergymen is jealousy. And how many scholars, who pride themselves on cool objectivity, are really moved more than they realize by emotion and prejudice?

This provoked the bold (that word *parrēsia* again!) biting response of Paul and Barnabas: "It was our duty to testify to the Jews first (Rom 1:16) but since you reject it, we turn to the Gentiles." At this point they no doubt intended to start a separate meeting for believing Jews and Gentiles. The phrase *Since you thrust it aside and judge yourselves unworthy of eternal life* deserves reflection. The words *judge yourselves unworthy* would ordinarily show humility. But here the implication is that the rejecters do not value their own souls. *Whoever fails to find me harms himself; all who hate me love death* (Prov 8:36). It is not that God or Paul condemns them "as unworthy of eternal life," but that they, by their own unbelief, condemn **themselves** as *unworthy of eternal life*. The phrase "eternal life" is not found in the OT but is frequent in the gospels and epistles. It is found only here in Acts (13:46 and 48). The concept of eternal life had come into Jewish thought in the intertestamental period.[16]

One of the two missionaries then quotes Isa 49:6: *I have made you a light for the Gentiles, that you may bring salvation to the ends of the earth.* In Isaiah 49 this wonderful prophecy refers to the Servant of the LORD. In Luke 2:32, Simeon applied these words to the baby Jesus, but here they are applied to his witnesses. This is no contradiction, for the prophecy will be fulfilled through *the Church which is His body*. Jesus said that his people would be his witnesses *to the end of the earth* (1:8). It is still the chief calling and marvelous privilege of the Body of Christ to be a *light to the nations to the ends of the earth*.

---

15   Schnabel, 586.

16   2 Mac 7:9; 4 Mac 15:3.

Paul's sermon delighted the Gentile proselyte members who *rejoiced and glorified* the message of the gospel of Christ by believing it. That is the human side. But the divine side was that they had been **appointed** (by God) to eternal life. This is as strong a statement of predestination as we find in the Bible. We do well not to water down or seek to evade the clear teaching of predestination.

The result of these conversions was that the *word of the Lord,* that is the message about Christ and his salvation, *spread through the whole region.* But the unbelieving Jews, the inevitable opposition, persuaded the town authorities to do what they could not: expel the evangelists. It is interesting that they stirred up *the devout women of high standing* against the apostles. The word *devout* indicates God-fearers in the synagogue who also happened to be wealthy and influential. It may be that their husbands were prominent in the town council. The word *persecution* may imply physical abuse, maybe one of the three times Paul was *beaten with rods* (2 Cor 11:25). Following the instructions of their Lord, the missionaries *shook off the dust from their feet,*[17] whether literally or figuratively, rejecting those who had rejected their message, and committing them to God's righteous judgment. But the disciples (always in Acts "disciples" = "believers in Christ") were filled with the Holy Spirit and His joy, the sign of true conversion.

Paul's sermon at Pisidian Antioch was the model synagogue sermon that he no doubt preached in varying forms whenever he preached to Jews. It is a model piece of expository preaching addressed to those who knew the Scriptures and respected its authority. Paul builds on what his hearers already know by emphasizing God's saving grace in the past and showing the fulfillment of prophecies about the Messiah in Jesus of Nazareth. He shows that the only ground of justification is the death and resurrection of Jesus Christ and makes a clear call for faith in this Christ. It parallels Peter's sermon in chapter 2 and is the Jewish version of the *kerygma* of 1 Cor 15:3-4.

Expository preaching of the Word will empty the church of scoffers but will fill it with believers. We must encourage our pastors to preach with the Bible in one hand and the needs of the people in the other hand, empowered by the Spirit to relate the one to the other.

---

17   As commanded by Jesus in Luke 9:5; 10:11; Matt 10:14.

Lessons for Life

1. Churches that foster a diversity of people in their body may be more open to cross-cultural missions.
2. The Holy Spirit is the mission strategist. We must be willing to commit our "best and brightest" to this great task.
3. The missionary call is first to God the Spirit, not to a country or a place. He will guide to the right location.
4. Missionaries are sent by the Spirit and released by their local church to His guidance.
5. Mission work is inevitably opposed by demonic forces who must be confronted openly in the power of the Spirit.
6. We, like Barnabas, should have the grace and humility to play "second fiddle."
7. In communicating the gospel, first establish common ground. Proceed from the known to the unknown.
8. The resurrection of Jesus must be a major part of our gospel witness.
9. The Law can condemn but cannot justify. Christ forgives and justifies those who believe.
10. Cultural sensitivity must not dominate necessary confrontation.
11. The besetting sin of many Christian workers is jealousy.
12. Joy in the midst of persecution was normal for the early church and should be normal for us today.
13. Preach with the Word with the Bible in one hand and the needs of the people in the other hand.

ACTS 14

PAUL AND BARNABAS IN ICONIUM, LYSTRA, AND DERBE

Acts 14:1-7

Evangelizing Iconium

1 Now at Iconium they entered together into the Jewish synagogue and spoke in such a way that a great number of both Jews and Greeks believed. 2 But the unbelieving Jews stirred up the Gentiles and poisoned their minds against the brothers. 3 So they remained for a long time, speaking boldly for the Lord, who bore witness to the word of his grace, granting signs and wonders to be done by their hands. 4 But the people of the city were divided; some sided with the Jews and some with the apostles. 5 When an attempt was made by both Gentiles and Jews, with their rulers, to mistreat them and to stone them, 6 they learned of it and fled to Lystra and Derbe, cities of Lycaonia, and to the surrounding country, 7 and there they continued to preach the gospel.

Iconium was the next major town, 80 miles (130 km) to the east on the Imperial Road (Via Sebastia), a four-day journey on foot. Politically, it was in the southern part of the Roman province of Galatia, and ethnically in the eastern extremity of Phrygia. Like Antioch it was a Roman colony. The Greek geographer Strabo called it "a well colonized town in a prosperous region."[1] Today there are no ruins to see; they are buried under the fourth largest city in Turkey, Konya.

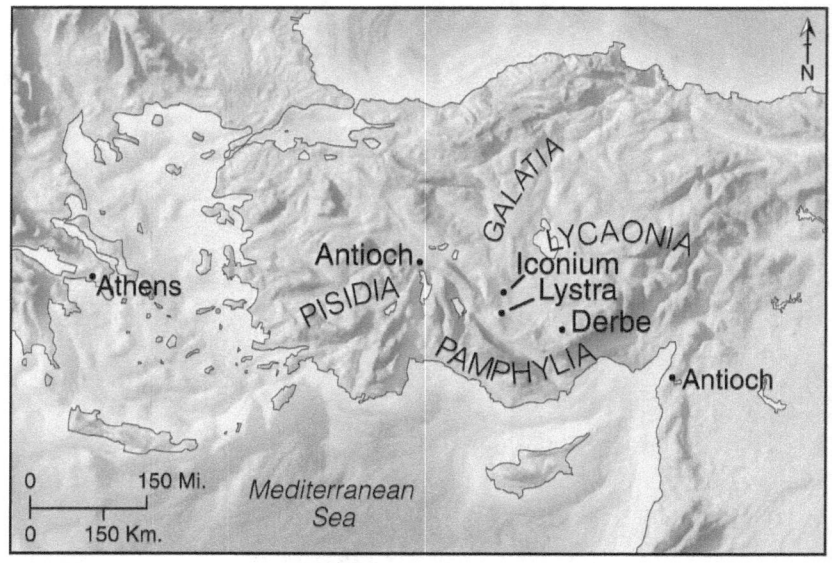

Paul and Barnabas in Galatia

The evangelization of Iconium was a repetition of the pattern in Antioch.[2] Paul and Barnabas went into the synagogue and no doubt gave a very similar message to the one given in Antioch. They spoke so effectively that a great number of Jews and Gentiles believed. It seems that they had an even greater response here than in Antioch. Though only the Spirit can bring one to conversion, He can and does use human zeal, persuasiveness, and effective homiletics. Let no one think **how** he speaks the message does not matter.

And then followed the inevitable opposition of unbelieving (literally disobeying) Jews who poisoned the minds of the Gentiles against the evangelists. Despite this opposition, Paul and Barnabas spent *a long time* there (weeks? months?) speaking boldly (as always!) for the Lord. In this city the Lord confirmed the truth of their message by granting them the ability to do miracles

---

1   Bruce, 316.

2   It makes more sense to translate *kata to auto* "as usual" (GNB, NET, NLT, and NRSV) rather than "together," which seems unnecessary. The phrase is rendered that way in I Mac 8:27. NRSV says, "The same thing happened" (Schnabel, 602).

(*signs and wonders*). These were probably healings and exorcisms of demons. Gal 3:5 implies that some of the Galatians themselves were also able to do miracles.

The message of Christ became known throughout the city and divided the populace into those for and those against the message of Christ. Someone has said that wherever Paul went, he caused either a revival or a riot. We should not be afraid of controversy; what we should fear is apathy.

Paul and Barnabas "hung in there" for as long as they could, but finally, the opposition was able to muster enough clout with the leaders of the city to organize a riot against the evangelists to stone them. When the evangelists heard of this plot, they fled to the region of Lycaonia to the south and east. The persecution only served to spread the good news in other places. When missionaries today are threatened with bodily harm and possible death, it is no disgrace or lack of faith to evacuate. Ministry is impossible under some circumstances.

∽∾

Acts 14:8-20

Stoned in Lystra

14:8-13 Paul and Barnabas Mistaken for Gods

8 Now at Lystra there was a man sitting who could not use his feet. He was crippled from birth and had never walked. 9 He listened to Paul speaking. And Paul, looking intently at him and seeing that he had faith to be made well, 10 said in a loud voice, "Stand upright on your feet." And he sprang up and began walking. 11 And when the crowds saw what Paul had done, they lifted up their voices, saying in Lycaonian, "The gods have come down to us in the likeness of men!" 12 Barnabas they called Zeus, and Paul, Hermes, because he was the chief speaker. 13 And the priest of Zeus, whose temple was at the entrance to the city, brought oxen and garlands to the gates and wanted to offer sacrifice with the crowds.

From the general statement of verse 7 *and there they continued to preach the gospel,* the narrative moves to a particular crisis in the mission at Lystra.

The four cities of Galatia decrease in importance, size, and degree of sophistication from west to east. The Romans planted a colony at Lystra in 25 BC to subdue the wild tribes of the Taurus Mountains on the south. The Imperial Highway (Via Sebastia) was extended 18 miles (29 km) south-southwest to its terminus at Lystra. The native people here were Lycaonians and they spoke their own language. There were also Greeks and Jews (at least Timothy's family lived here: Acts 16:1-3) living in the city. But there is no mention of a synagogue in either Lystra or Derbe. Today Lystra is an unexcavated mound of rubble in the midst of wheat fields near the village of Hatansaray.

For the first time, Paul and Barnabas encounter raw paganism. The incident began with an act of benevolence reminiscent of the healing of a lame man by Peter in Acts 3. Luke deliberately parallels much of the very language of that miracle in describing this one: a man *crippled from birth, looking intently at him,* and *stand up.* The results were the same; the lame man jumped up and began to walk. Luke is deliberately pointing out that Paul was just as powerful an instrument of God as Peter, one of the purposes of the book of Acts.

Notice that here the faith of the sick man was one of the conditions of his healing. We are reminded of the frequent word of the Lord Jesus *your faith has saved you* (Luke 5:20; 7:50; 8:48; 17:19; 18:42).[3] However we must not assume that faith in the afflicted is **always** a condition of healing, as some healers would have us believe.[4]

The reaction of the pagan Lycaonians was to interpret this miracle according to their own worldview. "Only the gods can do miracles like this; therefore these men must be gods. The gods sometimes disguise themselves

---

3   This phrase also occurs in Matt 9:22 and Mark 5:34 and 10:52, but it seems to be a particular favorite of Luke.

4   There is no mention of faith, either in the subject or the friends of the subject, in the cases of the man with the withered hand (Mark 3:1-6), the raising of the son of the widow of Nain (Luke 7:11-17), the blind and dumb man (Matt 12:22), the Gadarene demoniac, (Luke 8:26-39), the blind man at the pool of Siloam (John 9:1-8), the bent woman (Luke 13:10-13), the man with dropsy in the house of the Pharisee (Luke 14:1-5), and the healing of Malchus' ear (Luke 22:51). One of our chief objections to many so-called healers is the cruel accusation they level against those who are **not** healed at their meetings: "You do not have faith enough to be healed."

as humans. The way to honor the gods is by sacrifice." Not just that they are unknown gods, but "this older one is Zeus, and this younger one, the spokesman, must be Hermes" thus compounding error and folly with more error and folly. The priest of Zeus in the temple just outside the gates knew just what to do in such an emergency. He brought their very best, probably two bulls, properly garlanded,[5] to sacrifice to the two "gods."

Part of the Lycaonians' worldview may have been formed by the myth from that region about Zeus and Hermes recorded in Ovid's *Metamorphoses* (*8.620-724*). Zeus and Hermes, disguised as simple travelers, were searching for lodging in that area. They were refused a thousand times but finally one elderly couple, Philemon and Baucis, received them into their very poor house and did their best to make them comfortable. Strangely no matter how much they ate or drank, the supply of meat and wine did not diminish in the pots. The old couple trembled and tried to capture their only goose to feed the strangers, but the goose eluded them. The gods identified themselves and told the old couple they do not need the goose. The gods, Zeus and Hermes, then lead them out to a hilltop to witness the destruction of their stingy neighbors. Then they ask the couple what their reward shall be, and Philemon asks that they may be priests of Zeus and that, when their time comes to die, they may die in the same hour. Their hovel became a magnificent temple and their wishes were granted.[6]

Many a present-day missionary can tell stories, maybe not so dramatic, of how their innocent actions or words were interpreted in startlingly strange ways by the local people. Don Richardson tells one incident when he was attempting to bring the gospel to the Sawi people of New Guinea in his book *Peace Child:*

> On subsequent visits I expanded further on the life and ministry of Jesus, trying to establish His reality and relevance to their lives, but without apparent success ... Only once did my presentation win a ringing response from them. I was describing Judas Iscariot's betrayal of the Son of God. About halfway through the description I noticed they were listening intently . . . At the climax of the story Maum

---

5   One sees this sacrifice scene displayed on many carvings from the Roman world.

6   There are other evidences of a special connection to Zeus and Hermes in two inscriptions from the area (see Bruce, 321-322 for details).

whistled a birdcall of admiration. Kani and several others touched their fingertips to their chests in awe. Still others chuckled. At first I sat there confused. Then the realization broke through. They were acclaiming Judas as the hero of the story![7]

14:14-18 The Impromptu Sermon in Lystra

14 But when the apostles Barnabas and Paul heard of it, they tore their garments and rushed out into the crowd, crying out, 15 "Men, why are you doing these things? We also are men, of like nature with you, and we bring you good news, that you should turn from these vain things to a living God, who made the heaven and the earth and the sea and all that is in them. 16 In past generations he allowed all the nations to walk in their own ways. 17 Yet he did not leave himself without witness, for he did good by giving you rains from heaven and fruitful seasons, satisfying your hearts with food and gladness." 18 Even with these words they scarcely restrained the people from offering sacrifice to them.

The word *apostles* here means "missionaries," the equivalent word in Latin. The scene is comical, but to Barnabas and Paul, to call a human being "god" was blasphemy and they were horrified that they themselves were being deified. Instead of relaxing and enjoying the benefits the superstitious Lycaonians might render to them, like the two British soldiers in Kipling's "The Man who would be King," they tore their clothes and shouted like madmen. It had taken Paul and Barnabas some time to understand what was going on because they could not understand Lycaonian. Any cross-cultural evangelist can testify to the frustration, perils, and sometimes hilarity of ignorance of the local language.

They immediately launched into a witness about the true God-man, but

---

7   Judas was perceived by the Sawi as a clever hero because they honored treachery. Deceiving a man into thinking you were his friend and then killing him was much more admirable to the Sawi than simply killing him outright. The book goes on to tell of how Richardson discovered a cultural analogy to the gospel which spoke to the Sawi powerfully: the custom of bringing peace between warring tribes by the exchange of a baby called "The Peace Child." *Peace Child*. Glendale, California: Regal Books Division Gospel Light Publications, 1974. 203-204.

never got past the introduction. It is not clear whether Paul or Barnabas was speaking; Luke may be giving us the gist of what they both were saying in the confusion.

The missionaries are not afraid to call their piety *vain*. In Greek the word is *mataios*, "useless," "powerless." They appeal, not to the **falsity** of their worship and superstitions about the gods, but to their **uselessness** in helping them. This is an appeal to universal human pragmatism. "Does this god/religion really help you?" One appeal to primitive people, and even highly educated people, should be to ask them if their religion really helps them.

Paul and Barnabas immediately exhort them to turn to the living God (singular, and alive, in contrast to their dead gods, plural) *who made the heaven and the earth and the sea and all that is in them.* They do not quote the Old Testament to these tribesmen, but they summarize Genesis 1 in one phrase. Our problem today is that naturalistic materialistic evolutionistic thinking completely saturates the modern secular worldview. Except for Islam, other indigenous faiths somehow bypass the necessity of a Creator. That is one reason the gospel of Christ has made so little headway among Hindu and Buddhist cultures. We must solve this basic problem or our witness of Christ will be built on sand. We jump too quickly into the New Testament without first giving the basic truths of the Old Testament.

In past generations he allowed all the nations to walk in their own ways. Does this mean that *all the nations* were not accountable to the one true God because of their ignorance of him? No, it simply means that he abandoned them to *their own ways.* According to Romans 1:18-32, mankind originally knew the Creator God but turned away from him to idols, and God's judgment upon them was to let them go their own way. They are *without excuse* (Rom 1:20).

The next appeal is to the relevance of this Creator God to the Lycaonians. He is not only the God of Creation; he is the God who provides you every year with your very life by giving you rain and good harvests. They appeal first to what a simple agricultural people can understand. In theology we call this the "general revelation" of God who causes his sun to shine and his rain to fall even on his enemies and those who do not know him (Matt 5:45).

The evangelists could not get past the A and the B to Christ. The crowd was too fanatic, and too excited, to listen to them. Then the crowd has an amazing and frightening turnabout.

14:19-20 Stoned

19 But Jews came from Antioch and Iconium, and having persuaded the crowds, they stoned Paul and dragged him out of the city, supposing that he was dead. 20 But when the disciples gathered about him, he rose up and entered the city, and on the next day he went on with Barnabas to Derbe.

The zeal of the Jews from Antioch (100 miles, 160 km distant), and Iconium (18 miles, 30 km distant) is astonishing. They are not content with chasing the heretics out of their own towns; they pursue them even to pagan Lystra. Somehow they succeeded in turning the fickle Lycaonian crowd 180 degrees. "It is not likely that Zeus and Hermes would have visited Jewish synagogues in Antioch and Iconium! These guys are trying to pass themselves off as gods!" In rage at the "trickery" of the apostles, and chagrin at their own gullibility, the Lycaonians suddenly turn against them.

It is not clear who did the stoning—the Jews, the Lycaonians, or, most likely, both. Mob frenzy took over and stones started flying. One large stone hit Paul in the head and he collapsed, unconscious. Both of them must have been badly bloodied and bruised. They dragged Paul out of the city and left him for the wolves and the vultures.

But after the mob left, the believers gathered around him and he got up. Some think this was resuscitation from the dead, but that seems unlikely. Luke does not say he was dead; he says they thought he was dead. Some have wondered if this was the time Paul was taken up into the third heaven (2 Cor 12:2-4). This may have been a case of an out-of-the-body experience that many people now report in heart attack resuscitations. Paul may have been without a pulse for a time.

Where did these disciples come from? Although it is not impossible that some believers accompanied the apostles from Antioch and Iconium, Luke would probably have told us about that. These disciples must have been converts from the evangelizing Paul and Barnabas did in Lystra before this incident (verse 7).

The believers must have taken them back into their homes in the city, bandaged their wounds, and put them to bed. But it was too dangerous to stay there; the next day they departed, sore in every bone and muscle, for the three-day hike (60 miles, 96 km) to Derbe. Mission work was tough then, not for the weak or faint-hearted!

ceo

Acts 14:21-23

The Mission in Derbe and the Return Journey

21 When they had preached the gospel to that city and had made many disciples, they returned to Lystra and to Iconium and to Antioch, 22 strengthening the souls of the disciples, encouraging them to continue in the faith, and saying that through many tribulations we must enter the kingdom of God. 23 And when they had appointed elders for them in every church, with prayer and fasting they committed them to the Lord in whom they had believed.

Derbe was on the extreme southeast edge of Roman territory. Beyond, the road went through the non-Roman country of Commagene. Paul seems to prioritize Roman territory.

The account now becomes very abbreviated. We are not told any of the details of the mission in Derbe, only that they *discipled many* (the Greek uses the word *mathēteuō*, the same word in Matt 28:19 *disciple all nations*). Here it simply means to bring people to faith in Christ. Again, *disciple* means "believer." They did not have time for thorough "discipling" as we use that word today.

Paul and Barnabas were living testimonies to their own message. *Through many tribulations we must enter the kingdom of God.* Witherington points out that this is language more typical of Paul than of Luke (p. 428-29). What exactly does Paul mean by *the kingdom of God* here? Sometimes he uses it to mean "the present sphere of salvation" (Rom 14:17; 1 Cor 4:20) and sometimes something to be consummated in the future (1 Cor 6:9, 10; 15:24, 50). The latter could be "heaven" or "the kingdom of God on earth after the coming of Christ." Here it seems to mean that our present experience of salvation, until we enter heaven, will always be accompanied by trials.

This is no place to do a compete study of the subject of tribulation and hardship in the Christian life, but in a day of pragmatic religion and the "health and wealth gospel," we must frequently warn believers that we are **called** unto suffering (Phil 1:29; 1 Pet 1:6 and the whole book of 1 Peter).

Verse 23 describes the provision for rudimentary organization and leadership in the churches and furnishes an essential principle for church planting today. The missionary must work toward this goal, entrusting the newborn church to the Lord and to indigenous leadership. Paul did not get bogged down by spending years in pastoring his churches. The astonishing thing is that he could ordain elders so quickly. We can understand it better if we remember that the substructure for several of these churches was the synagogue and the structure of the early churches was built on the pattern provided by the synagogues. The first elders were appointed, not elected. How elders were selected in following years after the apostles moved on is not clear.

⤺⤻

Acts 14:24-28

Paul and Barnabas Return to Home Base and Report

24 Then they passed through Pisidia and came to Pamphylia. 25 And when they had spoken the word in Perga, they went down to Attalia, 26 and from there they sailed to Antioch, where they had been commended to the grace of God for the work that they had fulfilled. 27 And when they arrived and gathered the church together, they declared all that God had done with them, and how he had opened a door of faith to the Gentiles. 28 And they remained no little time with the disciples.

If one looks at the map, one realizes that Paul and Barnabas at this point are not far (only 150 miles, 240 km) from Paul's hometown Tarsus. Why did they not continue on that way for the return journey? The return route they chose was dangerous; Jews in all three cities had tried to kill them. The answer is that strengthening the new converts in Galatia and organizing them into churches with elders was more important than their personal convenience or physical safety.

The rest of the narrative is a simple travel itinerary of how they returned to the home base at Antioch (Syria). They were able to preach in Perga but there is no record of results. Perga later became the bishopric of western Pamphylia. It declined in the eighth century and the nearby seaport of Attalia took its place, which today is a thriving town, Antalya.

The missionaries ended their journey by making an official report to the assembly of believers in Antioch. **God** *had opened a door of faith to the Gentiles.* The "door" metaphor is typical Pauline language (1 Cor 16:9; 2 Cor 2:12; Col 4:3). Paul was very independent but he was happily accountable to the church that sent him out.

Lessons for Missionaries and Witnesses

1. Our hearers will always filter our message through their own worldview and often get it completely wrong.
2. We must tactfully confront the errors of false religion and false ideas.
3. We cannot preach the Redeemer without first preaching the Creator.
4. Those who witness for Christ will suffer persecution. All believers are called to suffering for Christ.
5. When missionary lives are in danger there is no shame in evacuation.
6. It is not enough to bring individuals to conversion. They must be discipled and encouraged and organized into churches with their own leaders.

ACTS 15

THE JERUSALEM COUNCIL

Chapter 15, roughly in the middle of the book of Acts, is the watershed of the book. All that precedes leads up to it, and all that follows is not possible without it. Indeed, if the Pharisaic party had won the debate, Christianity would not exist today except as an isolated sect of Judaism and might not have lasted more than a century or two.

We believe that this conference occurred in 49 AD and that Paul wrote the book of Galatians from Antioch soon after his return from the first missionary journey but before the Jerusalem Conference. It seems inconceivable that he would have failed to mention the decision of the conference to the Galatians since it settled the very problem Paul was trying to solve in the letter to the Galatians.

ᴐₑᴐ

Acts 15:1-5

The Problem

1 But some men came down from Judea and were teaching the brothers, "Unless you are circumcised according to the custom of Moses, you cannot be saved." 2 And after Paul and Barnabas had no small dissension and debate with them, Paul and Barnabas and some of the others were appointed to go up to Jerusalem to the apostles and the elders about this question. 3 So, being sent on their way by the church, they passed through both Phoenicia and Samaria, describing in detail the conversion of the Gentiles, and brought great joy to all the brothers. 4 When they came to Jerusalem, they were welcomed by the church and the apostles and the elders, and they declared all that God had done with them. 5 But some believers who belonged to the party of the Pharisees rose up and said, "It is necessary to circumcise them and to order them to keep the law of Moses."

The problem, narrowly put, was "Must the Gentiles be circumcised to be saved?" More broadly, "Must the Gentiles obey the law of Moses to be recognized as true believers" (verse 5)? There were three "boundary markers" or tests of the true Jew: circumcision, keeping the Sabbath, and observing the dietary restrictions. Circumcision (as well as baptism) was the initiatory rite essential for all males converted to Judaism and therefore the essential marker that included and implied the other two and indeed, commitment to obey the entire Law of Moses. To put it another way, the issue was "Do the Gentiles have to become Jews before they can become Christians?"

The men who came down from Judea were Judaizers, the same party that caused so much trouble for the new churches in Galatia. The Judaizers were Christian Jews who taught that Gentiles could not become true Christians without submitting to the Law of Moses. Opinions on the relationship of Galatians to Acts 15 vary, but it seems best to see Gal 2:12 *the coming of certain men from James* as parallel to *some men from Judea* in Acts 15:1.[1]

Today this particular issue may not be of much interest or relevance to us since the church of Christ is overwhelmingly Gentile, and few of us are tempted to be circumcised in order to be saved. If, however, we apply the principle more broadly, it is immediately apparent that many forms of Christianity demand that we have faith in Christ **plus something** to be saved. The Roman Catholic Church until recent decades denied that there was salvation outside the Roman Catholic Church, that is no salvation without

---

1   One problem with identifying these two groups of men as identical is that Acts 15:24 denies that they were authorized representatives of the apostles and elders in Jerusalem. It may be that they were indeed sent by James, but went beyond their authority in claiming that Gentiles could not be saved unless they were circumcised. F. F. Bruce leans to the view that the *men from Judea* were the same as the *false brothers* of Gal 2:4 (Bruce, 332). For a detailed comparison or harmony of the events of Acts with not only Galatians, but all of Paul's letters, see the table in Witherington, 445-449.

faith in Christ plus baptism, plus faithful attendance at Mass, plus avoiding mortal sin, etc. etc. There is a movement within Reformed theology today called "theonomy." Theonomists believe that the moral aspects of the Law of Moses are binding and applicable for all Christians today and that only this will free us from the moral laxity and sinfulness of the nation.[2] Others join movements like "Torah Keepers," who worship on Saturday and read only the Torah (the first five books of the Bible). The whole issue of the place of the Old Testament Law in the life of the Christian is still hotly debated today.

Since most of us know, especially from the book of Galatians, that the Judaizers were "bad guys," and we have no interest in their claim today, it is easy to dismiss them as unreasonable fanatics and thus fail to grasp the seriousness of the issue of Acts 15. It will help our understanding of the crisis of Acts 15 if we try to reconstruct and understand their point of view. Their point of view is concealed in the phrase *no small dissension and debate* of verses 2. They might have quoted verses like Gen 17:13b *My covenant in your flesh (referring to circumcision) is to be an **everlasting** covenant.* The sign of the Abrahamic Covenant was circumcision. If we Christians are the seed of Abraham, as Paul argues (Gal 3:7), then we must be circumcised. The sacred Torah, the Law of Moses, is said to be *an **everlasting** ordinance among the Israelites for the generations to come* (Exod 27:21).

Barnabas and Paul and Peter might have countered this argument with something like this: The Law was **for a specific people** (*the children of Israel*, Exod 19:3), **in a specific place** *there* (Jerusalem) *you must bring your burnt offerings*, Deut 12:5-6), **for a specific time** (*until the time of faith in Christ*, Gal 3:24-25). The Hebrew word *'olam* in verses like Gen 17:13 is not an absolute "forever," but usually means "an indefinitely long time."[3] Paul had already spoken to this issue most vehemently in the book of Galatians. We can imagine that some of the same arguments were used in the debate of the Jerusalem Conference.

---

2   Theonomists do not teach that one must keep the Law of Moses to be saved.

3   "That neither the Hebrew word (*'olam*) or the Greek word (*aiōn*) in itself contains the idea of endlessness is shown both by the fact that they sometimes refer to events . . . that occurred at a definite time in the past, and also by the fact that sometimes it is thought desirable to repeat the word, not merely saying 'forever,' but 'forever and ever.' Both words came to be used to refer to a long age or period . . ." (Allan A. Macrae, in *Theological Wordbook of the Old Testament*, Chicago: The Moody Bible Institute, vol 2, 673).

Many fine Protestant denominations practice infant baptism. They claim that infant baptism takes the place of circumcision, usually citing Col 2:11-12. Our question for them is this: If baptism takes the place of circumcision, why didn't Paul argue that point at this conference (or in Galatians for that matter)? It would have quickly silenced the Judaizers and there would have been no dispute.

Paul and Barnabas were sent by the church in Antioch to the apostles and elders in Jerusalem to settle this dispute. Jerusalem was still the "headquarters church." Some want to call this the first ecumenical council in church history, but that is a little off the mark. That term implies a gathering of representatives from numerous churches, whereas this conference was a gathering of the ruling authorities (*apostles and elders*) of the mother church.

On the way they stopped at churches in Phoenicia and Samaria and testified to the salvation of many Gentiles. This caused *great joy* (Luke can never resist a chance to mention the joy of salvation!) among these believers, none of whom asked whether the Gentiles had been circumcised. When they arrived in Jerusalem, they made the same report to the church, and some of them **did** raise the question of circumcision. Could some of the former Pharisees have been elders? If that were true, the circumcision issue was a very serious crisis indeed.

Acts 15:7-11

Peter's Speech

7 And after there had been much debate, Peter stood up and said to them, "Brothers, you know that in the early days God made a choice among you, that by my mouth the Gentiles should hear the word of the gospel and believe. 8 And God, who knows the heart, bore witness to them, by giving them the Holy Spirit just as he did to us, 9 and he made no distinction between us and them, having cleansed their hearts by faith. 10 Now,

therefore, why are you putting God to the test by placing a yoke on the neck
of the disciples that neither our fathers nor we have been able to bear? **11**
But we believe that we will be saved through the grace of the Lord Jesus,
just as they will."

Whether they were elders or not, the opinion of the former Pharisees was respected enough to allow *much debate.* Do we attempt to evade controversial issues in the church today by cleverly shutting out or shutting up troublesome people? It is better to let them have their say. Democracy started in pagan Greece, but the Christian church furnished the soil in which it eventually grew.

Luke records the gist of three speeches, one by Peter, one by Paul, and one by the moderator James. These are the persuasive arguments that resulted in the ruling of the council. Peter and Paul both cite the work of God. Peter reminds the assembled elders about the conversion of Cornelius and his family. They had heard Peter's message and believed. God enabled them to speak in tongues as proof that they had truly been converted and accepted by God and that the Spirit of God was dwelling in them. God made no distinction between *us* Jews and *them* (Gentiles). And all this occurred despite the fact that none of the Gentile converts were circumcised or keeping the Law.

Peter's conclusion is very sharp and surprisingly critical of the Law of Moses as *a yoke that neither we nor our fathers were able to bear.* To put that yoke on the Gentile converts is to *test God.* Peter has learned his lesson since his lapse mentioned in Galatians 2:11-14 when he refused to eat with converted Gentiles, and now he is just as strong as Paul against the Judaizers' demands. Peter says that to insist on law-keeping is to deny the grace of the Lord Jesus (verse 11). In the doctrine of salvation, grace and Law are polar opposites.

Acts 15:12

The Report of Barnabas and Paul

12 And all the assembly fell silent, and they listened to Barnabas and Paul as they related what signs and wonders God had done through them among the Gentiles.

Paul, the chief supporter of the anti-circumcision opinion, wisely takes a back seat. The name of Barnabas is mentioned first, a reversal of the order of the first missionary journey. In Jerusalem, Barnabas is still the head of the mission to Anatolia. The emphasis is not on what **they** had done, but on what **God** had done through them. They do not state debating points like Peter and James; they simply relate what God did.

As for the *signs and wonders,* we read of unspecified *signs and wonders* in Iconium (14:3), and two specific miracles, the blinding of Elymas, and the healing of the lame man in Iconium. Undoubtedly there were many other miracles that Barnabas and Paul recounted. But the greatest wonder of all was the salvation of so many Jews, God-fearers, and raw pagans. The point was that God saved a diversity of people without any demand that the converts keep the Law of Moses.

ᗢᗞ

Acts 15:13-21

The Ruling of James

13 After they finished speaking, James replied, "Brothers, listen to me. 14 Simeon has related how God first visited the Gentiles, to take from them a people for his name. 15 And with this the words of the prophets agree, just as it is written,

16 "After this I will return, and I will rebuild the tent of David that has fallen; I will rebuild its ruins, and I will restore it, 17 that the remnant of mankind may seek the Lord, and all the Gentiles who are called by my name, says the Lord, who makes these things 18 known from of old.'

19 Therefore my judgment is that we should not trouble those of the Gentiles who turn to God, 20 but should write to them to abstain from the things polluted by idols, and from sexual immorality, and from what has been strangled, and from blood. 21 For from ancient generations Moses has had in every city those who proclaim him, for he is read every Sabbath in the synagogues."

Apparently the whole assembly was still silent, impressed by the report of Barnabas and Paul. James, whose opinion may have been changed, or at least been more clearly focused, (see Gal 2:12), sums up the development of the emerging consensus and adds his own support by a quotation from Amos, as a representative of *the prophets.* As Bock comments, "James' point is not just about this one passage from Amos; rather, this passage reflects what the prophets teach in general, or what the book of the Prophets as a whole teaches."[4]

The most difficult issue, aside from various differences of wording in the quotation from Amos 9:11-12 between the Hebrew text, the Greek (Septuagint) text, and James' quotation, is the meaning of "the rebuilding of the tent of David."[5] The word *skēnē* might be rendered, as in the KJV, "tabernacle of David." Most take this phrase symbolically to mean the restoration of the dynasty of David in the coming of Messiah Jesus and the subsequent building of the Christian church (Marshall, Stott, among many). On the other hand, Amos may have been referring to the building of the eschatological temple in the messianic age. A literal temple was prophesied by Isaiah (2:2-3), Micah (4:1-2), Joel (3:18), and Ezekiel (chapters 40-48).[6] However one interprets the restoration and rebuilding of "the tent of David,"

---

4   Bock, 503.

5   We cannot adequately treat this rather difficult discussion here. See Bock, pages 503 and 504, for a good discussion.

6   Schnabel discusses this as a reference to the eschatological temple (639), but concludes that "The messianic temple, the restored 'tent of David,' is the community of all people who believe in Jesus as Israel's Messiah and Savior" (Schnabel, Acts chapter 15, Expanded Digital Edition (Grand Rapids: Zondervan, 2012, 31).

all agree that James' main point is the inclusion of the Gentiles as Gentiles, not Jewish proselytes.

This conclusion is based on 1) **the work of God**: God is saving the Gentiles (without requiring circumcision) and 2) **the word of God**: it was prophesied that Gentiles would believe in the true God (without requiring circumcision or law keeping).

James first summed up the testimony of Peter to the work of God. God visited in saving power (this is the significance of the Greek *episkepsatō*) to take out of the nations (*ethnoi*) *a people for His name,* that is "a people for his glory." The sovereign act of God in saving Gentiles for his own sake is stressed. For the first time the word *laos* ("people") is used for non-Jews. A new people of God is being formed. This is what God is still doing in this present age. He is still visiting the *ethnoi* of the world in saving power to take out from among them *a people for his name,* the Church of Christ (see 1 Pet 2:9-10). The salvation of Gentiles was predicted by the prophets, of which James only mentions one, Amos.

James' point is that Amos (and other prophets) predicted the salvation of the Gentiles. The issue of circumcision is not mentioned in the passage but James is saying that the Gentiles will be saved **as Gentiles**, not as converts to Judaism undergoing circumcision.

In verses 19-21 we have James' judgment or ruling. He does not mention circumcision directly but makes a sweepingly broad ruling: "Gentiles do not have to observe any of the laws of Moses, except for the following four restrictions." This is surprising. Many today would have James say, "Just keep the Ten Commandments," or "Just keep the moral aspects of the Law, not the cultural and ceremonial." Sabbath observance is not even mentioned. Legalism is an instinct that dies hard and many today cannot really accept the liberality of James' ruling.

The four prohibitions—defilement of idols, fornication, the strangled, and blood—present some difficulties as to their precise meaning and application. Most interpreters believe that three of the four have to do with what is called "table fellowship," that is to avoid eating either meat sacrificed to idols or meals in idol temples, and all meat not properly slaughtered so as not to drain the blood. If the animal is strangled the blood cannot drain properly. All these things would offend the Jewish believers and hinder relationships within the church. So for the sake of preserving fellowship and unity, the Gentile converts should voluntarily refrain from these things that offended the

Jews and the Jewish Christians. Verse 21 strongly supports this interpretation. Paul taught the same principle, but more broadly, in Romans 14:13-16, *not to put a stumbling block in our brothers' way.*

The inclusion of *porneia, fornication,* presents difficulties. First, why mention something so obvious, something already included in the Christian ethic (Matt 5:22; Mark 7:21; 1 Cor 6:18 and many others)? Second, fornication does not fit the other three stipulations all of which deal with dietary restrictions. Some interpreters produce evidence that *porneia* is a reference to marriage to close relatives prohibited in Lev 18:6 and following. Witherington is convinced that all four are references to feasts in pagan temples that involved cult prostitution (Witherington, 463).

Are the four prohibitions still in effect today? For example, must the German Christian refrain from his blood sausage and must the Masai believer stop drinking the blood of his cattle? To ask the question is to answer it: "No," at least for the first three. The four prohibitions did not seem to outlast the period when the Jewish believers were a significant number in all the Christian churches. We do not hear of these four rules being repeated in the epistles of Paul. It was a temporary ruling to solve a temporary problem.[7] However, the important principle as expressed by Paul still remains; we should avoid things that are lawful but that will cause unnecessary offence to our brothers in Christ and disharmony in the Body.

~~~

Acts 15:22-35

The Promulgation of the Decision

22 *Then it seemed good to the apostles and the elders, with the whole church, to choose men from among them and send them to Antioch with Paul and Barnabas. They sent Judas called Barsabbas, and Silas, leading men among the brothers,* **23** *with the following letter: "The brothers,*

---

7   Bock, however, says that "such limitations were observed in the church for some time." He cites references from Rev 2:14 to Eusebius (Bock, 507).

both the apostles and the elders, to the brothers who are of the Gentiles in Antioch and Syria and Cilicia, greetings. 24 Since we have heard that some persons have gone out from us and troubled you with words, unsettling your minds, although we gave them no instructions, 25 it has seemed good to us, having come to one accord, to choose men and send them to you with our beloved Barnabas and Paul, 26 men who have risked their lives for the name of our Lord Jesus Christ. 27 We have therefore sent Judas and Silas, who themselves will tell you the same things by word of mouth. 28 For it has seemed good to the Holy Spirit and to us to lay on you no greater burden than these requirements: 29 that you abstain from what has been sacrificed to idols, and from blood, and from what has been strangled, and from sexual immorality. If you keep yourselves from these, you will do well. Farewell."

30 So when they were sent off, they went down to Antioch, and having gathered the congregation together, they delivered the letter. 31 And when they had read it, they rejoiced because of its encouragement.

32 And Judas and Silas, who were themselves prophets, encouraged and strengthened the brothers with many words. 33 And after they had spent some time, they were sent off in peace by the brothers to those who had sent them. 35 But Paul and Barnabas remained in Antioch, teaching and preaching the word of the Lord, with many others also.

The ruling came from James, but it had the support of all the apostles and elders and *the whole church.* Presumably that included even the Pharisaic party. The Holy Spirit (verse 28) turned a severe problem threatening to destroy the young church into a victory that unified the church and made the worldwide mission to the Gentiles possible. They sent a four-man delegation consisting of the two missionaries, Paul and Barnabas, and two representatives from the Jerusalem church, Judas and Silas, to deliver the ruling to the churches in Antioch, Syria, and Cilicia. We know nothing else about Judas Barsabbas. Silas later became Paul's companion for the second and third missionary journeys in the place of Barnabas. Barnabas and Paul are commended as *men who have risked their lives for the name of our Lord Jesus Christ.* Missionaries should still be willing to risk their lives for their Lord. The roll of those who have risked their lives and even lost their lives in foreign lands is long indeed.

Luke has a copy of the decision and he quotes it word for word. The church of Antioch was greatly relieved and encouraged by this generous ruling. There is a tendency in many zealous churches throughout the world to multiply rules and "lay down the law" in an effort to keep the church pure. So many young churches in the developing world are permeated with a spirit of petty legalism and endless quarrels and splits over "the rules." Instead, we should make it a "rule" never to make rules, spoken or unspoken, unless they are absolutely necessary for the functioning of the body and the encouragement of God's people.

Prophets Judas and Silas (v. 32 and 33) and Paul and Barnabas (v.35) were sent from Jerusalem to Antioch to deliver and explain the decision of the Council. The result was rejoicing and encouragement (mentioned twice) and strengthening of their faith and unity. *After some days* Judas and Silas return to Jerusalem. Verse 34 is missing from the best manuscripts and so is omitted from versions after the King James. Paul and Barnabas remain in Antioch, setting the stage for the second missionary journey.

Lessons for Life

1. Problems in the church must be honestly confronted, not ignored or swept under the rug.
2. A forum must be provided for opinions and objections to be expressed openly.
3. Christians today are not under the Law of Moses, but they are under the Law of Christ (Gal 6:2; 1 Cor 9:21).
4. God is still today taking out from among the nations "a people for His Name."
5. We must not allow our liberty in Christ to stumble or offend our brothers and sisters in Christ.
6. Never make a rule in the church unless it is necessary for the functioning of the body or the encouragement of God's people.
7. Let us encourage one another.

Acts 15:36-16:40

The Second Missionary Journey

15:36-41 Paul and Barnabas Separate

36 And after some days Paul said to Barnabas, "Let us return and visit the brothers in every city where we proclaimed the word of the Lord, and see how they are." 37 Now Barnabas wanted to take with them John called Mark. 38 But Paul thought best not to take with them one who had withdrawn from them in Pamphylia and had not gone with them to the work. 39 And there arose a sharp disagreement, so that they separated from each other. Barnabas took Mark with him and sailed away to Cyprus, 40 but Paul chose Silas and departed, having been commended by the brothers to the grace of the Lord. 41 And he went through Syria and Cilicia, strengthening the churches.

This paragraph describes the selection of workers for the second missionary journey. The time is either the spring or summer of 49 AD, soon after the Jerusalem Conference.[8] At the start of the first missionary journey Barnabas was the leader. But now Paul is more prominent, and he makes the suggestion to visit all the believers that were converted on the first journey. Since they did not leave any missionaries behind to follow up on the converts, this was their minimum responsibility.

But there was a sharp disagreement[9] between Paul and Barnabas. Paul did not want to take John Mark because he had deserted them on the first journey. The book of Acts, and indeed the entire Bible, does not cover up the faults of its heroes. Barnabas cared for the worker, who happened to be his cousin,[10] but Paul cared more for the work. The confrontation must have been painful for both of them. Barnabas may have reminded Paul who it was

---

8   McRay, 75, and Hemer, 269.

9   The word *paroxusmos* indicates a heated argument. In the Greek OT of Deut 29:27 and Jer 39:37, it refers to God's wrath.

10   Col 4:10.

that rescued him out of suspicion and obscurity and introduced him into a place of important ministry. Paul may still have been resentful of Barnabas being swept away with Peter in the incident in Antioch (Gal 2:13). Who was right? In our judgment, Paul was wrong in not giving John Mark a second chance. Later Paul did recognize Mark as a trustworthy fellow-worker (Col 4:10; 2 Tim 4:11; Phm 24).

How often today there are serious disagreements between faithful zealous Christian workers! Our theory is that there are more apt to be disagreements between Christians than non-Christians because Christians are so earnestly involved in God's work and are often people of strong convictions, whereas non-Christians and lukewarm Christians believe less and so care less. Doing missionary work in teams is popular today, but it is "easier said than done."

Nevertheless, in the providence of God the disagreement produced two mission teams where there had been only one and may well have been the key to John Mark's recovery. Barnabas took John Mark and strengthened the believers in Cyprus and no doubt started other churches. This must have been part of the rehabilitation of Mark. The Coptic Church of Egypt is quite certain that Saint Mark was their founder. Few deny that he is the author of the gospel that bears his name. Without the encouragement of Cousin Barnabas, would these things have happened?

But Luke's purpose is to keep the spotlight on Paul; the name of Barnabas now disappears from the text of Acts and Paul chooses a new partner, Silas. Silas had a number of advantages. He was "a leading man" in the Jerusalem church (15:22) and was thus able to explain the decision of the Jerusalem Conference with knowledge and authority. He exercised the gift of prophecy (15:32), was fluent in Greek (15:32), and was able to serve as amanuensis for both Paul and Peter (1 Thess 1:1; 2 Thess 1:1; 1 Pet 5:12).[11] Unlike Barnabas, but like Paul, he had Roman citizenship.

---

11   An *amanuensis* was one who wrote letters for the one dictating the letter, a scribe. In Acts his name is the Greek *Silas;* in the epistles the Latin name *Silvanus* is used.

ACTS 16

A NEW CHURCH IN PHILIPPI

Acts 16:1-4

The Selection of Timothy

1 Paul came also to Derbe and to Lystra. A disciple was there, named Timothy, the son of a Jewish woman who was a believer, but his father was a Greek. 2 He was well spoken of by the brothers at Lystra and Iconium. 3 Paul wanted Timothy to accompany him, and he took him and circumcised him because of the Jews who were in those places, for they all knew that his father was a Greek. 4 As they went on their way through the cities, they delivered to them for observance the decisions that had been reached by the apostles and elders who were in Jerusalem.

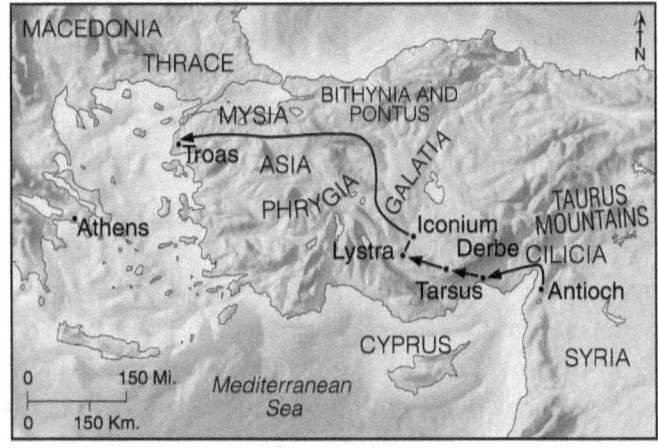

The Second Journey Begins

213

This time Paul takes the land route, apparently to strengthen the churches in Syria and Cilicia (15:41) and to deliver and explain the decision of the Jerusalem Conference. We wish we knew who started these churches and exactly where they were. We are reminded again that Acts is not a complete history of the early church. Paul may have had a hand in the founding of these churches (especially Cilicia) during the six silent years in Tarsus before Barnabas invited him to Antioch.

Paul and Silas must have gone through Paul's hometown of Tarsus and then up the rugged grandeur of the Cilician Gates to Tyana on the high dry Anatolian Plateau. From there it was about 80 miles (130 km) or four days walk to Derbe. Continuing on to Lystra Paul met one of his converts (1 Tim 1:2), Timothy, and persuaded him to accompany them. Every mature Christian worker should have his "Timothy," and every Christian should have his/her "Paul" as a mentor.

Some have found it unbelievable that Paul had Timothy circumcised. Did not the very document in their hands (the decree from the Jerusalem Conference) deny the need for circumcision of Gentiles? Is this the same Paul who railed against the Judaizers in the letter to the Galatians? The answer is that, among the Jews, Timothy was counted as a Jew, not a Gentile, because his mother was Jewish. In cases of mixed marriage even today, the rule for being recognized as a Jew for immigration to Israel is having a Jewish mother. This is a perfect illustration of the principle of 1 Cor 9:20. Paul circumcised Timothy in order to be able to preach the gospel of grace to Jews.

One may wonder how the Jewish community would have known whether Timothy was circumcised or not. We must remember that both the baths and the toilets were mostly public in those days and there was less concealment of private parts than we are used to in modern times.

5 So the churches were strengthened in the faith, and they increased in numbers daily.

Summary verses 16:5; 2:41; 6:7; 12:24; and 19:20 both divide the previous section (some call these "panels") from the next and serve to generalize what has been happening as a link to the next section. In Luke's mind the fourth panel of the book does not start with the departure from Antioch but with the first mission to new locations. We are finished with the work in

Galatia and now start the work in Greece. All summary verses report increased growth in numbers and strengthening in the faith.

There is relationship between strengthening and growth. If the churches are truly strong, they will grow on their own without the constant attention of the missionaries. Years ago Roland Allen protested against the mission station mentality of his time in a classic called *The Spontaneous Expansion of the Church*.[1] Today, church planting missionaries may need a longer time to get a church started than Paul had; but the principle of establishing local leadership and moving on is still necessary.

◦ℯℯ

Acts 16:6-10

The Trek Through Asia Minor and the
Macedonian Call

6 And they went through the region of Phrygia and Galatia, having been forbidden by the Holy Spirit to speak the word in Asia. 7 And when they had come up to Mysia, they attempted to go into Bithynia, but the Spirit of Jesus did not allow them. 8 So, passing by Mysia, they went down to Troas. 9 And a vision appeared to Paul in the night: a man of Macedonia was standing there, urging him and saying, "Come over to Macedonia and help us." 10 And when Paul had seen the vision, immediately we sought to go on into Macedonia, concluding that God had called us to preach the gospel to them.

This passage can be understood only with the aid of a map. The three missionaries were traveling west, probably through Antioch of Pisidia and Apollonia on the Imperial Road. The natural course continuing west would have taken them into the cities of the province of Asia: Colossae, Laodicia, Hieropolis, and eventually to Ephesus on the Aegean Coast. These were all important cities

---

1   Originally published in London by World Dominion Press in 1927. More recent republications are available.

and good strategy would have dictated that they be evangelized first. But the Holy Spirit stopped them, probably by a word of prophecy through Paul or Silas. So they turned north and actually had to curve back to the east a bit on the Roman road toward the cities of Nicea and Nicomedia in the province of Bithynia. Here again the Spirit stopped them (*the Spirit of Jesus* is the Holy Spirit.). So they turned west again until they came to Alexandria Troas (the full name) on the Aegean Coast. Troas is not to be confused with the ancient city of Homer's Troy, which was 16 km to the north. They may have evangelized Troas, for we find an assembly of believers there in Acts 20. Finally they get the guidance they need, the famous "Macedonian Call" in Paul's dream. As the word *concluding* shows, the guidance was indirect; they had to interpret the dream.

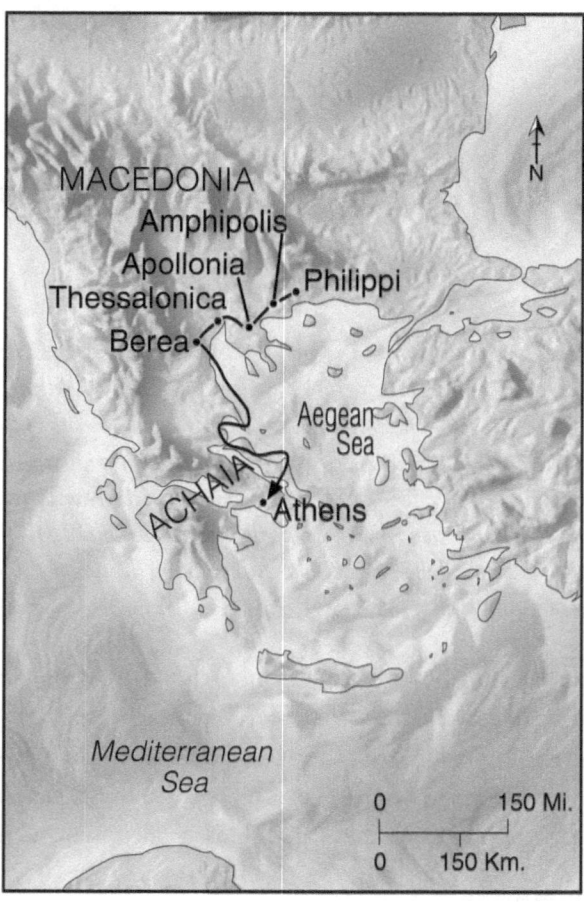

Ministry in Macedonia

This passage is very instructive on the matter of guidance for decisions in God's work. First, God does not usually reveal the whole plan from the beginning. Second, he sometimes allows his servants to wander with only negative guidance. (The distance from Iconium to Troas is about 360 miles [580 km] which would have taken at least twenty days on foot.) They walked for three weeks with no clear direction from God. Third, eventually the Spirit will give the guidance we need just when we need it.

The passage also reminds us that the Spirit is the strategist, not the mission or the missiologists. Strategic studies have their value, but the final word belongs to the Spirit. The cities of Asia and Bithynia were eventually evangelized, but this was not the work of Paul and company at that time. Maybe one reason for the journey to Troas was to add another member. Notice the little word *we* in verse 10. This shows that Luke joined Paul, Silas, and Timothy at this point. This first "we section" continues through the ministry in Philippi.

At this point the gospel crosses over into Europe, which is often hailed as a momentous turning point in church history and world history. But that could only be seen hundreds of years later; people at that time had no such concept as "Europe." Nevertheless, the gospel is now nearer Greece, the center of ancient culture, and one step closer to Rome, the ancient political center.

✺

Acts 16:11-15

The Conversion of Lydia

11 So, setting sail from Troas, we made a direct voyage to Samothrace, and the following day to Neapolis, 12 and from there to Philippi, which is a leading city of the district of Macedonia and a Roman colony. We remained in this city some days. 13 And on the Sabbath day we went outside the gate to the riverside, where we supposed there was a place of prayer, and we sat down and spoke to the women who had come together. 14 One who heard us was a woman named Lydia, from the city of Thyatira, a seller of purple goods, who was a worshiper of God. The Lord opened her heart to pay

attention to what was said by Paul. 15 And after she was baptized, and her
household as well, she urged us, saying, "If you have judged me to be faithful
to the Lord, come to my house and stay." And she prevailed upon us.

Apparently they spent one day sailing to the towering island (5,000 ft) of
Samothrace and one day sailing to Neapolis. They did not linger in the seaport
of Neapolis but soon crossed the 10 miles (16 km) over the coastal mountains
to the chief city of eastern Macedonia, **Philippi**. It was named after Philip II,
king of Macedon, father of Alexander the Great. It was made a Roman colony,
settled by many veterans, after the famous Battle of Philippi nearby in which
Antony and Octavian defeated Brutus and Cassius in 42 BC.

So far, Paul has always gone to the local synagogue first. But here, there
probably were not the required ten Jewish men to form a synagogue. But
there was a prayer meeting of Jewish women who gathered near a small stream
(Gangites) just west of town that rushes down from snow-capped mountains.
It is a quiet spot marked by a simple Greek Orthodox chapel commemorating
this event.[2]

Paul and his fellow-workers did not despise this opportunity just because
their audience was "only" women. It turned out there was a businesswoman
there by the name of Lydia. Her business was selling purple cloth, a luxury
item in the ancient world made from the madder plant grown near Thyatira
in Asia Minor. It was not just a small local business. She seems to have had a
substantial house with many servants. She provided the four evangelists with
a home base in Philippi. Whether she was married, widowed, or single we do
not know. She may have become interested in Judaism in her hometown of
Thyatira where there was a significant Jewish population.

The Lord opened her heart. The risen Lord Jesus was then and still is
working on earth to open hearts. How many Lydias have blessed the church
through the centuries and how we pray for many more.

Lydia must have persuaded her household (servants and maybe some
children) to believe for they were all baptized, maybe in the same river. She
immediately urged the four evangelists to stay at her house. Like Cornelius in
Acts 10:48, the new convert offers much needed hospitality as her contribution
to the missionary effort. She was a good steward of the wealth and property
the Lord had given her. Are we good stewards of our large houses today?

---

2   Schnabel thinks that they assembled at a stream outside the city gate, not the 1.5-mile
        distant Gangites (679). Did the Greek Orthodox Church get it wrong?

A memorial to the Jewish prayer meeting by the river (Acts 16:13)

Some of the ruins of ancient Philippi

Acts 16:16-24

The Imprisonment of Paul and Silas

16 As we were going to the place of prayer, we were met by a slave girl who had a spirit of divination and brought her owners much gain by fortune-telling. 17 She followed Paul and us, crying out, "These men are servants of the Most High God, who proclaim to you the way of salvation." 18 And this she kept doing for many days. Paul, having become greatly annoyed, turned and said to the spirit, "I command you in the name of Jesus Christ to come out of her." And it came out that very hour.

19 But when her owners saw that their hope of gain was gone, they seized Paul and Silas and dragged them into the marketplace before the rulers. 20 And when they had brought them to the magistrates, they said, "These men are Jews, and they are disturbing our city. 21 They advocate customs that are not lawful for us as Romans to accept or practice." 22 The crowd joined in attacking them, and the magistrates tore the garments off them and gave orders to beat them with rods. 23 And when they had inflicted many blows upon them, they threw them into prison, ordering the jailer to keep them safely. 24 Having received this order, he put them into the inner prison and fastened their feet in the stocks.

Whenever there is success in evangelism, the devil opposes the evangelists. The poor nameless slave girl was possessed by "a python spirit"[3] that enabled her to predict the future. Her owners made her "gift" into a profitable source of income. The famous oracle of Delphi was embodied in a huge snake (python) who represented the god Apollo. To a Bible reader the connection with the serpent of Genesis 3 is clear.

Just as the demons possessing the Gadarene demoniac confessed Jesus as *the Son of the Most High God* (Mark 5:7; Luke 8:28), so "the python spirit" confesses that *These men are servants of the Most High God, who proclaim to you a way of salvation* (a more literal translation). The terms *Most High God* and *a way of salvation* must have been misunderstood by the pagan crowds. To them Zeus was "the most high god," and there were many "ways of salvation." The

---

3   The literal Greek text is *pneuma pythuna* which the ESV renders "spirit of divination."

demon knows the real truth about *the Most High God* and must proclaim this truth through the slave girl. Under the power of the risen Christ, even the demons must acknowledge the truth (James 2:19). Even Christ's enemies will confess the truth in the Day of Judgment.

However, after many days the free publicity was more of a hindrance than a help. Paul became so troubled that he suddenly commanded the demon to *come out in the name of Jesus Christ.* It does not say that the girl believed, but we like to think that she, such a contrast to wealthy high-status Lydia, also became a member of the new church in Philippi.

Now Paul and Silas face a new problem: the rage of the owners of the prophetess. When Paul cast out the demon he also cast out their ill-gotten profits. The slave owners seized Paul and Silas and dragged them before the magistrates (Luke uses the correct term for the rulers of Philippi, *stratēgoi*) to the *bēma* (judgment platform) in the agora. They did not accuse them of destroying their livelihood, instead they tried a more effective accusation: *These men are Jews, and they are disturbing our city. They advocate customs that are not lawful for us as Romans to accept or practice.* They 1) Appealed to the prejudice against Jews. 2) They accused them of public disturbance (ironically it had been **their** slave girl who caused the disturbance) and 3) They attacked their preaching as contrary to the Roman way of life.

People might not care about religion but they get upset when their pocketbook is threatened. This is Paul's first persecution from a purely Gentile crowd. The next will be the incident of the silversmith riot in Ephesus (Acts 19). In both cases, loss of income triggered the opposition. Prejudice against foreigners and the alarm at perceived threats to local customs are still powerful obstacles to the gospel. People even today really are more protective of their way of life than their religion.

It must have been the roaring of the crowd that moved the magistrates (in this case two of them) to order Paul and Silas beaten with the rods called *fasces* (from which comes the word Fascist) by the *lictors*. Foreigners and strangers had no civil rights. This was one of three times Paul was *beaten with rods* (2 Cor 11:25). The two men staggered off to jail, bleeding profusely and in terrible pain. Why Paul and Silas did not claim their Roman citizenship, sparing themselves a painful beating, is a mystery. Perhaps they looked on this suffering as one of the *afflictions of Christ* (Col 1:24). Anyway, their submission to the beatings resulted in the salvation of a most unlikely member of the emerging church in Philippi.

Paul and Silas could have been beaten and released, but the magistrates also ordered them put in maximum security in the town jail, in the darkest innermost part with no water, no food, and no toilet facilities. Prisoners in ancient jails often begged their guards to have mercy and kill them. To add to the misery, they were put in painful stocks which immobilized the prisoner and spread his legs in a painful and awkward position. It was impossible to rest or sleep and there was no TV to pass the time. They had no idea of how long they would be there.

$$\backsim$$

Acts 16:25-34

The Conversion of the Philippian Jailer

25 About midnight Paul and Silas were praying and singing hymns to God, and the prisoners were listening to them, 26 and suddenly there was a great earthquake, so that the foundations of the prison were shaken. And immediately all the doors were opened, and everyone's bonds were unfastened. 27 When the jailer woke and saw that the prison doors were open, he drew his sword and was about to kill himself, supposing that the prisoners had escaped. 28 But Paul cried with a loud voice, "Do not harm yourself, for we are all here." 29 And the jailer called for lights and rushed in, and trembling with fear he fell down before Paul and Silas. 30 Then he brought them out and said, "Sirs, what must I do to be saved?" 31 And they said, "Believe in the Lord Jesus, and you will be saved, you and your household." 32 And they spoke the word of the Lord to him and to all who were in his house. 33 And he took them the same hour of the night and washed their wounds; and he was baptized at once, he and all his family. 34 Then he brought them up into his house and set food before them. And he rejoiced along with his entire household that he had believed in God.

Paul and Silas made the very best of a very bad situation. They were praying and singing hymns to God. Unbelievable. The other prisoners must have at first thought they were crazy but then realized that these men had a remarkable faith in a remarkable God. The other prisoners would not forget this incident as long as they lived. Maybe some were converted to Christ.

Nor would any of them forget the earthquake that was strong enough to spring the doors and pull chains out of the walls, but not strong enough to bring the roof down on their heads. The jailer was greatly alarmed. He grabbed his sword and headed for the jail. When he saw the open doors, he panicked and assumed all the prisoners had escaped and drew his sword to kill himself. The penalty for allowing prisoners to escape was death (Matt 28:11-15; Acts 12:19); if the jailor was a city slave, as Schnabel surmises, the execution might have been crucifixion. Then he heard Paul shout, *Do not harm yourself, for we are all here!* That was enough to bring the tough, hardhearted jailor to his knees and ask *Sirs, what must I do to be saved?"* In ancient times earthquakes were thought to be a sign of the wrath of the gods, and he knew the god of these two preachers must be very powerful and very angry. Philippi was small enough that he may have either heard their preaching or heard rumors of their preaching about salvation, and that may explain his question.

The jailer asked the right question, the best question of all possible questions, and the missionaries gave the right answer in the briefest words possible. This is all, in essence, that any person must do to be saved: **believe in the Lord Jesus**. More explanation will be necessary, but more than simple faith is never required of anyone. All else, confession, restitution, baptism, good works—will naturally follow genuine faith in the Lord Jesus. Faith alone in Christ alone is the kernel of the true gospel and we dare not complicate it or muddle it.

You will be saved, you and your household. Is this a universal promise that if we believe in Christ, our families will also be saved? We believe that this statement was a specific prophecy of what would happen to this particular man. The experience of millions of people whose families do not believe and indeed cast them out shows that we cannot claim this promise as absolute universal promise. Jesus warned us that, for many, their enemies would be those of their own house (Matt 10:36). Nevertheless, it will do no harm to remind the Lord of the promise to the Philippian jailor when we pray for our family members.

What started as the most miserable of nights became the most blessed of nights as their wounds were treated and food was set before them. The jailor could have gotten in trouble for helping prisoners and even feeding prisoners in his charge, but the joy of salvation overwhelmed all such fears. Paul and Silas had the privilege of explaining about the Lord Jesus and the way of salvation far into the night. The jailor and his family were so powerfully impressed that they believed that very night and asked for baptism (always the outward sign of true faith in Acts) the same night.

∽∾

Acts 16:35-40

Departure From Philippi

35 But when it was day, the magistrates sent the police, saying, "Let those men go." 36 And the jailer reported these words to Paul, saying, "The magistrates have sent to let you go. Therefore come out now and go in peace." 37 But Paul said to them, "They have beaten us publicly, uncondemned, men who are Roman citizens, and have thrown us into prison; and do they now throw us out secretly? No! Let them come themselves and take us out." 38 The police reported these words to the magistrates, and they were afraid when they heard that they were Roman citizens. 39 So they came and apologized to them. And they took them out and asked them to leave the city. 40 So they went out of the prison and visited Lydia. And when they had seen the brothers, they encouraged them and departed.

The magistrates did not know that the two troublemakers had already been released. Why the magistrates decided to release them is not clear; maybe they thought that one night in such a nasty jail was enough punishment. Maybe they had heard about the earthquake and feared divine retribution.

When the *police* (lictors) brought orders come to release them, Paul decides it is time for a little of his own righteous retribution. He demands that the two magistrates appear in person and apologize for beating Roman citizens publicly, and that without trial. The magistrates were rightly alarmed. It was illegal to beat a citizen without proper trial, and if this incident were reported to higher authorities, they would not only lose their positions, but also be severely punished. The humiliators had become the humiliated.

Before following the request of the magistrates that they leave the city, Paul and Silas (along with Timothy and Luke) go to Lydia's house where the Christians had gathered. The missionaries encouraged the little group who must have been shaken by these dramatic events. The house church in Philippi was one of Paul's favorite churches and one of his staunchest supporters (Phil 1:3-8; 4:15-18). We learn from the Book of Philippians the names of other believers in this church: Epaphroditus (Phil 2:2 f), Euodia and Syntyche (4:2), and Clement (4:3).

Luke was probably left in Philippi (where there was a famous medical school) and we pick him up again in Troas in the next "we section" (20:5). He must have been a great help to the church in Philippi.

Lessons for Life

1. Disagreements between earnest Christians happen. Disagree agreeably and let God work. There is no shame in re-forming mission teams.
2. Every mature Christian should have his "Timothy," and every growing Christian should have his "Paul."
3. We must be *all things to all men* for the sake of the gospel.
4. God does not lay out our course on a map but leads us step by step with red lights as well as green lights.
5. The Holy Spirit is the strategist; the missionary is the foot soldier.
6. God does great things through "weak" people. Women have always been very important in the mission of the church.
7. The Lord is still working to open hearts.
8. Followers of Christ will suffer the *afflictions of Christ.*
9. Joy in affliction is the most powerful testimony to Christ.
10. There is no other requirement for salvation than *Believe on the Lord Jesus.*

ACTS 17

THESSALONICA AND PAUL'S SPEECH IN ATHENS

Acts 17:1-9

Reasoning From the Scriptures in Thessalonica

1 Now when they had passed through Amphipolis and Apollonia, they came to Thessalonica, where there was a synagogue of the Jews. 2 And Paul went in, as was his custom, and on three Sabbath days he reasoned with them from the Scriptures, 3 explaining and proving that it was necessary for the Christ to suffer and to rise from the dead, and saying, "This Jesus, whom I proclaim to you, is the Christ." 4 And some of them were persuaded and joined Paul and Silas, as did a great many of the devout Greeks and not a few of the leading women. 5 But the Jews were jealous, and taking some wicked men of the rabble, they formed a mob, set the city in an uproar, and attacked the house of Jason, seeking to bring them out to the crowd. 6 And when they could not find them, they dragged Jason and some of the brothers before the city authorities, shouting, "These men who have turned the world upside down have come here also, 7 and Jason has received them, and they are all acting against the decrees of Caesar, saying that there is another king, Jesus." 8 And the people and the city authorities were disturbed when they heard these things. 9 And when they had taken money as security from Jason and the rest, they let them go.

Leaving Luke in Philippi, Paul, Silas, and Timothy continued west on the Via Egnatia to Thessalonica, the capital of Macedonia. Amphipolis was a district capital of some importance, one day's journey from Philippi, but Paul bypasses it for a more important city. The party seems to have stayed one night in Amphipolis, and one night in Apollonia. Today nothing but a few ruins and a plaque in Apollonia mark the passage of the first missionaries. Paul and Silas may have by-passed these two cities because they had no synagogue. They continued on to Thessalonica, *where there was a synagogue of the Jews.*

Thessalonica was the capital of the Roman province of Macedonia, the most strategic city for the spread of the gospel in northern Greece. At this large seaport, a major sea trade route met the Via Egnatia, the major east-west road through the Balkan Peninsula. It had been a free city since 42 BC.

Many think that Paul and Silas spent only three weeks in Thessalonica because of the *three Sabbath days* mentioned in verse 2. They may have spent some days before that and after that; nevertheless, the total time cannot have been much longer.

Paul went back to his familiar pattern of preaching Christ in the synagogue first. He did not just preach; he *reasoned* [1] and *explained* and *proved* that Jesus is the Christ from the Scriptures. These words all indicate a strong and earnest appeal to the mind as well as the heart. He was fully dependent on the power of the Holy Spirit but that did not stop him from doing his utmost to persuade with human reason.

As elsewhere, Paul always went to the local synagogue first and there his message was always the same *that it was necessary for the Christ to suffer and to rise from the dead, This Jesus whom I proclaim to you is the Christ* (the Messiah). Paul probably would have cited Psalms 2, 16, 110, and Isaiah 53. His message was totally Christ-centered.

In witnessing to Jews and Muslims today, we too can and should begin with the Old Testament and then move on to the *injil,* the Muslim word for "gospel." In the case of Hindus, Buddhists, Taoists, Shintoists, and animists, we must begin with God as Creator as Paul does later in this chapter in Athens. We must challenge their worldview before we can present Jesus as Savior and Lord.

Some of the Jews were persuaded as well as some of the God-fearers (*devout Greeks*) and many of the prominent Gentile women were persuaded that

---

1   Greek *dialegomai* may indicate that there was back-and-forth discussion.

Jesus of Nazareth was indeed the promised Messiah. In all three Macedonian cities where the team preached (Philippi, Thessalonica, and Berea), prominent women were an important segment among the converts.

But some of the Jews were jealous that so many had believed the message of the three evangelists and rounded up (and no doubt hired) some idlers (*agoraioi*) in the town plaza (*agora*) and used them to start a riot that would result in bringing the matter before the civic officials. The Jews attacked the house of Jason (though he had a Greek name, he may well have been Jewish) where the three were staying. Not finding Paul and Silas, they dragged (indicating some violence) Jason and other converts before the *politarchoi*. Again, Luke gets the title of the officials of Thessalonica exactly right. Thessalonica was governed by a city council of five *politarchoi*.

There were two accusations: first that *these men had turned the world* [2]*upside down* (a bit of an exaggeration, but it does show the revolutionary power of the gospel); and second that these heretical Jews were proclaiming a new king in defiance of the Roman emperor. The latter was a serious charge, since the penalty for treason against Caesar was death. Since Paul did teach the Coming of Christ (1 Thess 1:10; 2:19; 3:13; 4:13-17; 5:1-10, 23) and later told the Thessalonian believers that this Jesus would *come in flaming fire* (2 Thess 1:7-9) *to destroy the one who opposes and exalts himself above all that is called god* (2:4), the charge of treason against Caesar was understandable. There are no "theological" or religious charges; these would have meant nothing to the civil authorities.

Proclaiming Jesus as Lord is always a threat to every other institution of power, be it religious, social, or political. That is why we have had so many martyrs in the twentieth century; the church is growing rapidly in many places, and this always threatens the powers that be.

Since the *politarchs* did not have the defendants in court, they decided to rid themselves of a troublesome problem by banishing them from the city and enforcing this decree by taking a bond from Jason (a bond is an agreement to pay a sum of money if the conditions [in this case the continued banishment of Paul and Silas] are not met). Paul put his finger on the real agent behind this decision in 1 Thess 2:18: *Satan hindered us.*

---

2   The Greek word for "world" is *oikoumēne*, "the inhabited civilized world," and in this
     context meant "the Roman Empire."

The banishment of the apostles did not stop the persecution of the believers in Thessalonica (1 Thess 1:14-16). But despite the opposition and the very short time Paul and Silas spent among them, the church in Thessalonica became a model church and a great encouragement to the Apostle Paul.

ر‎حٰٮو

Acts 17:10-15

The Noble-Minded Bereans

10 The brothers immediately sent Paul and Silas away by night to Berea, and when they arrived they went into the Jewish synagogue. 11 Now these Jews were more noble than those in Thessalonica; they received the word with all eagerness, examining the Scriptures daily to see if these things were so. 12 Many of them therefore believed, with not a few Greek women of high standing as well as men. 13 But when the Jews from Thessalonica learned that the word of God was proclaimed by Paul at Berea also, they came there too, agitating and stirring up the crowds. 14 Then the brothers immediately sent Paul off on his way to the sea, but Silas and Timothy remained there. 15 Those who conducted Paul brought him as far as Athens, and after receiving a command for Silas and Timothy to come to him as soon as possible, they departed.

Again Paul and Silas are chased out of town. They continue about 50 miles (80 km) to the west, but this time a little south of the main road (Via Egnatia), to the city of Berea. Bruce points out that Paul may have wanted to go on westward to Rome (Rom 1:13; 15:22), but about this time Claudius had ordered the expulsion of all Jews from Rome (Bruce, 373).

One wonders why Paul persisted in going to the synagogues first, but in Berea this method was wonderfully vindicated. For the first time in a synagogue visit, the Jews were more *noble* than those of other synagogues. The word *eugenēs* means "well-born" but later meant "noble," "unprejudiced," or "fair-minded." In Modern Greek this word means "polite." The Bereans eagerly evaluated the Scriptures *daily* (not just on the Sabbath day) to see if what Paul was claiming about Jesus being the Christ might be true. Again the ultimate touchstone was the prophecies of the OT. This furnishes us today with a wonderful example of how we should evaluate all preaching and teaching. Is it "according to the Scripture"?

The result was that *many* (most?) of the Jews believed as did *not a few Greek women of high standing as well as men*. Notice again how Luke spotlights women believers. (One Greek text reverses the order in an attempt to "correct" the "improper" word order.) But just as the Jews from Antioch of Pisidia had pursued Paul as far as Lystra (chapter 4), the unbelieving Jews from Thessalonica hound the missionaries out of town. Again they agitate the pagan mob against the Nazarenes. Luke is again showing the unreasonableness, stubbornness, and underhanded methods of Jews who rejected Jesus. The situation is so dangerous that Paul must leave town immediately. It is not clear why Silas and Timothy are able to stay. Paul always put a high priority on teaching and training new believers, so it was providential that Silas and Timothy could be left for this purpose. Timothy was also able to serve as a messenger between the churches of Macedonia and Paul (1 Thess 3:6). Later both Timothy and Silas join Paul in Corinth (18:5).

This time the situation is so dangerous that Paul must not only leave the town but also leave the entire region. The brothers escort him to Athens. Some have thought that Paul went from the coast (perhaps from Dium) by ship to Athens. However, Luke always gives the ports of departure and arrival when he describes a sea-voyage and neither is mentioned here. It is more likely that they took the long overland route to Athens. Taking Paul to the sea may have been a trick to make pursuers think Paul had departed by ship.

Lessons for Life

1. Preaching the gospel is not only an emotional appeal; there must also be the persuasion of the mind.
2. Preachers must appeal to the Scriptures and hearers must evaluate their messages from the Scripture.
3. We can expect opposition and false charges when we preach the gospel.

Acts 17:16-34

Paul's Encounter With the Athenian Philosophers

17:16-21 Preaching in the Marketplace

16 Now while Paul was waiting for them at Athens, his spirit was provoked within him as he saw that the city was full of idols. 17 So he reasoned in the synagogue with the Jews and the devout persons, and in the marketplace every day with those who happened to be there. 18 Some of the Epicurean and Stoic philosophers also conversed with him. And some said, "What does this babbler wish to say?" Others said, "He seems to be a preacher of foreign divinities"—because he was preaching Jesus and the resurrection. 19 And they took him and brought him to the Areopagus, saying, "May we know what this new teaching is that you are presenting? 20 For you bring some strange things to our ears. We wish to know therefore what these things mean." 21 Now all the Athenians and the foreigners who lived there would spend their time in nothing except telling or hearing something new.

This story is one of the most interesting accounts in the Book of Acts. First it takes place in the most famous cultural and intellectual center of the ancient world, Athens. Second, the pattern of synagogue preaching is broken by the witness in the *agora* (marketplace) and the speech before the Areopagus, the religious court of Athens. Third, though Paul preaches Christ, he does so in an entirely different way than in the previous evangelistic sermons that Luke has related to us.

The political and cultural peak of Athens was now three to four hundred years in the past. Politically Athens was conquered by Rome in 146 BC and had lost population, in Paul's time down to between 10,000 and 30,000. Culturally there were no longer architects like Phidias (who built the Parthenon), playwrights like Euripedes, or philosophers like Socrates and Plato. Nevertheless, Athens was a free city and still highly respected as the premier university city of the Roman Empire. Philo wrote that the Athenians were "keenest in intellect" and Josephus said that the Athenians were "the most god-fearing of the Greeks." Even today the Parthenon in Athens is a splendid reminder of the glory that was Greece.

Paul no doubt had time to tour the magnificent sights of the city and maybe even attend a play by Sophocles in the theater of Dionysius in the shadow of the Parthenon. But Luke mentions none of these things. What Paul **saw** (the Greek word *theoreō* indicates a careful look and long consideration) was a city filled with idols. The word *kateidōlos* occurs only here in Greek literature and means literally "under idols;" we might say "submerged in idolatry." There were over 3,000 temples, shrines, statues, and altars. Here were all the gods of the Greek pantheon carved in marble and ivory and overlaid with gold and silver. Paul had to pass a forest of *herms*, square pillars topped with heads of the god Hermes, to enter the *agora*. This greatly *provoked* him. The word used is *paroxunō*. As John Stott points out, this is the same word used in the Greek OT for the Holy One of Israel being *provoked* by the sin of man, particularly idolatry.[3] This was not a sudden fit of exasperation but a deep grief that moved Paul to action.

Those of us who have lived in a Christian culture for many generations may have forgotten the terrible burden that polytheism imposes upon its subjects. Kanzō Uchimura, one of the great Japanese Christians of the Meiji Era (1868-1911), describes eloquently his pre-Christian "spiritual darkness" and "gross superstition":

> I believed, and that sincerely, that there dwelt in each of the innumerable temples its god, jealous over its jurisdiction, ready with punishment to any transgressor that fell under his displeasure." Then Uchimura lists the various gods and their various stipulations: "One God would impose upon me abstinence from the use of eggs, another from beans, till after I had made all my vows, many of my boyish delicacies were entered upon the prohibition list." After he became a Christian (a fascinating story well worth reading), he described the blessed relief from paganism:

> The practical advantage of the new faith was evident to me at once. . . I was taught that there was not but *one* God in the Universe, and not many—over eight millions—as I had formerly believed. The Christian

---

3   Deut 32:16 and Isa 65:2-3 are typical of 52 uses of the word in the OT. Stott, *Acts*, 278.

monotheism laid its axe at the root of all my superstitions. All the vows I had made, and the manifold forms of worship with which I had been attempting to appease my angry gods, could now be dispensed with by owning this *one* God . . . No more use of saying my long prayers every morning to the four groups of gods situated in the four points of the compass; of repeating a long prayer to every temple I passed in the streets; and of observing this day for this god and that day for that god . . . Monotheism made me a new man. *I resumed my beans and eggs.* I thought I comprehended the whole of Christianity, so inspiring was the idea of one God.[4]

Those of us who live in cities like Kamakura in Japan, or Bangkok in Thailand, or Varanasi in India, may become accustomed to the temples and idols surrounding us. We are told that they must be respected as great art. (There is no denying that many of them **are** great art.) We are no longer disturbed, and we are little burdened for overwhelming masses under demonic control. We do not want to "rock the boat" with anything so crass as pointing out the inadequacy of their idolatry. But notice the subtlety and grace with which Paul suggests that their "unknown gods" need to be replaced by something better.

Even in Athens Paul went first to the synagogue and *reasoned* (again the same word as in 17:2, often indicating a give-and-take style of debate), after his usual pattern. But Luke does not give the results. It is possible some of the converts mentioned in verse 34 came from the synagogue. But for the first time it is recorded that he also went into the large *agora* every day and in both conversation with by-passers and what we would today call open-air evangelism, *preached the good news about Jesus and the resurrection.* Since Paul was all alone, and had no friends to stand with him, this was a remarkable display of zeal and courage.

Today our Christian conscience is being smothered by the idolatry that surrounds us. There is the bombardment of the modern world: lurid TV, magazines, and cinema flaunting idols of sex, food, drugs, designer clothes, new cars, and exotic holidays. The gods of this age have blinded our minds to the glory of Christ (2 Cor 4:4). Modern paganism is obsessed with self-sufficiency and inner peace but is blind to its real source. Secular consumerism and hedonism are the Epicureanism of our age.

---

4   Kanzō Uchimura, *How I Became a Christian: Out of My Diary*, Tokyo, Kyōbunkan, 1971, from 1895 Japanese edition, 22-23 and 28-29.

Ruins of the agora (marketplace) of ancient Athens.

The Parthenon was completed in 438 BC. In the time of Paul, it contained a huge statue of the goddess Athena.

The lovely maidens of the Erechtheion, a small temple near the Parthenon, dating from about 430 BC.

Where are our *agoras* today, places where people gather to relax, loaf, converse? Is there a local café, or pub, or park, street corner, or shopping mall in our area? Do we ever take the gospel outside the four walls of our churches? Do we have the Spirit-given courage to do this type of thing? May God give us more of the same spirit Paul had!

Some of the Epicurean and Stoic philosophers also conversed with him. Even after the passage of more than two millennia, the Epicureans and Stoics are still studied in courses of the history of philosophy and these words can be found in our English dictionaries. The **Epicureans** believed that the gods were far away and cared nothing for mankind. They denied life after death or judgment in the afterlife. Their chief virtue was *ataraxia*, a state of mind denoting tranquility, even in the face of life's reverses, and that the ideal life is to devote oneself to pleasure. Today the word "epicurean" means one who indulges the pleasures of the flesh, but originally the Epicureans put more emphasis on the pleasures of the mind. Diogenes summed up their philosophy of life as "Nothing to fear in god, nothing to fear in death, Good (pleasure) can be attained, Evil (pain) can be endured."[5]

The **Stoics** agreed with the Epicureans that there is no afterlife and that the gods do not dwell in temples made by man. The Stoics believed that the deity (*logos*) was the soul of the material world as the human mind is the soul of its body. *Logos* determines the course of all things, and the world goes through endless cycles of destruction and rebirth. Their ethic was "follow nature; follow reason." They had a higher sense of duty and virtue than the Epicureans. The chief virtue of life was *autarcheia*, independence and self-sufficiency, even in the face of suffering. (Being impassive in the face of misfortune is the meaning of the word today.) Neither philosophy believed in a personal God, just as skeptics and atheists today. How modern much of this sounds!

The Stoics and the Epicureans were contemptuous of Paul's witness in the marketplace. The word translated *babbler* is *spermologos*, literally a "seed gatherer," and meant a sparrow or small bird that eats seeds. In Athenian slang it came to mean one who picks up scraps of knowledge here and there and misapplies it in a ragbag of nonsense. Most commentators think the philosophers misunderstood Paul to be preaching two new gods, one Jesus, and the other (his female consort?) *Anastasis*, (the word for resurrection). As

---

5   Witherington, 514.

in Lystra, the message is badly misunderstood by the hearers. In Lystra these superstitious rustics thought that Paul and Barnabas were gods; in Athens, the cultured despisers thought Paul was preaching new gods. Even today our non-Christian hearers misunderstand, misrepresent, and disdain our message.

The philosophers took Paul to "the Areopagus" so they could hear more clearly away from the confusion of the bustling *agora*. If one climbs up to the rocky crag Areopagus high above the ancient ruins of the *agora* to the west of the Parthenon, one can see a plaque commemorating this event. But for a number of reasons we believe that the "Areopagus" (which means "the Hill of Ares") was not this hill which would take the group at least an hour of hard climbing to ascend, but the ancient court or council by that name which met at the Royal Porch (*stoa*) in the northwest corner of the *agora*. In verse 22 Paul is made to stand *in the midst* of the Areopagus and that expression is strange if the hilltop is meant. Similarly in verse 33, he *went out from* the Areopagus, which describes an exit from a building, not a descent from a mountain.

This was not a formal legal trial but an informal inquiry. The ancient Areopagus Court, in Paul's time much diminished in its powers, still had authority over cases of homicide, education, and **religion**. One of the charges is ominous: preaching foreign deities. Socrates had been put to death by this very court for that very offense and for "corrupting the morals of the youth of Athens." Josephus writes that "the penalty (in Athens) for introducing a foreign god was death."[6] It seems that this was a hearing to determine whether this new religion was a threat to Athenian society. On the other hand, verse 21 seems to indicate that one of their chief motives was curiosity. Like many modern people who are not serious inquirers, the Athenian philosophers loved to debate novel religious ideas, keeping real commitment at a comfortable distance.

17:22-34 Paul's Speech in the Areopagus Court

22 *So Paul, standing in the midst of the Areopagus, said: "Men of Athens, I perceive that in every way you are very religious.* **23** *For as I passed along and observed the objects of your worship, I found also an altar with this inscription: 'To the unknown god.' What therefore you worship as unknown, this I proclaim to you.* **24** *The God who made the world*

---

6   *Against Apion* 2.262-268. Cited from Schnabel, 727.

and everything in it, being Lord of heaven and earth, does not live in temples made by man, 25 nor is he served by human hands, as though he needed anything, since he himself gives to all mankind life and breath and everything. 26 And he made from one man every nation of mankind to live on all the face of the earth, having determined allotted periods and the boundaries of their dwelling place, 27 that they should seek God, and perhaps feel their way toward him and find him. Yet he is actually not far from each one of us, 28 for "'In him we live and move and have our being'; as even some of your own poets have said, "'For we are indeed his offspring.'

29 Being then God's offspring, we ought not to think that the divine being is like gold or silver or stone, an image formed by the art and imagination of man. 30 The times of ignorance God overlooked, but now he commands all people everywhere to repent, 31 because he has fixed a day on which he will judge the world in righteousness by a man whom he has appointed; and of this he has given assurance to all by raising him from the dead."

32 Now when they heard of the resurrection of the dead, some mocked. But others said, "We will hear you again about this." 33 So Paul went out from their midst. 34 But some men joined him and believed, among whom also were Dionysius the Areopagite and a woman named Damaris and others with them.

This passage is a marvelous example of how Paul could, among the most sophisticated Greeks, become "a Greek to the Greeks." His speech uses a slightly elegant style of Greek (impossible, of course, to convey in translation), with alliteration and assonance,[7] following Greek rules of rhetoric,[8] replete with references to classical poets, and starting with a superb "point of contact." Though clothed in language that would have been intelligible to this audience, the essential religious content is thoroughly Jewish and Christian, and does not shrink from hard truths the Athenian philosophers would find unpalatable.

---

7   Alliteration is repetition of words beginning with the same consonant sound or letter: for example *pistin paraschōn pasin* in v. 31. Assonance is repetition of words of similar internal sounds such as *zoein kai pnoein* in v. 25.

8   See Witherington, page 518. The *exordium* (opening), v. 22-23a; the *propositio* (the point he wishes to prove), v. 23b; the *probatio* (argument or proof), v. 24-29; the *peroratio* (concluding exhortation), v. 30-31. Paul also used Greek rhetoric before Jews, as we saw in the sermon in Antioch of Pisidia (chapter 13), and as we will see in a series of trials before secular rulers.

The point of contact was an altar Paul had observed in his tour of the city inscribed to an "Unknown god" (*Agnōstō Theō*). This inscription both demonstrated his remark that the Athenians were either remarkably pious or very superstitious (the word *deisidaimonesteros* can mean either) and furnished an opening to the subject of the One True God. It shows the pathetic fear and futility behind polytheism. The Athenians tried to appease all the gods, but lest one be neglected and curse the city, they also built an altar to "an unknown god." Many of the commentators list the references to such altars in ancient literature and archaeology.[9] We ourselves have seen a block of marble in the ruins of Pergamum (present day Bergamo in Turkey) bearing the inscription "*Theois Agn[nōstois]*" ("to unknown gods"). The portion in brackets is missing but *Agnōstois* is a very likely restoration of the missing letters. The remark did not insult the philosophers, for they too considered themselves above the superstitions of the uneducated populace.

While visiting Pergamum in present day Turkey, I was able to photograph an inscription "To unknown gods," similar to an altar that Paul noticed in Athens. Half of the word "unknown" is missing.

What therefore you worship as unknown, this I proclaim to you. The word *worship* might better be translated with a softer word like "venerate" or "honor." The veneration was simply building the altar; it is not likely that

9   Bruce, 380-381, is most thorough.

sacrifices or regular prayers were offered to this "unknown god." The bold statement "I am going to proclaim to you the unknown god" was the main point of the speech.

What follows seems more like notes of main points because no proof or explanation is offered. Paul simply assumes the God of Creation when he puts creation in the relative clause *who made the world and everything in it.* Was there more of an explanation preceding this sentence? The Greeks did not have a clear idea of creation. The Stoics believed that *Logos* indwelt all things and that the physical world was its body. The Epicurians followed the older teaching of Democritus that the original elements of the universe, called atoms, moved through the void by themselves to form the world as we know it. (These ideas sound very similar to modern naturalism and evolutionary thought.) Nevertheless, the philosophers do not seem to dispute the point of a Creator God. In modern mission we need to establish the concept of *the God who made the world and everything in it* before we proclaim the God of salvation.

Paul quickly moves on to make seven points about this Creator God: 1) He is Lord of heaven and earth and therefore 2) He does not dwell in man-made temples 3) He does not need to be served by mankind but on the contrary 4) He is (continually) giving to mankind life and breath and all that is necessary to sustain that life. 5) He made all peoples (*ethnoi*) from one man for two purposes: 6) To dwell on all the earth in their appointed places and appointed times and 7) To seek the Creator-Sustainer-Sovereign God.

The speech majors less on God as Creator and more on his relationship to mankind. Paul does not mention abstract terms or attributes of God such as love, mercy, and omnipotence, but instead describes God by what he **did and does**. The God that Paul presents here is completely the opposite of the Greek ideas of the gods who **did** very little and lived in shrines and temples and needed to be appeased by constant sacrifices.

The Greeks believed that they had sprung from their native soil and that they were superior to all other peoples whom they called "barbarians." In many cultures we quite frequently encounter a nationalistic or ethnic pride that says in effect, "We do not need the Christian God of the West. We have no connection with your God. He is OK for you, but we have our own religion." The thrust of the speech before the Areopagus is that, on the contrary, God continually sustains your life and existence and made your nation from one man and you have a responsibility to seek this God. In our evangelistic preaching we frequently fail to establish the relationship of our audience to the True God and their responsibility to him. But without this foundation preaching salvation is meaningless.

Paul says that though it is not easy to find God (it is like groping [*pseilafaō*, a verb often used of the blind]), yet he is not far away. He is not in the *intermedia* (where the Greeks thought the gods dwelt in splendid isolation from the lower world of suffering where mankind dwelt), but he is *not far from each one of us*. The general *all mankind* has become the very personal *each one of us*.

Now Paul finishes his argument with two quotations from **their** "scriptures," two Greek poets. The Greek philosophers, of course, even though they were foremost in the world in their day in profound thought and wisdom, were ignorant of God's revelation in the Hebrew Scriptures. No use quoting Genesis or naming Adam (the *one man* of verse 26). The Greeks did believe that their poets spoke by a kind of "inspiration" from deities called the Muses.

Three things surprise us here. It is like discovering wholly unknown facets of a person we thought we knew fairly well. First, it is surprising that Paul even knew about passages from the Greek poets, let alone be able to quote them accurately from memory. Second, that a strict Pharisee like Paul would bother studying the godless pagan poets of Greece. Third that he should be so "careless" as to invite confusion of Zeus with Yahweh.

To consider point three, the phrase, *For in him we live and move and have our being* is a line from a hymn to Zeus by Epimenides of Crete.[10] *We are his offspring* is a quotation from Aratus, a native of Paul's hometown of Tarsus. The word *his* refers to Zeus. Paul takes a risk here that his audience will think he is talking about the head god in the Greek pantheon or assume the Stoic ideas of a pantheistic Zeus. Perhaps he knows that everything else he is saying about the true God will prevent any such confusion.

Christianity from the beginning has adopted pagan words for God and filled them with new meaning. Our English word "god" was originally polytheistic, and the Japanese Bible's word for "God" is *kami*, still in common

---

10   See the complete text in Greek in Bruce, p. 384. Interestingly Paul quotes the second line of the hymn, "Cretans are always liars, wicked beasts, lazy gluttons" in a completely different context in Tit 1:12.

use for the "Eight Million gods" of Shinto. The Greek word for both the pagan gods and the One True God is *theos*.

Missionaries and evangelists today usually do not study, let alone quote in an evangelistic message, any such thing as the Koran, the Bhagavad Gita, or the sutras of Buddhism. But this passage teaches us that we would be wise to master the literature, especially the religious literature, of the country we are attempting to reach for Christ and to quote it if that literature will illustrate our point. No religion is 100% error; it would never have survived if it were completely wrong. So we can always find many elements of truth in the proverbs, poems, and traditions of our audience to support our message. Nothing touches the heart like a quotation from the soul of a people; it will bring a knowing smile and a grudging nod.

Verse 29 concludes the argument and returns to the point of verse 24. If God sustains our life and we cannot live or move or exist without him, and if we are his children, how foolish it is to think that we can, even with the genius of human skill and reason, make "gods" out of gold, silver, and stone! However much the philosophers might have frowned at some of Paul's previous points, they would be nodding their heads vigorously at this point. If Paul had closed there, they might have applauded him warmly. But he goes on to "spoil" the speech with his *peroratio* or concluding exhortation in verses 30 and 31.

> *The times of ignorance God overlooked, but now he commands all people everywhere to repent, because he has fixed a day on which he will judge the world in righteousness by a man whom he has appointed; and of this he has given assurance to all by raising him from the dead.*

The theme of ignorance is again mentioned, as in verse 23. Does this mean that people living in the times of ignorance will be saved? If this is the same Paul who wrote Rom 1:18-32, it cannot mean that their ignorance of God will give them a free pass into heaven. God's "overlooking" of the sin of pre-Christian generations does not mean he condoned their sin or forgave their sin during the times of ignorance but rather that he did not punish those sins at that time. This is similar to what Paul said to the pagan Lycaonians in Acts 14:16: *In past generations he allowed all the nations to walk in their own ways.*

But now refers to an important shift in salvation history marked by what Paul has not yet mentioned, the death and resurrection of Jesus the Son of God. Because of that colossal event, not only the Athenians hearing this message, but *all people everywhere* must **repent** because one day each one will stand before the Man who will righteously judge all mankind.

Many people seek God only when they are in trouble. As the Japanese saying has it, *"Komatta toki Kamidanomi"* ("In time of trouble invoke the deities"). The implication is that no one needs God or religion unless one is in trouble. Why put up an umbrella unless it is raining? In such a culture, we preachers tend to fall into a pattern of presenting the gospel only as the solution to people's problems. What corrects this lopsided gospel is pointing out the fact that God **commands** repentance. It is not an optional offer subject to the whim and preference or perceived needs of sinners.

The day has been appointed and the Man has been appointed. The proof is in the resurrection of that Man. Paul had mentioned the name Jesus in the *agora* (v. 18), but here it is just *a man whom he has appointed. And of this he has given assurance to all by raising him from the dead.* The mention of resurrection broke up the meeting with ridicule and scorn.

Did not Paul realize that at the founding of the Court of Areopagus, the god Apollo denied resurrection? "When once a man dies, there is no resurrection."[11] Paul has violated the founding charter of this court! To the Greeks the soul was divine, the body was earthly and evil, and any resurrection of this body was not only impossible, but disgusting.

Was Paul's speech before the Areopagus a failure? The philosophers laughed him out of court. No church was born in Athens at this time. A popular view apparently first proposed by William Ramsay was that when Paul got to Corinth, he repented of his failure to preach the cross and of depending on *excellence of speech or wisdom* in Athens and that this is the background for 1 Cor 2:1-2. This theory cannot be disproved but it must be pointed out that the speech before the Areopagus was not the complete gospel but was more what we today call "pre-evangelism." It must also be noticed that there were **some** converts. *But some men joined him and believed, among whom also were Dionysius the Areopagite and a woman named Damaris and others with them.*

None of the philosophers believed, but one member of the Court of Areopagus named Dionysius did believe. A woman named Damaris must have heard the gospel in the synagogue or the *agora* and Luke does not fail to mention the chief woman convert. There may have been other women among

---

11   Bruce, 387, quoting some lines from Aeschylus in *Eumenides.*

the *others* since the masculine gender of that word could also include females. Paul's work in Athens was not a failure. Within a few decades a strong church was born there.

Lessons for Life

1. This chapter is a wonderful example of "buying up" opportunities to preach the gospel.
2. What is the *agora* in our community?
3. We need Paul's rare combination of intellectual learning and evangelistic zeal.
4. We must know and use the religious literature and proverbs of the people we are trying to reach.
5. In mission work we must begin where the people are instead of using a canned "one size fits all" approach.
6. We cannot preach the God of salvation until we establish the God of creation.
7. Our gospel is not just a "positive message." It must tactfully and tastefully make clear the distinctions with errors such as idolatry.
8. Repentance is not optional. It is commanded by the God who will judge all mankind.
9. We do not preach the resurrection enough in evangelism. It is an essential part of every sermon in the book of Acts.

ACTS 18

MINISTRY IN CORINTH

Acts 18:1-17

Putting Down Roots in Corinth

From the faded glory of Athens, the most important city of Greece culturally, Paul now moved on, only fifty miles (80 km) to the west to the most populous and dynamic **commercial** city of Greece, Corinth. Corinth was by far the most strategic and cosmopolitan city Paul had yet visited. Here one could rub shoulders with Persians and Iberians, Carthaginians and Gauls in a way second only to great Rome itself. That may be why God in his providence had allowed Paul to be ejected from lesser cities and to settle down unmolested in Corinth for eighteen months.

Corinth had been completely destroyed in the Roman invasion of 146 BC, lain in ruins for a century, and then been completely rebuilt as a Roman colony by Julius Caesar in 44 BC. It commanded both the north-south route through the narrow neck of land connecting the Pelopennese to the south with the heartland of Achaia to the north, and the east-west traffic by sea between the Saronic Gulf on the east and the Corinthian Gulf on the west. Today a canal 3.9 miles long cut hundreds of feet down to sea-level joins the two gulfs. In ancient times one either had to go 200 miles around the Pelopennese or transfer one's cargo to wooden carriages that could be dragged along a road with grooves for the wagon wheels.

Corinth was also **a great religious center** with shrines and temples dedicated to *many gods and many lords* (1 Cor 8:5). Among them the most prominent was the temple of Aphrodite on the summit of *Acrocorinthos* looming 2,000 feet high to the south of the city. At the foot of the mountain was a temple to Melicertes, the patron god of seamen. In the ruins of the ancient town, a few columns of the temple to Apollo still stand.

Corinth was also an important **athletic center**. Every two years it hosted the Isthmian Games in honor of Poseidon (Neptune), the god of the sea. It was in his first letter to the Corinthian Christians that Paul used the famous metaphor of the Christian discipline as *running in a race* (1 Cor 9:24-27).

All these factors enabled Corinth to become a notorious **center for sexual profligacy**. Strabo claimed that the temple of Aphrodite boasted 1,000 cult prostitutes. Even by the permissive standards of the ancient world, Corinth was infamous for loose morals. In Greek to "Corinthianize" was to live a grossly immoral life.

No wonder Paul came to Corinth *with weakness, in fear, and in much trembling*. Stott points out that this was the reason Paul determined to refuse to use *persuasive words of men's wisdom* (Greek rhetoric), but instead preach nothing among them *but Jesus Christ and him crucified*. (1 Cor 2:1-5). For us today as well, the only thing that will prevail over overwhelming spiritual darkness is "Jesus Christ and him crucified." The idolatry and immorality of secular Corinth also explain why the Corinthian Church had such terrible problems with both.

18:1-6 The Team Gathers in Corinth

1 After this Paul left Athens and went to Corinth. 2 And he found a Jew named Aquila, a native of Pontus, recently come from Italy with his wife Priscilla, because Claudius had commanded all the Jews to leave Rome. And he went to see them, 3 and because he was of the same trade he stayed with them and worked, for they were tentmakers by trade. 4 And he reasoned in the synagogue every Sabbath, and tried to persuade Jews and Greeks.

5 When Silas and Timothy arrived from Macedonia, Paul was occupied with the word, testifying to the Jews that the Christ was Jesus. 6 And when they opposed and reviled him, he shook out his garments and said to them, "Your blood be on your own heads! I am innocent. From now on I will go to the Gentiles."

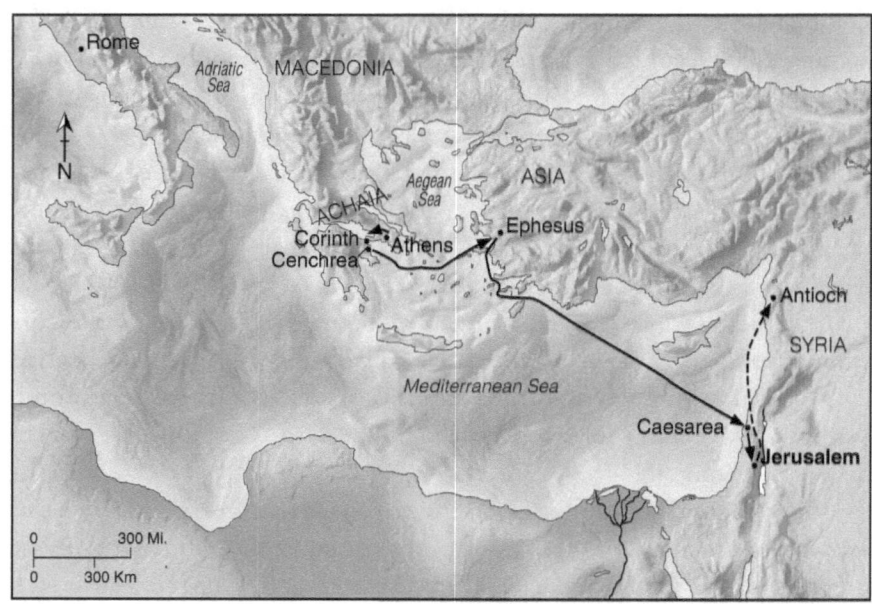

Ministry in Corinth and Ephesus

When he had to, Paul evangelized alone, as he did at Athens. But in the strategic and formidable city of Corinth, God encouraged him by assembling capable and loyal helpers. If the great apostle Paul needed human help, how much more do we?

Again and again we will see what a blessing this remarkable couple, Aquila and Priscilla, was to the baby churches! How encouraged Paul was to meet them! They were of the same trade (tentmaking), the same faith (Christian Jews), and maybe even the same tribe (as Manuscript D has it) as Paul.

The sentence *Claudius had commanded all the Jews to leave Rome* gives us a point of contact with Roman history. The Roman historian Suetonius (Life of Claudius 25:4) wrote that it was because "the Jews were making constant disturbances at the instigation of Chrestus." "Chrestus" seems to be a mistaken spelling of "Christ." This seems to mean that the gospel of Christ was causing such dissension among the Jews of Rome that the dispute became a public nuisance, and the impulsive Claudius ordered all Jews to leave Rome. The expulsion order occurred in the year 49. The German scholar Harnack speculated that Priscilla and Aquila had been foundation members of the church in Rome and that they were the co-authors of the book of Hebrews (Bruce, 390).

The fact that Paul went back to his trade of tentmaking shows that he had run out of funds. He may have found employment in the shop of Aquila and Priscilla weaving the coarse goat hair of his native province into a black cloth called cilicium. Tents and awnings would have been in great demand during the Isthmian Games and may have had some nautical applications. While their hands were busy making tents, the three artisans must have had marvelous conversations about their conversions, the traditions of the life of Christ, and "war stories" of the battle for the gospel in Rome and Anatolia and Macedonia and Athens.

Paul spent his weekdays making tents and his Sabbath days reasoning in the synagogue that Jesus of Nazareth was the Messiah. Today one can see a white marble lintel in the ruins of Corinth inscribed Synagogē Hebraion in Greek capital letters. This may have been the very stone Paul and his friends passed under to enter the synagogue every Sabbath day.

When his partners Silas and Timothy arrived from Macedonia, they probably brought with them contributions from the churches in Macedonia (Phil 4:15-16), which enabled Paul to devote full time to gospel preaching.

But here too, as in every synagogue, the Jews eventually opposed and reviled Paul's "heresy." Paul cut his ties with them in the traditional emphatic manner of shaking out his garments and again turned to the Gentiles. The Gentiles were not very far away. In fact, to the exasperation of the unbelieving Jews, he only moved his evangelistic operations next door! Today many of us are so fearful of confrontation or offending people that we can hardly imagine the strong language Paul used in bidding the synagogue farewell. We must be careful lest our tact become a cover for our cowardice.

18:7-11 Eighteen Months of Harvest in Corinth

7 And he left there and went to the house of a man named Titius Justus, a worshiper of God. His house was next door to the synagogue. 8 Crispus, the ruler of the synagogue, believed in the Lord, together with his entire household. And many of the Corinthians hearing Paul believed and were baptized. 9 And the Lord said to Paul one night in a vision, "Do not be afraid, but go on speaking and do not be silent, 10 for I am with you, and no one will attack you to harm you, for I have many in this city who are my people." 11 And he stayed a year and six months, teaching the word of God among them.

God encouraged his servants in three ways. First, he provided, through Titius Justus, a "god-fearer" Gentile and no doubt a convert to Christ or at least a serious inquirer, a place for the emerging church to meet. Second he yielded many conversions, including Crispus the synagogue ruler and his entire family. Third, the Lord spoke again to Paul to encourage him to stay.

Church planting missionaries are always requesting prayer for the three "P's:" People, Place (to meet), and Pastor. In Corinth God provided the first two. **Many** who were hearing were as a result of hearing were believing, and as a result of believing, were being baptized. As always in Acts, baptism was the normal and expected sign of genuine faith. The past continuous (imperfect) tenses of these verbs show that the growth of the church was a process that took a little time. The text seems to indicate that the conversion of Crispus and his household was a key to the conversion of many others. We always pray for key converts in church planting. Were Gaius and Erastus (Rom 16:23) among them?[1]

Latin inscription in Corinth to one of the believers, "Erastus, city treasurer (Aedile)," mentioned in Romans 16:23. A remarkable corroboration of that passage.

---

1   There is a large deeply incised inscription commemorating *Erastus Aedile* in the ruins of Corinth to this day. *Aedile* was the title of an official who was in charge of public buildings, the police, and other municipal functions.

An inscription that might have been the lintel of the entrance to the synagogue in Corinth. The first half of the word "synagogue" is missing. One can make out the Greek capital letters ΓΩΓΗ ΗΕΒΡ (GOGE HEBR). Traces of Jewish synagogues in ancient ruins are rare.

This is the judgment seat (Bema) where Paul was arraigned before Proconsul Gallio.

Three times Acts records direct revelation from God to Paul. (Four times if we include Paul's conversion.) In Troas (16:9-10) the Lord Jesus gave critical guidance. Here in Corinth he gave Paul vital encouragement. And during the storm on the voyage to Rome, God gave Paul reassurance that he would indeed arrive in Rome (27:23-24).

Why did Paul need special encouragement at this point in Corinth? First, though there has been much fruit during his work up to this point, Paul has been run out of every town and synagogue he has visited, often under life-threatening conditions. Though a few believed in Athens, he was really laughed out of town. Second, the Corinthian correspondence shows that Paul was often under much stress, bordering on depression, in his relations with the fruitful but taxing work in Corinth. We have already mentioned 1 Cor 2:1-5 and the incredible pressure of the ungodly atmosphere in Corinth. Later there would be serious problems in the church that form the content of 1 Corinthians. 2 Corinthians is full of Paul's despair and anxiety over the situation in Corinth (see especially 2 Cor 2:1-13). Perhaps God, knowing the pressure of Paul's past persecution, and anticipating the future pressures of the work in Corinth, appeared to him in a dream to prevent his collapse.

The Lord said *Do not be afraid but go on speaking and do not be silent, for I am with you* . . . Even a zealous witness can become so discouraged or fearful that he or she lapses into silence. The Lord then gives two reasons. First, he promised that *no one will attack you or harm you.* When the charges did come the proconsul quickly dismissed them. Second, *I have many people in this city.* The thought that the Lord has many as yet unsaved people who belong to him in a given location has encouraged many a missionary. The result was that Paul could settle down and spend eighteen months teaching the converts. In mission work evangelism is not enough; the converts must be thoroughly grounded in their faith.

18:12-17 Paul Before Proconsul Gallio

> *12 But when Gallio was proconsul of Achaia, the Jews made a united attack on Paul and brought him before the tribunal, 13 saying, "This man is persuading people to worship God contrary to the law." 14 But when Paul was about to open his mouth, Gallio said to the Jews, "If it were a matter of wrongdoing or vicious crime, O Jews, I would have reason to accept your complaint. 15 But since it is a matter of questions about words and names and your own law, see to it yourselves. I refuse to be a judge of these things." 16 And he drove them from the tribunal. 17 And they all seized Sosthenes, the ruler of the synagogue, and beat him in front of the tribunal. But Gallio paid no attention to any of this.*

Gallio furnishes us with another confirmation point from secular history and an important benchmark to date Paul's ministry. Gallio was the son of the elder Seneca and the brother of Seneca the philosopher.[2] We know from fragments of an inscription found in Delphi mentioning "my friend Gallio proconsul of Achaia" that dates from the twenty-sixth acclamation of Claudius as emperor that Gallio became Proconsul of Achaia no later than May 51.[3] Again Luke gets the title right. Achaia (the southern half of present-day Greece) had been governed as an imperial province for which the correct title was *praefect* (as was the case with Pilate in Judea) until 44 AD. Since then the correct title was *proconsul,* just as Luke records here. By May of 52 AD, Gallio had left office for health reasons, so Paul's appearance before the judgment seat of Gallio has to date within that year.

The Jews could stand no more. They had lost the ruler of their synagogue and no doubt many parishioners to this pernicious sect. They attempted to bring a legal charge against Paul as they had done in every other city where he had split their synagogues. The charge was that Paul was *persuading* the people to worship God (not *the gods*) outside the law. The law they were referring to is not Roman law but the Torah, the Law of God.

Paul opened his mouth to defend himself but before any words came out, Gallio broke in and dismissed the case. He refused to get involved in a religious dispute over which he had no legitimate jurisdiction. For the first time, Paul is completely vindicated by a civil authority. It was just as the Lord had promised; this time the charge did not stick, and the accusers got their just reward.

One can see a good portion of the remains of the *bēma* where Paul stood before Gallio in the *agora* of ancient Corinth to this day.

Who were *they* who beat Sosthenes? It seems unlikely that either the Jews or the Christians would beat the ruler of the synagogue. It is much more likely that these were either the marshals responsible for order in the court (the bearers of the *fasces*?) or bystanders who hated the Jews and saw a chance to give them a good thrashing for bringing a frivolous lawsuit. Gallio no doubt smiled in amusement.

Was this the same Sosthenes mentioned in 1 Cor 1:1 as the co-originator of that epistle? If so, he changed from an enemy of Paul to a trusted disciple

---

2   See more detail in Bruce, 394.

3   The evidence is very complex. See Bruce, 395, for details.

and fellow worker of Paul, and Paul robbed the synagogue of a chief elder. Despite the fierce opposition in Corinth, the gospel is triumphing through the power and protection of God.

⌒ℓℯ⌒

Acts: 18:18-23

Transition From Corinth to Ephesus

18 After this, Paul stayed many days longer and then took leave of the brothers and set sail for Syria, and with him Priscilla and Aquila. At Cenchreae he had cut his hair, for he was under a vow. 19 And they came to Ephesus, and he left them there, but he himself went into the synagogue and reasoned with the Jews. 20 When they asked him to stay for a longer period, he declined. 21 But on taking leave of them he said, "I will return to you if God wills," and he set sail from Ephesus.

22 When he had landed at Caesarea, he went up and greeted the church, and then went down to Antioch. 23 After spending some time there, he departed and went from one place to the next through the region of Galatia and Phrygia, strengthening all the disciples.

Here Luke abbreviates a period of about a year and a half and travel of at least 1,750 miles (2,800 km). The passage serves as a transition between the two most important cities of Paul's missionary work, Corinth and Ephesus. It marks the transition between the second and third missionary journeys, though Luke does not seem to divide his material that way.[4]

Gallio arrived in Corinth in May or June of 51 AD and Paul most likely appeared before his *bēma* shortly after. If he stayed *many days* after that in Corinth (18:18), and the total time he spent in Corinth was eighteen months (18:11), it seems most likely that he sailed for Syria via Ephesus when the sailing season opened in early March 52 AD. It is remarkable that this request to stay came from the synagogue even **after** he had reasoned with them about Jesus the Messiah.

In verse 22 *the church* he *went up to* was not the church in Caesarea but the church in Jerusalem. The words "go up" and "go down" are a standard reference to travel to and from Jerusalem. (The same way of speaking of travel up to and down from Tokyo, the capital of Japan, is rigidly maintained in Japanese speech.) He only greets the church there and then hurries on 350 miles (560 km) north to Antioch where he spent *some time* there on missionary "furlough." This period may have lasted until the spring of 53 when travel was again possible through the Cilician Gates and through the highlands of Anatolia. As on the start of the second journey, Paul spent quite a bit of time *strengthening all the disciples* in Derbe, Lystra, Iconium, Antioch of Pisidia, and then proceeded on to Ephesus, the capital of the Province of Asia, the very thing he had been forbidden by the Spirit to do some four years earlier.

There are several unanswered questions in this section. Why does he go to so much trouble to visit Jerusalem and Antioch? Why not stay and minister in receptive Ephesus? Why did the Paul who preached the gospel of grace take a Jewish vow which involved cropping (the word means "cut with scissors," not "shave with a razor") his head? Why is the visit to the church in Jerusalem (his fifth visit to Jerusalem) not dealt with in more detail?

We cannot answer the other questions, but the haircut and the vow deserve some discussion. Most commentators think that this was the Nazirite Vow described in Num 6:1 and following. Paul may have been a Christian and

---

4   This whole passage is still part of Panel 5 of Acts, marked off by summary statements at 16:5 and 19:20. See Longenecker, 234; 244-246.

"free from the Law," but he chose to follow one of the rituals of the Law. The Jews took the Nazirite Vow either to thank God for something or to ask God for something. Paul may have been thanking God for the birth and growth of the church in Corinth and for being able to minister unmolested for such a long time. He *became as a Jew* that he might *win Jews* (1 Cor 9:20-21). Could his shorn head have made such an impression of the Jews in the synagogue in Ephesus that they were eager to listen to him?[5] Was he also trying to impress the Jewish Christians in Jerusalem and/or trying to appease his Jewish enemies there? The hair of the Nazirite Vow had to be burned with proper cleansing ritual at the temple in Jerusalem. [6]

∽

Acts 18:24-28

Eloquent Apologist Apollos in Ephesus

24 Now a Jew named Apollos, a native of Alexandria, came to Ephesus. He was an eloquent man, competent in the Scriptures. 25 He had been instructed in the way of the Lord. And being fervent in spirit, he spoke and taught accurately the things concerning Jesus, though he knew only the baptism of John. 26 He began to speak boldly in the synagogue, but when Priscilla and Aquila heard him, they took him aside and explained to him the way of God more accurately. 27 And when he wished to cross to Achaia, the brothers encouraged him and wrote to the disciples to welcome him. When he arrived, he greatly helped those who through grace had believed, 28 for he powerfully refuted the Jews in public, showing by the Scriptures that the Christ was Jesus.

Now Luke, leaving his hero Paul "on furlough" (now called "home assignment" or "home ministry"), introduces Paul's "furlough substitute." Paul did not

---

5   Stott, 301.

6   See more detail on the Nazirite Vow in Longenecker, 488.

arrange this assignment, nor had he ever even met Apollos, but in some ways Apollos was the equal or superior of Paul in his fervency and persuasive power.

Apollos was a Christian Jew from Alexandria in Egypt, the second most important city in the Roman Empire. Jews were very numerous there; in fact they occupied two of the five wards of the city. Two hundred years prior, the Jewish Scriptures had been translated into Greek in this city (the Septuagint). Alexandria was the home of the famous Philo and it is possible Apollos had met him or even been taught by him. The Coptic Church of Egypt traces its origin to Saint Mark in the mid first century. Could it have been Mark himself who *catechized* (the Greek word used here for *instructed*) Apollos in the *way of the Lord*? This explains how he could speak *accurately* about Jesus. How is it that he knew nothing about Christian baptism but *knew only the baptism of John*? Notice here the similarity with the following section, Acts 19:1-10. Apollos himself had never been baptized in the name of Christ, yet he was a Christian missionary! Only Matthew, among the synoptic gospels, mentions baptism for disciples of Christ.[7] If Apollos knew only the gospel of Mark, his ignorance of Christian baptism is more understandable.[8]

It does seem, however, that Apollos had heard some form of the Great Commission, for he came across the sea to Ephesus to preach the gospel of Christ. We are told four things about him. First, he was a learned or eloquent man (the word *logikos* can be translated either way). He was probably trained in Greek rhetoric and had considerable gifts of debate and persuasion, maybe even more than Paul himself. Second, he had a thorough knowledge of the Scriptures (*competent in the Scriptures*). "Scriptures" at that time of course meant the Old Testament Scriptures. Third, he was *fervent in spirit*. This could mean either fervent (literally *boiling*) in his human spirit or fervent in the Holy Spirit. Notice the same phrase in Rom 12:11. Fourth, he was accurate in his teaching.

Here is a rare combination of qualities which we should desire. Usually, the scholarly studious types are not eloquent and fervent, and the zealous fervent types are short on accuracy, education, and detailed knowledge. The ideal evangelist or missionary or preacher is both! If we are weak in one side, let us ask God to strengthen us so that we can be like Apollo.

---

7   That is, a baptism distinct from the baptism of John the Baptist. Matt 28:19. Mark 16:10 is part of a later addition.

8   This assumes that Mark 16:16 was, as most scholars believe, a later addition.

God allowed Apollos to preach but he did correct his deficiencies through his servants Priscilla and Aquila. Notice which name comes first (again). Priscilla may have done most of the talking. They tactfully made the necessary corrections privately. In too many cases familiar to us, Christians either gossip about the pastor's shortcomings or criticize him in bitter public confrontation. Apollos was humble enough to receive their suggestions and he became an even better preacher. He had a ministry of *watering* what others had *planted* (I Cor 3:6). He was eager to go on to Corinth in this capacity and the believers in Ephesus did not selfishly keep him to themselves, but were happy to write him a letter of introduction and recommendation. The happy result was *When he arrived, he greatly helped those who through grace had believed, for he powerfully refuted the Jews in public, showing by the Scriptures that the Christ was Jesus.*

Paul was not jealous of Apollos' work but was grateful to God for providing such wonderful help. Verse 28 shows that Apollos' combination of natural and spiritual gifts made him a powerful apologist for the faith. We need people like Apollos today in every people group and nation.

Lessons for Life

1. We may think religious and moral conditions are appalling today. They were worse then.
2. God is able to provide wonderful partners at just the right time for evangelism and church planting.
3. Be like Priscilla and Aquila: hospitable, sacrificial, flexible, tactful.
4. Christian workers may sometimes have to support themselves with their own hands.
5. God gives encouragement just when we need it. Even godly workers can be subject to severe stress and discouragement.
6. God can use people even if their knowledge of the gospel is not perfect. But he does not leave them in ignorance or error.
7. Be like Apollos: combining knowledge and zeal, teachable, bold, eager to use our gifts in mission.

ACTS 19

PAUL IN EPHESUS

Acts 19:1-41

The Riot in the Amphitheater

Paul's three-year ministry in Ephesus (20:31; roughly from the summer of 52 to the spring of 55AD) brings us to the climax of his church planting activity. He was able to settle down and teach for two uninterrupted years at the Hall of Tyrannus (19:10). During this period, which includes his trip into Macedonia and Achaia, he wrote I and II Corinthians and the Epistle to the Romans.

Ephesus, with a population of between 200,000 and 250,000, was the fourth largest city in the empire after Rome, Alexandria, and Antioch of Syria. It was a "free" city and the capital of the senatorial province of Asia; the Roman proconsul lived there. It was the nerve center of Roman communications to the East and though its harbor was constantly silting up, was a major commercial center. The colossal temple of Artemis, one of the seven wonders of the ancient world, brought worshippers and tourists from all over the empire. Even today the ruins of Ephesus are magnificent and the best preserved of all the cities mentioned in Acts or the Seven Churches of Revelation. For Paul it was the key center to spread the gospel throughout the Province of Asia (19:10). It later became an important Christian center and a major ecumenical council, the Council of Ephesus (431 AD).

19:1-7 The Encounter With Disciples of John

1 And it happened that while Apollos was at Corinth, Paul passed through the inland country and came to Ephesus. There he found some disciples. 2 And he said to them, "Did you receive the Holy Spirit when you believed?" And they said, "No, we have not even heard that there is a Holy Spirit." 3 And he said, "Into what then were you baptized?" They said, "Into John's baptism." 4 And Paul said, "John baptized with the baptism of repentance, telling the people to believe in the one who was to come after him, that is, Jesus." 5 On hearing this, they were baptized in the name of the Lord Jesus. 6 And when Paul had laid his hands on them, the Holy Spirit came on them, and they began speaking in tongues and prophesying. 7 There were about twelve men in all.

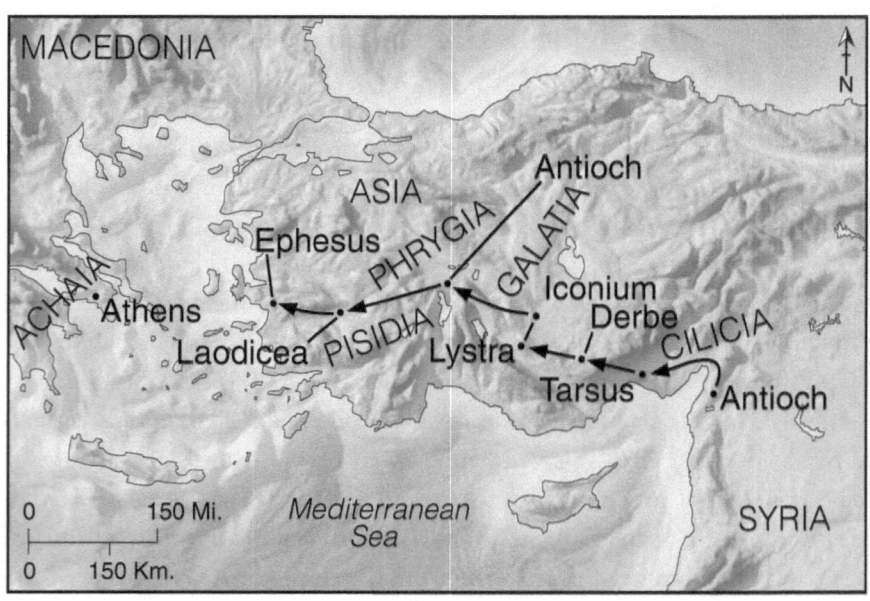

The Third Journey Begins

While Apollos was in Corinth, Paul arrived from his quick trip back to Jerusalem and Antioch (18:21-23). He returned to Ephesus by the overland route through the Cilician Gates and the four cities of Galatia.

Upon arriving in Ephesus, he encountered a group of disciples of John the Baptist who had not heard of either the baptism in the name of Christ or the baptism of the Holy Spirit, reminding us of the condition of Apollos (18:25) but differing significantly from him in that according to verse 4 they had not even heard of Jesus Christ. The existence of these disciples is a testimony to the power and extent of the Baptist's ministry.[1] It is not clear why Aquila and Priscilla and Apollos had not enlightened these men. It may be that they had, like Paul, just arrived in Ephesus. There is debate over whether these twelve men were *Christian* believers. Stott and Longenecker conclude that they were not, because they had not received the Spirit (v. 4). It may be more accurate to say that they were true *believers* in all that had been revealed up to the time of John the Baptist, but seriously deficient in knowledge of Christ, the one whom the Baptist foretold. These twelve men were still living in the pre-Pentecost Old Testament faith and as such, must be brought into the full post-Pentecost New Testament faith. The purpose of this brief narrative seems to show the gathering of scattered remnants of believers into one unity of practice and belief. This incident demonstrates again our contention that the Book of Acts is a book of transition.

The King James Version caused much confusion on the doctrine of the Holy Spirit by mistranslating verse 2 *Have ye received the Holy Ghost **since** ye believed?* More recent versions correct this error to read *Did you receive the Holy Spirit **when** you believed?* The point is important because the mistranslation supported the Pentecostal contention that the reception of the Holy Spirit is a "second work of grace" that occurs after one receives Christ. When the passage is properly understood, it becomes a powerful testimony to just the opposite conclusion: when one believes in Christ, he/she also receives the Holy Spirit. "The norm of Christian experience, then, is a cluster of four things: repentance, faith in Jesus, water baptism, and the gift of the Spirit. Though the perceived order may vary a little, the four belong together and are universal in Christian initiation."[2]

Why then do not all Christians speak in tongues and prophesy when they are baptized and receive the Holy Spirit? Our answer is that speaking in tongues in the Book of Acts was an indisputable, but not universal, demonstration of the inclusion of those who had previously been outsiders into the true church.

---

1   "The Baptist movement (that is the John the Baptist movement) seems to have
     continued well into the fourth century A.D." Witherington, 569.

2   Stott, Acts, 305. His discussion of this passage is excellent.

Speaking in tongues is mentioned in Acts only three times: in **Acts 2 Jews** who believed in Jesus as Messiah spoke in tongues when the Spirit came. **In Acts 10** a new group, **Gentiles**, spoke in tongues even before they were baptized, showing a sovereign work of God to include them in the new Body. Here a minor miscellaneous sub-group, **disciples of the Baptist**, is shown to now, after their baptism in the name of Christ, to be genuine believers in Christ and members of the one Body. Ironically the gifts of tongues and prophecy, then a unifier of the church, has now become a divider of the church.[3]

19:8-10 The Evangelization of Ephesus and Asia

8 And he entered the synagogue and for three months spoke boldly, reasoning and persuading them about the kingdom of God. 9 But when some became stubborn and continued in unbelief, speaking evil of the Way before the congregation, he withdrew from them and took the disciples with him, reasoning daily in the hall of Tyrannus. 10 This continued for two years, so that all the residents of Asia heard the word of the Lord, both Jews and Greeks.

To the very end of his free ministry, Paul entered the synagogue first.[4] Again Paul spoke boldly, reasoning and persuading, the same two verbs that are used again and again to describe his preaching. The subject of his earnest preaching is, as that of Philip in 8:12, and Paul again in 28:23, 31, the kingdom of God. Is there a distinction between preaching the gospel and preaching the kingdom of God? My conclusion is that "to preach the kingdom" is to preach the king of that kingdom, not just in the narrower version of the gospel concerning the life, death, and resurrection of Jesus (cf. 1 Cor 15:1-4), but also including the second coming and reign as king.

The Jews in Ephesus seem to have been more open to the gospel than the synagogues Paul had preached in up to now. He was so well received in this synagogue that he was invited to stay (18:20). But after three months, even

---

3   I think that there were really four groups that needed a sign of inclusion (tongues). The Samaritans received the Holy Spirit when the apostles laid hands on them (8:17) and though the passage does not mention tongues, it is possible that they too spoke in tongues to demonstrate that they had indeed received the Spirit.

4   "The Jewish community in Ephesus was a large one, the largest in the area, and had been there since the third century B.C. "Witherington, 574.

here, the inevitable opposition arose. Just as in Corinth, where Paul transferred his evangelism to the house of Titius Justus, in Ephesus he found a place to preach and teach every day in the lecture hall of one Tyrannus ("Tyrant"). "Since it is difficult (except in certain bleak moments of parenthood) to think of any parent naming his or her child 'Tyrant,' the name must have been a nickname given by the man's students or tenants."[5] Whether he was the owner of the hall or the philosopher/teacher of a private school we do not know. Such a site has not yet been discovered in the ruins of Ephesus but would be a wonderful discovery.

The Western text adds that Paul spoke every day from 11:00 AM to 4:00 PM, the time when businesses closed and everyone took a siesta. The business day began at dawn and continued until 11:00 AM. During this time Paul would have been busy at his trade, and then used his siesta time to preach the gospel. If this is reliable information, and we believe that it is, we must be impressed with two things: first Paul's hard work and diligence, and second, the power of his preaching to draw people even during siesta!

Here Paul was able, as in Corinth, to settle down for an extended period to evangelize by teaching. In a day when many preachers consider it a hardship to preach once a week, Paul's example is a challenge to our laziness. When did he have time for preparation? How did he avoid undue repetition lecturing every day for two years? It was during this period that he wrote at least two of his four letters to the Corinthians, including our 1 Corinthians. No wonder he seems overwhelmed in 2 Cor 11:27-28 *I have labored and toiled and have often gone without sleep . . . Besides everything else, I face daily the pressure of my concern for all the churches.*

Another important point is that **evangelism by teaching** was the heart of his ministry. Paul's evangelism included *the whole counsel of God* (20:27). So much modern evangelism, packaged in ten-minute plans of salvation, seems shallow and stunted by comparison. Paul had plenty of emotion and persuasive power, but he also appealed to the mind as well as the heart. His evangelism had solid content.

The sentence *so that all the residents of Asia heard the word of the Lord, both Jews and Greeks* proves the effectiveness of his method. *All* here is not a "100% all;" it means "many" or "most." Still quite impressive. Paul may

---

5   Longenecker, 495.

have done some of this work himself, but what no doubt happened is that his disciples, like Epaphras, founded the three churches of the Lycus Valley, Laodicea, Hierapolis, and Colossae (Col 1:6-8; 2:1; 4:12-13). Other converts and disciples must have taken the gospel to Smyrna, Pergamum, Thyatira, Sardis, and Philadelphia (Rev 2 and 3). There were also churches in Magnesia and Tralles, not mentioned in the Bible.[6]

19:11-16 The Miracles and the Jewish Exorcists

11 And God was doing extraordinary miracles by the hands of Paul, 12 so that even handkerchiefs or aprons that had touched his skin were carried away to the sick, and their diseases left them and the evil spirits came out of them. 13 Then some of the itinerant Jewish exorcists undertook to invoke the name of the Lord Jesus over those who had evil spirits, saying, "I adjure you by the Jesus whom Paul proclaims." 14 Seven sons of a Jewish high priest named Sceva were doing this. 15 But the evil spirit answered them, "Jesus I know, and Paul I recognize, but who are you?" 16 And the man in whom was the evil spirit leaped on them, mastered all of them and overpowered them, so that they fled out of that house naked and wounded.

17 And this became known to all the residents of Ephesus, both Jews and Greeks. And fear fell upon them all, and the name of the Lord Jesus was extolled. 18 Also many of those who were now believers came, confessing and divulging their practices. 19 And a number of those who had practiced magic arts brought their books together and burned them in the sight of all. And they counted the value of them and found it came to fifty thousand pieces of silver. 20 So the word of the Lord continued to increase and prevail mightily.

This passage has a theme of what is now called "power encounter," a battle with demonic forces. The great William Ramsey confessed that this section impressed him, "not of weighed and seasoned history; but of popular fancy; and I cannot explain it on the level of most of the narrative."[7] Ramsey's skepticism may reflect more the rationalist bias of the Western mind of that era, rather than the reality of spiritual battle that believers today face in the so-

---

6   Mentioned in the letters of Ignatius as First Century churches. Schnabel, 794.

7   *St Paul the Traveler and Roman Citizen*, 208.

called "third world." For Paul, both the opposition of demons and the miracles of God were frequent realities.

Ephesus, for all the glory of its commercial and political power, was a center of magic and the occult. "Ephesus was the home of all sorts of magic and superstition, and the phrase 'Ephesian writings' *(Ephesia grammata)* was common in antiquity for documents containing spells and magical formulae."[8] God knew what would impress these superstitious people, so he used *extraordinary miracles* to win them to Christ. The *handerkerchiefs* (*soudaria*) were sweatbands or cloths that laborers wore wrapped around their foreheads.[9] This hints at an extraordinary incidental picture of Paul the laborer, toiling with his hands in the heat. The *simikinthia* were aprons that craftsmen wore. It was not that Paul sent out such items for healing purposes, like some American radio evangelists do in return for a contribution, but that others, Christian or non-Christian, were using these articles to heal people and cast out demons. God, accommodating himself to their superstition and worldview, used them to effect real cures. We are reminded of people being healed by Peter's shadow (5:15) and the woman who was healed when she touched Jesus' robe (Matt 9:20; 14:36). The fact that Luke records these "dubious" incidents is part of his strategy throughout Acts to show that Paul was just as important as Peter.

Then some Jewish exorcists (the word is used only here in the NT) tried to "cash in" on the power of the name of Jesus. Jewish exorcists were famous in antiquity.[10] They, especially a priestly family, had special access to the divine names, and magic involved the repetition of powerful names to manipulate the named gods to curse or cure.[11] Personal faith or allegiance to the "god" was not needed.

Sceva was not *the* high priest, but *a* high priest and may have assumed that title as a renegade from a priestly family to impress the gullible. His seven sons attempted to cast out a demon by calling upon *the name of Jesus whom Paul preaches*. The demon's reply is ironic: *Jesus I know, and Paul I know, but*

---

8   Longenecker, 496.

9   I am reminded of the *hachimaki* that Japanese laborers tie to their foreheads.

10   Witherington, 580.

11   The Paris Papyrus 574 includes the following spell: "I adjure you by the Jesus the God of the Hebrews," and also "Hail God of Abraham, hail God of Isaac, hail God of Jacob, Jesus Chrestus, Holy Spirit, Son of the Father." Cited from Witherington, p. 580, note 87.

who are you? The demonic knowledge of the true identity of Jesus reflects incidents in the gospels like Matt 8:29. Then one demon jumped on the seven men and sent them howling in fear from the house, *naked and wounded.* God used a demon to rebuke the demonic charlatans. As in the demon stories in the gospels, even the demons are compelled to confess the Name, here with a flair that shows that God has a sense of humor. The story quickly spread in Ephesus and the vicinity; they were all seized with a healthy fear of God and acquired a great respect for the name of Jesus.

The fear of God seized even the Christian believers for they *openly confessed their evil deeds* (NIV). Some Christians brought their scrolls (*biblia*) of magic incantations and formulae and burned them in public. It is hard to imagine true Christians practicing the occult arts, but the text plainly states that these penitents were *believers.* Pastors and missionaries in many primitive places might not find their failure so strange. Even those who have been carefully catechized and baptized are sometimes guilty of the most flagrant sins and need a severe shock to jar them loose from their complacency. Believers anywhere may find it hard to make a clean break with the past and syncretism (the mixture of religions) is common in almost every country that the gospel has been preached.

Their repentance was drastic, though some may have thought them overly zealous. Why not sell the books and give the money to the church? The total value of the burned up scrolls was estimated at 50,000 drachmae. A drachma was one day's wages for a laboring man and so if a man earned 350 drachmae a year (a few days off for holy days and festivals) it would take him 143 years to buy all these magic books. Their repentance was genuine and it was decisive. This is the kind of godly fear and repentance and revival that is needed in so many churches today. Maybe we should have a bonfire once a year where Christians can burn their dirty books, their ungodly clothes, and their X-rated CDs and videos.

The result of this repentance, and indeed the result of all the spiritual power that God was pouring out through Paul and his fellow-workers, was that *the word of the Lord continued to increase and prevail mightily.* This is a **summary verse** (see also 6:7; 9:31; 12:24; and 16:5) that divides the fifth and sixth panels or major segments of Acts. Here is the climax of the blessing of the triumphant gospel ministry of Paul. From now on things "go downhill" into what Witherington calls "troubles, travels, and trials."[12]

---

12   Witherington, 583.

Lessons for Life

1. The norm of Christian initiation (becoming a Christian) includes repentance, faith in Christ, and water baptism in the name of Jesus.
2. God is concerned to bring all believers into one Body. In Acts the gift of tongues was a sign of that unity and must not be used now so as to sow disunity.
3. Effective evangelism includes: speaking boldly, persuasion, thorough teaching, hard work, and spiritual power.
4. The power of God not only converts unbelievers but also cleanses compromising believers.
5. Powerful evangelism radiates to surrounding areas.

19:21-22 Travel Plans

21 Now after these events Paul resolved in the Spirit to pass through Macedonia and Achaia and go to Jerusalem, saying, "After I have been there, I must also see Rome." 22 And having sent into Macedonia two of his helpers, Timothy and Erastus, he himself stayed in Asia for a while.

Paul concentrated diligently on the evangelism of Ephesus and the Province of Asia for two years, but he did not neglect the churches across the Aegean Sea. He was led by the Spirit to visit Philippi, Thessalonica, and Berea in Macedonia, and Athens and Corinth in Achaia before he visited Jerusalem again.[13] Paul seems drawn to Jerusalem like a moth to the flame, but despite the danger, he seems to have two purposes in mind: first to testify of Christ before his countrymen, for whom, despite being refused and persecuted by

---

13   The NIV here simply says *decided*, assuming that the word *pneuma* in the phrase *etheto en to pneumati* is a reference to his own human spirit. We prefer, with Bruce, the KJV, ESV, NASB, RSV, and NRSV to understand *en to pneumati* here to be a reference to the Holy Spirit. We will encounter a similar ambiguity in 20:22.

them again and again, he still had a tremendous burden (Rom 9:1-3); and second because he was very concerned to deliver the collection for the relief of the poor saints in Jerusalem which he mentions repeatedly in his letters of this time (Rom 15:25-28; 31; 1 Cor 16:1; 2 Cor 8 and 9, esp. 9:2). Acts says very little about this project except for a brief mention in Paul's speech in 24:17. Paul also expressed his desire to visit Rome (Rom 15:24; 28), which was confirmed by the Lord in the vision in Jerusalem (Acts 23:11). The word used here translated *must* is the Greek *dei,* which often, and especially in Luke's writings, connotes a divine compulsion.

Paul by now has a number of disciples. He sends Timothy and Erastus ahead to prepare his visits to the churches of Greece. Timothy was Paul's son in the faith and his closest fellow worker. He is mentioned in the NT as having worked with Paul in Philippi, Berea, Thessalonica, Corinth, Rome, and Ephesus. During the period of the Pastoral Epistles Timothy was Paul's representative (bishop?) in Ephesus. Erastus was a common Latin name and it seems unlikely that he is the same person mentioned as *aedile* of Corinth in Rom 16:23, but that is not impossible. Erastus is mentioned as a helper of Paul at the end of Paul's life in 2 Tim 4:20.

19:23-41 The Riot of the Silversmiths

23 About that time there arose no little disturbance concerning the Way. 24 For a man named Demetrius, a silversmith, who made silver shrines of Artemis, brought no little business to the craftsmen. 25 These he gathered together, with the workmen in similar trades, and said, "Men, you know that from this business we have our wealth. 26 And you see and hear that not only in Ephesus but in almost all of Asia this Paul has persuaded and turned away a great many people, saying that gods made with hands are not gods. 27 And there is danger not only that this trade of ours may come into disrepute but also that the temple of the great goddess Artemis may be counted as nothing, and that she may even be deposed from her magnificence, she whom all Asia and the world worship."

28 When they heard this they were enraged and were crying out, "Great is Artemis of the Ephesians!" 29 So the city was filled with the confusion, and they rushed together into the theater, dragging with them Gaius and Aristarchus, Macedonians who were Paul's companions in travel. 30 But when Paul wished to go in among the crowd, the disciples would not let him. *31 And even some of the Asiarchs, who were friends of his, sent to him and were urging him not to venture into the theater. 32 Now some cried out one thing, some another, for the assembly was in confusion, and most of them did not know why they had come together. 33 Some of the crowd prompted Alexander, whom the Jews had put forward. And Alexander, motioning with his hand, wanted to make a defense to the crowd. 34 But when they recognized that he was a Jew, for about two hours they all cried out with one voice, "Great is Artemis of the Ephesians!"*

35 And when the town clerk had quieted the crowd, he said, "Men of Ephesus, who is there who does not know that the city of the Ephesians is temple keeper of the great Artemis, and of the sacred stone that fell from the sky? 36 Seeing then that these things cannot be denied, you ought to be quiet and do nothing rash. 37 For you have brought these men here who are neither sacrilegious nor blasphemers of our goddess. 38 If therefore Demetrius and the craftsmen with him have a complaint against anyone, the courts are open, and there are proconsuls. Let them bring charges against one another. 39 But if you seek anything further, it shall be settled in the regular assembly. 40 For we really are in danger of being charged with rioting today, since there is no cause that we can give to justify this commotion." 41 And when he had said these things, he dismissed the assembly.

Archaeology and ancient literature corroborate the accuracy of this fascinating incident. The colossal marble temple of Artemis, one of the seven wonders of the Ancient World, had four times the floor area of the Parthenon of Athens. Pliny says that the temple was 115 m long and 55 m wide,[14] larger than an American football field. There were 127 columns 20 m high. "I have seen the walls and Hanging Gardens of ancient Babylon," wrote Philon of Byzantium, "the statue of Olympian Zeus, the Colossus of Rhodes, the mighty work of the high Pyramids and the tomb of Mausolus. But when I saw the temple at Ephesus rising to the clouds, all these other wonders were put in the shade."[15] The temple was one of the greatest worship centers and tourist attractions of the Ancient World and the cult of Artemis or Diana was one of the most popular.

---

14   The precise dimensions vary slightly from source to source.

15   http://unmuseum.mus.pa.us/ephesus.htm.

Ephesus was very proud of its official role as *neokoros*, (v. 35) literally "temple-sweeper," which came to mean "guardian of the temple." The use of this technical term required accurate knowledge of the city of Ephesus.

We are not then surprised to learn that craftsmen in Ephesus had for centuries done a brisk business in selling miniature shrines of the temple that people could place in their homes to worship Artemis, or bury in their graves. Those that have been discovered by archaeologists are crude terra cotta, but molds for the silver models have also been discovered. It is not surprising that the silver itself did not survive the plunders of the centuries.

The sacred stone that fell from the sky (v. 35) is mentioned in ancient sources and seems to have been a meteorite that was venerated as a divine object in the first of five temples at this site for centuries before the temple of Paul's time was built.[16]

The Asiarchs of verse 31 is indeed an accurate title for the holders of high office in the free cities of Asia.[17] The mention of proconsuls plural *(anthupatoi* in Greek) in verse 38 raises the interesting possibility that this incident occurred soon after the assassination by poisoning of Proconsul M. Junius Silanus in October of 54 AD. Before his successor could be put in place, Helius and Celer, two of the officials in charge of emperor's affairs in Asia, were acting as temporary proconsuls. Bruce, however, rejects this idea and thinks that "the plural is generalizing," ("there are such people as proconsuls").[18] Likewise the grammateus or "town clerk" who quieted the crowd was indeed the correct title for chief executive officer of the town council. He also served as the principle liaison officer between the city government and the Roman authorities.[19] Luke never fails to give the correct titles of government officials of the precise period that he is writing about.

About that time there arose no little disturbance concerning The Way (v. 23). The Christians did not yet have a name for their religion. The word "Christian" was still a slur on the lips of their opponents (11:26). They called themselves "The Way,"[20] perhaps after the word of their Lord who

---

16   Ibid.

17   Bruce, 418.

18   Bruce, 421.

19   Bruce, 420.

20   See also Acts 9:2; 19:9, 23; 24:14 and compare 18:25-26.

said, I am the Way (John 14:6). It implies that there is no other true way **to** life or way **of** life. The gospel of Christ is not just a means of salvation, it is a way of life, not just orthodoxy, but orthopraxy, not just the correct beliefs, but right behavior.

Wherever the gospel has great success, it also has powerful opposition. In Luke's mind, opposition was a sign of the truth of the gospel (compare 2 Thess 1:4-5). The gospel was so widespread in Ephesus and vicinity that sales of miniature temples of Artemis were starting to fall off. Demetrius the silversmith knew just how to provoke the most basic instincts of his fellow craftsmen. He probably exaggerated for effect, but the statement that *not only in Ephesus but in almost all of Asia this Paul has persuaded and turned away a great many people, saying that gods made with hands are not gods* was not far from the actual situation. So many people had abandoned idol worship and had turned to Christ that their livelihoods were in danger. The gospel of Christ had the power to shake the foundations of the most widespread and powerful cult of that day.

One could wish that souvenir sellers and travel agents in Nikko, Japan and the tourist trade of Bangkok would suffer because so many converts to Christ were abandoning their pilgrimages to these holy sites.

The harangue of Demetrius also betrays the fact that Paul did not just preach a "positive message." He spoke against the pagan gods by saying that that gods made with hands are not gods, just as he did in Athens. He was not afraid to imply that the whole magnificent edifice of the Artemision, with its overwhelming popularity, and centuries of tradition and entrenched economic power, was based on a lie. Do we have that courage today or do we pussyfoot around the plain truth lest we offend someone?

Finally Demetrius appeals to their pride, both personal and corporate: our trade will come into disrepute. This was a powerful motive in a shame/honor culture. Not even a prostitute likes to think her trade is any less honorable than any other. As for collective pride, *the temple of the great goddess Artemis may be counted for nothing, and that she may even be deposed from her magnificence, she whom all Asia and the world worship.* For centuries this great goddess and this great temple had been the glory of Ephesus throughout the ancient world. Is the worship of Artemis to be threatened or lost? It is no wonder that the crowd was enraged and were crying out, "Great is Artemis of the Ephesians"!

*The theater in Ephesus. It is still there! These very stones rang with the cry
"Great is Artemis of the Ephesians"! The road beyond led to the ancient port.*

Today Artemis and her temple have vanished. "Artemis" is just another
forgotten name that students memorize for their study of ancient history. Her
colossal temple is today a marshy hole in the ground with a few pathetic
stones piled one on top of another to suggest an ancient column. The 127
magnificent marble columns and the thirteen-step foundation were quarried
through the centuries by Christians and Turks for other construction. The
very site was forgotten and only discovered in 1869 by the diligent efforts of
John T. Wood from the British Museum.

How tenacious we human beings are to maintain the pride of our nation,
our culture, our religion! So often the gospel is rejected out of hand, not
because it is proved to be false, but because it clashes with tribal or national
pride. "To be a Turk is to be a Muslim!" "To be a Thai is to be a Buddhist!"
"A true Indian is Hindu." "Christianity is fine, but we Japanese have our own
religions." "If the whole nation converted to Christ, the distinctive identity
and pride of our country would be lost." The liberal Christians applaud and
promote such a sentiment and look with horror on anyone like a missionary

who would be so unenlightened as to attempt to persuade people to change their religion. Yet, as happened with the great temple of Artemis, *Every plant, which my heavenly Father has not planted, shall be rooted up* (Matt 15:13).

The next paragraph of the incident marks a crisis for the Christians in Ephesus, especially for Gaius and Aristarchus, who happened to be in the wrong place at the wrong time. Paul seems to have been safely elsewhere, though it was only the intervention of his less impulsive disciples, and, interestingly, some of his friends among the Asiarchs, that prevented his plunging into the fray.

In the safety of retrospect, the scene must have been told and retold in the churches with broad smiles at its more humorous aspects. A crowd gathered at the outcry of the silversmiths and rushed into the theater. It is still there, the semi-circular rows of seats much as they were then, and still useable as an amphitheater holding 25,000 people. Because there is nothing to pull down or fall over in an earthquake, the amphitheaters are the most durable structures in the ruins of any ancient Greek city. Most of the excitable crowd were not sure why they had rushed into the theatre; there was no order, nothing to see, and no agenda. *Now some cried out one thing, some another; and the assembly was in confusion, and most of them did not know why they had come together.* In the confusion one of the Jews, Alexander, perhaps thinking the hostility was against the Jews, or that the crowd did not differentiate between the Jews and "the Way," attempted a defense, but he only succeeded in provoking the fanatical crowd into a frenzy, who for two hours shouted themselves hoarse with the mantra *Great is Artemis of the Ephesians!*

What Luke is telling Theophilus and any readers of this book is that much of the opposition to the gospel of Christ is not because it is false, but because of primitive fear and irrational superstition that spook men to shout for two hours like madmen. "Great is Artemis of the Ephesians"! Shouting a slogan does not make it so, but rather leads one to suspect that the shouters are trying to make something they fear is untrue true by the sheer volume of their voices drowning the opposition in waves of noise. One is reminded of the frenzied shouts of "Allahu Akbar!" in present-day riots in the Middle East.

Eventually the shouting must have started to die down from weariness, laryngitis, and thirst. The town clerk stepped in to quiet the rabble and dismiss the crowd. His first point was to affirm their chant, but then to point out that it is not a profitable use of time to belabor that of which everyone is already convinced. Second, and more seriously, you have no proper legal charges against these men. Third, if there is a charge, Demetrius and his fellows must bring it before the city courts; or, if the charge is serious enough, before one of the Roman proconsuls. Fourth, we Ephesians are in danger of being charged with illegal assembly and riot and having our status and privileges as a free city taken away by the Emperor. This last point was most telling and must have sobered even the most fanatic.

And when he had said these things, he dismissed the assembly. The disciples must have gathered around Paul, with their nerves still jangling, and with "Great is Artemis of the Ephesians!" still ringing in their ears, to give thanks to God for their deliverance. Soon after, Paul wrote to the Corinthians that he had fought with beasts at Ephesus (1 Cor 15:32). Irrational fear turns men into beasts.

Paul, who has had the starring role up to now, is now literally and figuratively "off the stage." He was helpless to do anything in this crisis and almost rashly brought down a lynching upon himself, but God overruled to keep both him and his disciples safe.

Lessons for Life

1. If our gospel succeeds in converting many people, we can expect violent and powerful opposition. If we are not making somebody mad, maybe we are not doing our jobs.
2. Our gospel is not just a positive message. We at times must say plainly and boldly, gods made with hands are not gods.
3. Opposition to our faith is perfectly understandable, especially when it threatens people's pocketbooks, or national pride, or entrenched way of life.
4. God is able to protect his people, even in a riot, even when things are entirely out of our control.

ACTS 20

FINAL FAREWELLS

Acts 20:1-38

20:1-6 The Trip to Greece and Troas

1 After the uproar ceased, Paul sent for the disciples, and after encouraging them, he said farewell and departed for Macedonia. 2 When he had gone through those regions and had given them much encouragement, he came to Greece. 3 There he spent three months, and when a plot was made against him by the Jews as he was about to set sail for Syria, he decided to return through Macedonia. 4 Sopater the Berean, son of Pyrrhus, accompanied him; and of the Thessalonians, Aristarchus and Secundus; and Gaius of Derbe, and Timothy; and the Asians, Tychicus and Trophimus. 5 These went on ahead and were waiting for us at Troas, 6 but we sailed away from Philippi after the days of Unleavened Bread, and in five days we came to them at Troas, where we stayed for seven days.

The unifying feature of this chapter is four farewells: to the believers of Ephesus, to the churches in Macedonia and Achaia, to the church in Troas, and to the Elders of the Ephesian Church. This chapter marks the end of Paul's free mission ministry, at least in the Book of Acts. From chapter 21 through 28 he is under arrest.

The Christians have survived the riot in Ephesus, but it seems Paul can no longer minister openly in Ephesus. Instead of using the Hall of Tyrannus, he called the believers to meet him privately *and after encouraging them, he said farewell and departed for Macedonia.* The four farewells in this chapter consist largely of Paul's *paraklēsis,* which can be translated comfort (for sorrow), or encouragement (for fear or anxiety), or exhortation (for lethargy or carelessness). The word is used in verses 1, 2, and 12, and though not occurring there, certainly is what is happening in verses 17-38, the farewell to the Ephesian elders. It may well be that we are to take the speech of verses 17-38 as a sample of the kinds of things he may have said in all four locations, especially his personal example in persevering for the gospel even in the face of suffering, and in warning them against false teachers and false teaching.

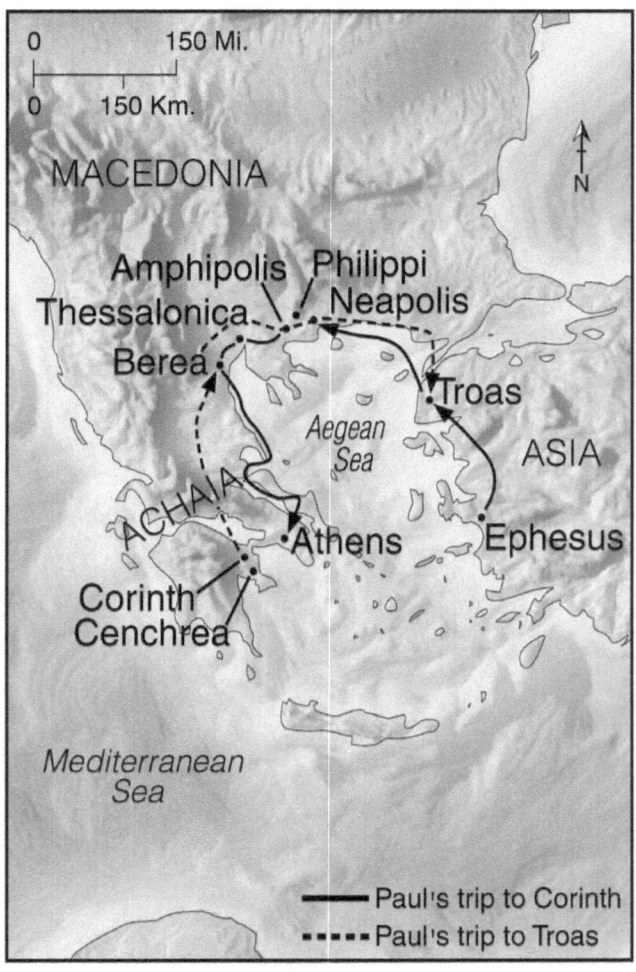

Through Macedonia and Achaia

The account in verses 1-6 is very abbreviated, a brief travel diary. Paul and his helpers must have visited the churches of Macedonia (Philippi, Thessalonica, and Berea) before going on to Greece (the more popular name for the Province of Achaia). Except for Philippi, we have these cities mentioned in verse 4 as the hometowns of his seven co-workers. Luke may have represented Philippi.

We may know more of the details about Paul's activities and state of mind during this period by studying 2 Corinthians. It was during this period that that epistle was written from Macedonia and Romans was written from Corinth, where Paul stayed three months, perhaps the winter of 56/57.[1] It may also be at this time that Paul traveled as far as Illyricum (present day Croatia on the coast of the Adriatic Sea, Rom 15:19).

The threats against Paul are growing more deadly. The unbelieving Jews are no longer content to simply evict him from the synagogues; now there is a plot to kill him on the ship bound for Syria. It would have been easy to bind and gag him and throw him overboard some dark night. In the providence of God, the plot became known to Paul and his friends and he makes an abrupt change of plans to reverse his course back to Macedonia.[2] As the following chapters demonstrate, Paul is not afraid to walk into danger to follow the will of God, but here he takes a troublesome and radical change of course to avoid danger.

Verse 4 gives us the names of seven of Paul's traveling companions. If, as seems very likely, they are bearing the relief funds for the poor saints in Jerusalem (Rom 15:25-26; 1 Cor 16:1-4; 2 Cor 8 and 9), each man may have been not only a disciple of Paul, but also a personal representative of his own church. Luke joins the party at verse 5, (notice the word *we* or *us* is resumed), where we left him last in Philippi (16:17). Including Paul there is a party of nine men. Such a large number of traveling companions would ensure more security for the funds. No checks in the mail or wire transfer in those days! Verse four incidentally informs us of the growing unity, strength, and maturity of the Christian churches.[3]

---

1   Bruce, 423.

2   The word for "plot,"*epiboulē*, is often used for a plot to kill: Acts 9:24; 23:30; Est 2:22; 3 Mac 1:2, 6. We have three mentions of plots against Paul being discovered in time in Acts: 9:24, this passage, and 23:16.

3   See more detail on these points in Stott, 318. "The fruits of mission became the agents of mission."

All but Secundus of Thessalonica are mentioned elsewhere in the NT. More detailed commentaries like Schnabel (p. 833) list the references where their names may be found. Simple computer searches of the Bible text will turn up the same information. The lesson for us is that Paul did not work or travel alone but always with men who were his disciples. The recent emphasis on teams in mission work is a healthy application of this principle.

It is not clear why the party split up briefly to meet again in Troas. The *we* of verse 6 seems to refer only to Luke and Paul. Paul avoided traveling alone if possible.

20:7-12 The Breaking of Bread in Troas and the Incident of Eutychus

> *7 On the first day of the week, when we were gathered together to break bread, Paul talked with them, intending to depart on the next day, and he prolonged his speech until midnight. 8 There were many lamps in the upper room where we were gathered. 9 And a young man named Eutychus, sitting at the window, sank into a deep sleep as Paul talked still longer. And being overcome by sleep, he fell down from the third story and was taken up dead. 10 But Paul went down and bent over him, and taking him in his arms, said, "Do not be alarmed, for his life is in him." 11 And when Paul had gone up and had broken bread and eaten, he conversed with them a long while, until daybreak, and so departed. 12 And they took the youth away alive, and were not a little comforted.*

Troas is not to be confused with Troy, which was the ancient city of the Iliad only 25 km to the north. The official name of this port city on the Aegean Sea was Alexandria Troas. The coastal region there, part of the Province of Asia, was called Troas or the Troad. From Alexandria Troas Paul, Silas, and Timothy had embarked for Macedonia on the second missionary journey in response to the vision of the man of Macedonia (16:8-11).

Troas was a seaport of considerable size in ancient times, as the extensive area of present-day ruins attests. Seleucid kings once resided here. By the time of Paul, the city had been made a Roman colony like Philippi and Corinth. This exempted its citizens from poll and land taxes. No mention is ever made of evangelism in Troas or the establishing of a church, but now there is a church in Troas. This church may have been started during Paul's two-year stay in Ephesus when *all the Jews and Greeks in Asia heard the word of the Lord* (19:10).

The nine travelers and the believers of Troas gathered on the first day of the week (Sunday evening) to *break bread*. This is the first indication in the New Testament of the custom of meeting on Sunday to worship.[4] The "breaking of bread" is a technical term for what later became known as the Eucharist, or Lord's Supper. As in other mentions of the Lord's Supper in the New Testament, it was combined with a communal meal called the Agape (1 Cor 11:17-34).

The place where they were gathered, an *upper room,* evokes memories of the first Lord's Supper and the gathering of the first believers in Jerusalem (Luke 22:12; Acts 1:13). Witherington believes that the phrase "upper room" indicates a modest room in an *insula* or apartment building that would indicate a lower income setting.[5]

Paul may not have droned on until midnight without interruption. The word for *he prolonged his speech* is *dialegomai*, which can mean either "instruct" or "converse," or "discuss" just as we use the word "dialog" today. In any case, the lateness of the hour and the stuffiness of the room from many burning oil lamps caused a shocking accident. A young man by the name of Eutychus ("Lucky") dozed off, fell into a deep sleep, and fell out of the third-floor window to his death. It was not like the incident in chapter 14 in Lystra when Paul was thought to be dead; the wording leaves no doubt that Eutychus was actually dead. Doctor Luke probably confirmed the medical facts personally. *His life is in him* would then indicate, not that he was not dead, but that a miracle through Paul had given him life again.

We miss the shock of it because we have read the story many times and we know the happy ending. But accidents like this, especially in the context of a Christian event or meeting, can cast a terrible pall and even doubts toward God. We know of a case of attempted suicide in a Christian school in Japan where a young girl, apparently mentally disturbed, thought God was telling her to walk out a second-floor window. She had a soft landing and was not seriously hurt. Eutychus was a case of carelessness rather than deliberate self-destruction, but the shock and dismay are powerful.

---

4   The other mention of worship on the first day of the week is 1 Cor 16:2.

5   Witherington, 607. A wealthy person would entertain in a ground floor *triclinium*.

Paul threw himself on the boy (reminiscent of Elisha in 2 Kings 4:34-35) and brought him back to life by the power of God. A terrible tragedy, which might have caused loss of faith, was suddenly turned into rejoicing and wonder and a powerful stimulus to faith. Paul, just like Peter (9:40-42), was empowered to raise the dead. There can be no doubt about the gospel he was preaching.

Now that everyone was thoroughly awake and had something to eat (this second *breaking of bread* refers to an ordinary meal), they listened to Paul and the next thing it was daylight! This meeting was important! It was the last time they would see Paul for a long time, and it was an incredible privilege to sit at the feet of such a great man. Everyone lost track of time. They finished the night more energized than if they had slept all night. In Western cultures today people live, wake, and sleep by the clock. We would never stay up all night, especially to listen to a man talk! Maybe we are missing something the early Christians had.

20:13-16 The Voyage to Miletus

> *13 But going ahead to the ship, we set sail for Assos, intending to take Paul aboard there, for so he had arranged, intending himself to go by land. 14 And when he met us at Assos, we took him on board and went to Mitylene. 15 And sailing from there we came the following day opposite Chios; the next day we touched at Samos; and the day after that we went to Miletus. 16 For Paul had decided to sail past Ephesus, so that he might not have to spend time in Asia, for he was hastening to be at Jerusalem, if possible, on the day of Pentecost.*

This section, verses 13-16, is a good example of Luke's personal travel diary in the "we" sections that dominate the last nine chapters of Acts.

Why did Paul decide to walk 30 miles (50 km) to **Assos** on the south coast of the Troad peninsula? Luke does not tell us. Maybe he wanted to meditate on a problem or needed privacy to pray. Those on the boat could have taken advantage of northerly winds during the day to go a short distance along the Aegean Coast. Then before the wind ceased in late afternoon and evening, they would put in to the nearest harbor for the night. Luke lists each port; each seems to mark one day's journey.

From Troas to Miletus

The ship arrived at **Miletus**, a major port some 62 miles (110 km) walk from Ephesus,[6] and apparently was scheduled to stay there for about a week. This gave Paul an opportunity to send for the elders of the Ephesian churches for final instructions and exhortations. Paul seems anxious to get to Jerusalem by Pentecost, and he now has about thirty days left until Pentecost. It is not clear why being in Jerusalem during Pentecost was so important to him. Paul did not want to go to Ephesus and become entangled in a long and difficult

6   Schnabel, 838, note 27.

second farewell there. Also, it might have been dangerous to appear openly in the city. Another possibility may simply be that his ship was not scheduled to stop in Ephesus.

20:17-38 The Farewell Speech to the Ephesian Elders

17 Now from Miletus he sent to Ephesus and called the elders of the church to come to him. 18 And when they came to him, he said to them:

"You yourselves know how I lived among you the whole time from the first day that I set foot in Asia, 19 serving the Lord with all humility and with tears and with trials that happened to me through the plots of the Jews; 20 how I did not shrink from declaring to you anything that was profitable, and teaching you in public and from house to house, 21 testifying both to Jews and to Greeks of repentance toward God and of faith in our Lord Jesus Christ. 22 And now, behold, I am going to Jerusalem, constrained by the Spirit, not knowing what will happen to me there, 23 except that the Holy Spirit testifies to me in every city that imprisonment and afflictions await me. 24 But I do not account my life of any value nor as precious to myself, if only I may finish my course and the ministry that I received from the Lord Jesus, to testify to the gospel of the grace of God. 25 And now, behold, I know that none of you among whom I have gone about proclaiming the kingdom will see my face again. 26 Therefore I testify to you this day that I am innocent of the blood of all, 27 for I did not shrink from declaring to you the whole counsel of God. 28 Pay careful attention to yourselves and to all the flock, in which the Holy Spirit has made you overseers, to care for the church of God, which he obtained with his own blood. 29 I know that after my departure fierce wolves will come in among you, not sparing the flock; 30 and from among your own selves will arise men speaking twisted things, to draw away the disciples after them. 31 Therefore be alert, remembering that for three years I did not cease night or day to admonish every one with tears. 32 And now I commend you to God and to the word of his grace, which is able to build you up and to give you the inheritance among all those who are sanctified. 33 I coveted no one's silver or gold or apparel. 34 You yourselves know that these hands ministered to my necessities and to those who were with me. 35 In all things I have shown you that by working hard in this way we must help the weak and remember the words of the Lord Jesus, how he himself said, 'It is more blessed to give than to receive.'"

36 And when he had said these things, he knelt down and prayed with them all. 37 And there was much weeping on the part of all; they embraced Paul and kissed him, 38 being sorrowful most of all because of the word he had spoken, that they would not see his face again. And they accompanied him to the ship.

Paul, for reasons we have discussed, did not want to visit Ephesus again but he felt it essential that he give a final word of parting and exhortation to the elders of the church in Ephesus. He is particularly burdened about the heresy that he foresees will ravage this church (v. 29).

Anyone who has started a church or a Christian organization knows the concern Paul felt at the point of turning over a work that has been his "baby" for so long. Some Christian workers or missionaries never do come to the point where they are able to "cut the umbilical cord." Paul was always turning over churches to their own leadership and *commending them to God and to the word of his grace* (v. 32), and we must be willing to follow his example.

It is instructive to study the words used for these leaders. First, they are called "elders," that is *presbuteroi* in Greek. This word later morphed into the English word "priest" and came to denote a full-time clergyman who alone is qualified to perform the sacraments, and, on the Old Testament model of that word, was a mediator between God and the laity. The New Testament elders (always plural) were themselves laity who had a special designation by the Spirit to serve as leaders of the local church or churches. The word church is in the singular but there may have been a number of separate meeting places in Ephesus.

Second, the elders are called *episkopoi* (literally "overseers," v. 28), which denotes their authority and their responsibility to watch over the flock. Later this term came to mean "bishop" in a hierarchical structure as one in charge of many churches and many priests in a given district. But it is clear from this passage that in the earliest churches, *presbuteroi* and *episkopoi* are the same.

Third, although the noun "pastor" (*poimēn*) is not used here as in Eph 4:11, the verb *poimainō* is used as the key imperative in v. 28: they are to *Be shepherds of the church of God* (NIV) or better, *shepherd the church of God* (NRSV). In modern times we usually have one pastor in charge of one church and distinguish between pastor and elders, but in NT times the three terms were equivalent and they apparently functioned together in what we might today call a "pastoral team."[7] As yet there is no hint of "full time seminary educated pastorate;" in fact, Paul's example and exhortation in v. 35 assumes that they will work with their hands.

We have not forgotten our dictum that Acts is a book of "description not prescription," but it makes us uneasy the further our modern practice departs from the apostolic example.

This is the only speech in Acts that is spoken to Christian believers. It is a precious insight into Paul's intense burden for his churches and their leaders. Almost every word and phrase is so like Paul.[8] This point is important to rebut skeptical scholars who claim that the Book of Acts is a work of fiction and that this speech in particular was "put in the mouth of Paul."

Analyses of the structure of the address vary after verse 22, but all agree that in verses 18-21 Paul speaks of his ministry in the past in Ephesus. This paragraph is marked the phrase "You know" and refers to the past. In verses 22-24 he speaks of being *constrained by the Spirit* to go to Jerusalem and there he will suffer *imprisonment and afflictions*. This section is marked by the phrase "I know" and refers to the future. Verses 25-38 move into the heart of Paul's message: an exhortation to the elders. This longer section, while returning to his personal example again in verses 27 and 34-35, is marked by imperatives: *Keep watch! Be shepherds! Be on your guard! Remember!*

Though Paul claims humility (v. 19), it may strike some cultures as immodest and indeed prideful for Paul "to blow his own horn" so much in stressing his personal example of hard work and faithfulness in ministry. What we can say in response is that, for Paul, what he **did** was just as important as what he **said**. His message always was, *be imitators of me, as I am of Christ* (1 Cor 11:1). That is his argument in this passage: "I served God this way; I want you to do the same." "I did my part and must now leave you, now you must do your part and do as I have done." Paul was not shy about what he expected of his disciples.

There is another possible explanation for the defensive nature of Paul's appeals to his example. In the time (almost a year?) that he was absent from

---

7   The Presbyterian form of church government holds that the "pastor" is one of the elders, a "teaching elder" as distinct from those who are "ruling elders."

8   Witherington (610) lists thirteen terms or concepts reminiscent of Paul's writings.

Ephesus, there may well have been attacks by his opponents, maybe some of them within the church, as was the case in Corinth and indeed in most of his churches. He says in v. 19 that *I was severely tested by the plots of the Jews* (NIV). This comes as a bit of a surprise, because Luke has not mentioned such troubles in Paul's ministry in Ephesus or Asia. But Paul may have been imprisoned in Ephesus, and flogged, maybe several times (2 Cor 11:23-24). Writing from Ephesus, he spoke of *many adversaries* in 1 Cor 16:9 and that he was in danger *every hour* (1 Cor 15:30).

Not only does Paul expect the elders of Ephesus to be humble and endure trials, but also (v. 20-21) not to dilute the message. They, like he, must not hesitate to preach and teach anything that will be profitable to the people. They must minister not only publicly, but also *from house to house.* They must not shy away from or depart from the central message of the gospel: *repentance toward God and faith in our Lord Jesus Christ.*

Paul does not use the word "repent" or "repentance" often in his epistles as part of the terms (conditions) of salvation (except in Rom 2:4 and 2 Tim 2:25). The original text of this verse gives a clue that he may have thought of repentance and faith as two sides of the same coin: both nouns are included with one Greek definite article, literally *the repentance and faith;* this construction usually indicates that the two items are thought of as one.

In this day, too many of us preachers are desperately eager to preach "seeker sensitive" messages. In other words, we tell people what they want to hear and avoid what they do not want to hear. While being fully aware of what people **want** to hear, we must never neglect what they **need** to hear, and that, at the core, is the gospel of repentance and faith. We must beware lest we slide into being nothing more than "people-pleasers," *adulterating the Word of God* (2 Cor 4:2 NASB).[9]

In verses 22-24 Paul testifies to seemingly contradictory messages: the Spirit is compelling him to go to Jerusalem, but at the same time giving messages through prophets *in every city . . . imprisonment and afflictions await me.* We will have more to say about this seeming contradiction when we discuss the question raised in chapter 21 as to whether going to Jerusalem

---

9   Paul refused to dilute the truth (1 Thess 2:5; Gal 4:16; 2 Cor 2:17; 4:2).

was not a mistake that ended his itinerant evangelism. At this point it is important to observe that in the phrase *constrained by the Spirit (dedemenos . . . to pneumati),* the word *pneumati* can refer either to Paul's own human spirit or to the Holy Spirit. The older English versions (KJV, ASV, NASV) chose the former option ("spirit") and more modern versions (RSV, NRSV, NIV, JB) as well as most modern commentators choose the latter ("Spirit"). We had the same ambiguity in 19:21. In favor of the "human spirit" option is the fact that the qualifying word "holy" is missing. But this is true in many places where the reference is clearly to the Holy Spirit (Matt 4:1; John 3:6; Acts 8:29; Gal 5:25; 1 Tim 4:1 among many). In favor of the latter is the fact that there is divine compulsion in the word *dei* ("must") in 21:4. Also the phrase *dia tou pneumatos* in that verse certainly refers to the Holy Spirit. The Spirit is directing Paul's travel plans.

Paul escapes when he can, but if the Spirit is directing him to Jerusalem, he will go even if it means the loss of his life. The only thing that matters to him is finishing the race and completing the work the Lord Jesus had given to him, the greatest work in the world, testifying to the gospel of the grace of God. It is a searching question to ponder whether we can honestly repeat Paul's words in v. 24 as our own.

In verses 25-31 Paul's exhortation moves into high gear in an emotional appeal. He expects that none of them will see him again. That will be true whether he is killed in Jerusalem or whether he survives; even if he lives, he considers his work in the Aegean Sea area finished; from now on he will move on to Italy and Spain. There is no record that he ever visited Ephesus after this. The Pastoral Epistles make clear, however, that Paul kept in touch with Ephesus through his disciples Timothy and Tychicus.

The *therefore* in v. 26 marks a forceful transition. Because this is the last time, Paul wants them to know, in a highly emotional and solemn testimony, that he has finished his work in Ephesus. He is *innocent of the blood* of the unsaved, a phrase reminiscent of Ezekiel 3:17-21. If this strong language seems an exaggeration to us, maybe we do not appreciate how seriously Paul took his commission from the risen Christ. He did not preach superficially; he took time to teach *the whole counsel* (NRSB *purpose*) *of God,* that is the plan of God for this age and the age to come, such as we find in Romans 9-11 and the Thessalonian epistles. He taught full-orbed doctrine such as we find systematically expounded in the book of Romans and Ephesians and scattered throughout his other epistles. The implication is that these elders are to continue to do the same in-depth evangelism and teaching.

Now the stage is set for five solemn imperatives: 1) Keep watch over yourselves. 2) Keep watch over the flock. 3) Shepherd the church of God. 4) Be on your guard! 5) Remember my warnings about false teachers. All five charges seem to be a counter to the rise of *fierce wolves* (who) *will come in among you, not sparing the flock; and from among your own selves will arise men speaking twisted things, to draw away the disciples after them.* 1 and 2 Timothy (written to Timothy in Ephesus) and Rev 2:1-7 show that Paul's fears were not unfounded. The letter to the church in Ephesus in Revelation 2 shows that in general these elders must have heeded Paul's earnest warnings about false teaching (Rev 2:6 *But you have this in your favor: You hate the practices of the Nicolaitans, which I also hate.*)

Keep watch over yourselves (NIV) sounds remarkably similar to Paul's imperative to Timothy in 1 Tim 4:16. The shepherds cannot protect the sheep if they do not first protect themselves. The worst trials the church faces are usually internal; pastors and elders fall into adultery, or they misappropriate church funds; they fall into addiction or pornography or adultery or run off with the church secretary. The sad fact is that this type of thing happens all too often and decimates the morale of the churches.

It is worth noting again that these men were made elders, not by human appointment but by the designation of the Holy Spirit. Also, they were appointed not "over" the flock but "among" (*en hō*) the flock (v. 28). Their job is to **shepherd** the flock. Real life shepherds have two chief responsibilities: feeding or leading the flock to pasture and protecting the flock from dangers of predators, disease, and going astray.[10] The elders of the church likewise have two chief responsibilities: teaching the Word of God and protecting the church from spiritual dangers.

Verse 28 has three important textual/exegetical problems: 1) Is it the "church of God" or the "church of the Lord"? 2) Is "church" the universal

---

10   Most modern cultures know little or nothing about sheep and shepherding. We recommend the classic by Phillip Keller; *A Shepherd Looks at Psalm 23* (Zondervan, 1996) for insight into what a real-life shepherd does and the application of the metaphor to pastoring the church.

church or the local (Ephesian) church? 3. Is *dia tou haimatos tou idiou* "through his own blood" or "through the blood of his own (dear one)"?

1. Our best textual authorities have chosen the reading *tēn ekklēsian tou theou* over *tēn ekklēsian tou kuriou* ("the church of God" and "the church of the Lord") because first, *the church of God* is supported by reliable manuscripts (but so is the latter alternative). Second, it is the more difficult reading. One can surmise why a scribe might change the reading to "Lord" because the "the blood of God" (at the end of the verse) is a strange and startling concept, and one cannot surmise why a scribe would insert such an unusual expression. Third, Paul often uses the phrase *church of God* (nine times) but never *church of the Lord.*

2. Most of our versions translate *which he obtained* (*peripoieomai*) **through his own blood.** This translation is of course legitimate and if best, gives us a good verse to support the doctrine of the deity of Christ. We prefer the less popular alternative: **through the blood of His Own** (= *his Dear One*).[11] This rendering removes the jarring reference to *the blood of God* and still supports the main point: the church is precious and must be protected at all costs; it was bought with the highest price that could ever be paid, the life-blood of "the Dear One," the Son of God. The corollary is that the church is the most important and valuable thing in the universe and deserves our best and most sacrificial efforts.

3. Was Paul here thinking of the redemption of the local church in Ephesus or the universal church? We cannot say for sure. In the earliest letters of Paul he uses the word *ekklēsia* for local churches. In later letters, like Ephesians and Colossians, he also writes about the universal church. The usual theological formulation is to say that redemption for the whole universal church came through the blood of Christ, but it gives a more particular and sharper significance to realize also that each local church is precious (just as is each individual believer) because it was redeemed by the blood of the Lamb of God.

In verses 32 to 35 Paul commits his "baby" to the care of God (and its new caretakers), and to the message of **the grace of God**. This message is able

---

11   See Bruce, 434, for support for this alternative.

to first Build them up and mature them in faith. Second, Guarantee them a heavenly inheritance with all the saints, those who have been sanctified by that grace. So many preachers, distressed at immoral trends in society and apostasy in religion, spend too much time railing at the darkness outside and the sins of the flock inside. The net effect is to produce a sense of doom and despair and guilt. While there must always be a warning and a convicting element to our preaching, we must remember that what builds people and churches is not the condemnation of God but the grace of God. The motivation for the **do** is the **done.**

Paul then returns, as he began, to a defense of his ministry. In a nutshell, he says that he is not guilty of covetousness. He had testified in another place (Rom 7:7) that he had been slain by the tenth commandment *Thou shalt not covet.* Apparently this was a temptation that he was determined to avoid and he here testifies that he did not covet anyone's *silver or gold or apparel.* These were the three chief "liquid assets" in the ancient world. Like Samuel (1 Sam 12:3) in his farewell speech, no one could accuse him of "being in it for the money." He had supported himself by working with his own hands (a disgrace for any philosopher or teacher worth his salt). He apparently expected these elders to do the same, and to use any wealth they did not need for their own support to help the weak, that is those unable to support themselves adequately. This final exhortation is supported by quoting a saying of the Lord Jesus himself: *It is more blessed to give than to receive.* This saying is not found in the gospels, but Luke preserves this gem by including it in Acts.[12]

Do we Protestant preachers and professors in theological schools really believe and practice these verses? Do we realize how contemptuous the watching world is of any hint of materialism or avarice in a church worker? Are we really concerned about the poor in our churches, or is that only the responsibility of the government? Sri Lankan Christian leader Ajith Fernando, in his fine commentary on this section, laments the effect of modern materialism and "convenience" on the poorer churches:[13]

> This pattern (of making convenience a major goal in life) has posed a
> major problem to churches in the poorer countries. They send some of

---

12   This proves that the sayings of Jesus were already known and circulating in some form, either oral or written by the mid 50's AD.

13   Ajith Fernando, 542.

their most capable people to richer countries for education, and these people return expecting convenience. They have become soft and do not want to suffer; when they do, they resent it. Not only do they end up having ineffective ministries, they also drag the church down to their low level of commitment. We should work hard at trying to restore a sense of the glory of suffering in the church.

Lastly in verses 36-38 we have the tearful parting. One can picture this band of brothers kneeling on the sands of the shore in fervent prayer, within sight of that magnificent stadium near the harbor, and then the final goodbyes with many hugs and kisses and much loud crying.[14] Some of our societies find such a demonstrative display of raw emotion undignified and unbecoming. We bottle up our emotions and pass off our discomfort with a smile or a joke. Perhaps the early Christians had a richer, simpler humanity and would find us cold and uncaring.

The theater in Miletus is in good condition. The ruins of the ancient baths also remain. The theater and the bath were essential amenities of civilization in ancient Greek cites. In Paul's time the coastline was nearby to the left in this photograph.

---

14   The word *klauthmos* indicates crying out loud, not silent weeping.

Lessons for Life

1. The ministry of *paraklēsis* (comfort, encouragement, exhortation) is vital.
2. It is always wise to flee from danger (20:3) unless we have leading from God to walk into danger (20:22-24).
3. The early Christians gathered each first day of the week to "break bread." The Lord's Supper is important.
4. Paul's miracles, like bringing Eutychus back to life, authenticate his gospel and doctrine and put him on a par with Peter.
5. Church planters must work for the day when we can entrust the church to its own local leadership.
6. We should be able to say to our people, "Imitate me as I imitate Christ."
7. The early church had a plurality of elders, also called "overseers," whose job was "pastoring."
8. We must never dilute the gospel of repentance toward God and faith in our Lord Jesus *Christ* or yield to the temptation to be "people-pleasers."
9. There is much about the "theology of suffering" to be gleaned from this passage. God's way is seldom the easy or convenient way.
10. Our evangelism and teaching should include "the whole plan of God."
11. The church is God's church, not ours, and it is incalculably precious. Its leaders are under the most solemn obligation to protect the church, purchased with the blood of the Son of God.
12. The elders cannot watch over the church unless they watch over themselves first.
13. The Christian worker must beware of covetousness and materialism as if it were the plague.

ACTS 21-28

TESTIMONY AND SUFFERING

Some years ago I was preaching through the Book of Acts in my church in Japan. I had gotten as far as chapter 19 and was wondering if I should continue chapter by chapter through the rest of the book, because all of the "good" material was about finished. About that time we left on home assignment and we turned the church over to a young Japanese pastor. To my surprise, he picked up where I had left off and finished preaching through the book.

This got me to pondering seriously the value and purposes of the last eight chapters. Paul's itinerant mission and church planting are over; now he is under arrest and what we have is "just" a series of trials before various officials. The program of Acts 1:8 does not seem to be moving toward fulfillment anymore. Indeed, most commentaries cover this section in far less detail than the first two-thirds of the book, either from weariness or impatience or the pressure of a deadline. The last third of the book typically ends up composing only one sixth of the commentary.

I started from two premises: 1) The ultimate Author of Scripture is the Holy Spirit. 2) The Holy Spirit does not waste time or space. Each chapter and verse is there for a good reason and is "profitable" (2 Tim 3:16). Therefore, if some parts of Scripture seem less profitable to me, I must study them until I do understand their purpose and profitability.

The result of this study was a realization of the purpose of God for Paul expressed in Acts 9:15-16. If Acts 1:8 is the programmatic statement of the book as a whole, Acts 9:15-16 gives the rationale for chapters 21-28. The

Lord's word to Ananias, in convincing him to visit the arch inquisitor Saul was, *This man is my chosen instrument to carry my name before the Gentiles and their kings and before the people of Israel. I will show him how much he must suffer for my name.* Two elements of God's plan for the rest of Saul's life are expressed here: 1) testimony before the Gentiles and their kings and before the Jewish people and 2) suffering for the sake of Christ. Though we have had both of these elements in chapters 13-20, chapters 21-28 seem to fulfill this commission *par excellence.*

First, there is a chance for Paul to give his salvation testimony of how the risen Lord Jesus had appeared to him before a large crowd of unconvinced Jews in the very heart of their nation, the temple in Jerusalem (chapter 22). Chapter 23 follows quickly with a chance to testify before the Senate of Israel, the Sanhedrin, the same body that condemned Jesus of Nazareth to death. In chapter 24 there is a testimony before a Gentile "king," Felix, and in chapter 25 before another "king," Festus, and in chapter 26 a full testimony of his conversion before the half-Jewish king Agrippa. And in chapters 27 and 28, Paul is protected on his way to testify of Christ before the greatest king of all, the emperor in Rome. Through his arrest, Paul was given amazing and strategic opportunities for testimony to Christ and for defense of the faith. The fact that none of the hearers of these testimonies seem to have believed him and accepted his message does not diminish their value. God was glorified even though the message and the messenger were rejected (Ezek 2:5-7; 3:11).

Second, these chapters are a record of the suffering of imprisonment and the frustration of continual misunderstanding and rejection and delay. Paul is a "little Christ," and he follows his Lord in similar sufferings, as indeed to some extent, do all believers. If we think this is not worth our perusal and meditation, perhaps we need to take a course in the theology of suffering, a much-neglected topic in our modern church.

ACTS 21

PAUL'S ARREST IN THE TEMPLE

Acts 21:1-16

The Journey to Jerusalem

1 And when we had parted from them and set sail, we came by a straight course to Cos, and the next day to Rhodes, and from there to Patara. 2 And having found a ship crossing to Phoenicia, we went aboard and set sail. 3 When we had come in sight of Cyprus, leaving it on the left we sailed to Syria and landed at Tyre, for there the ship was to unload its cargo. 4 And having sought out the disciples, we stayed there for seven days. And through the Spirit they were telling Paul not to go on to Jerusalem. 5 When our days there were ended, we departed and went on our journey, and they all, with wives and children, accompanied us until we were outside the city. And kneeling down on the beach, we prayed 6 and said farewell to one another. Then we went on board the ship, and they returned home.

7 When we had finished the voyage from Tyre, we arrived at Ptolemais, and we greeted the brothers and stayed with them for one day. 8 On the next day we departed and came to Caesarea, and we entered the house of Philip the evangelist, who was one of the seven, and stayed with him. 9 He had four unmarried daughters, who prophesied. 10 While we were staying for many days, a prophet named Agabus came down from Judea. 11 And coming to us, he took Paul's belt and bound his own feet and hands and said, "Thus says the Holy Spirit, 'This is how the Jews at Jerusalem will bind the man who owns this belt and deliver him into the hands of the Gentiles.'"

12 When we heard this, we and the people there urged him not to go up to Jerusalem. 13 Then Paul answered, "What are you doing, weeping and breaking my heart? For I am ready not only to be imprisoned but even to die in Jerusalem for the name of the Lord Jesus." 14 And since he would not be persuaded, we ceased and said, "Let the will of the Lord be done."

15 After these days we got ready and went up to Jerusalem. 16 And some of the disciples from Caesarea went with us, bringing us to the house of Mnason of Cyprus, an early disciple, with whom we should lodge.

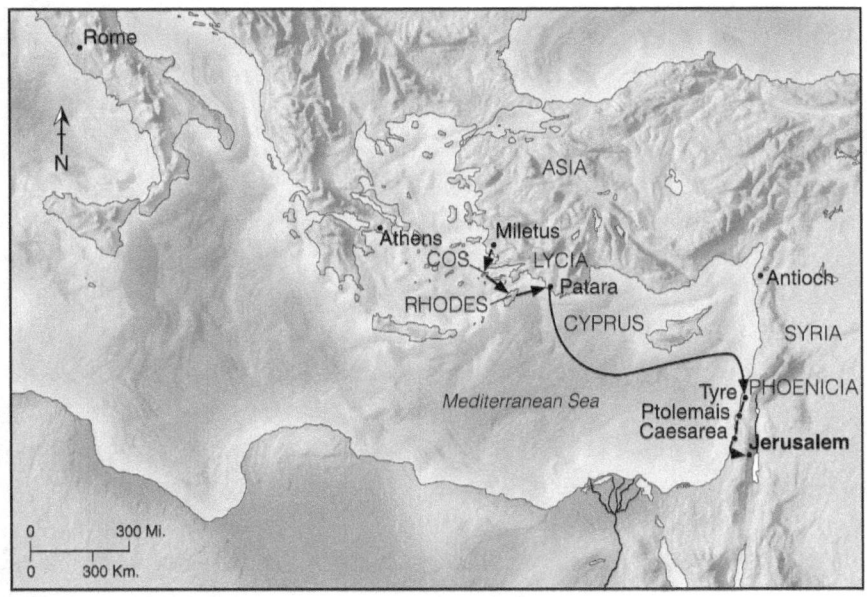

Paul's Return to Jerusalem

Luke continues his personal travel journal on the ship south along the Aegean coast of Asia Minor. It probably took one day to the island of Cos, the home of the famous medical school founded by Hippocrates. By the next night they were in the port of Rhodes on the northeast tip of the island of Rhodes, where they might have marveled at the one of the seven wonders of the ancient world, the Colossus, a bronze statue dedicated to the sun god Helios 104 feet in height (31 m) guarding the inner harbor.[1] From there the

---

1   The popular legend that ships could sail beneath the outspread legs of the statue is false. But the city was still magnificent. Strabo said that he knows of no city so splendid in harbor, walls, and streets (ISBE, vol. IV, "Rhodes," 2589.)

ship continued east to Patara, an important port on the mainland where the excellent ancient harbor can still be seen.

In Patara the party changed ships for a larger vessel headed straight east southeast across 400 miles of open sea to Tyre, skimming the west point of Cyprus halfway. This might have taken about five days.

After landing at Tyre, they sought out the local disciples (Christians), and stayed seven days. The Phoenician churches mentioned in Tyre and Ptolemais (v. 7) were no doubt a result of the evangelism by scattered believers mentioned in 11:19. The believers were getting messages from the Spirit which they interpreted that Paul was in danger if he went to Jerusalem and that he should not go.[2] The warning will get even more explicit in the next paragraph. In a scene reminiscent of the departure from Miletus, the believers, this time with women and children, knelt on the sandy beach to pray, no doubt for the safety of the nine men in the party.

The ship's next stop was Ptolemais, the ancient Acco, and the Crusaders' Acre, near the modern Israeli town of Haifa, and then on to Caesarea, where the sea voyage ended. In Caesarea they were lodged in the house of Philip (the Evangelist, to distinguish him from Philip the Apostle). We last left this Philip some twenty years previously at Caesarea in 8:40. Unlike Paul, he seems to have been married and settled with four daughters, who all had the gift of prophecy, and a house large enough to accommodate nine guests. God has his own best for each of his workers. Again, Luke never fails to mention the contribution of women to the gospel effort.

But the dramatic center of this whole section comes, not from one of the four daughters, but from Agabus, who made a special trip from Jerusalem to warn Paul: *Thus says the Holy Spirit, "This is how the Jews at Jerusalem will bind the man who owns this belt and deliver him into the hands of the Gentiles."* This is the same Agabus of 11:28 who accurately predicted a famine that would affect the whole Roman Empire. He mimes the captivity of Paul in the manner of an Old Testament prophet.[3] The *zōnei* with which Agabus bound his own hands and feet was not a leather belt, but a long strip of cloth which was wound around the waist several times and could be used to carry money.

---

2   The imperfect tense of the word for "say" indicates repeated action: they were telling him repeatedly not to go to Jerusalem.

3   Compare Ahijah tearing Jeroboam's cloak into twelve pieces (1 Kings 11:29f.), Isaiah going naked and barefoot for three years (Isa 20:3f.), and especially Ezekiel, who prophesied using a number of symbolic actions (chapters 4 and 5).

The total effect was so powerful that the whole company, both the local believers and the other eight companions of Paul, wept and *urged him not to go up to Jerusalem.* Paul must have been either a very stubborn or a very resolute man to withstand this kind of pressure. *What are you doing, weeping and breaking my heart? For I am ready not only to be imprisoned but even to die in Jerusalem for the name of the Lord Jesus.*[4] Since we know that Agabus' prophecy did come true, how shall we evaluate Paul's decision here? Why is the Holy Spirit seeming to give contradictory messages about going up to Jerusalem?

First there were the "go to Jerusalem" messages: Acts 19:21(at Ephesus): *Now after these things had been accomplished,* **Paul resolved in the Spirit** *to go through Macedonia and Achaia, and then to go on to Jerusalem* (NRSV). Acts 20:22 (at Miletus): *And now,* **compelled by the Spirit***, I am going to Jerusalem, not knowing what will happen to me there* (NIV).

Then there were "do not go to Jerusalem" messages: Acts 20:23 (at Miletus): *the* **Holy Spirit** *warns me that prison and hardships are facing me.* Acts 21:4 (in Tyre): **Through the Spirit** *they urged Paul not to go on to Jerusalem.* Acts 21:10-11 (in Caesarea): Prophetic mime of **Agabus**: *he took Paul's belt, tied his own hands and feet with it and said, "The Holy Spirit says, "In this way the Jews of Jerusalem will bind the owner of this belt and will hand him over to the Gentiles."*

How are we to resolve this "contradiction"? We could say that the references to *pneuma* in 19:21 and 20:22 refer not to the Holy Spirit but to Paul's human spirit. In this case the "contradiction" disappears. We prefer, however, to interpret these two verses with a capital "S," Spirit, and resolve the "contradiction" by other means. As we look at the "Do not go" messages more carefully, we see that they do not really tell Paul not to go but rather that, if he does go, he will be imprisoned and suffer many trials. Paul plainly told the Ephesian elders exactly that (20:22-23). Agabus (21:10-11) made the point of imprisonment more graphic and more specific. This leaves only the earnest advice of the believers in Tyre (21:4) "do not go up to Jerusalem." We think that what they said was an interpretation of what the Spirit said; the Spirit was not giving a prohibition, but a warning, which Paul's friends then interpreted as a prohibition. Paul was not getting a red light, but a flashing

---

4   The word *break* (*sunthrupto*) was used of pounding laundry with stones to get it clean.

yellow light. He will go to Jerusalem even if he is thrown in prison, and even if he dies (21:13).

What do we do, especially if we have been raised in a "consensus" society to follow the group and never "make waves," but we know God wants us to do something different? Many third-world Christians face this dilemma when they must endure the opposition of their families to their faith in Christ. But what about confusion and disagreement caused by opposition from godly, earnest, fellow believers? How can I be sure that I am right and that their advice, however well meant, is wrong? Only much prayer and a clear conviction of the Spirit's guidance will steady us in such a storm.[5] Meanwhile it is some comfort for those in such situations today to realize that even the greatest of early believers, including those who had the benefit of the gift of prophecy, had differences of opinion on the will of the Lord.

There is, however, an underlying motif at work in these chapters that explains the will of God for Paul at a deeper level. It seems to be the will of God for Paul to experience in a measure the same sufferings that Jesus experienced by going up to Jerusalem where he would be rejected and killed. The parallels, so well summarized by Stott, are too numerous to dismiss as coincidence:

> Both Jesus and Paul (1) were rejected by their own people, arrested without cause, and imprisoned; (2) were unjustly accused and willfully misrepresented by false witnesses; (3) were slapped in the face in court; (4) were the hapless victims of secret Jewish plots; (5) heard the terrifying noise of a frenzied mob screaming "Away with him"; and (6) were subjected to a series of five trials – Jesus by Annas, the Sanhedrin, King Herod Antipas, and twice by Pilate; Paul by the crowd, the Sanhedrin, King Herod Agrippa II and by the two procurators, Felix and Festus.[6]

This list illuminates the Lord's word to Ananias in 9:16: *I will show him how much he must suffer for my name.* As it turned out, Paul would indeed suffer many things during his itinerant missions. After finishing his missionary

---

5   Could it be this was the problem Paul was wrestling with on his solo walk from Troas to Assos (20:13-14)?

6   Stott, 336, in comments on 21:18 and following. Jesus also appeared before Caiaphas, which would make six trials.

journeys, he would go up to Jerusalem to suffer as Jesus himself suffered in Jerusalem. Perhaps we can, through Paul's sufferings in these chapters, better understand what it means for Paul to "die with Christ" and something of what he meant in Col 1:24: *I am now rejoicing in my sufferings for your sake, and in my flesh I am completing what is lacking in Christ's afflictions for the sake of his body, that is, the church.*

How little we modern Christians understand suffering as the will of God! If the church of the first three centuries went overboard in seeking martyrdom, we go to the opposite extreme and think that any suffering or even discomfort is failure, either a result of our sin and carelessness, or the lapses of those around us, or the failure of God to protect us. We are **called** to suffering (Phil 1:29; 1 Pet 2:21).

The companions of Paul, including Luke, Agabus, and Philip, and all the other believers who might have been present, on hearing Paul's resolve even to die for Christ, acquiesced and gave their blessing: *the will of the Lord be done.*

Paul must have been heartened by the generous hospitality and concern for his welfare from the believers in Tyre, Caesarea, and now, in v. 16, with Mnason the Cypriote, *an early disciple.* It is possible that the stay at Mnason's house was between Caesarea and Jerusalem, but it is more likely that Mnason lived in Jerusalem and that his house became the lodging for the whole party of nine during their time in the Holy City. Again and again in the gospels and Acts, we are given examples of practical godliness in offering hospitality to Christian workers. Later, Paul would write that no woman could be enrolled as a widow for church support unless she had *shown hospitality and washed the saints' feet* (1 Tim 5:20), and that hospitality was one of the qualifications for elders (1 Tim 3:2; Tit 1:8).

Acts 21:17-26

Paul Sponsors Four Men With a Vow

*17 When we had come to Jerusalem, the brothers received us gladly. 18
On the following day Paul went in with us to James, and all the elders
were present. 19 After greeting them, he related one by one the things that
God had done among the Gentiles through his ministry. 20 And when
they heard it, they glorified God. And they said to him, "You see, brother,
how many thousands there are among the Jews of those who have believed.
They are all zealous for the law, 21 and they have been told about you that
you teach all the Jews who are among the Gentiles to forsake Moses, telling
them not to circumcise their children or walk according to our customs.
22 What then is to be done? They will certainly hear that you have come.
23 Do therefore what we tell you. We have four men who are under a
vow; 24 take these men and purify yourself along with them and pay their
expenses, so that they may shave their heads. Thus all will know that there
is nothing in what they have been told about you, but that you yourself
also live in observance of the law. 25 But as for the Gentiles who have
believed, we have sent a letter with our judgment that they should abstain
from what has been sacrificed to idols, and from blood, and from what has
been strangled, and from sexual immorality." 26 Then Paul took the men,
and the next day he purified himself along with them and went into the
temple, giving notice when the days of purification would be fulfilled and
the offering presented for each one of them.*

Verse 18 marks the end of this "we section." The next "we section" starts at
27:1. Luke may have remained with Paul during this time, but had no direct
participation in the events of the intervening chapters. Paul wastes no time in
fulfilling his mission; he and his companions went to meet with James and
the elders. James, as we have seen in chapter 15, is the head of the church in
Jerusalem. None of the apostles are mentioned (Peter, John, et al), and we may
guess that they are out on the mission to preach the gospel in "all the world."
Paul gave a thorough report of what God had done (an exemplary way to put
it; not what **Paul** had done or what **they** had done) on the third missionary
journey. Nothing is said about the collection for the poor saints which Paul

had been spending so much effort on.[7] When James and the elders heard Paul's report, *they praised God*. All might have been well if that had been the end of the session.

But now James mentions the success of the gospel among the Jews in the homeland by saying that *many thousands* of Jews have believed.[8] He further claims that all of these Jewish converts to Messiah Jesus *are zealous for the law*. This comes as a bit of a surprise to us modern Gentiles because we have known for two millennia that the New Covenant supersedes the Old, that we are "not under the law." These Palestinian Jews were suspicious of Paul because they had heard that he was teaching *all the Jews who are among the Gentiles to forsake Moses, telling them not to circumcise their children or walk according to our customs*. Was there any substance to this rumor? Nowhere in the New Testament is it recorded that Paul actually taught Jewish believers to abandon the Law of Moses. They were free to observe it or to ignore it as they felt best. However, passages such as Gal 5:2, where Paul sternly warns Gentile Christians not to be circumcised, could easily have been misconstrued to apply also to Jewish believers. Passages from his letters like Rom 6:14-15 and Gal 5:18 (which are written to both Jewish and Gentile believers in Christ) might easily confirm the suspicions of the Jewish Christians in Jerusalem that Paul was teaching Jews to *forsake Moses*.

James and the elders have a clever plan to defuse the suspicions against Paul. He will pay the expenses and join in the purification rites in the temple of four men who are completing a vow. Because these men will have their heads shaved, it is assumed by most commentators that this is the Nazirite Vow of Num 6:1-21. During the period of the vow, the Nazirite must abstain from all alcoholic drinks and must not cut his hair or allow himself to be ceremonially unclean. At the end of his vow period, he must offer the sacrifice of a year-old male lamb, a year-old female lamb, and a ram and a basket of unleavened bread at the tabernacle (later the temple) and have his hair shaved

---

7   It is a puzzle why Luke fails to mention this collection, except in passing in 24:17. Is Luke trying to cover up a failure? Was it not received, as Paul had worried (Rom 15:31), or was it received, but lukewarmly, and not achieving the results hoped for by Paul? Or is there no particular significance to the fact that Luke fails to mention the collection?

8   The Greek word *muriades* means "ten thousands" in the strict sense and "a very large number, not precisely defined" in the loose sense (BDAG). Since a precise number is not attached to the word (as in Acts 19:19), probably the latter is meant.

off and burned *before the LORD*. Apparently, Paul is joining in customs which are not stipulated in Numbers 6, such as being purified in the temple himself on the third and seventh days and paying the expenses of the Nazirites. Many commentators believe that Paul's purification was necessary because he was recently returned from the unclean lands of the Gentiles.[9] The three sacrificial animals would be a considerable expense for a person of modest income and it was considered a great act of piety among the Jews to stand the expenses of such persons.[10]

Since the whole scheme backfired badly and resulted in the arrest of Paul and the endangerment of his life, was not this a mistake? First, was it a mistake on the part of James and the elders to make the request, and second, was it a mistake for Paul to agree to their request?

The first question can, in our opinion, be answered in the affirmative. James was trying to make Paul appear to be what he was not. Was it really true that Paul himself was **always** *living in obedience to the law*? Did he never travel on the Sabbath Day? Did he always have kosher food available? He himself testifies that he became *to those who are without law as without law* but that he was under the *law of Christ* (1 Cor 9:21). How could the author of Gal 5:1 where he calls the Law *a yoke of slavery* be passed off as a proponent of the Law of Moses?[11] The whole idea was more worthy of a clever politician than the head of the Christian church, the scheme of the flesh instead of the leading of the Spirit.

Why then did Paul go along with it? We believe that though Paul was right to go to Jerusalem, but that he was wrong to go along with this dubious scheme.[12] Although he was courageously independent most of the time, here he may have set aside his personal convictions in order to obey church authority and foster harmony in the church. Besides, Paul was desperately

---

9   This purification is mentioned in the Talmud, *m. Oholoth* 2:3. Paul would no doubt have skipped this purification if he had not been asked to stand with the four men.

10   Josephus records that Herod Agrippa I paid expenses for sacrificial animals for many Nazirites (*Ant.* 19.294).

11   It is because of difficulties like these that liberal scholars believe that the author of Acts is trying (falsely) to present Paul as a Torah-abiding Jew (which his epistles show that he is not).

12   Most conservative commentators defend Paul's decision here, but for a view that thinks Paul made a big mistake, not only to enter the temple for vows, but even to go up to Jerusalem. See James Boice's commentary on Acts, pages 363-70. Boice believes that the offering of animal sacrifices after the death of Christ is particularly problematic.

anxious that his relief collection be accepted and that there be harmony in a church that was dangerously divided in basic practices.

∽

Acts 21: 27-40

Paul Captured: The Riot in the Temple

27 When the seven days were almost completed, the Jews from Asia, seeing him in the temple, stirred up the whole crowd and laid hands on him, 28 crying out, "Men of Israel, help! This is the man who is teaching everyone everywhere against the people and the law and this place. Moreover, he even brought Greeks into the temple and has defiled this holy place." 29 For they had previously seen Trophimus the Ephesian with him in the city, and they supposed that Paul had brought him into the temple. 30 Then all the city was stirred up, and the people ran together. They seized Paul and dragged him out of the temple, and at once the gates were shut. 31 And as they were seeking to kill him, word came to the tribune of the cohort that all Jerusalem was in confusion. 32 He at once took soldiers and centurions and ran down to them. And when they saw the tribune and the soldiers, they stopped beating Paul. 33 Then the tribune came up and arrested him and ordered him to be bound with two chains. He inquired who he was and what he had done. 34 Some in the crowd were shouting one thing, some another. And as he could not learn the facts because of the uproar, he ordered him to be brought into the barracks. 35 And when he came to the steps, he was actually carried by the soldiers because of the violence of the crowd, 36 for the mob of the people followed, crying out, "Away with him!"

37 As Paul was about to be brought into the barracks, he said to the tribune, "May I say something to you?" And he said, "Do you know Greek? 38 Are you not the Egyptian, then, who recently stirred up a revolt and led the four thousand men of the Assassins out into the wilderness?" 39 Paul replied, "I am a Jew, from Tarsus in Cilicia, a citizen of no obscure city. I beg you, permit me to speak to the people." 40 And when he had given him permission, Paul, standing on the steps, motioned with his hand to the

*people. And when there was a great hush, he addressed them in the Hebrew
language, saying:*

Paul almost got home free. He had to go to the temple twice, on the
third day and seventh day, in the process of purification. But on the seventh
day he happened to be recognized by some Jews from Asia, probably Ephesus,
who immediately raised the alarm. *Men of Israel, help! This is the man who
is teaching everyone everywhere against the people and the law and this place.
Moreover, he even brought Greeks into the temple and has defiled this holy place.*
If only it were not Pentecost, a festival that brought the Jews from Asia, and if
only Paul had not agreed to help the four men, and if only, in a large throng
of jostling pilgrims, Paul had not been noticed, none of this would have
happened. Bad luck? In any unfortunate incident or tragedy, the "if onlys"
torment the victims. "If only my daughter had left the house a minute earlier,
or a minute later, she would not have been killed by that drunk driver." But all
this is happening, not by chance, but **in the providence of God**.

The accusations could not have been more inflammatory. Paul's teaching
was perceived by the Jews of Asia to be anti-Jewish, anti-Torah, and anti-
Temple. At first "The Way" of Jesus of Nazareth was seen as another sect of
Judaism, and though opposed by the Sanhedrin, was being tolerated, especially
since the Jewish Christians in Judah were *all zealous for the Law*. But Paul
preached to Gentiles and worse, did not teach them to observe *the customs* of
Judaism. The second charge, that he defiled the temple by bringing a Gentile
beyond the *soreg*, the barrier separating the Court of the Gentiles from the
Court of the Women, was serious indeed, in fact punishable by death.[13] Of
course Paul had done no such thing as bringing Gentiles into forbidden areas
of the temple, but fanatics do not stop to check the facts. Paul is in real danger
of being beaten to death by the mob.

The mob quickly grew to include *all Jerusalem*. The rumor spread rapidly
from the temple at the very heart of the densely crowded city, shouted from

---

13   Two of the original inscriptions on this barrier have been discovered. One is in Greek
      and reads: *"No foreigner may enter within the barricade which the surrounds the temple and
      enclosure. Anyone who is caught doing so will have himself to blame for his ensuing death."*
      (Cited from Stott, 344.) This is the only area where the Roman authorities allowed the
      Jews to exercise the death penalty. Even Roman citizens were not exempt.

quarter to quarter, and the stampede was on, most not knowing what or why.[14] Perhaps this riot worked out to Paul's deliverance, however, for it attracted the attention of the jittery Roman troops overlooking the temple courts from the Fortress Antonia, which towered over the northeast corner of the temple walls. Another factor that helped Paul was that he had to be dragged out of the sacred inner courts into the Court of the Gentiles to prevent the spilling of blood in the holy place. The Roman troops had time to rescue Paul before he was killed.

The commander himself led the charge down one of the two stairways that descended to the large plaza from the Antonia Fortress. The Romans were very anxious to seize control before a riot started in ever-volatile Jerusalem. *When the rioters saw the tribune and the soldiers, they stopped beating Paul.* If the beating had continued, Paul would soon have been dead. This is an ironic scene. The unclean Roman Gentiles are playing the role of the righteous to rescue Paul from "pure" Jewish zealots.

After chaining Paul to a soldier by each arm, the troops carried him through the angry mob up the stairs into the safety of the fortress. The frenzied crowd screamed *Away with him!* just as a similar crowd had screamed at Pilate *Away with this man!* some thirty years earlier in this very city (Luke 23:18).

Paul said to the tribune, *Exestin moi eipein ti pros se? Is it permitted for me to say something to you?* The tribune was surprised that he spoke Greek, the *lingua franca* of the eastern Mediterranean. The commander had his own misconception and jumping-to-a-conclusion: *Are you not the Egyptian who recently stirred up a revolt and led the four thousand men of the Assassins out into the wilderness?*

This is a remarkable instance where the book of Acts corresponds with secular history. According to Josephus, about the year 54 AD a false prophet from Egypt came to Jerusalem and led a crowd of 30,000 people to the Mount of Olives and promised that when the walls fell down at his command, they could rush in and seize the city. Procurator Felix dispatched his troops to disburse them. They killed 400 and captured 200.[15] The Messianic pretender escaped. The Talmud mentions his name as Ben Stada.

---

14   As in the riot in Ephesus, *Some in the crowd were shouting one thing, some another.* Chapters 1 and 2 of Josephus' *Jewish Wars* describe just such mass protests and riots when the Jews thought their customs were being violated.

15   Josephus, *Jewish Wars*, 2.261-63. Josephus' "30,000" is suspect; Luke's 4,000 is much more likely. It could be that there was a simple error of one letter in the transmission of Josephus' text to turn "3,000" into "30,000." See Bruce, 452. This man was only one of many would-be Messiahs in that period.

Paul is quick to claim his rights as a Roman citizen. *I am a Jew, from Tarsus in Cilicia, a citizen of no obscure city. I beg you, permit me to speak to the people.* Most of us would have been glad to get as far away from that mob as possible, but Paul still has an aching burden for his people. He now has an admirable opportunity: a large audience of his people in the very heart of the nation and an ideal vantage point on the stairway to address them. When he spoke to them in Aramaic,[16] the common speech of the Jews of the day of Jesus in Palestine, they fell silent to listen.

Lessons for Life

1. The guidance of the Spirit may sometimes set us at odds, not only with non-Christian friends and relatives, but also with well-meaning fellow believers. We need courage to stand against the consensus at times.
2. As "little Christs," part of our destiny is *to know the fellowship of His sufferings* (Phil 3:10).
3. The ministry of hospitality is so important to encourage church workers.
4. There may be tension with church leaders and temptation to compromise our deepest convictions.
5. We will be victims, as Christ and Paul were, of misunderstanding and misconception.
6. God can preserve us, even in the most dangerous circumstances, and even if we have made mistakes that put us in those circumstances. His purposes will prevail, even through the mistakes of ourselves and others.
7. Sometimes Christians are so estranged from their own people that they are tempted to cut themselves off from them. Do we, like Paul, have a burden for the salvation of our own people?

---

16   It is possible that Paul actually spoke in Hebrew, but it is most likely that the reference to *Hebrew language* here actually meant Aramaic. See the detailed discussion by Bock, 658.

ACTS 22

PAUL'S SPEECH TO THE TEMPLE CROWD

Acts 22:1-30

Paul's Apologia Before the Temple Crowd

Paul, even though he must have been terribly bruised and bloodied, seized a golden opportunity to address a large crowd of zealous Jews and many of the residents of Jerusalem. This is the second of three accounts of his conversion. The first in chapter 9 was in the third person and the second and third (chapters 22 and 26) are Paul's first person accounts, here before a large Jewish crowd, and in chapter 26 before King Agrippa and Governor Festus. Paul skillfully modified the two accounts slightly to fit the respective audiences. Details come out that are not in chapter 9.

This is the first of five apologia or defenses of the faith in these chapters: (1) Before the Jewish crowd in the temple court (chap. 22). (2) Before the Sanhedrin in Jerusalem (chap. 23) (3) Before Governor Felix in Caesarea (chap. 24). (4) Before Governor Festus and King Agrippa II in Caesarea. (5) To the Jewish leaders in Rome (chap. 28).

22:1-5 "A Hebrew of the Hebrews"

1 "Brothers and fathers, hear the defense that I now make before you."
2 And when they heard that he was addressing them in the Hebrew language, they became even more quiet. And he said:

305

*3 "I am a Jew, born in Tarsus in Cilicia, but brought up in this city,
educated at the feet of Gamaliel according to the strict manner of the
law of our fathers, being zealous for God as all of you are this day. 4 I
persecuted this Way to the death, binding and delivering to prison both
men and women, 5 as the high priest and the whole council of elders
can bear me witness. From them I received letters to the brothers, and I
journeyed toward Damascus to take those also who were there and bring
them in bonds to Jerusalem to be punished.*

Every word of Paul's opening statement is calculated to identify himself
with the people he is addressing and win their hearts. First, he spoke in the
language of their hearts and homes, *Hebraisti.* Almost all commentators say
this means Aramaic, one of the Semitic family languages used from Palestine
and Syria to Mesopotamia. Aramaic is to Hebrew as Italian is to Latin. Bruce
aptly comments: "(It is) as though an audience of Irish or Welsh nationalists,
expecting to be addressed in English by someone believed to be a traitor to
the national case, suddenly become aware that they were being addressed in
the Celtic vernacular."[1] The crowd is so startled it falls silent. Paul did not
have a PA system and they would need to be quiet to hear his words. Bruce's
comment would have even more force if *Hebraisti* meant "Hebrew," a now
archaic language but probably still comprehensible to this audience.[2]

Second, he addresses them politely and formally *Men, brothers, fathers,*
exactly as Stephen had done in 7:2. One marvels at Paul's composure and
lack of anger. He would have been justified at giving them a good tongue-
lashing in an angry tirade that began with some choice words more suitable
to their true character. Third, he says *I am a Jew.* Most of them already knew
that, but that is his whole point in this section. Notice that he does not say,
"I **was** a Jew." Fourth he gives his Jewish pedigree. He is not just any Jew but
has impeccable credentials. "I was born in Tarsus but brought up in Jerusalem
(our Holy City). I was educated at the feet of the renowned Gamaliel (whose
memory you all revere and whose sayings you all quote, the first to be called
Rabban, an honor even greater than the title *Rabbi.* By the way if you had

---

1   Bruce, 454.

2   As the entry under the word *Hebrais* (ἑβραις) in the latest (third edition) of Danker's
     lexicon (BGAD) notes, a minority of scholars hold that the word does mean "Hebrew,"
     not "Aramaic."

even one tenth of his irenic and tolerant spirit, you would not be acting like animals right now)."

Paul goes on to assert that he was punctiliously trained in the law of their fathers and was, in his youth, just as zealous for the Law as his audience. Notice that Paul is speaking of his past; he cannot say that he has the same zeal for the Torah now. The proof of his zeal is that he persecuted apostates from the Law, the sect of the Nazarenes, the followers of the false Messiah, and as a result of his zeal, some of them (not just Stephen) were put to death. This must have been a matter of deep sorrow and regret for Paul for the rest of his life.

To sum up, Paul is saying to these rabid Jews, "I was just as you are now. I understand your indignation." Now the stage is set for him to tell them why he changed from a persecutor of Christ to a preacher of Christ.

22:6-11 The Lord of Glory Blinds the Misguided Zealot

6 As I was on my way and drew near to Damascus, about noon a great light from heaven suddenly shone around me. 7 And I fell to the ground and heard a voice saying to me, 'Saul, Saul, why are you persecuting me?' 8 And I answered, 'Who are you, Lord?' And he said to me, 'I am Jesus of Nazareth, whom you are persecuting.' 9 Now those who were with me saw the light but did not understand the voice of the one who was speaking to me. 10 And I said, 'What shall I do, Lord?' And the Lord said to me, 'Rise, and go into Damascus, and there you will be told all that is appointed for you to do.' 11 And since I could not see because of the brightness of that light, I was led by the hand by those who were with me, and came into Damascus.

Paul could never forget the shattering crisis that changed his life forever. He must have told the story hundreds of times, and just as we never tell our stories in precisely the same words, each of the three versions in Acts varies slightly. In fact, we would be suspicious if all three were exactly the same.

The three-fold repetition of Paul's conversion underlines the importance of testimony. It strengthens the faith of the testifier. It holds the interest and attention of people who may react negatively to abstract religious arguments or presentations. For Paul it was a bridge to the hearts of both Jews and Gentiles. People will listen to a story of a changed life. Testimony must not serve to boost the ego of the witness but should be a humble witness to the power of God.

We learn for the first time here that the time was *about noon*. The words from heaven are slightly different in that the Lord calls himself *Jesus **of** Nazareth whom you are persecuting*. Paul may have added this word for the benefit of this audience to make it clear just which Jesus had spoken to him. Or this may have been the actual word of the Lord himself and the words *of Nazareth* were dropped in the account in chap. 9.

This account says that the men accompanying Paul saw the light from heaven but did not hear the voice from heaven, whereas chapter 9 says they saw no one (notice it does not say they did not see the light) but they did hear the voice. There is a difference in the case of the word for "voice" (*phōnē*) in 9:7 and 22:9 which follows *akouō*, the word for "hear." In 9:7 it is genitive and simply means "hear" (whether understanding occurs or not). In 22:9 it is accusative and means "hear with understanding." The bystanders heard something but did not understand what was said, just as the bystanders in John 12:28-29 heard a voice from heaven but did not hear it as intelligible speech and some thought that it was thunder.

We also learn for the first time that the Lord's directions to go into the city of Damascus and await further instructions were in response to Paul's question *What shall I do, Lord?* Also, Paul here ascribes the cause of his blindness to *the brilliance of the light*. The Greek for this phrase is *apo tēs doxēs tou phōtos*, "from the **glory** of the light." The basic meaning of the word *doxa* is "brightness." Paul saw Jesus in his risen glorified state, the same Jesus that Peter, James, and John saw on the mount of transfiguration. This puts Paul on the same level as Peter and John.

This is the heart of the matter. Paul was not converted from a fire-breathing Pharisee into a flaming apostle of Christ by arguments or logical reasoning. He was really at first quite an unwilling miserable convert who was overwhelmed, indeed blinded, by a special appearance of the Christ of glory. He had no choice but to obey.

22:12-16 The Role of Ananias, a Pious Jew

> *12 "And one Ananias, a devout man according to the law, well spoken of by all the Jews who lived there, 13 came to me, and standing by me said to me, 'Brother Saul, receive your sight.' And at that very hour I received*

my sight and saw him. 14 And he said, 'The God of our fathers appointed
you to know his will, to see the Righteous One and to hear a voice from his
mouth; 15 for you will be a witness for him to everyone of what you have
seen and heard. 16 And now why do you wait? Rise and be baptized and
wash away your sins, calling on his name.'

The account of the role of Ananias in healing Paul's blindness and of
baptizing him is slightly different than the account in chapter 9. In chapter 9
Ananias was simply a disciple. Before this Jewish audience he is identified as
a devout observer of the law and highly respected by all the Jews living there.
The objections of Ananias and his debate with the Lord are omitted here. But
there are additions to the words of Ananias to Paul: The God of our fathers
appointed you to know his will, to see the Righteous One, and to hear a voice
from his mouth; *15 for you will be a witness for him to everyone of what you have*
seen and heard. 16 And now why do you wait? Rise and be baptized and wash
away your sins, calling on his name. Phrases such as *The God of our fathers* and
the Righteous One are used to appeal to this Jewish audience.

You will be a witness for him to everyone of what you have seen and heard.
Here Ananias relayed to Paul an abbreviated form of what God had told him
in 9:15. The word "witness" picks up the key word of the programmatic verse
of the book of Acts, 1:8. Everyone (*pantas*) means "all kinds of people" and is a
summary of the Gentiles and their kings and the people of Israel of 9:15. Paul
in this way avoids the poison word "Gentiles." *What you have seen and heard*
refers primarily to the vision of the exalted Jesus." That is the reason why Paul
repeated it every chance he got and why it is recorded three times in this book.

Rise and be baptized and wash away your sins, calling on his name. This
sentence offers a number of exegetical alternatives depending on one's choices
among possibilities in the Greek text. The second and third imperatives, be
baptized and wash your sins away, are in the middle voice and could be or
permissive: "let yourself be baptized and let your sins be washed away." Another
problem is how we interpret the phrase *calling on his name.* The English
translation leaves the meaning of the Greek aorist participle ambiguous. It
could be a temporal participle "after" you call upon his name.[3] It could be
a participle of means: "by calling upon his name." In this case the participle

---

3   The aorist participle usually indicates antecedent action, that is, action previous to the
     main verb. Usually though the aorist temporal participle **precedes** the verb it modifies.

would modify only the third imperative: "Wash away your sins by calling upon his name." It could be a participle of attendant circumstances: "the whole process of baptism, washing of sins, and calling on the Lord's name is portrayed as a single complex event."[4] We prefer either the second or third of these three alternatives, with a slight preference for the second.

Perhaps the reason for this "slight preference" is our theological bias on the connection between baptism and cleansing from sin or forgiveness. We do not believe that the act of baptism as a sacrament washes away sin, but is rather a symbol of the cleansing or washing away of sin which has already transpired through faith (expressed here by "*calling on his name*;" cf. Rom 10:13).

22:17-21 The Lord Appears to Paul in the Temple

17 "When I had returned to Jerusalem and was praying in the temple, I fell into a trance 18 and saw him saying to me, 'Make haste and get out of Jerusalem quickly, because they will not accept your testimony about me.' 19 And I said, 'Lord, they themselves know that in one synagogue after another I imprisoned and beat those who believed in you. 20 And when the blood of Stephen your witness was being shed, I myself was standing by and approving and watching over the garments of those who killed him.' 21 And he said to me, 'Go, for I will send you far away to the Gentiles.'"

Paul made many visits to the temple; this incident probably occurred on his first visit to Jerusalem after his conversion (9:26-30). This paragraph is unique to this chapter; it is not found in either of the other two accounts in Acts 9 or 26.

This is the second of six occasions when God revealed himself directly to Paul in a dream or a vision.[5] This puts him ahead of Peter, to whom only one vision is ascribed in the book of Acts (chapter 10). The first two

---

4   Mikeal C. Parsons and Martin M. Culy, *Acts: A Handbook on the Greek Text*. Waco, Texas, Baylor University Press, 2003, 429.

5   In chronological order there was the Damascus Road vision (Acts 9:3-8), this vision (*ekstasis*) in the temple, the dream in Macedonia (16:9), the dream in Corinth (18:9-10), the appearance of an angel of God by night on the storm-tossed ship, and Paul's being *caught up into Paradise* (2 Cor 12:2-4). We do not know the time of the last, though some speculate it might have happened as an out-of-the-body experience when Paul was stoned in Lystra (Acts 14:19).

are trances or visions and the next three are dreams. In both of the first two appearances, especially this one, Paul argued with the Lord, reminiscent of Ananias' protests in 9:10-16. The command *Make haste and get out of Jerusalem quickly, because they will not accept your testimony about me* is unique to this account. Paul protests, in effect, that he was best qualified to witness to the Jewish leadership because he had once been a zealous supporter of their cause. The Lord replies that he must leave Jerusalem because the Jews there will not listen to his testimony.

No matter how much we may think we are suited for a certain ministry, only the Lord knows where we will be most effective. He also knows that it is useless, maybe dangerous, to testify to some people *because they will not accept your testimony about me.* "I understand your burden for your own people but My mission for you is to preach to the Gentiles."

22:22-30 Paul is Rescued From a Manic Crowd and From Scourging

22 Up to this word they listened to him. Then they raised their voices and said, "Away with such a fellow from the earth! For he should not be allowed to live." 23 And as they were shouting and throwing off their cloaks and flinging dust into the air, 24 the tribune ordered him to be brought into the barracks, saying that he should be examined by flogging, to find out why they were shouting against him like this. 25 But when they had stretched him out for the whips, Paul said to the centurion who was standing by, "Is it lawful for you to flog a man who is a Roman citizen and uncondemned?" 26 When the centurion heard this, he went to the tribune and said to him, "What are you about to do? For this man is a Roman citizen." 27 So the tribune came and said to him, "Tell me, are you a Roman citizen?" And he said, "Yes." 28 The tribune answered, "I bought this citizenship for a large sum." Paul said, "But I am a citizen by birth." 29 So those who were about to examine him withdrew from him immediately, and the tribune also was afraid, for he realized that Paul was a Roman citizen and that he had bound him.

30 But on the next day, desiring to know the real reason why he was being accused by the Jews, he unbound him and commanded the chief priests and all the council to meet, and he brought Paul down and set him before them.

The Jewish crowd now demonstrated the truth of the Lord's word *they will not accept your testimony about me.* When the crowd heard the words that Paul had been sent to the **Gentiles**, they exploded with fury anew, *shouting and throwing off their cloaks and flinging dust into the air.* They may have been trying to throw the dust at Paul.

Why did the word "Gentiles" trigger such an uproar?[6] Did not the Jews themselves have very successful missions among the Gentiles to convert them to Judaism? Were there not Gentile proselytes in almost every Jewish synagogue? The answer seems to be that Paul was preaching a faith that did not require the Gentiles to enter faith through the gate of Judaism: circumcision, obedience to the Law and attendance at the temple (21:21 and 21:28). It may also have reminded them of the accusation that Paul had brought a Gentile into the holy precincts. Notice, however, that these are not Paul's words; he is quoting the words of the Lord Jesus, and it is that Lord that these Jews are again vilifying and rejecting. One is reminded of the rejection of Jesus in the synagogue of his hometown of Nazareth when he said that in the days of prophets God had, on two occasions, by-passed the Jews and saved Gentiles (Luke 4:24-29).

That said, there is something irrational about the behavior of this Jewish crowd. Recall that one of Luke's purposes in the book of Acts is to explain, by relating certain parts of the history of the early church, why the Jews rejected their own Messiah. In this chapter he is pointing out that much of their objection was fanatical unbelief, irrational prejudice, and mob psychology.

The Roman tribune, completely ignorant of what Paul had said or the reason for the riot, took Paul into the safety of the Fortress Antonia and prepared to get the truth out of this "criminal." In those days, the quickest way to get the truth out a suspect was to flog him with the fearful *flagellum*, the same brutal instrument that had been used against Jesus. It was a whip with thirteen leather thongs embedded with bits and bone and metal. One stroke made the back a bleeding, quivering pulp.

---

6   The Greek text says literally *"they listened to him as far as this word."*

But here the resemblance to the sufferings of Christ abruptly ended when Paul claimed his Roman citizenship.[7] It was legal to flog slaves and non-citizens, but flogging a Roman citizen would have gotten this commander in serious trouble, and even putting an uncondemned citizen in chains was illegal. This explains why Paul was released so quickly. Again we have the irony of Paul the Jew being rescued from his own people by the unclean Gentile dogs, who were only trying their best to preserve law and order.

We can only speculate as to what Paul might have said if he had not been so rudely interrupted. He might have gone on to quote Scripture and speak more directly of Jesus as he did in the Acts 13 sermon in Antioch of Pisidia or in the same vein as Peter did on the day of Pentecost. It is instructive that he did not do what we might have done, that is to defend himself directly against the charges of 21:28 by denying that he had ever taught *against our people and the law and this place.* Neither did Paul attempt to deny the falsehood that he had taken Trophimus into the holy place. Instead, he went first to the underlying issue: the shattering and undeniable experience he had experienced on the Damascus Road.

When we defend ourselves against false accusations, we are on weak ground, but we are on strong ground when we address underlying issues and stress what actually happened and why. In this way we follow the example of our Lord Jesus, who in his trials, had almost nothing to say in his defense (1 Pet 2:23; 3:9, 14-17).

The commander of the legion realized that this was a religious problem, and so he decided to bring Paul before the religious experts the next day.

---

7   By the time of Paul, many non-Romans were granted Roman citizenship as a favor for special services to the state or as rewards for other meritorious deeds. Since Paul was *born a citizen,* his father must have been a Roman citizen, but we have no idea how that happened, or how far back in Paul's line the citizenship might have extended.

Lessons for Life

1. We must make every effort to tailor our speech to impress the particular audience we are addressing. This includes addressing people in their heart language and requires intimate knowledge of their culture and worldview.
2. Even though we have every right to be angry when unjustly accused, we, either as individuals or a church, must refrain from responding in like manner.
3. Testimony is more powerful than self-defense, theological argument, or even sound sermons, as necessary as these are. The word "witness" is the key word of this chapter.[8]
4. We must accept the fact that sometimes people will not believe our testimony.

---

8   The word "witness," either as noun or verb, occurs five times in this chapter, more than any other chapter of Acts.

ACTS 23

PAUL BEFORE THE SANHEDRIN

Acts 22:30-23:11

The Inquest Before the Sanhedrin

30 But on the next day, desiring to know the real reason why he was being accused by the Jews, he unbound him and commanded the chief priests and all the council to meet, and he brought Paul down and set him before them.

1 And looking intently at the council, Paul said, "Brothers, I have lived my life before God in all good conscience up to this day." 2 And the high priest Ananias commanded those who stood by him to strike him on the mouth. 3 Then Paul said to him, "God is going to strike you, you whitewashed wall! Are you sitting to judge me according to the law, and yet contrary to the law you order me to be struck?" 4 Those who stood by said, "Would you revile God's high priest?" 5 And Paul said, "I did not know, brothers, that he was the high priest, for it is written, 'You shall not speak evil of a ruler of your people.'"

6 Now when Paul perceived that one part were Sadducees and the other Pharisees, he cried out in the council, "Brothers, I am a Pharisee, a son of Pharisees. It is with respect to the hope and the resurrection of the dead that I am on trial." 7 And when he had said this, a dissension arose between the Pharisees and the Sadducees, and the assembly was divided. 8 For the Sadducees say that there is no resurrection, nor angel, nor spirit, but the Pharisees acknowledge them all. 9 Then a great clamor arose, and

some of the scribes of the Pharisees' party stood up and contended sharply,
"We find nothing wrong in this man. What if a spirit or an angel spoke
to him?" 10 And when the dissension became violent, the tribune, afraid
that Paul would be torn to pieces by them, commanded the soldiers to go
down and take him away from among them by force and bring him into
the barracks.

11 The following night the Lord stood by him and said, "Take courage,
for as you have testified to the facts about me in Jerusalem, so you must
testify also in Rome."

Though we have counted this appearance before the Sanhedrin as one of the
five "trials" in this portion of Acts, strictly speaking it is not a trial, but an
arraignment or inquest to determine what the charges are against Paul. Here is
another chance for Paul to explain his conversion or witness to the Lord Jesus.
But the hearing soon collapsed into physical violence and a rowdy fracas.

We do not see Paul at his best here. First, he seems to be speaking out of
order by making his opening statement before the presiding officer can either
accuse him or ask him questions or even call the meeting to order. Second,
when he was slapped on the mouth, he reacted with a perfectly understandable
but unwise outburst against his tormentor. Both of his statements here
were perfectly true; the problem was that he spoke out of turn and in an
inflammatory manner both times. When Jesus was arraigned before this same
body, he only spoke when questioned and did not resort to name-calling or
any tricks to escape (Luke 22:66-70).

Paul's statement about always living with a clear conscience was true even
before his conversion when he was persecuting the believers in the Nazarene
even to the point of death because he sincerely thought he was doing the
will of God.[1] Conscience is sometimes a faulty compass. Paul's point is
that he has done nothing against the will or the law of God, certainly not
such an outrageous thing as to desecrate the temple by bringing Gentiles
into forbidden areas. His statement is a pre-emptive strike to defend himself
against any accusation.

---

1   *A time is coming when anyone who kills you will think he is offering a service to God* (John
16:2, NIV). An appeal to his clear conscience is so typical Paul: Acts 24:16; Rom 9:1;
1 Cor 4:4; 2 Cor 1:12; 2 Tim 1:3. No other NT writer, with the exception of the author
of Hebrews, even mentions "conscience," but Paul uses it often.

Paul's minor offence triggered the temper of the high priest, who ordered his unruly mouth slapped into submission. This was of course an unbelievable offense against the rights of the accused and the law (as Paul pointed out) and against any semblance of proper procedure. It set the scene for the debacle that followed.

But Paul did not help matters by name-calling. His called his accuser *a whitewashed wall* (not a whited sepulcher), perhaps a proverb having its origin in Ezek 13:10-16 where lying prophets concealed the real condition of apostate Israel. So the epithet meant a religious fraud or hypocrite. That was right on the mark with this high priest, whose name was Ananias. He was high priest from 47-66 AD. Josephus records that he was corrupt; he promoted bribery and stole from the tithes paid to the temple.[2] "The Talmud reproduces popular lampoons of his gluttony."[3]

It may well be that Paul had never seen the reigning high priest, since he had not been in the sessions of the Sanhedrin for over twenty years. This lends some credence to his apology in verse 5 that he did not know it was the high priest. The reason for this ignorance is variously attributed to Paul's allegedly poor eyesight, or that the high priest was not wearing his customary vestments and insignia of rank, or even that it was a sarcastic remark meaning, "I did not know that a person giving such a command could possibly be the high priest." If Paul had never met this high priest, it is explanation enough.

Next Paul, again without waiting for any questions or charges, seized the initiative with a clever trick to divide the Sanhedrin and divert attention from himself. He cried out *Brothers, I am a Pharisee, a son of Pharisees. It is with respect to the hope and the resurrection of the dead that I am on trial.* What he said about being a Pharisee was perfectly true. The second part of his statement seems strange. Nobody was accusing him of his hope in the resurrection from the dead.[4] He is referring, somewhat elliptically, to his faith in the resurrection of Jesus of Nazareth. This was an important underlying issue; if Jesus had not risen and appeared to him, he would never have been converted into a

---

2   *Antiquities*, 20.103.

3   Bruce, 464.

4   This is the first of four references to the theme of *the hope of Israel* in the latter chapters of Acts. See also 24:15, 26:6-7, and 28:20.

Christian missionary and never been accused by the Jewish mob. Even so he phrased it in such a way that it triggered their favorite argument.

The doctrine of general resurrection is referred to clearly in the OT only in Isa 26:19 and Dan 12:2. It developed into a generally popular doctrine among many Jews, including the Pharisees, in the 400-year intertestamental period. The Sadducees, in some ways liberal, and in some ways conservative, relied only on the Torah, the five books of Moses, and denied not only the resurrection, but also the immortality of the soul. The latter is evidently the meaning of their denial of angel or spirit. The word "angel" here is not what the Bible usually means by "angel," but the departed human spirit (see Acts 12:15).

The result was a disgraceful dissension in which the Pharisees forgot the main issue and sided with Paul, their fellow-Pharisee. Paul was the rope in a tug-of-war between the Pharisees and the Sadducees.

Nobody looks good in this incident except the Romans. The most eminent and most authoritative body in Israel perpetrated this ridiculous travesty of justice and common civility. One of Luke's purposes is to answer the question: If Jesus really is the Messiah, why did his own people not receive him? Here his answer, simply recording what happened in this incident, is: "What can you expect from such a troop of squabbling baboons?"

We are afraid our hero Paul does not look good here. Some commentators try to excuse him, as if he could do no wrong. Nevertheless, he certainly did not follow the example of his Lord *who when he was abused, he did not return abuse; when he suffered, he did not threaten; but he entrusted himself to the one who judges justly* (1 Pet 2:22).

Those who do defend Paul here, however, can refer to verse 11. The Lord himself again appeared to Paul and the Lord did not scold Paul but instead gave him a wonderful encouragement and said in effect: "Do not be discouraged. This is all part of my plan. I wanted you to testify in Jerusalem. I also want you to testify in Rome and this is part of my plan to get you to Rome (without paying for passage!)." Did Paul recall here what he had written to the Romans: *We know that in all things God works for the good of those who love him, who have been called according to his purpose?*

Paul needed this gracious intervention of the Lord. His nerves must have been frazzled by the violence of both the mob and the Sanhedrin. He may have wondered whether he made the right decisions in coming to Jerusalem and in agreeing to the scheme of James that required him to enter the temple. He had a wonderful chance for a testimony to Christ, but he knows of no one who believed his testimony. He may have felt guilty about his less than Christlike conduct before the Sanhedrin. Now the grace of the Lord has strengthened him for the next trial and for about five years of captivity.

ᘓℯᘔ

Acts 23:12-22

The Plot to Assassinate Paul

12 When it was day, the Jews made a plot and bound themselves by an oath neither to eat nor drink till they had killed Paul. 13 There were more than forty who made this conspiracy. 14 They went to the chief priests and elders and said, "We have strictly bound ourselves by an oath to taste no food till we have killed Paul. 15 Now therefore you, along with the council, give notice to the tribune to bring him down to you, as though you were going to determine his case more exactly. And we are ready to kill him before he comes near."

16 Now the son of Paul's sister heard of their ambush, so he went and entered the barracks and told Paul. 17 Paul called one of the centurions and said, "Take this young man to the tribune, for he has something to tell him." 18 So he took him and brought him to the tribune and said, "Paul the prisoner called me and asked me to bring this young man to you, as he has something to say to you." 19 The tribune took him by the hand, and going aside asked him privately, "What is it that you have to tell me?" 20 And he said, "The Jews have agreed to ask you to bring Paul down to the council tomorrow, as though they were going to inquire somewhat more closely about him. 21 But do not be persuaded by them, for more than forty of their men are lying in ambush for him, who have bound themselves by an oath neither to eat nor drink till they have killed him. And now they are ready, waiting for your consent." 22 So the tribune dismissed the young man, charging him, "Tell no one that you have informed me of these things."

Paul is in deadly peril. The danger is underlined by the fact that some Jews[5] had taken an oath to neither eat nor drink until they had killed Paul. One could not be more deadly serious than that. Some would most likely die in the assassination attempt. Second, there were forty of them, enough to easily overpower a squad of Roman soldiers escorting Paul. Third, the assassins acted quickly, the same day the Sanhedrin had failed to do any harm to Paul. Fourth, they were willing to risk the wrath of Rome in what would most certainly have caused a bloody reprisal. This is the kind of Jewish fanaticism that led to the rebellion of 66 AD and the annihilation of the Jewish state in 70 AD.

The big point of the story, however, is how the plot was foiled by the providence of God. We wish Luke had told us a little more. We would like to know more about Paul's family. This is the only reference in the Bible to any of his family. Why was his nephew in Jerusalem? Was his home Tarsus or Jerusalem? Was he studying in Jerusalem as Uncle Paul had done? How old was the *young man*?[6] How did he happen to hear of the plot?

Concerning the last question, we do not need to assume that the young man was present at the planning meeting of the conspirators. Somehow, in the providence of God, he heard about or overheard the plot. Maybe he heard a small group or two discussing the plan after the main meeting. The conspirators may have been careless in their talk, confident that none of their fellow Jews would betray them to the Romans. We have a similar instance of providence in preserving God's people in the story of how Mordecai overheard a plot against the King of Persia (Esther chapter 2).

---

5   The addition of the word 'some' in some lesser manuscripts and ancient translations makes the text more accurate. The conspirators would not have approached the Pharisees who had tried to defend Paul.

6   The first word used, in v. 17, is *neanias,* which means, according to BDAG, "a young man from about the 24th to the 40th year." The word in verses 18 and 22 is *neaniskos,* which would normally indicate the diminutive of *neanias,* but according to BDAG this word is equivalent to *neanias* and covers the same age range. Philo says a *neaniskos* was a young man between 24 and 28. However, the word is often used in the Septuagint to translate the Hebrew *na'ar,* which often refers to teenage boys such as Joseph (17 years old in Gen 37:2) and Jonathan's boy servant who chased arrows (1 Sam 20:22). Since the commander *took him by the hand* (v. 19), this *young man* must have been a teenager.

It is not strange that the young man had access to Paul. Paul was under house arrest in the fortress of Antonia and he would have been able to receive visitors, especially family, in his state of custody. This would be true for the next five years.

∽ced∼

Acts 23:23-35

The Military Escort out of Danger

23 Then he called two of the centurions and said, "Get ready two hundred soldiers, with seventy horsemen and two hundred spearmen to go as far as Caesarea at the third hour of the night. 24 Also provide mounts for Paul to ride and bring him safely to Felix the governor." 25 And he wrote a letter to this effect:

26 "Claudius Lysias, to his Excellency the governor Felix, greetings. 27 This man was seized by the Jews and was about to be killed by them when I came upon them with the soldiers and rescued him, having learned that he was a Roman citizen. 28 And desiring to know the charge for which they were accusing him, I brought him down to their council. 29 I found that he was being accused about questions of their law, but charged with nothing deserving death or imprisonment. 30 And when it was disclosed to me that there would be a plot against the man, I sent him to you at once, ordering his accusers also to state before you what they have against him."

31 So the soldiers, according to their instructions, took Paul and brought him by night to Antipatris. 32 And on the next day they returned to the barracks, letting the horsemen go on with him. 33 When they had come to Caesarea and delivered the letter to the governor, they presented Paul also before him. 34 On reading the letter, he asked what province he was from. And when he learned that he was from Cilicia, 35 he said, "I will give you a hearing when your accusers arrive." And he commanded him to be guarded in Herod's praetorium.

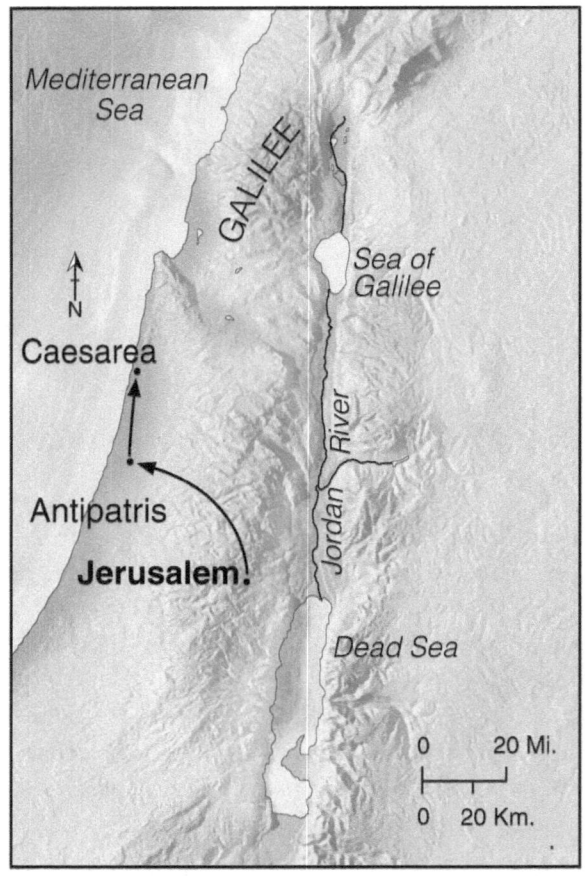

Imprisonment in Caesarea

The Commander (Tribune) in charge of the garrison in Jerusalem acted decisively and swiftly, in the best tradition of the Roman army. The Romans did not do things by halves! They must leave by night as soon as the army can get organized. To counter the threat of forty Jewish assassins, Claudius Lysias assigned 470 fully armed soldiers, including regular foot soldiers, cavalry, and spearmen,[7] to whisk Paul away to the safety of Caesarea, 66 miles (106 km) from Jerusalem. Paul was given *mounts* (plural); he rode on one and one was available for his baggage, and maybe a third as a relief mount. The modern

---

7   The meaning of this very rare word *dexiolaboi* is obscure; "spearmen" is as good a guess
     as any.

equivalent would be a a motorcycle escort. He must have marveled, even laughed, at this magnificent escape, perhaps contrasting it with his ignominious escape from Damascus many years before in a basket! He may have chuckled wondering how long the conspirators would keep their vow not to eat or drink.

Witherington points out that there may have been good reasons for Lysias to commit such a large force to protect Paul and to march by night.[8] First fanatics like these forty, like the *sicarii* (21:38) were volatile and dangerous. Second the route to be traveled to Caesarea was particularly dangerous. Recently an imperial slave carrying a large sum of money had been attacked and robbed on this road.[9] Later, in 66 AD, an entire Roman legion was almost annihilated by Jewish rebels in the narrow confines of this road. One might also point out that Lysias was in charge of maintaining order in Jerusalem and Paul was obviously a threat to that order every hour he remained in the city. It was not just pity for Paul that provided such an invincible escort.

Antipatris was a Roman military base 31 miles (50 km) from Jerusalem, and safely distant from the hungry assassins. The escort continued, after a day of rest, with the 200 cavalrymen to Caesarea, where the Roman governors of Judea maintained their headquarters in a large palace. The letter was immediately given to Felix the procurator and Paul was officially remanded to his custody.

The NIV renders the Greek phrase *grapsas epistolēn exousan ton **tupos** touton* in v. 25 as *He wrote a letter as follows:* indicating a precise quotation, but the ESV translates: *He wrote a letter to this effect* indicating that this text is an approximation of what was written. Either interpretation of *tupos* is possible, but one eminent scholar argued persuasively that *tupos* here is not "pattern" but "verbatim copy."[10] Many have accused Luke of making up this letter, as some ancient historians were wont to do, assuming that Luke would never have had access to the letter. However, Felix may have read, or had read, the letter in Paul's presence since ancient readers always read out loud. It was almost certainly written in Latin, not Greek, so in that sense our version is not a precise duplicate. It is very possible that the letter became part of Paul's case dossier, and may have been read in court on other occasions when Luke was present. Both Paul and Luke would have known rudimentary Latin.

---

8   Witherington, 696-97.

9   Josephus, *War* 2.228; *Ant.* 20.113).

10   See Bruce 471 and Witherington, 698. The scholar was E. A. Judge.

The content of the letter is concise and clear. Theophilus may have smiled at the way Claudius Lysias covered his terrible mistake of chaining and almost flogging a Roman citizen by making his discovery of Paul's citizenship prior to and not after the rescue operation. Except for that little inaccuracy, the account is true and makes the tribune look good in the eyes of his superior. Today we call the slant public figures put on their press releases "spin." How little things have changed!

Lysias does make the important point that he has so far not found any *aitia* (charge) against Paul worthy of capital punishment or even of confinement. This recalls the case of Jesus, of whom Pilate said three times *I find no fault in this man* (Luke 23:4, 14, 22). The case had nothing to do with Roman law but only of Jewish religious law. Therefore the accusers must present their charges and their case before the governor. Now the stage is set for the trial before Felix in chapter 24.

The whole point of the chapter may be summed up in the verb in verse 24 *diasōsōsi: they **brought him safely** to Felix.* "Complete deliverance" is the theme of all of these chapters through to the end of the book.[11] It was really the providence of God that rescued Paul from the plot of the forty assassins and delivered him safely in such magnificent style to Caesarea.

Lessons for Life

1. As the Japanese proverb has it, "*Saru mo ochiru.*" "Even a monkey will fall." The meaning is that even experts sometimes make a mistake. Here Paul, a courageous saint and an outstanding Christian leader, makes some mistakes. But the Lord in his mercy not only does not mention his mistakes, but rather encourages him in the stress of this severe ordeal.

2. We or our church may well suffer false accusation, threats, even violence. Our Lord suffered this way and so do we. But God is able to protect us in perilous situations.

3. The providence of God is a marvelous thing for the protection of his people.

---

11   The same verb occurs again in Acts 27:43 and 44 and 28:1 and 4, sometimes translated "escape."

ACTS 24

PAUL BEFORE FELIX

Acts 24:1-9

The Accusation

1 And after five days the high priest Ananias came down with some elders and a spokesman, one Tertullus. They laid before the governor their case against Paul. 2 And when he had been summoned, Tertullus began to accuse him, saying:

"Since through you we enjoy much peace, and since by your foresight, most excellent Felix, reforms are being made for this nation, 3 in every way and everywhere we accept this with all gratitude. 4 But, to detain you no further, I beg you in your kindness to hear us briefly. 5 For we have found this man a plague, one who stirs up riots among all the Jews throughout the world and is a ringleader of the sect of the Nazarenes. 6 He even tried to profane the temple, but we seized him. 8 By examining him yourself you will be able to find out from him about everything of which we accuse him."

9 The Jews also joined in the charge, affirming that all these things were so.

Antonius Felix was the sixth procurator of Judea since Pontius Pilate. He had been born a slave but was a friend of Emperor Claudius in their boyhood days and was freed by Claudius' mother Antonia. His brother Pallas, also a freedman, and very wealthy, had much power in Roman political circles. Felix was appointed to a post under the previous governor of Judea, Cumanus, in

48 AD and was made governor of Judea when Cumanus was deposed in 52 AD. We are now at the year 57 AD, so Felix has been governor of Judea for about five years.

It was not an easy task. During this time rebellions, messianic movements, and assassinations were increasing throughout Palestine.[1] Felix put down these uprisings with excessive brutality and so the Jews hated him. It was the Jewish protest against his slaughter of Jews in a Greek-Jew riot in Caesarea in 59 AD that brought about his dismissal as governor. Tacitus described him as "a master of cruelty and lust who exercised the powers of a king with the spirit of a slave."[2] He seems to have presumed upon his high connections in Rome, but now that Nero was Emperor he had to be a little more careful.

The High Priest Ananias and his allies in the Sanhedrin lost no time in lodging charges against Paul before the governor. They hired a lawyer named Tertullus, who may have been Roman or a Romanized Jew, who could plead their case with elegant Latin. This may be a summary of what he actually said; if so, he spent half his time flattering Felix in the *exordium* or opening remarks. Maybe Felix winced a bit, realizing that the *peace* and *reforms* Tertullus alluded to had been secured by shedding a lot of Jewish blood. Everything in Tertullus' opening was standard courtroom rhetoric typical of lawyers of those times.[3] The last line *But, to detain you no further, I beg you in your kindness to hear us briefly* was quite common in such speeches. Paul is up against a professional prosecutor and he has no defense lawyer to stand with him.

Next follow three accusations: 1) This man is a troublemaker who endangers the peace of the empire. 2) This man is a ringleader in the sect of the Nazarenes (who as you know are troublemakers). 3) This man defiled the temple. Accusations one and three were very serious and could have resulted in the death penalty.

We have found this man to be a plague. The implication is that this movement is a dangerous epidemic which is spreading rapidly and must be eradicated.

He is a ringleader of the sect of the Nazarenes. Each of the three key words here has a negative flavor. The word for sect is *hairesis*, which simply meant

---

1   See Josephus, *Jewish Wars*, chapters 12 and 13.

2   Cited by Longenecker, 539 from Tacitus' *Historiae* 5.9.

3   Witherington lists a number of supporting references in note 272, 705.

"sect" with no negative connotations, but the usage here anticipates the later meaning of "heresy."[4]

The accusation that Paul tried to *profane the temple* was a lie. The words *we seized him* should have been "the mob in the temple tried to beat him to death but your Roman soldiers took him into custody." Luke's readers of course see through these false charges.

By examining him yourself. . . Tertullus ends lamely. He has produced no witnesses to back up the charges and now he wants Felix to do his work for him. The High Priest and his henchmen form a chorus that echoes the charges that Tertullus had made. Paul is greatly outnumbered and no one is standing with him.

∽✆∍

Acts 24:10-21

Paul's Defense

10 And when the governor had nodded to him to speak, Paul replied:

"Knowing that for many years you have been a judge over this nation, I cheerfully make my defense. 11 You can verify that it is not more than twelve days since I went up to worship in Jerusalem, 12 and they did not find me disputing with anyone or stirring up a crowd, either in the temple or in the synagogues or in the city. 13 Neither can they prove to you what they now bring up against me. 14 But this I confess to you, that according to the Way, which they call a sect, I worship the God of our fathers, believing everything laid down by the Law and written in the Prophets, 15 having a hope in God, which these men themselves accept, that there

---

4   This word was undergoing a transition of meaning in NT times. In Acts 5:17; 15:5; and 26:5 it refers to the distinctive parties within Judaism, the Pharisees and the Sadducees. But here and in 24:14 and 28:22 it refers to the sect of the Nazarenes and has a definite pejorative cast. In 1 Cor 11:19 and Gal 5:20 it means "factions" with a negative meaning. In 2 Peter 2:1 the second century meaning used by Christian apologists such as Ireneus of "heresy" is apparent.

will be a resurrection of both the just and the unjust. 16 So I always take pains to have a clear conscience toward both God and man. 17 Now after several years I came to bring alms to my nation and to present offerings. 18 While I was doing this, they found me purified in the temple, without any crowd or tumult. But some Jews from Asia— 19 they ought to be here before you and to make an accusation, should they have anything against me. 20 Or else let these men themselves say what wrongdoing they found when I stood before the council, 21 other than this one thing that I cried out while standing among them: 'It is with respect to the resurrection of the dead that I am on trial before you this day.'"

Now it is Paul's turn. Paul's *exordium* (formal greeting) is brief, respectful, and truthful. Paul was glad to make his defense before Felix because, despite his lust and greed and cruelty, Felix had been in Palestine long enough to understand something of the nature of the Jews and their controversies and was well acquainted with the Jesus movement. Against the vague charge that he is a *troublemaker all over the world* Paul narrows the time frame to the twelve days since he arrived in Jerusalem and the location to the temple. He had not tried to foment a disturbance either *in the temple or in the synagogues or in the city.*

As for the charge that he is *a ringleader of the sect of the Nazarenes,* he must admit (*homologeō*) that that he is indeed *a follower of the Way which they call a sect.* He does not say "a follower of Jesus the Christ." Perhaps in this situation a less inflammatory, indirect expression was sufficient to convey the meaning to Felix. "The Way" might have been, in the light of John 14:6, a title of Christ. Paul then emphasizes the common ground with his accusers. He, like they, believes the Scripture "from cover to cover" and he shares the popular Jewish hope *in the resurrection of both the just and the unjust.*[5] He does not bring up their differences or get entangled in a discussion of the claims of Jesus to be the Messiah. That would not have been appropriate before this secular judge. All that Felix needs to know is that on a very basic level he and his "sect" are within basic Jewish doctrine. This "sect" is not an illegal religion but still considered by the Romans to be within the umbrella of Judaism, a *religio licita* (legal religion).

---

5   This verse is of special interest, as it is the only place in the speech or writings of Paul
     where he affirms a belief in the resurrection of the **unsaved** as well as the saved. He
     may be preparing Felix and his court to consider their own resurrection and consequent
     judgment. Compare John 5:28-29.

Thirdly, Paul denied that he had desecrated the temple. He had simply come to Jerusalem to bring his people the relief for the poor (mentioned only here in Acts) and to present offerings in the temple (as requested by James). "I was ceremonially clean when they found me in the temple courts doing this." "I did not defile the temple; I was ceremonially clean according to their Law." (If they want to accuse someone of desecrating the temple they might start with the mob that beat me up in the temple court.) He denied that he had started a riot. It was the Jews from Asia who started the riot.

"Where are my accusers? Where are the witnesses who saw me 'desecrating the temple'? And why were there no formal charges from the Sanhedrin?" The dual claim that there are no witnesses and no charges is Paul's most powerful argument. According to Roman law the case should have been dismissed immediately. There were no witnesses.[6]

Paul adroitly admitted to a minor fault. He might be blamed for causing a ruckus in the Sanhedrin by shouting out *It is with respect to the resurrection of the dead that I am on trial before you this day.* It was clever of Paul to admit a lesser fault. First it commended his truthfulness to admit a fault, because "we all err." Second, that fault was not relevant to this trial; it was a **theological** issue that was the real basis of their animosity against him.

൞

Acts 24:22-27

Felix' Non-Decision

22 But Felix, having a rather accurate knowledge of the Way, put them off, saying, "When Lysias the tribune comes down, I will decide your case." 23 Then he gave orders to the centurion that he should be kept in custody but have some liberty, and that none of his friends should be prevented from attending to his needs.

---

6   Why didn't the Jews bring the Asian witnesses with them? Was it not because they knew no one had seen Paul do anything wrong and that their case would quickly be lost? Their case is transparently flimsy; all they can do is hope that Felix will be afraid they will report him to Rome.

> *24 After some days Felix came with his wife Drusilla, who was Jewish, and he sent for Paul and heard him speak about faith in Christ Jesus. 25 And as he reasoned about righteousness and self-control and the coming judgment, Felix was alarmed and said, "Go away for the present. When I get an opportunity I will summon you." 26 At the same time he hoped that money would be given him by Paul. So he sent for him often and conversed with him. 27 When two years had elapsed, Felix was succeeded by Porcius Festus. And desiring to do the Jews a favor, Felix left Paul in prison.*

Felix should have dismissed the case for lack of provable charges and credible witnesses. Instead he temporized. If he thought the testimony of Lysias the commander was really necessary, he could have had him in court within two days at most. Felix is on the horns of a dilemma. He is well acquainted with the Way, so he knows that the charges against Paul are nonsense. But the governors of Judea always had to juggle a balancing act; they could not afford to antagonize the Jewish Sanhedrin lest they accuse him to Rome. The threat *If you release this man, you are no friend of the emperor* (John 19:12) was enough to intimidate Pontius Pilate. Indeed, it was Jewish complaints against Felix concerning how he brutally suppressed a riot in Caesarea two years later that caused his removal from his post. That is why he was anxious to curry the favor of the Jews.

Paul was under a not too uncomfortable house arrest, except, as was standard Roman custom, his friends had to take care of his needs. Felix used Paul to provide diversion for his young (about 18) and beautiful wife Drusilla. Drusilla was the daughter of King Agrippa I who had beheaded James (12:1). This was Felix' third marriage. Felix had rescued her from an unhappy marriage to the king of Emesa through the persuasion of a Cyprian sorcerer. As one Syriac version says, it may have been the request of Drusilla to meet Paul.

Paul was a celebrity of sorts and the movement he represented was excitingly controversial. Paul faithfully spoke about faith in Christ Jesus. Paul's speech must have included a review of the life of Christ, his death and resurrection, and an appeal to believe in Christ. God was enabling Paul to fulfill Acts 9:15 by witnessing to Christ before royalty. Paul also reasoned about righteousness, self-control and coming judgment, precisely what this sinful pair needed. We are attracted to the suggestion of Stott that the righteousness (dikaiosunē) mentioned here might have been the "justification" expounded in Romans 3 and 4.[7] Self-control, which often has the connotation of sexual

---

7   Stott, 364. It is just as likely, and indeed the opinion of most commentators, that *dikaiosunē* here refers to moral uprightness as in Rom 6:13 *instruments of righteousness.*

self-control, may have been a word to explain "sanctification" to a couple like Felix and Drusilla. If so we would have the three tenses of salvation: justification in the past, a deliverance from sin in the present, and preservation from judgment in the afterlife.

Paul's boldness in frankly discussing these topics is remarkable, but it fits everything we know about the apostle Paul. Felix had Paul's fate in his hands and could have sent him back to the Jews any time, but Paul is still courageous enough to give him the whole gospel without pulling any punches. If every Christian had this kind of courage in witnessing for Christ, there would be a revolutionary impact on the whole world.

It was probably the prospect of judgment that alarmed Felix; the word *emphobos* indicates more than ordinary fear, so he delayed again.[8] His delay and indecision on the issue of what he would do with Christ was more fatal than his decision on what he would do with Paul. It is ironic that the most powerful man in the land was such a weak and indecisive temporizer. He often sent for Paul and enjoyed hearing him talk about Christ and the faith, but he never came through to a decision to believe in Christ. Of course it would most likely have meant the loss of everything: his position, his wealth, his lustful lifestyle, and maybe even his pretty wife. [9]

How familiar this is to any Christian worker! We all can think of "Felixes" who attend church or Bible studies for years and love to discuss religion, even shed tears and seem to be under conviction at times; but who never cross the line that divides death from life; *Ever learning, and never able to come to the knowledge of the truth* (2 Tim 3:7). They may have this excuse or that excuse and protest, "I wish I could believe what you believe," but at the end of the day they are unwilling to forsake a sinful lifestyle or risk the loss of their present worldly advantages.

We learn in verse 26 that Felix's interest was not all curiosity. He was hoping Paul would give him a bribe! Is this not a problem for Christians

---

8   Again we observe that the preaching of judgment is the missing note in contemporary evangelism.

9   Ajith Fernando, in his comments on this chapter (p. 587), notes three reasons from Felix' behavior why it is hard for the rich and powerful to enter the kingdom of God: 1) They are able to camouflage their insecurity by pretending to be in control of their lives. 2) The rich and powerful are often slaves to an insatiable greed. 3) Those who are at the top feel that they must please other people if they want to stay at the top.

throughout the world! Entrenced corruption is an enormous drain on the economies of most of the countries of the so-called third world. Paul's example here is instructive for Christians who are faced with the dilemma of whether to pay a bribe for a good cause, say to get government approval for the purchase of land for a church. Paul did not pay even though it might have meant his freedom for ministry and mission!

Paul was confined for two years in the palace in Caesarea. A waste of precious time? Yet our stops and our starts and our languishing in "uselessness" for a time are all in the hands of our wise and sovereign God. A few scholars think he wrote the epistle to the Philippians at this time.[10]

In the midst of these chapters on the trials of Paul before various authorities, we might reflect on the problem we believers will all face: we are citizens of two kingdoms. We are expected by the people around us to be loyal to our family, clan, tribe, and country. Yet we have become citizens of Christ's kingdom and sometimes there are severe conflicts between the demands of our two loyalties. How do we respond when we are accused of destroying the family by being baptized and refusing to burn incense to the ancestors, or of being traitors to our country and its tradition? We can only respond as Paul did, doing all he could to observe the demands of his culture but never compromising essential truths or practices of a Christ-follower. We have a prior allegiance that we owe to Christ; we must be prepared to undergo conflict and perhaps even persecution and death. We must obey God rather than man (Acts 5:29).

---

10   Gerald Hawthorne, after a lengthy discussion of the possibilities as to the place from which the Epistle to the Philippians was written, concludes that "Philippians was written by Paul from a prison in Caesarea about A.D. 59-61" (Philippians, Word, 1983, xliii). Carson, Moo, and Morris lay out all the evidence for Caesarea, but tentatively favor Ephesus (*An Introduction to the New Testament*, Zondervan, 319-321).

The Roman aqueduct in Caesarea.

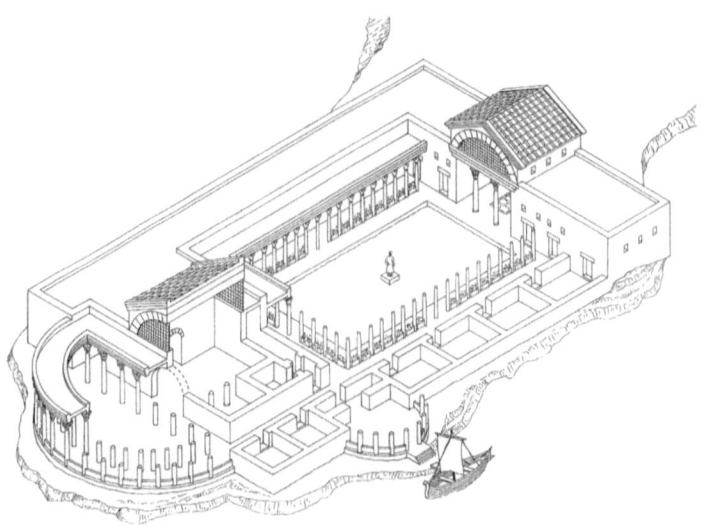

Diagram of the Palace (Praetorium) of the Roman governor in Caesarea that was built to extend out into the sea. Paul may have been imprisoned here. An image used by permission of Ritmeyer Archaeological Design (UK).

Lessons for Life

1. Sometimes our most severe trials and most dangerous moments will give us our best opportunities for witness.
2. When unjustly accused, either as individuals or as a church, we need to defend ourselves with quiet dignity and complete reliance on our God.
3. Those who seem to have everything; power, wealth, and glamorous wives, are really the most helpless and wretched and miserable of all (Rev 3:17).
4. We need Paul's amazing death-defying boldness in our witness for Christ.
5. Some people are *ever learning and never able to come to the knowledge of the truth.* Procrastination only hardens the heart until decision is impossible.
6. We cannot advance the work of God by paying bribes demanded of us by corrupt officials.

ACTS 25

PAUL APPEALS TO CAESAR

Acts 25:1-12

Paul Appeals to Caesar

1 Now three days after Festus had arrived in the province, he went up to Jerusalem from Caesarea. 2 And the chief priests and the principal men of the Jews laid out their case against Paul, and they urged him, 3 asking as a favor against Paul that he summon him to Jerusalem—because they were planning an ambush to kill him on the way. 4 Festus replied that Paul was being kept at Caesarea and that he himself intended to go there shortly. 5 "So," said he, "let the men of authority among you go down with me, and if there is anything wrong about the man, let them bring charges against him."

6 After he stayed among them not more than eight or ten days, he went down to Caesarea. And the next day he took his seat on the tribunal and ordered Paul to be brought. 7 When he had arrived, the Jews who had come down from Jerusalem stood around him, bringing many and serious charges against him that they could not prove. 8 Paul argued in his defense, "Neither against the law of the Jews, nor against the temple, nor against Caesar have I committed any offense." 9 But Festus, wishing to do the Jews a favor, said to Paul, "Do you wish to go up to Jerusalem and there be tried on these charges before me?" 10 But Paul said, "I am standing before Caesar's tribunal, where I ought to be tried. To the Jews I have done no wrong, as you yourself know very well. 11 If then I am a wrongdoer and have committed anything for which I deserve to die, I do not seek to escape death. But if there is nothing to their charges against me, no one can give me up to them. I appeal to Caesar." 12 Then Festus, when he had conferred with his council, answered, "To Caesar you have appealed; to Caesar you shall go."

Two dreary years have passed. Suddenly there is a change of procurators. Emperor Nero replaced Felix with Festus in his fifth year, 59 AD.[1] Josephus tells us that Felix was relieved of his command because he mishandled a riot between Syrian Gentiles and Jews in Caesarea. His soldiers killed many Jews and plundered the rich homes of many Jews. Felix ("Lucky") lost his position but escaped punishment because of the influence of his wealthy brother Pallas.[2]

Festus was a better man than most of the governors that preceded him or followed him. If he had not died after only two years in office, the history of the Jewish War with Rome might have been different.

As he breaks upon the scene in chapter 25, we are at first impressed with his energy and decisiveness. He went immediately to Jerusalem to meet the Jewish leadership. Whether he was briefed by the preceding administration about the matter of the Jewish prisoner Paul we cannot be certain, but the prosecution of Paul is the first order of business for the chief priests and Jewish leaders. It is astonishing that after a lapse of two years, their first item of business is still Paul. One might think that their hatred of Paul might have been dulled by the passage of time, but they immediately raise the case with Festus as if the temple incident had happened only yesterday. The defenders of the Law of Moses, which includes "Thou shalt not murder," are still plotting to ambush Paul and kill him on his way to Jerusalem in blatant violation of not only the law of God but also of their own rules of procedure in criminal cases.

Boice reflects on "the corrupting effects of religion when it is not actually in contact with God."[3] Mankind generally thinks of religion as a good thing but when it is corrupted, nothing is worse. Some of the worst crimes and

---

1   A simple way to remember which comes first and which comes second: though the first two letters of their names are identically "Fe," the "L" of Felix precedes the "S" of Festus alphabetically.

2   Josephus *Antiquities*, 20.173-184.

3   Boice, 395.

injustices in history have been and even now are being perpetrated by those who think they do God service.[4]

Providentially Festus refused the request of the Jewish leadership to transfer Paul to Jerusalem for trial. Perhaps he had been told of the plot of the forty assassins two years earlier. But he promised to hold court on this matter shortly in Caesarea. This he did the very next day after his arrival there.[5]

The Jews again presented the same accusations against Paul that they had used two years earlier. Again they have no proof of these many serious charges against him. *Neither against the law of the Jews, nor against the temple, nor against Caesar have I committed any offense.* "Treason against Caesar" has been added. This is the trial of Christ all over again. He too was accused of heresy against the Law of Moses when he plucked grain on the Sabbath day. He too was accused of sacrilege when he insulted the temple by talking about its destruction. He too was charged with treason against Caesar by claiming to be a king.

Verse 9 reveals Festus' fatal defect: he wanted to do the Jews a favor. Festus is Felix all over again. He asked Paul if he would be willing to go up to Jerusalem to stand trial. He knew this would be very pleasing to the Jewish leadership.

To this Paul gave a vigorous refusal (verses 10-11). *To the Jews I have done no wrong, as you yourself know very well. If then I am a wrongdoer and have committed anything for which I deserve to die, I do not seek to escape death. But if there is nothing to their charges against me, no one can give me up to them. I appeal to Caesar.* Later, Agrippa pointed out that Paul might have been freed if he had not appealed to Caesar (26:32). Did Paul make a mistake in appealing to Caesar? Yes, it would serve to get him to Rome, as the Lord had promised him (23:11). But he could have journeyed there on his own after being released by Festus. There are two factors that may have forced Paul to make this drastic step.

First, Paul trusted that Felix would not turn him over to the Jews and might eventually set him free. Second he may have hoped that the new procurator would do the right thing and free him for lack of evidence. But

---

4   John 16:2.

5   *Kathisas epi tou bēmatos,* "sitting on the judgment rostrum," was the official act that opened a legal trial.

when he saw that Festus also was eager to please the Jews, and indeed asked him to consent to being tried in Jerusalem (something Felix had never done), he realized that he was in serious danger under Festus. In short, he could not trust Festus. He knew that if he were sent to Jerusalem, he would not likely arrive there alive. And even if he did survive the trip, he would not survive a trial in the fanatic city of Jerusalem.

A second reason to appeal to Caesar might be that Paul saw a chance to testify to Christ before the greatest king of all, Emperor Nero and his officials. Nero, under the influence of his counselors Seneca and Burrhus, was still on his best behavior, and had not yet become the monster that history remembers. Indeed, the first five years of his reign were fondly recalled as a mini golden age for Rome.

The right of a Roman citizen to appeal to the highest authority in cases that were *extra ordinem*, that is, outside the ordinary cases of the law, went all the way back to the very founding of the state. The conditions under which appeal could be made varied from time to time, but as Bruce states: "Luke's account of Paul's appeal conforms with what is known of conditions in the late fifties of the first century."[6] When Paul said the words *Kaisara epikaloumai* (*ad Caesarum provoco* in Latin), Festus had no choice under Roman law; he had to grant that request. He must have been secretly relieved because Paul's case was a sticky issue that would bring bad consequences for him no matter which way he decided. You have appealed to Caesar. To Caesar you will go!

၁၉၁

Acts 25:13-22

Festus Tells Agrippa II and Bernice About Paul

13 Now when some days had passed, Agrippa the king and Bernice arrived at Caesarea and greeted Festus. 14 And as they stayed there many days, Festus laid Paul's case before the king, saying, "There is a man left

---

6   Bruce, 489.

*prisoner by Felix, **15** and when I was at Jerusalem, the chief priests and the elders of the Jews laid out their case against him, asking for a sentence of condemnation against him. **16** I answered them that it was not the custom of the Romans to give up anyone before the accused met the accusers face to face and had opportunity to make his defense concerning the charge laid against him. **17** So when they came together here, I made no delay, but on the next day took my seat on the tribunal and ordered the man to be brought. **18** When the accusers stood up, they brought no charge in his case of such evils as I supposed. **19** Rather they had certain points of dispute with him about their own religion and about a certain Jesus, who was dead, but whom Paul asserted to be alive. **20** Being at a loss how to investigate these questions, I asked whether he wanted to go to Jerusalem and be tried there regarding them. **21** But when Paul had appealed to be kept in custody for the decision of the emperor, I ordered him to be held until I could send him to Caesar." **22** Then Agrippa said to Festus, "I would like to hear the man myself." "Tomorrow," said he, "you will hear him."*

This Agrippa was the son of King Agrippa I (whose demise is recorded in Acts 12), the grandson of Aristobolus and Mariamne, and the great grandson of Herod the Great. Through his grandmother Mariamne he had claim to the Hasmonean line and Jewish lineage. Like his father he was raised in the Roman imperial court with Claudius. When his father died in 44 AD he was only 17, too young to be entrusted with the whole kingdom of his father so he was safely made king of a minor principality in present day Lebanon (Chalcis) in 50 AD, and in 53 AD exchanged that for four minor kingdoms in present day Lebanon and Syria. His capital was in Caesarea Philippi and he held the title of king. Still later, in 55 AD, Nero added much of Galilee to his kingdom. But most of the land of Palestine, Samaria, and Judea, remained in the control of a series of Roman procurators, the present governor being Festus. King Agrippa II was one of the better Herods. He tried to be a bridge between the Romans and the Jews, making earnest appeals to the Jews not to rebel against Rome.[7] He died childless at the end of the century, the last of the Herodian line.

Agrippa's relationship with his sister Bernice, who accompanied him on this occasion, was a subject of much scandal and gossip. She went through

---

7   Josephus, in *Wars,* Book 2. 345-401, records a very long speech of this Agrippa, who with tears tried to persuade the Jews not to rebel against Rome.

a series of marriages; her second was to her uncle, Herod of Chalcis. After his death she lived with her brother Agrippa. Later she married the king of Sicily, then returned to Agrippa, and later was the mistress of both Emperor Vespasian and Emperor Titus.

These two "royals" of dubious morality arrived to pay their respects to the new procurator of Judea. Festus wasted no time in bringing up Paul's case. Witherington is not impressed with Festus' self-serving explanation of the situation to Agrippa and Bernice (verses 14-21).[8] First, Festus blamed Felix for not resolving the problem sooner (v. 14), and in that he is correct. Then, in verses 15-16 he portrays himself as the great upholder of Roman law. Next he pointed out that he had acted with great dispatch in bringing the case to a hearing (v. 17). In verses 18 and 19 he cited the incompetence of the accusers, who seem to have no grounds for their charges except some religious controversy about a certain Jesus, who had died but *whom Paul asserted to be alive.* (This is a little different than the resurrection that Paul claimed; it could mean that Jesus had never really died. Here we have a little insight as to how the strange idea of resurrection might have been reinterpreted by typical pagans at that time.) Festus next admitted that he was at a loss how to handle this case (v. 20), but that Paul had forced a solution by appealing to Caesar (v. 21).

Strictly speaking, Festus had no reason to tell Agrippa about the case. If Paul had not appealed to Caesar, he would be asking Agrippa, who was quite knowledgeable about Jewish affairs and religion, for advice. But now there is no reason to tell Agrippa about Paul except to make entertaining conversation and impress Agrippa with what a good job he was doing. Although Agrippa did not rule the large territory that his father had, he knew that Agrippa had the ear of influential people in Rome.

Agrippa could not resist. He certainly had heard of the Jesus movement, and very likely had even heard of Paul, and now he has a chance to interview that notorious character in person. The stage is set for the testimony of Paul before Agrippa (25:23-27 and chapter 26).

Festus was a better man than Felix, and he did take up Paul's case with energy and dispatch, but he, like Felix was a "man-pleaser;" they both wanted *to do the Jews a favor.* How often do we fall into the same trap? We know what the right thing to do is, but we fail to fulfill our responsibility because we are afraid of men. Boice asks:

---

8   Witherington, 728-29.

How are we going to stand when the world says, "You have to go along to get along. Nobody who is rigid ever gets ahead. If you tell the truth, your competitor is going to get the edge on you, and pretty soon you'll be broke."? [9]

Paul is an amazing contrast to Festus here. He is the accused, the prisoner, but he is confidant and refuses to give in to the fear of man. How bold he is when he sticks a needle in Festus: I have not done any wrong to the Jews, as you yourself know very well (v. 10). The secret of Paul's boldness is expressed in verse 11: If then I am a wrongdoer and have committed anything for which I deserve to die, I do not seek to escape death. Boice quotes a passage from the great Russian writer Aleksandr Solzhenitsyn's The Gulag Archipelago on how some survived under the interrogations:

> At the very threshold, you must say to yourself:: "My life is over, a little early to be sure, but there's nothing to be done about it. I shall never return to freedom. I am condemned to die—now or a little later. But later on, in truth, it will be even harder, and so the sooner the better. I no longer have any property whatsoever. For me those I love have died, and for them I have died. From today on, my body is useless and alien to me. Only my spirit and my conscience remain precious to me."
>
> Confronted by such a prisoner, the interrogation will tremble. Only the man who has renounced everything can gain that victory. [10]

Paul was one who had renounced everything. For him the machinations of the Jews and the compromising and temporizing of Festus and even the court of the Roman emperor held no fears.

---

9   Boice, 398.

10   Boice, 400. Cited from Aleksandr Solzhenitsyn, *The Gulag Archipelago, 1918-1956* (New York: Harper & Row, 1973), 130.

Lessons for Life

1.   Though we are witnesses, we are not reckless martyrs. We do not
     need to throw our lives away needlessly. We should assert whatever
     rights we are entitled to as citizens.
2.   There is nothing worse than corrupt religion.
3.   Only the fear of God will deliver us from the fear of man. Only
     the one who is willing to die for his faith is really free to live for his
     Lord.

∽∾

Addendum on Persecution

Question 1. Why are Christians being persecuted as never before?

We have seen the rise of religious fanaticism in recent decades with
murder, rape, civil violence, burning of churches and Christian homes. The
motivation for these acts of violence has many sources. The most obvious
one is **political**. General Zia-ul-Haq in Pakistan and Ayatollah Khomenei
in Iran are examples of those who in the name of Islam sought to renew
the Islamic community by political revolution. The conflict between North
and South Korea is motivated by political ideology. In each case Christians
who are politically powerless suffer the most indirect attacks on them and
their property. In the case of Islamic persecution, the implementing of the
"blasphemy laws," as in Pakistan in 1986, has been abused with devastating
effect on the Christian community.

Zeal for purity of religious faith and practice has in many cases been
the cause of persecution, usually with ethnic rivalry fueling the strife. The
never-ending clash between Israeli Jews and Palestinian Arabs, with Christians
caught in the crossfire, is the classic case of Christians being treated as second-
class citizens by both sides. In Iraq, Christians were identified with the hated
American occupiers and suffered accordingly. In India persecution under the
BJP government is severe.

At a deeper level, all persecution of believers in Christ is due to **the opposition of the unseen forces of Satanic darkness** (Acts 26:18; Ephesians 6:10-20). Satan attacks Christ by attacking his Body on earth, the Christians. Saul of Tarsus was a tool of Satan at the execution of Stephen and in the persecuting of believers in Jesus unto death (Acts 22:4). Saul was arrested from his fanatical violence only by his dramatic conversion on the road to Damascus.

Question 2. How should Christians respond to persecution?

It has been estimated that more Christians have been martyred for their faith in the twentieth century than in all previous nineteen centuries put together. If the age is indeed drawing to a close, will the twenty-first century be any different? We have much guidance in the book of Acts by studying how Paul reacted to persecution.

First, he had a genuine **love for his enemies** and was burdened for their salvation (Rom 9:1-3). He did not try to avenge himself for the injustices done to him. He lived out the Sermon on the Mount in a life of holiness.

Second, he was **confident and courageous**. He was sure of his calling as an apostle and was never ashamed of the gospel of Christ (Rom 1:16). His boldness in his trials in the latter chapters of Acts is breathtaking.

Third, he was **humble** enough to admit his failings (23:5; 26:11).

Fourth, he **engaged the opposition** to plead his case and the truth of the gospel. He gave his conversion testimony three times, each time at great length. While trying to avoid argument, he appealed to reason (26:25) and sought to clarify misunderstandings (25:8; 26:4-5).

Fifth, **he did what he could to escape** persecution. He claimed his rights as a Roman citizen (16:37; 22:25). He notified the Roman commander of the plot of the assassins (23:17). He appealed to Caesar, claiming his rights as a Roman citizen (25:11).

Sixth, despite point five, he was perfectly **willing to suffer and sacrifice** his life in obedience to the will of God (20:24). He considered suffering part of his calling as a Christian (Phil 1:29).

Luke sets Paul forth as an ideal model of how to endure sufferings as a faithful servant of the Lord Jesus Christ, a pattern for all pastors and lay leaders and ordinary believers in these turbulent and frightful times.[11]

---

11   This addendum was written by the co-author of the first edition of this book, Dr. Bruce Nicholls, now deceased.

ACTS 26

PAUL BEFORE AGRIPPA

Acts 25:23-27

The Grand Entrance of Agrippa and Bernice

23 The next day Agrippa and Bernice came with great pomp and entered the audience room with the high ranking officers and the leading men of the city. At the command of Festus, Paul was brought in.

24 Festus said: "King Agrippa, and all who are present with us, you see this man! The whole Jewish community has petitioned me about him in Jerusalem and here in Caesarea, shouting that he ought not to live any longer. 25 I found he had done nothing deserving of death, but because he made his appeal to the Emperor I decided to send him to Rome. 26 But I have nothing definite to write to His Majesty about him. Therefore I have brought him before all of you, and especially before you, King Agrippa, so that as a result of this investigation I may have something to write. 27 For I think it is unreasonable to send on a prisoner without specifying the charges against him."

This chapter brings us to Paul's fifth and final defense. Luke evidently considers it the most important of the five because it is the longest.[1] The word "trial"

---

1   The five defenses are: 1) Before the crowd in the temple (chap. 22) 2) Before the Sanhedrin in Jerusalem (chap. 23) 3) Before Governor Felix in Caesarea (chap. 24) 4) Before Festus in Caesarea (chap. 25) 5) Before Felix and King Herod Agrippa II in Caesarea (chap. 26). In the first and last of these defenses, Paul gives the account of his conversion; these mark the second and third times the Damascus Road conversion is related.

is not appropriate for this final hearing because there are no formal charges and no verdict. Festus is anxious to find some suitable charges to bring against Paul so that he will not look so foolish as to send an accused prisoner to the emperor without specific charges (v. 27). Paul is allowed, indeed invited, to tell his story before an august assembly of not only King Agrippa and his sister Bernice, but also before *the military tribunes and the prominent men of the city.* The city of course is Caesarea, the seat of the Roman government in Palestine, and one of the most Gentile cities in the land. Some of the *prominent men of the city* may have been Jews, but the audience is predominantly Gentiles of the highest rank.

The Roman love of splendor made this a dramatic scene indeed. Luke calls it *phantasia,* "pomp," the word that Arabic still uses for "parade." Agrippa and Bernice would have been wearing their royal robes of purple and gold tiaras on their heads. The tribunes and their guards would have been in dress uniform and the leading men of the town in their best finery. When they were all seated according to their rank, *Paul was brought in.* The contrast must have been striking. Paul, whom one source says was a homely bow-legged little man, in his plain robes and chained hands was standing before the "crowned heads" and elegant courtiers.[2] But the "pomp and circumstance" did not faze Paul one bit; as Barclay remarks, ". . . from the moment he speaks it is Paul who holds the stage."[3] In that day, Theophilus may have been impressed that Paul spoke before such famous persons; but today we know their names only because Paul appeared before them.

The presence of other local VIPs reminds us that this hearing is not just a zeal for justice but also a desire for entertainment. Paul, like it or not, was being used as a curiosity to entertain the elites. As long as he can tell what God did for him, he does not mind. *For it seems to me that God has put us apostles on display at the end of the procession, like men condemned to die in the arena. We have been made **a spectacle** to the whole universe, to angels as well as to men* (1 Cor 4:9).

Festus opens proceedings by briefly reviewing the situation for Agrippa. *The whole Jewish people has petitioned me, both in Jerusalem and here, shouting*

---

2   Paul is described in the apocryphal *Acts of Paul and Thecla* as "baldheaded, bowlegged, strongly built, small in size, with meeting eyebrows, a rather large nose, full of grace, for at times he looked like a man and at times had the face of an angel."

3   Barclay, 175.

that he ought not to live any longer. "Something about this man has upset the whole Jewish community, and they are vociferously demanding that he be put to death. I have listened to their accusations against this man, but, as far as I can see, he has done nothing worthy of death. He has appealed to Caesar and I must send him to Rome, but I am embarrassed to have no specific charges to present to his Majesty (the Greek word is *kyrios,* 'lord.'). Maybe you, King Agrippa, can help me out."

One would think that Agrippa would ask "What are the charges?" but somewhat incongruously, no charges are mentioned. Instead Paul is permitted to speak (26:1) whatever he wants. He does, however, mention the underlying reason for the animosity of the Jewish leaders against him in 26:21.

ᴄⱸᴐ

Acts 26:1-23

Paul's Apologia

26:1-8 Paul, Jewish Advocate of the Jewish Hope

2 "King Agrippa, I consider myself fortunate to stand before you today as I make my defense against all the accusations of the Jews, 3 and especially so because you are well acquainted with all the Jewish customs and controversies. Therefore, I beg you to listen to me patiently.

4 "The Jews all know the way I have lived ever since I was a child, from the beginning of my life in my own country, and also in Jerusalem. 5 They have known me for a long time and can testify, if they are willing, that according to the strictest sect of our religion, I lived as a Pharisee. 6 And now it is because of my hope in what God has promised our fathers that I am on trial today. 7 This is the promise our twelve tribes are hoping to see fulfilled as they earnestly serve God day and night. O king, it is because of this hope that the Jews are accusing me. 8 Why should any of you consider it incredible that God raises the dead?

In the opening of his speech, Paul delivers what in the rhetoric of the time was called *captatio benevolentae*, the address to the personage being addressed and an appeal to listen patiently.[4] Usually this part was larded with generous flattery (see 24:2-3), but Paul is genuinely happy (*makarios*, the word translated "blessed" in the Beatitudes) and thankful to be able to present his testimony before the most benevolent Herod, because he is "Jewish" himself and is familiar with the religious controversies of the Jews and perhaps even knows a bit about Jesus of Nazareth and the persecution of his followers. After two years of silence, Paul at last has a chance to speak and testify to what God had done for him. This is a golden opportunity to speak before kings (Matt 10:18; Acts 9:15) and Paul makes the most of it.

First Paul declares that he is a "Hebrew of the Hebrews," indeed a member of the strictest and most zealous of the Jews, a Pharisee. "The Jews of Jerusalem can all testify that I was nurtured from childhood in their sacred traditions. I am one of them. Why are they accusing me of believing the most central promise of our religion"?

Paul had said that he would make his defense against all the accusations of the Jews, but instead of mentioning the surface accusations of defiling the temple and so forth, he gets to the root of their animosity. *And now I stand here on trial because of my hope in the promise God made to our fathers.* His point is that "the Jews are accusing me because of our common hope (the word occurs here three times), the great Jewish hope from ancient times, the coming of the Messiah." Paul does not mention the word Messiah, or use the name of Jesus, but he knows that Agrippa is able to fill in the gaps.

Why is it thought incredible by any of you that God raises the dead? This question seems a bit strange. First, it seems that Paul is jumping to an unrelated topic, and that a very strange topic. Second, most people in Paul's audience would have thought resurrection to be *incredible* indeed.[5] As for the first objection, Paul may be using a technique of raising a question in their minds that he will elucidate plainly in verse 23. As for the second, Paul does indeed run the risk here of being thought *mad*, as Festus blurts out in interrupting him the next time he mentions resurrection (verse 24). But if one believes in a God who will raise the dead, and that God has raised Jesus of Nazareth, who appeared to Paul personally, resurrection loses its "incredibility."

---

4   The rhetorical analysis comes from Witherington, 739.

5   See our comments in Acts 17 on the Greek attitude toward resurrection.

26:9-11 Paul the Zealous Persecutor of Heretics

9 "I myself was convinced that I ought to do many things in opposing the name of Jesus of Nazareth. 10 And I did so in Jerusalem. I not only locked up many of the saints in prison after receiving authority from the chief priests, but when they were put to death I cast my vote against them. 11 And I punished them often in all the synagogues and tried to make them blaspheme, and in raging fury against them I persecuted them even to foreign cities.

"As they (the Jews accusing me) are now, so once was I. I understand their motivation perfectly." There is no more powerful and persuasive testimony than that of the convert, especially the testimony of the religious zealot concerning his former religion. He cannot be accused of ignorance of the beliefs of the other side. So give the Japanese Buddhist the biography of Ryoun Kameya, the Jōdō Shinshū monk who converted to Christ, and to the Hindu the biography of Sadhu Sundar Singh.

This paragraph gives more detail and intensity than the parallel account of Paul the persecutor in 22:4-5. Paul tried to force the Christians to blaspheme. The reference to having some put to death is more explict than the account in chapter 22.[6] On what occasions could Paul have voted to have Christians put to death? It does not seem that the use of the word "vote" is metaphorical for simple assent or approval (compare 8:1). Only the Sanhedrin had the power of passing the death sentence (for religious cases only) and most commentators feel that Paul was too young (in his pre-conversion days) to be a member of the Sanhedrin. It may be that Paul was casting his vote for death in a sub-committee or investigating committee of the Sanhedrin. In any case the memory of his causing the death of precious fellow believers in his post-conversion days must have been exceedingly painful to him and made his claim to be the chief of sinners (I Tim 1:15) to be more than a rhetorical exaggeration.

---

6   The word "forced" is in the imperfect tense in the Greek, and could mean either
     that Paul **tried** (but failed) to force Christians to blaspheme (to deny that Christ was
     Messiah and Lord), or that from time to time, he actually succeeded in forcing them to
     blaspheme.

26:12-18 The Light From Heaven and the Commission From the Lord

12 "In this connection I journeyed to Damascus with the authority and commission of the chief priests. 13 At midday, O king, I saw on the way a light from heaven, brighter than the sun, that shone around me and those who journeyed with me. 14 And when we had all fallen to the ground, I heard a voice saying to me in the Hebrew language, 'Saul, Saul, why are you persecuting me? It is hard for you to kick against the goads.' 15 And I said, 'Who are you, Lord?' And the Lord said, 'I am Jesus whom you are persecuting. 16 But rise and stand upon your feet, for I have appeared to you for this purpose, to appoint you as a servant and witness to the things in which you have seen me and to those in which I will appear to you, 17 delivering you from your people and from the Gentiles—to whom I am sending you 18 to open their eyes, so that they may turn from darkness to light and from the power of Satan to God, that they may receive forgiveness of sins and a place among those who are sanctified by faith in me.'

In each retelling of Paul's conversion we get a little more detail. Now the light from heaven is brighter than the sun. Here all of the company fell to the earth, not just Paul. Paul explains to these Gentiles that the voice he heard was in Aramaic ("Hebrew" in our ESV text); the Jewish audience of chapter 22 would have assumed that. Here for the first time we have the intriguing phrase *It is hard for you to kick against the goads.*[7] This proverb has not been found in Aramaic or Hebrew sources, but it is rather common in Greek classical literature where the meaning is "it is useless, indeed painful, to resist the will of the gods."[8] Many have interpreted "the goads" to mean "the goads of a guilty conscience," but Bruce says:

---

7   "Goad" is a term used for the sharp stick used to prod oxen yoked to a plow or cart, an image instantly recognizable in any agricultural society before the twentieth century. The evidence for including this phrase in Acts 9:5, as the KJV does, is very weak. None of the major manuscripts include it there.

8   "One must not fight against a god, [89] who raises up some men's fortunes at one time, and at another gives great glory to others. But even this [90] does not comfort the minds of the envious; they pull the line too tight and plant a painful wound in their own heart before they get what they are scheming for. It is best to take the yoke on one's neck and bear it lightly; kicking against the goad [95] makes the path treacherous." Pindar, Pythian Odes 2. See other references listed by Bruce, 501.

The "goads" against which Paul was told it was fruitless for him to kick were not the prickings of an uneasy conscience over his persecuting activity but the new forces which were now impelling him in the opposite direction . . . [9]

In light of the classical Greek background of the saying, it is interesting that Paul includes it for his Gentile audience but not for his Jewish audience in Acts 22. In the mouth of the glorified Lord Jesus it would mean, "It is useless to try to resist me."

This version of Paul's conversion story includes a more detailed commission of the Lord given in verses 16 and 17. In chapters 9:6 and 22:10 the Lord's directions were *Now get up and go into the city, and you will be told what you must do.* Entirely new information is given in verse 18: *I am sending you to open their eyes, so that they may turn from darkness to light and from the power of Satan to God, that they may receive forgiveness of sins and a place among those who are sanctified by faith in me.* First comes a terse command, "Stand." We are taken back to Ezek 2:1-4 when Ezekiel was prostrate before God but told to stand and that God would send him to the people of Israel as a prophet. The word send is also key in the call of Isaiah (Isa 6:8).

There are three key verbs in verse 16: I have **appeared** to you (past), I will **deliver** you (future), and I now **send** you (present). Christ says he will appoint Paul *as a servant and witness to the things in which you have seen me and to those in which I will appear to you.* Like his Lord, Paul is a "servant of Yahweh" (Isaiah 42, 49, 53), a light to the nations (49:6), indwelled by the Spirit (42:1), and vitally involved in the suffering which brings redemption (52:13-53:12). Notice that Paul is to be a witness not only of what he is now experiencing but also of **what I will show you** (NIV). This phrase will be fulfilled in the unique doctrines the Lord later gave through the Apostle Paul such as justification by faith (Romans 3 and 4), oneness with Christ in his crucifixion and resurrection (Romans 6), details on the rapture of the church (I and II Thessalonians), and the Church as the Body of Christ (Eph 1-3). Too often the prophetic role of Paul in receiving the revelation of the Lord is diminished to purely human opinion or innovation as if Paul were the inventor of "Pauline theology."

---

9   Bruce, 501.

(I will) deliver you from your people and from the Gentiles. This promise was the secret of Paul's unfailing boldness and courage and confidence in an unending series of threats on his life. Perhaps the most important single lesson we can learn from the book of Acts is boldness. We are immortal until our work is done. The promise was not that Paul would be able to retire to a rocking chair at age sixty-five. His "retirement" was martyrdom about the year 64 AD.

I am sending you *18 to open their eyes, so that they may turn from darkness to light and from the power of Satan to God, that they may receive forgiveness of sins and a place among those who are sanctified by faith in me.*

Verse 18 always reminds me that this verse was printed on the prayer card of a certain missionary in Japan, now deceased, and I never fail to thrill at the power and grandeur of these words. Can there be any more significant work for a human being? This promise is exactly what had happened to Paul himself and is what he desires for Agrippa, and Festus, and all listening to these words. Paul's own eyes had been **opened** when he was still a blind raging wolf ravaging the church, utterly convinced that Jesus of Nazareth was a false Messiah. He had been **turned from the darkness** of his error to **the light** of the truth in Christ. He had been turned from being **a servant of Satan** to **a servant of God**. He had received forgiveness for his sins, even the sin of killing Christians. He had been made an heir of the kingdom and had been **sanctified** or made fit for his present calling and his future glory. Though our conversions may not be as dramatic as the conversion of the Apostle Paul, these wonderful words are the purpose of God for every true believer and the heart of our appeal in witness to the world.

26:19-23 Paul's Obedience to the Vision, the Rationale for His Actions and the Reason for the Jewish Enmity

19 "Therefore, O King Agrippa, I was not disobedient to the heavenly vision, 20 but declared first to those in Damascus, then in Jerusalem and throughout all the region of Judea, and also to the Gentiles, that they should repent and turn to God, performing deeds in keeping with their repentance. 21 For this reason the Jews seized me in the temple and tried to kill me. 22 To this day I have had the help that comes from God, and so I stand here testifying both to small and great, saying nothing but what the prophets and Moses said would come to pass: **23** *that the Christ must suffer and that, by being the first to rise from the dead, he would proclaim light both to our people and to the Gentiles."*

Paul now summarizes the main point of his defense, which is not only a defense but also an evangelistic appeal. He is saying in effect: "The reason I have gotten into this trouble is my obedience to the Lord who appeared to me. I had no choice. From that time to this, I have preached to the Jews in Damascus where I was converted, to the Jews in Jerusalem and Judea, and to Gentiles all over the eastern part of the empire." It was a tough message demanding genuine repentance (verse 20.) The meaning of "repentance" is fleshed out as *turning to God* (compare 1 Thess 1:9) and *performing deeds in keeping with repentance* (compare 1 Thess 1:10). Paul emphasizes faith more than repentance in his epistles, but note Rom 2:4 and 2 Tim 2:25 as two clear references to repentance for unbelievers. The reference to *proving repentance by their deeds* reminds us of the preaching of John the Baptist (Luke 3:8-14; Matt 3:8;), recorded in most detail by Luke. Luke, along with Matthew, emphasizes repentance more than any other NT writer. It is mentioned eleven times in Acts, by Peter (2:38; 3:19) and Paul (17:30; 20:21; and this passage). In our appeals for faith we must not forget to demand genuine repentance that is marked not only by words but also by deeds.

For this reason the Jews seized me in the temple and tried to kill me.

"Despite this false accusation that the Jews have been alleging against me these two years, the heart of the matter is that this message of repentance is the **real** reason the Jews insist on killing me. They are convinced that they are right and need no repentance." People today think that they are basically good people and are offended by any claim that they need to repent.

Now in verses 22 and 23 Paul moves to what is rhetorically known as *propositio* or the key central point, here introduced by *therefore*.[10] "1) I am line with the deepest roots of Jewish tradition. Everything I preach is nothing other than what was predicted by Moses (the greatest figure in the Jewish religion) and the prophets. "Why then are the Jews attacking me for

---

10   Witherington, 748. ESV ignores the word *oun*, "therefore." The KJV is better: "Having therefore obtained help of God."

preaching the fulfillment of the predictions of their greatest prophet and the other prophets?" 2) Specifically, the focus of their predictions was the promise of Messiah (*the Christ*) and his sufferings (a reference to the cross) and his resurrection and that he would proclaim the light of salvation to both Jews and Gentiles. (This fleshes out the somewhat vague references to the Jewish *hope* in verses 7 and 8.)

Again the resurrection is the constant center of the apostolic preaching, perhaps slightly more prominent in Acts than the cross.[11] Here it is not just the resurrection of the Messiah; he is just the *first* to be raised. Paul fills out the details in the great exposition of the resurrection of Christ and the believer in Christ in 1 Cor 15, especially 15:20, *Christ the first fruits.* To Paul the *kerygma* included not only the resurrection of Christ but also the resurrection of those who believe in him.

ᴄᴇᴏ

Acts 26:24-29

Interruption by Festus and a Lively Exchange Between Paul, Festus, and Agrippa

24 And as he was saying these things in his defense, Festus said with a loud voice, "Paul, you are out of your mind; your great learning is driving you out of your mind." 25 But Paul said, "I am not out of my mind, most excellent Festus, but I am speaking true and rational words. 26 For the king knows about these things, and to him I speak boldly. For I am persuaded that none of these things has escaped his notice, for this has not

---

11   The actual word "cross" appears only once in Acts: 2:23; though to be sure synonyms like "tree" (5:30; 10:39; 13:29) and references to Christ's "sufferings" "murder" or "crucifixion" occur in eight of the ten evangelistic speeches in Acts. Even here the translation *that the Christ would suffer* is a paraphrase. The word "suffer" in the Greek text here is not a verb but an adjective *patheitos* which means "subject to suffering." This word highlights a little more sharply the bone of contention with Jews to this day: they cannot believe that Messiah would be "subject to suffering."

*been done in a corner. **27** King Agrippa, do you believe the prophets? I*
*know that you believe." **28** And Agrippa said to Paul, "In a short time*
*would you persuade me to be a Christian?" **29** And Paul said, "Whether*
short or long, I would to God that not only you but also all who hear me
this day might become such as I am—except for these chains."

A speaker knows he is getting through when he is abruptly interrupted as Paul
is cut off here by Festus. This talk of resurrection is incredible (v. 8) to Festus, as
it was to any sensible Roman or Greek. He has a certain sympathy for Paul but
is not just making a friendly jibe; he thinks that Paul, though a man of great
learning, is out of his mind. We sometimes hear skeptics dismiss doctrines like
resurrection and other miracles as the superstitions of a gullible, pre-scientific
age. Not so, resurrection was a tough sell even in those "primitive" times.

Paul replies that he is not insane. "What I am saying is true and rational.
It becomes true and rational when you see the real thing, as I and others have
seen the risen Christ." He thinks King Agrippa must have heard about these
things (including the unsolved mystery of the disappearance of Jesus' body
from a sealed and guarded tomb and the reports of a number of appearances
of the risen Christ to his disciples). *This has not been done in a corner.* The word
"this" seems to refer to the crucifixion and resurrection considered together.

Paul then turns to King Agrippa in a direct appeal to believe, an
unbelievable act of boldness. Paul cares more about the salvation of Agrippa
and the others than he cares about his own release. It is not now Paul before
Agrippa but Agrippa before Paul. He asks not, "Do you believe in Jesus as
Messiah"? but "Do you believe the prophets?" Agrippa senses he is being
trapped. If he admits that he believes the prophets, Paul will lead him into
believing in Christ. The embarrassed king fends Paul off with a deft bit of
humor. *Do you think that in such a short time you can persuade me to be a*
Christian? (NIV). The word "time" is supplied but is likely the correct sense.

We cannot hear Agrippa's tone of voice in the ancient record. Is he
joking? Is he being sarcastic? Is he angry? "The tone is sophisticated annoyance
by a slightly embarrassed king."[12] His retort has its own logic. He really needs
more time talking with Paul about the prophets and Jesus of Nazareth if he
is to believe. But if he were really interested, he would have called Paul in
for a private session. Agrippa is afraid that repentance and conversion would

---

12   W. J. Larkin, *Acts* (Downers Grove, IL: Intervarsity Press, 1995), 365, cited by
      Witherington, 751.

probably cost him his position and require him to give up a sinful life. So it is with the high and mighty of this world; they are imprisoned in their own gilded cages.

Paul gracefully lets the king off the hook with a bit of humor of his own: *Whether short or long, I would to God that not only you but also all who hear me this day might become such as I am—except for these chains.*

Paul would say the same to all who have read these words through the centuries.

൦ℓ൦

Acts 26:30-32

Conclusion: "This Man is Innocent"

30 Then the king rose, and the governor and Bernice and those who were sitting with them. 31 And when they had withdrawn, they said to one another, "This man is doing nothing to deserve death or imprisonment." 32 And Agrippa said to Festus, "This man could have been set free if he had not appealed to Caesar."

The king rises to leave (kings outrank governors) and that is the signal that the show is over. There is no hint that Paul's courageous witness has left any permanent impression, but there may well have been later conversions from among that audience. We never know what God will do with our testimony. Luke was probably in that audience and overheard the remarks of the departing guests. There seems to have been agreement that Paul had done nothing worthy of death; indeed he had done nothing deserving even imprisonment. For the third time a Roman tribunal has found Paul innocent. This is probably a deliberate parallel to the three times Pilate found Jesus innocent (all three in Luke 23). Like Jesus, the unbelieving Jews hated (Paul) without a cause (John 15:25). Theophilus must understand that three high-ranking Roman authorities have found Paul innocent and that the Jews really had no case against him.

Agrippa's final remark reinforces the opinion of the assembled guests. This man is not doing anything that deserves death or imprisonment. Witherington, based on the opinion of Sherwin-White, an expert in ancient Roman law, disagrees with most commentators who say that Festus' hands were bound and that he had no choice but to send Paul to Rome.[13] Since there were no credible charges, Festus had the legal authority to acquit Paul and dismiss the case. The decision to send Paul to Rome had no legal basis but was a political choice based on three factors: dodging a troublesome case, fear of alienating the Jews, and a fear of somehow reducing the prestige of the Emperor. Paul was the victim of a miscarriage of justice, but he does not protest; he knows it is the Lord's will that he testify of Christ at the court of Emperor Nero (23:11). Now he will get free transportation to Rome, courtesy of the Roman government.

Lessons for Life

1. We should preach the gospel not only to the poor and lowly but also the "high and mighty."
2. Be ready to seize opportunities to testify of what Christ has done for you.
3. Use the testimonies of those converted out of the religion(s) of your target audience.
4. God can convert even "the chief of sinners."
5. "Pauline theology" came from the Lord, not from Paul but through Paul.
6. Do not neglect two crucial "R's" in evangelism: Resurrection and Repentance.
7. The three keys to successful evangelism are boldness, boldness, and boldness, well-tempered with sensitivity to the audience, wit, and wisdom.

---

13 Witherington, 752.

ACTS 27

PAUL SAILS FOR ROME, THE STORM, AND THE SHIPWRECK

Acts 27:1-44

Saved Through the Storm

Now at last Paul is underway for Rome, the destination of his dreams, the center of empire, and the place of the Lord's destiny for him (23:11). But the party of three (Paul, Luke, and Aristarchus) is shipwrecked on the way and their lives endangered. However, God in his providence sees them safely through all the way to Rome.

Why does Luke use up his precious manuscript space with details that seem to have little to do with his evangelistic and theological purposes in Acts?[1] We might rather know what happened in the trial before Caesar than the details of how he got to Rome. Did Luke reach toward the end of his story, see that he had more precious vellum left than he had anticipated, and decide to spin out the yarn in a little more detail? A number of scholars have suggested better reasons, none of which is without merit.

---

1   "There is no more detailed record of the working of an ancient ship in the whole of classical literature." Thomas Walker, *The Acts of the Apostles* (Chicago: Moody, 1910), 543, cited by Stott, 385.

First, some suggest that a story of shipwreck or peril at sea was a staple of the literary conventions of the time. The more skeptical think that Luke latched on to a good sea story and inserted Paul into it in such a way as to make his hero look good. If so, it would be an amazing coincidence that Luke found a story that moved Paul in just the direction he needed to go! Or that the story would be told with the vividness and attention to detail that only an eyewitness record can account for. But it cannot be denied that Luke may have had an eye to the sheer interest or entertainment value of an exciting story. (Is our preaching and teaching so dull that we can never tell a good story?) The story does serve to make Paul look good and indeed brings out aspects of his character in a "secular" practical situation that we have not seen before. Stott astutely suggests that this account is part of the "journey motif in a kind of recapitulation of the sufferings of Christ." Just as Luke, from 9:53 of his gospel on, details Jesus' journey to Jerusalem, so, here Luke highlights Paul in his journey to Rome.[2]

Another more prosaic possibility is that all of the "we" sections of Acts (16:10-17; 20:5-15; 21:1-18; and 27:1-28:16) tend to be more detailed on both events and items of itinerary.[3] The third "we" section (21:1-18), an account of the return voyage of the third missionary journey, gives details of ports visited and especially times of travel between points which are very much like chapter 27.

Perhaps the best explanation of the length of this passage is theological. Luke, under the Spirit, was again emphasizing God's providential protection of Paul to fulfill his own purpose. This may have meant more to ancient readers than to modern readers. There was a concept in ancient times that those who suffered shipwreck had incurred the wrath of the gods and were being punished. We have an indication of this concept in 28:4 where the Maltese islanders said, when Paul was bitten by a snake, *No doubt this man is a murderer. Though he has escaped from the sea, Justice has not allowed him to live.* This was not just the belief of "barbarians;" it was common among Greco-Romans of all classes.[4] Paul's survival would have been interpreted as God's approval of his messenger and the messenger's gospel message.

---

2   Stott, 385.

3   Longenecker (458) observes that "the ministry at Philippi receives the greatest attention (thirty verses) in this fifth panel" and "Luke devotes more space to the mission in Philippi than he does to any other city on Paul's second and third missionary journeys." His point is that the "we" sections contain greater detail from eyewitness Luke.

4   Marshall, 401.

27:1-12 Fair Sailing to Crete

1 And when it was decided that we should sail for Italy, they delivered Paul and some other prisoners to a centurion of the Augustan Cohort named Julius. 2 And embarking in a ship of Adramyttium, which was about to sail to the ports along the coast of Asia, we put to sea, accompanied by Aristarchus, a Macedonian from Thessalonica. 3 The next day we put in at Sidon. And Julius treated Paul kindly and gave him leave to go to his friends and be cared for. 4 And putting out to sea from there we sailed under the lee of Cyprus, because the winds were against us. 5 And when we had sailed across the open sea along the coast of Cilicia and Pamphylia, we came to Myra in Lycia. 6 There the centurion found a ship of Alexandria sailing for Italy and put us on board. 7 We sailed slowly for a number of days and arrived with difficulty off Cnidus, and as the wind did not allow us to go farther, we sailed under the lee of Crete off Salmone. 8 Coasting along it with difficulty, we came to a place called Fair Havens, near which was the city of Lasea.

9 Since much time had passed, and the voyage was now dangerous because even the Fast was already over, Paul advised them, 10 saying, "Sirs, I perceive that the voyage will be with injury and much loss, not only of the cargo and the ship, but also of our lives." 11 But the centurion paid more attention to the pilot and to the owner of the ship than to what Paul said. 12 And because the harbor was not suitable to spend the winter in, the majority decided to put out to sea from there, on the chance that somehow they could reach Phoenix, a harbor of Crete, facing both southwest and northwest, and spend the winter there.

In the first paragraph (verses 1-3) the salient feature is the good will that Julius, the centurion in charge of the prisoners, showed toward Paul. Again a centurion turns out to be a good man, a helper of the gospel. Julius' favor will have important implications in the rest of the story. He was probably one of the *speculatores*, a special body of imperial guards who had police and escort responsibilities.[5]

The first ship was from Adramyttium, a port not far from Troas in Asia Minor, and it seems to have been a coaster returning to its homeport. The reason it hugs the shore is that the prevailing winds, especially in the fall of the

---

5   Longenecker, 558.

year, were from the west and north. The ship kept close to shore for some
shelter from the winds that were partially blocked by the high mountains of
the Taurus Range and also to take advantage of offshore breezes that blew
during the night. The "lee" (the side away from the wind) of Cyprus is the
north side of Cyprus. It is hard for modern people to grasp how much at the
primitive ships of those times were at the mercy of the winds. There was no
such thing as a direct route to Rome that would be routinely plotted by a
modern navigator.

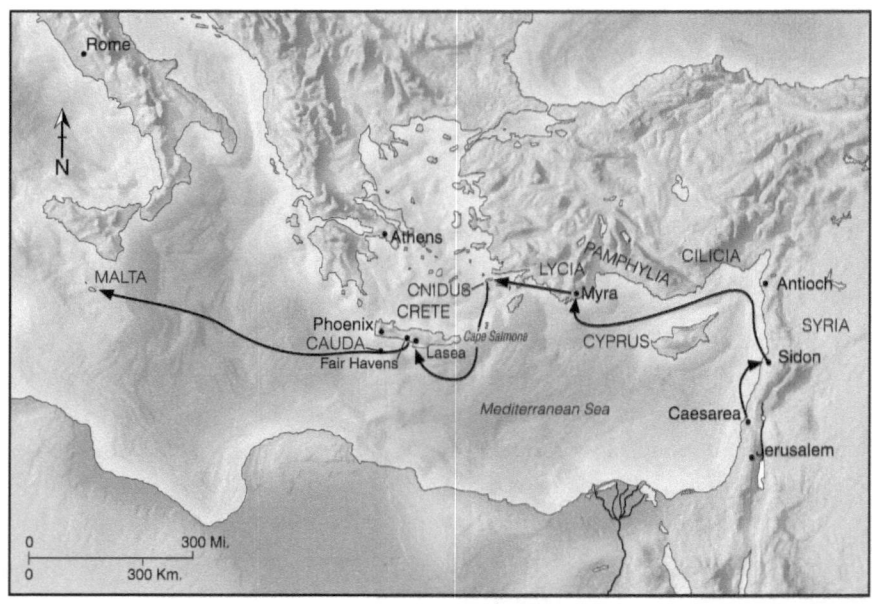

Voyage to Rome, Shipwreck

At Myra they transferred to a much larger ship called *annona*, especially
designed to carry grain from Egypt to Rome.[6] These ships were of vital
importance to the political survival of the Roman emperors and every effort was
made to ensure an adequate grain supply to feed the masses in Rome. The ships
were under direct imperial control under the command of an officer like Julius
but were operated by private owner/captains (the *naukleros* of verse 11). Myra,
along with Patara, a little further to the west on the coast of Lycia (southwest
coast of Turkey today), was an important port on the grain shipment route.

---

6   There is a splendid picture of such a ship on page 256 of Ramsey.

This is a model of the ancient Roman grain ship called "annona." These ships carried wheat from Egypt, the breadbasket of the Empire, to Rome to feed the masses. Courtesy of The Model Shipyard, Mossel Bay, South Africa

As far as Myra the voyage was routine and making good time. But now we have the first hint of difficulties and delays. When the grain freighter reached the western tip of the southwest Anatolian peninsula (Cnidus), the ship hit contrary winds from the west and north. They diverted south to sail along the south side of Crete (in this case the "lee" of Crete is the south coast) to get some shelter from the winds. When they reached a small bay called "Fair Havens" (which is still called "*Kali Limenes*" = "Fair Havens") in the middle of the south coast of Crete, they realized they had a problem.

Much time had passed, and the voyage was now dangerous because even the Fast was already over. We know from ancient records that sailing the Mediterranean Sea after September 14 was considered dangerous and from November 11 through the winter, voyages were prohibited. "The Fast" was the Day of Atonement (*Yom Kippur*), still one of the most important holy days in the Jewish calendar. If, as many commentators believe, this was the year 59 AD, the Day of Atonement fell on October 5 that year, far past the safe point of mid-September. The centurion (who was in charge), following the advice of the navigator and the owner, decided to sail to Phoenix (the modern village of Loutros), a better port on the south coast of Crete only fifty miles to the west, which had a more sheltered harbor.

On the face of it this seemed to be a sensible decision, but Paul was opposed. *Sirs, I perceive that the voyage will be with injury and much loss, not only of the cargo and the ship, but also of our lives.* Paul was not responsible for the ship and as a prisoner had no authority. Except for the favor of Julius, he would not have been consulted at all. But what is the opinion of a passenger against all the experience of the professionals?

This advice does not come from a divine revelation because, as it turned out, there was no loss of life. Paul's advice may be an example of what is called in 1 Cor 12:8 the spiritual gift of *the word of wisdom.* Paul may not have been a professional sailor, but he had already sailed some 3,000 miles as a passenger in eleven voyages recorded in Acts alone, not to mention the three shipwrecks he had suffered before this one (2 Cor 11:25), including *a day and a night in the deep.* He is now a veteran sea traveler and is all too keenly aware of the dangers of late autumn winds.[7]

27:13-26 The Storm

> **13** *Now when the south wind blew gently, supposing that they had obtained their purpose, they weighed anchor and sailed along Crete, close to the shore.* **14** *But soon a tempestuous wind, called the northeaster, struck down from the land.* **15** *And when the ship was caught and could not face the wind, we gave way to it and were driven along.* **16** *Running under the lee of a small island called Cauda, we managed with difficulty to secure the ship's boat.* **17** *After hoisting it up, they used supports to undergird the ship. Then, fearing that they would run aground on the Syrtis, they lowered the gear,*ᵉ *and thus they were driven along.* **18** *Since we were violently storm-tossed, they began the next day to jettison the cargo.* **19** *And on the third day they threw the ship's tackle overboard with their own hands.* **20** *When neither sun nor stars appeared for many days, and no small tempest lay on us, all hope of our being saved was at last abandoned.*
>
> **21** *Since they had been without food for a long time, Paul stood up among them and said, "Men, you should have listened to me and not have*

---

7   Witherington, 754.

set sail from Crete and incurred this injury and loss. **22** *Yet now I urge you to take heart, for there will be no loss of life among you, but only of the ship.* **23** *For this very night there stood before me an angel of the God to whom I belong and whom I worship,* **24** *and he said, 'Do not be afraid, Paul; you must stand before Caesar. And behold, God has granted you all those who sail with you.'* **25** *So take heart, men, for I have faith in God that it will be exactly as I have been told.* **26** *But we must run aground on some island."*

The decision to proceed seemed vindicated when they got a *gentle south wind.* But it was if they had been lured into a trap because they had not gone very far before a fearful gale force wind called *Euroaquilo* swept down from the mountains of Crete to the north. In ancient times the maritime wind compass was divided into twelve sections and each had a nickname.[8] As the following narrative shows, this storm was powerful enough to seriously endanger the ship.[9] The crew could no longer control the ship and they were driven helplessly before a ferocious wind and mountainous seas.[10]

The crew did five things to try to save the ship. They hauled in the ship's boat (with much difficulty), which was normally towed behind the ship. They passed cables under the ship to strengthen the hull.[11] They lowered the sea anchor, a canvas cone that would of course not reach bottom, but served to slow the drift and steady the ship somewhat. The storm only got worse, so the

---

8   A compass circle with the names of the winds has been found in Thugga, North Africa. From the north there is *septentrio, aquilo,* and then *euroaquilo* (a hybrid Greek-Latin word). The *euroaquilo* was 60 degrees to the east of north. Bruce, 518.

9   The Greek word is *typhonikos* (whirlwind), derived from *Typhos,* the sea monster with a hundred heads. Coincidentally this word sounds like the characters for "big wind" in Chinese and Japanese, from which we get our word "typhoon."

10   Unless you have experienced it, you cannot understand the awesomeness of a storm at sea. The author has experienced several big storms on a US Navy ships, one a typhoon off the coast of Japan. The crests of huge waves are twenty degrees above eye level, the wind is shrieking and blowing rain horizontally, mountains of water cascade across the bridge, the ship rolls violently back and forth thirty degrees, and everything not securely fastened crashes back and forth violently with each roll of the ship. If this is a frightening experience in a large steel ship, what must it be in a smaller wooden ship?

11   Literally the word is "underbelts," but exactly how they were applied is uncertain. The ropes or chains would pass under the ship crosswise to hold the hull together laterally. This operation could be accomplished by lowering strong cables at the bow and then walking them aft until they were secured at the desired location.

next day they threw some of the cargo (wheat) overboard to lighten the ship. One is reminded of the storm in Jonah. The crew is becoming increasingly desperate. And fifth, as a final act of desperation, they threw some of the ship's tackle overboard. The word is vague; perhaps they jettisoned the heavy single mainsail and maybe the large yardarm that held it up. But nothing seemed to help. *When neither sun nor stars appeared for many days and no small tempest lay upon us, all hope of our being saved was at last abandoned.* The clouds obscured the sun and stars for two whole weeks and so they had no idea of their location. Both crew and passengers must have huddled miserably below decks, most so seasick they could hardly move; in an unending purgatory, with the terror of expecting the ship to break up any moment or to be dashed on the reefs or rocks of some unknown land. They were in numb despair and had given up all hope of being saved.

It was at this point that Paul was able to give hope to the passengers and crew. Resisting the temptation to say, "I told you so," Paul says:

> **21** *"Men, you should have listened to me and not have set sail from Crete and incurred this injury and loss.* **22** *Yet now I urge you to take heart, for there will be no loss of life among you, but only of the ship.* **23** *For this very night there stood before me an angel of the God to whom I belong and whom I worship,* **24** *and he said, 'Do not be afraid, Paul; you must stand before Caesar. And behold, God has granted you all those who sail with you.'* **25** *So take heart, men, for I have faith in God that it will be exactly as I have been told.* **26** *But we must run aground on some island."*

Paul has received a word from the Lord, just at the point when all hope was lost and they were all resigned to die. The angel's first words, *Do not be afraid, Paul* show that despite the promise of 23:11, Paul too was afraid and wondering why God didn't do something to help them.[12] No one will be lost but they must run aground on some island. The angel gives just enough information to give courage and hope. Other details are unimportant. The chief reason for the deliverance is that Paul must stand before Caesar. But for the sake of Paul, everyone on board will be saved. This is one of the key themes of the story.

---

12   The negative imperative in the present tense has the sense of "stop doing what you are doing," here "stop fearing."

27:27-44 Shipwreck on Malta

27 When the fourteenth night had come, as we were being driven across the Adriatic Sea, about midnight the sailors suspected that they were nearing land. 28 So they took a sounding and found twenty fathoms. A little farther on they took a sounding again and found fifteen fathoms. 29 And fearing that we might run on the rocks, they let down four anchors from the stern and prayed for day to come. 30 And as the sailors were seeking to escape from the ship, and had lowered the ship's boat into the sea under pretense of laying out anchors from the bow, 31 Paul said to the centurion and the soldiers, "Unless these men stay in the ship, you cannot be saved." 32 Then the soldiers cut away the ropes of the ship's boat and let it go.

33 As day was about to dawn, Paul urged them all to take some food, saying, "Today is the fourteenth day that you have continued in suspense and without food, having taken nothing. 34 Therefore I urge you to take some food. For it will give you strength, for not a hair is to perish from the head of any of you." 35 And when he had said these things, he took bread, and giving thanks to God in the presence of all he broke it and began to eat. 36 Then they all were encouraged and ate some food themselves. 37 (We were in all 276 persons in the ship.) 38 And when they had eaten enough, they lightened the ship, throwing out the wheat into the sea.

39 Now when it was day, they did not recognize the land, but they noticed a bay with a beach, on which they planned if possible to run the ship ashore. 40 So they cast off the anchors and left them in the sea, at the same time loosening the ropes that tied the rudders. Then hoisting the foresail to the wind they made for the beach. 41 But striking a reef, they ran the vessel aground. The bow stuck and remained immovable, and the stern was being broken up by the surf. 42 The soldiers' plan was to kill the prisoners, lest any should swim away and escape. 43 But the centurion, wishing to save Paul, kept them from carrying out their plan. He ordered those who could swim to jump overboard first and make for the land, 44 and the rest on planks or on pieces of the ship. And so it was that all were brought safely to land.

The name of the sea given by the ESV as *"Adriatic"* is an error.[13] The word is *"the Sea of Adria"* (NRSV), which denoted that region of the central Mediterranean between Italy, Greece, Malta and Crete.

---

13 The Adriatic is the relatively narrow sea between Italy and the Balkan Peninsula.

The sailors may have suspected they were near land when they heard the crashing of waves against the shore (it was night). Soundings confirmed a rapidly decreasing depth of water. Now that the water was shallow enough, they could put down anchors to keep the ship from being dashed on the rocks, and wait for daybreak.

Under the cover of darkness, and pretending to put out more anchors, some of the sailors abandoned the tradition of the sea and tried to escape on the ship's boat. Catastrophes always bring out the worst and the best in human nature.[14] Again Paul has a word of wisdom: *Unless these men stay in the ship, you cannot be saved. Then the soldiers cut away the ropes of the ship's boat and let it go.*

God had promised they would all be saved but that does not prevent Paul from using the human wisdom available to him. The sailors would be needed to run the ship safely onto the shore.

Then for the fourth time Paul takes the initiative for the good of all. He encourages them to eat, for most had not eaten for many days, either from despondency or seasickness, and they would need all their strength to swim ashore. Before, Paul had given a witness to the true God by reporting what the angel of God had said to him; now he gives thanks to God before them all and starts eating some bread. All 276 people follow his example![15]

The saying has it that "Some are so heavenly minded they are no earthly good." Quite the opposite, in situations of despair, only the heavenly minded are any earthly good. We must mix our spirituality with common sense and practicality. Saving souls out of the fire of hell may be the main thing, but sometimes God wants us to help put out the earthly fire.

Now the crew sees their chance; there is a sandy beach and they will run the ship up onto it and be safe. They cut loose the stern anchors and untied the steering oars (one on each side) so they could keep the ship headed straight in. All worked well until they hit what was probably a sandbar, and the ship's bow stuck fast while the stern was being pounded to pieces by the waves.

---

14   As I write, the catastrophic hurricane Katrina has flooded New Orleans, and the point is being abundantly illustrated on the TV news.

15   The number is no exaggeration and shows the size of these grain freighters. Interestingly, the historian Josephus was shipwrecked on a similar ship in the same area within a few years of this incident. Out of 600, only 80, including Josephus, survived (*Life of Josephus*, 3.15).

Another crisis is prevented, in the providence of God, when the centurion Julius, wishing to save Paul, prevents his soldiers from killing the prisoners (this is the first time we know that there are other prisoners). The soldiers no doubt feared they would put to death if any of the prisoners escaped. For the sake of Paul, all are spared.

But now it is every man for himself! The remarkable thing is that no one drowned in the heavy surf. Either they were able to swim ashore, or be helped ashore by others, or were able to cling to planks from the disintegrating ship and be pushed ashore by the surf. And so it was that all were brought safely to land.

ᴄᴇᴏ

General Reflections and Application

God's Providence

Though some have gone too far in making this incident into an allegory of salvation, it does fit the theme of "salvation for all" in the book of Acts. The theme is **the providence of God** in preservation, protection, and salvation, whether spiritual or physical.

It has been a long time since we have had a miracle in the book of Acts. If we make a chart or list of the miracles in Acts, we soon see that there have been no miracles since Eutychus was raised from the dead in chapter 20. From chapters 21 through 27, we have no miracles, though we do have two appearances of the Lord to Paul. Why was Paul not delivered from the Roman prison in Caesarea miraculously like Peter was in chapters 5 and 12 and as Paul himself was in Philippi (chap. 16)? Though we again have two accounts of miracles, maybe three, in chapter 28, we have the impression that miracles are decreasing in frequency toward the end of the book.

The providence of God, however, is in many ways more remarkable than the miracles of God. When God does a miracle, he can work directly and immediately without the "trouble" of using intermediate agents. When he acts in providence, he uses a host of factors like weather, or the vagaries of ocean currents, or the actions of unbelieving sailors, or any of numberless actions and reactions to achieve his purposes. He seems to do this without "pulling any strings" or directly setting aside natural law and natural events to effect the desired outcome. From our human point of view, then, providence is much more "difficult" than miracle. To use an absurdly simple example, it is easier to prepare one's own breakfast (acting directly) than to train a chimpanzee to prepare one's breakfast.

We can illustrate the difference between deliverance by miracle and deliverance by providence if we contrast Acts 27 with the storm on the Sea of Galilee in the gospels (Matt 8:18-27; Mark 4:35-41; Luke 8:22-25). In that case Jesus wakened and stilled the storm instantly with a word. There was instant deliverance by a fantastic miracle. In Acts 27 God did not answer for fourteen miserable days, but was all the while using the natural movements of wind and sea to move the ship to its appointed haven.

Consider some of the "points of providence" that God used not only to preserve Paul and his party but also to speed them on their way to Rome. First they found a ship headed for Rome that was large enough to survive rough weather. Second, Paul himself, though not acting under any special divine guidance, was an agent of the ship's preservation; he encouraged and fed the passengers and crew when they were in despair, and he prevented the escape of the crew when the ship went aground. Third, the ship was driven straight west, precisely the direction they needed to go. (It could, for example, have been driven to shipwreck on the North African coast.) Fourth, the ship did not miss Malta and drift into the western Mediterranean where they might have died either from the breaking up of the ship or starvation or striking a rocky coast. (Look at the map; Malta is really small!) Fifth, the ship did not break up in the fourteen days of drifting, even though it took a severe pounding. Sixth, the ship did not break up on a rocky shore of Malta (Malta has very few sandy beaches) but made a bull's eye into what is today called St. Paul's Bay, a natural harbor on the northeast side of Malta that had a sandy beach. Seventh, even though the ship went aground and was being destroyed by the surf, not one of the 276 on board died. The very breaking up of the ship provided large pieces of wood that the people could use to ride the surf ashore.

In our lives today, true miracles are rare, but what we sometimes call "miracle," the providence of God, is a daily experience. If providence is more remarkable than miracle, why are we always longing for miracles and overlooking the providence of God in the midst of everyday life?

Leadership

Leadership seminars are popular today in the western world, both in the church and in the business world. Many Christian speakers decry a "lack of leadership" in the church. In any country we are often all too keenly aware of a lack of honest leadership or true statesmanship in our political leaders, whether autocratic dictators or democratically elected legislatures and prime ministers. How often leaders disappoint their longsuffering subjects! How few are truly admired and respected! How long has it been since we have had a Mahatma Ghandi or a Sun Yat-sen or an Abraham Lincoln?

Paul the Apostle furnishes us with an excellent model of leadership in Acts 27. First, Paul was constantly **concerned** more **for the common good** than for his own comfort. It was not enough that he and his companions ate some bread; Paul urged everyone to have something to eat. He warned the centurion and the captain that they were subjecting the ship to danger. He encouraged the entire body of crew and passengers when God gave him a revelation that they would be saved. Second, Paul was **aware of the situation**, especially the dangers. He warned the centurion that they could not survive if the sailors escaped. Third, Paul **took the initiative** to rectify the situation. He spoke up when he thought setting out to sea from Fair Havens was dangerous. He had no special authority; he could have pleaded that he was not in charge and that it was none of his business. Fourth, Paul had the **courage** that we have seen throughout the book of Acts to speak up decisively in the above situations. Fifth, anticipating 28:3, Paul was **humble** enough to help in the gathering of sticks to build a fire. Many in positions of high status or position consider it beneath their dignity or station in life to dirty their hands with manual labor. *Whoever wants to become great among you must be your servant.* (Mark 10:43). "Servant leadership" is much talked about in the church these days; how much is it really practiced?

Vindication of the Accuracy of the Book of Acts

The most striking commentary on the accuracy of this chapter is a remarkable book by James Smith of Scotland titled *The Voyage and Shipwreck of St Paul* (originally 1848, fourth edition of 1880 published by Longmans). Stott gives some detailed information on James Smith:

> (Smith) was a soldier by profession, a keen yachtsman of thirty years experience, an eminent amateur geologist and geographer, and a Fellow of the Royal Society. He lived successively in Gibraltar, Lisbon, and Malta, and spent the winter of 1844-45 in Malta while investigating Paul's voyage. He was widely read, he familiarized himself with the weather patterns of the Mediterranean, and he made a study of navigation and seamanship in both the ancient and the modern worlds. His general conclusion was that Acts 27 was the work of an eyewitness who nevertheless was a landlubber, and not a professional seaman: 'no sailor would have written in a style so little like that of a sailor; no man not a sailor could have written a narrative of a sea voyage so consistent in all its parts, unless from actual observation.'[16]

Witherington also cites Smith's work:

> One of the most convincing portions of Smith's detailed study of Paul's journey is the calculation of how long it would take a ship of the sort Paul was on, in the face of a northeaster, to drift from Cauda to near the mouth of Saint Paul's Bay at Malta at the point called Koura. The distance is some 475 miles, and Smith's detailed comparison of nautical accounts from this region showed that it was likely to take right at fourteen days to drift this far. This is a rather striking confirmation of the accuracy of Luke's account.[17]

As we have gone through the book of Acts, we have again and again been impressed with Luke's painstaking accuracy concerning place names and particularly the precise titles of local officials. Here at the end of the book, we have one more indication that this book was not a "pious fiction."

---

16   Stott, 386.

17   Witherington, 771, citing Smith's work pp. 124-27.

ACTS 28

PAUL ON MALTA AND HIS ARRIVAL IN ROME

Acts 28:1-31

Rome at Last!

28:1-10 "Unusual Kindness" on Malta

1 After we were brought safely through, we then learned that the island was called Malta. 2 The native people showed us unusual kindness, for they kindled a fire and welcomed us all, because it had begun to rain and was cold. 3 When Paul had gathered a bundle of sticks and put them on the fire, a viper came out because of the heat and fastened on his hand. 4 When the native people saw the creature hanging from his hand, they said to one another, "No doubt this man is a murderer. Though he has escaped from the sea, Justice has not allowed him to live." 5 He, however, shook off the creature into the fire and suffered no harm. 6 They were waiting for him to swell up or suddenly fall down dead. But when they had waited a long time and saw no misfortune come to him, they changed their minds and said that he was a god.

7 Now in the neighborhood of that place were lands belonging to the chief man of the island, named Publius, who received us and entertained us hospitably for three days. 8 It happened that the father of Publius lay sick with fever and dysentery. And Paul visited him and prayed, and putting his hands on him, healed him. 9 And when this had taken place,

371

the rest of the people on the island who had diseases also came and were
*cured. **10** They also honored us greatly, and when we were about to sail,*
they put on board whatever we needed.

Malta is a small island 58 miles south of Sicily and 158 miles from the North
African coast. It is only 18 miles long and 9 miles wide. Rome acquired the
island in 218 BC from Carthage and made it part of the province of Sicily. It
was known for growing cotton and making cotton fabric.

The Maltese, who today speak an Arabic dialect, at that time were
descendants of Phoenicians who had settled the island as early as 1000 BC.
At the time of Paul they spoke a dialect called Punic and were related to
the Carthaginians, made famous by Rome's desperate wars with that North
African power. In verse 2 the word *native people* is *barbaroi* in Greek. This did
not mean they were primitive; the word simply means "foreigner." During the
age of Augustus the word came to be used for all tribes which had no Greek
or Roman civilization.[1] This account reminds us of the encounter of Paul
and Barnabas with the more primitive Lycanonians in Acts 14. Like them, the
Maltese were superstitious. When a snake bit Paul and Paul did not die, they
concluded that he must be *a god.* The Lycaonians thought Paul was a god and
then thought he was an imposter; the Maltese thought he was a criminal and
then thought he was a god. The *unusual kindness* of the native Maltese is one
more evidence of the providence of God in protecting and providing for the
physical needs of Paul and his companions, Luke and Aristarchus. They could
have been met on a strange shore by savage brutes who sold them into slavery.
Shipwrecked sailors are at the mercy of the first people they encounter.[2] The
temperature was probably in the 50s (Fahrenheit, 10 Celsius) and without the
big bonfire, death from hypothermia was very possible.

Paul would not have been bitten if he had warmed himself by the fire and
let the "lower castes" gather the firewood, or assume a "leadership" position
and supervise others in the gathering of firewood. We see here his humility
and Christian character in helping with a small but important task.

The snake is called *echidna,* which is incorrectly translated "viper,"
designating a poisonous snake. The word can refer to any kind of snake. It is
possible that this was a poisonous snake and that God miraculously preserved

---

1   Liddell and Scott *Intermediate Greek-English Lexicon.*

2   The "wreckers" of Cornwall, England were infamous for preying on the many
     shipwrecks which occurred on their coasts.

Paul from the effect of the venom. I suspect that this was not a poisonous snake. First there are no poisonous snakes on the little island of Malta today.[3] Second and most convincing to me, a poisonous snake does not clamp on; it strikes with its fangs and leaves two tiny holes in the skin through which it has injected the venom and withdraws before the victim realizes what has happened to him. The fact that Paul had to shake the snake off shows that it was not a poisonous snake. As far as the islanders thinking it was a poisonous snake, then as now, many people think all snakes are poisonous.[4]

Paul and his company, (no doubt including Julius the centurion and his soldiers), were invited by the chief official of the island, a Roman by the name of Publius,[5] to stay three days at his estate until more permanent winter quarters could be found. Publius' father was sick with a fever and Paul was able to exercise his gift of healing and so make a powerful impression for Christ.[6] This is the first miracle since the healing of Eutychus in Troas (chap. 21). Again, God in his providence puts Paul and company in contact with a man of more than necessary kindness and again the gospel reaches a high government official. There is no mention of preaching, but we cannot imagine Paul failing to take advantage of this splendid witnessing opportunity.

When this had taken place, the rest of the people on the island who had diseases came and were cured. The news of the healing spread and many who were sick came and were being healed. The gospel had a powerful debut on this little island, the first nation in Europe to embrace Christianity. The 400,000 Maltese are still 97% Christian and with higher rates of church attendance than the rest of Europe.[7]

---

3   It is possible that at that time there were poisonous snakes and that they have since become extinct.

4   "Pliny the elder indicates it was a common belief, even among the educated, that all snakes were poisonous and that they were often agents of divine vengeance." Witherington, 778. T. E. Lawrence (Lawrence of Arabia) tells in his book *Revolt in the Desert* (London, 1927) of a similar encounter with a snake. "When the fire grew hot, a long black snake wound slowly out into our group; we must have gathered it, torpid, with the twigs" (p. 107, cited by Bruce, 531).

5   The name, which is really a title meaning "first," has been found on an ancient inscription from an island near Malta (ISBE, *Publius*, 2501).

6   The fever and dysentery of the father may well have been caused by a microbe in goat's milk, known traditionally as "Malta Fever" (Bruce, 533).

7   Patrick Johnstone and Jason Mandryk, *Operation World* (Paternoster Publishing, 2001), 431.

They also honored us greatly, and when we were about to sail, they put on board whatever we needed. The word *honored us greatly* in Greek is *honored us with many honors.* The noun often means a monetary gift, so the honor no doubt consisted of funds to replenish the pockets of shipwreck victims who had lost everything. Not only that but the grateful islanders replenished all the supplies they had lost. Again the providence of God is the thread that connects all of chapters 27 and 28. They are now ready to continue the voyage to Rome.

28:11-16 From Malta to Rome

11 After three months we set sail in a ship that had wintered in the island, a ship of Alexandria, with the twin gods as a figurehead. 12 Putting in at Syracuse, we stayed there for three days. 13 And from there we made a circuit and arrived at Rhegium. And after one day a south wind sprang up, and on the second day we came to Puteoli. 14 There we found brothers and were invited to stay with them for seven days. And so we came to Rome. 15 And the brothers there, when they heard about us, came as far as the Forum of Appius and Three Taverns to meet us. On seeing them, Paul thanked God and took courage. 16 And when we came into Rome, Paul was allowed to stay by himself, with the soldier who guarded him.

Paul and his party had to wait for the opening of seafaring in the spring to resume their journey. This would bring us to early February, probably in the year 60 AD. They got passage on a grain ship from Alexandria, which had no doubt spent the winter in a harbor in Malta. This ship had a twin figurehead of two popular gods, Castor and Pollux, patron gods of sailors and travelers, whose zodiac constellation Gemini ("Twins") is clearly visible in the night sky at that time of year, believed to be a sign of good fortune in a storm.[8] Pagan gods meant nothing to Paul, whose Bible prohibited astrology, and who depended on the God of heaven, not the stars in the heavens.

The ship stayed three days in Syracuse, the ancient Greek (Corinthian) colony and the chief port of Sicily, called by Cicero "the greatest of Greek cities and the most beautiful of all cities." But Luke never mentions the local sights; his purpose is to get Paul to Rome.

---

8   Witherington, 781.

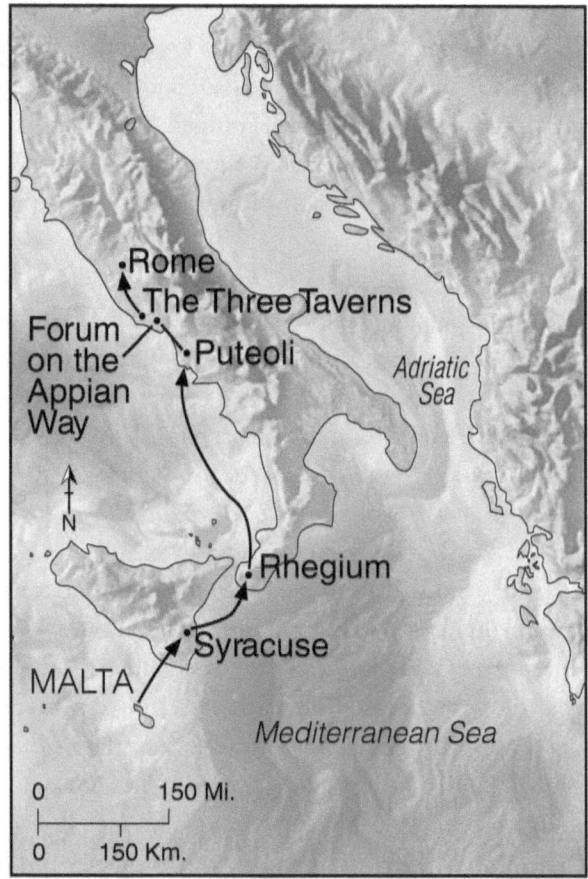

Paul Arrives in Rome

Paul and his companions sail north up the coast of Sicily and cross the strait of Messina to Rhegium, another ancient Greek colony, on the toe of the boot of Italy.[9] Now that they have landed in Italy, they must have heaved sighs of relief; there is little chance that storms will delay them now. The very next day they got a south wind, and avoiding the infamous rock of Scylla and the whirlpool of Charybdis in the strait, make the best time of the entire dreary voyage, cruising the 180 miles to Puteoli in one day.

---

9   There is a textual problem on whether they "weighed anchor" (NRSV) (*periaireō* = "take away") or "made a circuit" (ESV) (*perierchomai*). This is one of many cases where our ignorance of the precise text makes little difference.

Puteoli (modern Pozzuoli), inhabited by some 100,000 people, was the second most important harbor in Italy. It was located on the north part of what we know today as the Bay of Naples. Paul and the passengers gazed on Mount Vesuvius and Herculaneum and Pompeii and hundreds of wealthy villas ringing the beautiful bay as the ship came into harbor. Within twenty years, both cities would be buried under volcanic ash in the eruption of Mount Vesuvius in 79 AD.

There we found brothers and were invited to stay with them for seven days. Luke is interested in the precious believers who hosted them for a week, not the magnificent scenery. Up to now, Paul has been the great pioneer missionary; now he benefits from the fruit of the labor of other witnesses. We know that Christians had existed in Rome for many years, but this verse indicates a spread of the faith to other cities of Italy. There were also Christians in Herculaneum and Pompeii at this time.[10] We can only speculate on the origin of the church in Rome but Acts 2:10 gives the best clue: Jews from Rome who were present at the Day of Pentecost must have carried the gospel of Christ back to Rome.

And so we came to Rome. Wait a minute, you still have 130 miles to go! Why is this sentence here and not in verse 16? Perhaps Luke was thinking "Rome" included the *ager Romanus,* the whole territory belonging to Rome and its founding tribes.[11] Or, much better, we can translate *kai houtos* in verse 14 as "and this way" (anticipating what follows, as is the case in 1:11), rather than "and so" looking backward.[12]

Now their feet and hearts felt lighter as they started the five day hike to Rome. Two stopping places are mentioned: The Forum of Appius (*Appii Forum*) and Three Taverns (*Tres Tabernae*). After a trek inland on the Via Campania, they joined the Via Appia, the famous highway which led straight as a string to Rome. They might have gotten an overnight ride on a canal boat at the Pontine Marsh, arriving at *Appii Forum* 43 miles south of Rome.[13] There some of the brothers from Rome, somehow receiving word that Paul was on his way, came out two days walk to meet him. This was the standard

---

10   Bruce, 535.

11   Witherington, 786.

12   Witherington, 787.

13   Teikichi Haraguchi, *Fukuin o Tsutaeta Michi,* (Roads that Carried the Gospel) 26. Untranslated Japanese book published by Nazare Kikaku in Tokyo, 2004.

way to greet a ruler or very important person in ancient times; Paul was a VIP to these brothers, and he was greatly pleased and encouraged. *On seeing them, Paul thanked God and took courage.* Others of the Roman church who either started later or tired on the way joined them at Three Taverns, only one day's walk from Rome.

And when we came into Rome, Paul was allowed to stay by himself, with the soldier who guarded him. Verse 16 marks the end of the travelogue and the end of this "we" section. Luke and Aristarchus probably stayed with Paul for some time in Rome.[14] He is not regarded as a dangerous prisoner by the Roman authorities because they gave him the most lenient form of military custody, house arrest. We are told in verse 30 that he lived in his own rented quarters, which we should probably imagine as an apartment in one of the *insula* (apartment buildings) in Rome. A detached house in Rome would have been prohibitively expensive. He was constantly chained to a Roman soldier who stood a four-hour shift. It is hard for us to imagine a lack of privacy such as Paul experienced here, but there is a strong hint in Phil 1:13 that this is the way the gospel spread among the whole Praetorian Guard. If the Western text (reflected in the KJV translation) expansion of verse 16 is correct, "the centurion delivered the prisoners to the *stratopedarch* ("captain of the guard"), most likely the Praetorian prefect Afrianus Burrus himself.[15] Sextus Afranius Burrus had been Nero's tutor and was now his advisor. For the first eight years of Nero's rule, he and Seneca the Younger helped maintain a stable government.[16] Paul is tantalizingly close to the actual interview with Emperor Nero himself.

28:17-29 Preaching to the Jewish Leaders in Rome

17 After three days he called together the local leaders of the Jews, and when they had gathered, he said to them, "Brothers, though I had done nothing against our people or the customs of our fathers, yet I was delivered as a prisoner from Jerusalem into the hands of the Romans. 18 When they had examined me, they wished to set me at liberty, because there

---

14 Col 4:10-14 and Philemon 23-24.

15 Witherington, 788.

16 Wikipedia, The Free Encyclopedia under "Sextus Afranius Burrus."

was no reason for the death penalty in my case. 19 But because the Jews objected, I was compelled to appeal to Caesar—though I had no charge to bring against my nation. 20 For this reason, therefore, I have asked to see you and speak with you, since it is because of the hope of Israel that I am wearing this chain." 21 And they said to him, "We have received no letters from Judea about you, and none of the brothers coming here has reported or spoken any evil about you. 22 But we desire to hear from you what your views are, for with regard to this sect we know that everywhere it is spoken against."

23 When they had appointed a day for him, they came to him at his lodging in greater numbers. From morning till evening he expounded to them, testifying to the kingdom of God and trying to convince them about Jesus both from the Law of Moses and from the Prophets. 24 And some were convinced by what he said, but others disbelieved. 25 And disagreeing among themselves, they departed after Paul had made one statement: "The Holy Spirit was right in saying to your fathers through Isaiah the prophet:

26 "'Go to this people, and say,
"You will indeed hear but never understand,
and you will indeed see but never perceive."
27 For this people's heart has grown dull,
and with their ears they can barely hear,
and their eyes they have closed;
lest they should see with their eyes
and hear with their ears
and understand with their heart
and turn, and I would heal them.'
28 Therefore let it be known to you that this salvation of God has been sent to the Gentiles; they will listen."

Paul has hardly moved into his new quarters when, within three days, he invites some of the leaders of the Jewish community in Rome to his quarters. Since he cannot go to them, they must come to him. Paul was the apostle to the Gentiles (Rom 11:13; Gal 2:8) and he had announced twice before that he was "giving up" on the Jews and turning to the Gentiles (13:46; 18:6), but here he is again, in accordance with his own dictum *To the Jew first* (Rom 1:16), inviting, not pagan Gentiles or brothers in Christ, but Jews as his very first guests. The theme of the Jews and their reaction to the gospel looms more important in Luke's purposes for the book of Acts than we may appreciate. As we have had occasion to state many times in this commentary, one of the key purposes in writing the book is to answer the question: "If, as you claim, Jesus is the true Messiah, why didn't the experts on Messiahs, the Jews, accept him as Messiah?" This section will give another answer to that question.

The Jewish community in Rome has been estimated to have been as many as 50,000 in the early first century, but may have been reduced to about 20,000 after the expulsion edict of Claudius in 49 AD.[17] We have the names of thirteen synagogues that occur in inscriptions from the time.[18] There was even a "Jewish district" on the north side of the Tiber.[19] Paul no doubt continued to see such large numbers of his people as a bridge to the Gentiles for the gospel.

First, however, Paul assumes that they have heard bad reports about him, and he must defend himself against the accusations against him and clear his name if he is to gain an audience. A relationship of trust and credibility must be established before any serious witness can begin. Today we call this "earning the right to be heard." We cannot plunge into evangelism without first securing the confidence of our hearers.

In the first meeting with the Jewish leaders, Paul seeks to establish three points: First, I am innocent of doing anything against Jewish customs. Second, The Roman auhtorities investigated and found no grounds for the death penalty. Third, I am not here to bring any charges against my people. *But because the Jews objected, I was compelled to appeal to Caesar. . .* more fully, "When the Jews requested that I be tried in Jerusalem and I realized they would ambush me and kill me, I had no choice but to appeal to Caesar."

The use of the word *the Jews* seems a little peculiar here, because both the speaker and his hearers are Jews. What Paul meant was, "The Jewish leadership in Jerusalem." Some have thought that, in using expressions like this, and in blaming the Jews so plainly for the death of Jesus, Luke was a first century anti-Semite.[20] *The Jews,* meaning the "Christ-and-Christianity-opposing

---

17 Witherington, 795.

18 Haraguchi, 6. Some were named after great men like Augustus, some after places like Rhodes, some after names symbolizing Judaism like "Hebrew," and some after foreign cities like Tripoli.

19 Philo, *Legatio ad Gaium* 155-57, cited by Witherington, 795.

20 A whole book, *The Jews in Luke-Acts* by Jack T. Sanders (Philadelphia: Fortress, 1987), was written to make this point. For a more balanced view of Luke's view of the Jews, see Robert L. Brawley, *Luke-Acts and the Jews* (Atlanta: Scholars Press, 1987).

Jews," is quite frequent in Acts (I count 23 times, as in 13:45 and 17:13), but the term *the Jews* is just as frequently used either in a favorable or neutral sense (as in 17:1 and 19:10).

It is because of the hope of Israel that I am wearing this chain. Paul again, as in 26:6, 7 asserts that the real reason for the enmity of "the Jews" and his resulting arrest was that he believed in *the hope of Israel.* In 23:6 and 24:15 *the hope of Israel* was the hope of resurrection. Here *the hope of Israel* means "the coming of Messiah."[21] So being interpreted, this sentence means, "It is because of Jesus the Messiah that I am an accused prisoner." Paul called himself a "prisoner of Christ" in Eph 3:1; 4:1 and Philemon 1 and 23.

The reply of the Jewish delegation is peaceful and neutral. Surprisingly, they have not heard anything about the charges against Paul as Paul had assumed. They profess to have heard nothing of what was only recently the top item on the agenda of the Sanhedrin in Jerusalem. The only thing they know is *for with regard to this sect we know that everywhere it is spoken against.* Instead of assuming the truth of the rumors, these Jews are very fair-minded and want to hear from Paul what this "sect" (*hairesis*) really believes. They want to hear more, so they set a day and come in even larger numbers.

Again Paul has a golden opportunity to witness for Christ. His explanation and the ensuing discussion lasted all day. One must give credit to these Jews for patiently hearing Paul out. Paul did not hold back anything. *He expounded to them, testifying to the kingdom of God and trying to convince them about Jesus both from the Law of Moses and from the Prophets.* John the Baptist and Jesus had announced the arrival of the kingdom predicted in the Prophets. Ajith Fernando says that "Preaching the kingdom of God presents the greater purpose of God rather than just what God can do to an individual."[22] Paul must have quoted all the texts he could think of from both the Law of Moses (Deuteronomy 18 for example) and the Prophets concerning Messiah and then how Jesus fulfilled these predictions. Paul's knowledge (recitation from memory, because it is very unlikely that he had access to OT scrolls) was so extensive that it took most of

---

21 As we have seen in previous comments, *the hope* as resurrection and *the hope* of Messiah are two interrelated concepts. Longenecker, 570, and Stott, 398, also take *the hope* here to mean "the hope of Messiah."

22 Fernando, 630-31. He goes on to say: "If the truth of the kingdom were added to our evangelistic preaching our evangelism would yield much stronger Christians . . . if the grand picture of the kingdom is firmly rooted in their minds, they will never forsake the Lord of the universe for a smaller, less powerful deity."

the day to make his appeal. We get a glimpse of what such a presentation might have been like in Peter's sermons in Acts 2 and 3 and Paul's synagogue sermon in Antioch (Acts 13). *And some were convinced by what he said, but others disbelieved. They disagreed among themselves.* Again, as in every case when the gospel was preached to Jews in Acts, some believed, and some did not believe. We would like to know what percentage believed, but Luke does not tell us. Perhaps half believed and half did not. So one answer to the problem of why the Jews did not believe is that some of them, perhaps a good many of them, **did** believe.

Another answer is given in the long quotation from Isaiah 6. The unbelief of the Jews was no surprise to God; in fact he had predicted this reaction some 700 years prior to the cross. Jesus had used the same passage twice when confronted with the unbelief of his people in Mark 4:12 (parallel to Matt 13:13 and Luke 8:10), and on a different occasion summed up Jewish unbelief in John 12:40. Stott, in dealing with this passage, cites J. A. Alexander: "there are three distinguishable agencies expressly or implicitly described, the ministerial agency of the prophet, the judicial agency of God, and the suicidal agency of the people themselves."[23] In the Acts passage, it is the third that is most prominent. In other words, even though they had heard with their ears, understood with their minds and seen with their eyes, *This people's heart has grown dull, and with their ears they can barely hear, and their eyes they have closed; lest they should see with their eyes and hear with their ears, and understand with their heart and turn, and I would heal them.* In other words, they did not want to believe so they closed their ears, eyes, and hearts lest they believe. Unbelievers do not want to believe because *We do not want this man to reign over us* (Luke 19:14). So another reason many Jews did not believe in Jesus was willful, inexplicable "suicidal" stubbornness in the face of clear evidence.

We wonder at Paul's "lack of tact" in citing this passage against the unbelieving group and saying nothing in praise of the convinced group. It was at this point that the Jewish delegation all got up and left, heatedly debating among themselves.[24] Once again there is a split decision on the issue of Jesus

---

23   Stott, 399.

24   Verse 29, "and when he had said these words, the Jews departed and had great disputing among themselves" is missing in modern versions like the NIV and ESV because this verse comes from the Western text only and is not in the other major manuscripts. It was adopted by the Byzantine text family and so came into the KJV. However, as we have frequently noticed, the Western text "expansions" are often reasonable and may represent what may have actually happened.

of Nazareth. Paul is not afraid to use tough passages to exercise "tough love," which may later prick the conscience.

T. J. Bach was a missionary to Venezuela and Colombia and later the general director of The Evangelical Alliance Mission (TEAM, in Bach's time SAM, Scandinavian Alliance Mission) for eighteen years. The first time he was handed a gospel tract on a street in Copenhagen, he exploded "Why do you bother other people with your religion? I'm quite able to take care of myself." He snatched the tract, ripped it in two, crumpled it up, and stuffed it in his pocket. The young man who had given Bach the tract said nothing but turned toward a doorway and bowed his head in prayer. Bach noticed in astonishment that he had tears on his cheeks. Later, alone in his boarding room, he could not forget the incident. Out of curiosity he fished the mutilated paper out of his pocket and carefully put it back together. Before he was finished reading the message he was on his knees asking God to forgive his sins.[25] The conversion of T. J. Bach illustrates this possibility.

Therefore let it be known to you that this salvation of God has been sent to the Gentiles; they will listen. And listen they did! Though not in overwhelming numbers at first, within less than three hundred years there were enough Roman Christians to make Christianity the religion of the emperor and the majority religion of the empire. Paul had earlier pondered the connection between the rejection of the gospel by the Jews and its acceptance by the Gentiles:

> *Again I ask: Did they* (Israel, the Jews) *stumble so as to fall beyond recovery? Not at all! Rather, because of their transgression, salvation has come to the Gentiles to make Israel envious. But if their transgression means riches for the world, and their loss means riches for the Gentiles, how much greater riches will their fullness bring! I am talking to you Gentiles. Inasmuch as I am the apostle to the Gentiles, I make much of my ministry in the hope that I may somehow arouse my own people to envy and save some of them. For if their rejection is the reconciliation of the world, what will their acceptance be but life from the dead?* (Rom 11:11-16)

This passage brings out three points. First, in making such a remark that the Gentiles would listen, Paul hoped to stimulate the Jews to jealousy and faith. "If the Gentiles believe Jesus is the Messiah and they are so radically changed

---

25   Tom Watson, Jr. *T.J. Bach a Voice for Missions* (Chicago: Moody Press, 1965), 14-15.

by this belief, maybe we should reconsider our opinion of Jesus." Second, the transgression of the Jews in crucifying their Messiah and their continued unbelief, in the providence and sovereignty of God, enabled the gospel of salvation to go to the Gentiles. Third, there will come a day when the Jews do believe (11:26) and that will be *life from the dead* for the whole world. Today there are hundreds of "Messianic synagogues" of Hebrew Christians and more Jews believing in Jesus as the Christ than at any time in history. That the Jews still exist at all as a distinct people is a miracle of God. God was not "through with the Jew" at the end of Acts and he has still not written them off as hopeless.

*The salvation of God has been sent to the Gentiles, **and they will listen** may be seen as the open-ended ending of the book of Acts. *The salvation of God* started in Jerusalem, and has spread throughout the eastern Mediterranean, and has reached Rome. Now it will spread from Rome to all the corners of the empire. And, on a scale that would have astonished Peter and Paul, in the great missionary centuries from 1700 to 2000 it will continue to spread *to the ends of the earth*, a world of hundreds of nations and thousands of people groups in a population over 7.8 billion and growing. If the gospel does not seem quite so triumphant where we serve, let the apostle's words ***they will listen*** reverberate in our hearts.

28:30-31 Incomplete Postscript on What Happened to Paul

> **30** *He lived there two whole years at his own expense, and welcomed all who came to him, **31** proclaiming the kingdom of God and teaching about the Lord Jesus Christ with all boldness and without hindrance.*

Paul's *proclaiming of the kingdom of God* had no need of a pulpit or a large congregation. The word "proclaim" is the familiar *kērussō*, "to announce as a herald," in this context to share the gospel as something new to those who had never heard it. These meetings must have been one-on-one or small group situations. God somehow brought people to him. Paul also *taught about the Lord Jesus Christ*. This implies that he instructed those he led to Christ. Some have said that preaching is aimed at the will and teaching is aimed at the mind. He did not teach "Christianity," he taught *the Lord Jesus Christ*. We pray and sing to "Jesus," but Paul used Jesus' full title, which included the now neglected word "Lord."

Did not Paul feel the pain and discouragement of not being able to travel freely as he used to and preach the gospel in yet other lands, maybe Spain and the north coast of Africa? Was it not hard for such an energetic active man to be so confined "wasting time" in detention? To the contrary, Paul seems to be quite busy preaching and teaching the gospel to those whom God brought to him in his rented quarters. This was the period during which Paul led a runaway slave, Onesimus, to Christ and sent him back to his master Philemon. There must have been many other converts of whom we know nothing. As we have noted, this was the period when the gospel spread throughout the Praetorian Guard (Phil 1:13). Indeed, Phil 1:12-25 opens a window on his faith and joy during this period of confinement. As a result of Paul's imprisonment *Christ is being preached, and in this I rejoice* (Phil 1:18). It is astonishing that one of the key themes of Philippians—joy—could come out of such a seemingly depressing situation.

Time in "jail" may have deepened Paul's insight into the Person of Christ and the reality of the Body of Christ. Many centuries later, an English tinker by the name of John Bunyan wrote eleven books while he was in jail, one of them, next to the Bible, the all-time best seller, *Pilgrim's Progress.*[26]

Few of us will be thrown in jail for our faith. But most of us will have to deal with the slowly increasing confinement of aging. One by one our faculties weaken: sight, hearing, mobility. The day comes when we must relinquish our car keys. We may be confined to one room and then our whole world may shrink to the size of one bed. Some are imprisoned in bodies whose mind no longer functions. Meditation on how Paul had greater freedom and spiritual fruitfulness in prison may well strengthen us for the trials of old age.

A Personal Note to Luke

Well, Luke, as we come to the end of your inspiring book, I must confess a little disappointment. Why did you cut it off without telling us what happened in Paul's trial before Caesar Nero, which the Lord promised one night during the storm (27:24)? Did Paul ever get to Spain? Did you intend Acts to be an open-ended volume in which future generations would add thousands of volumes on how the gospel spread?

---

26   There is more detail on how Bunyan made the best of his time in jail, including making a flute out of the leg of a stool and playing it when the jailors were away, in Fernando, 630.

The last four words of your book are so great: μετα πασης παρρησιας ακωλυτως (*meta pasēs parrēsias akōlutōs*)! "With all boldness unhindered!" If there is one lesson we learn from your book, it is boldness—boldness to preach the gospel even in the most intimidating circumstances, boldness even in the face of persecution and death, confidence even when thrown in jail for years. "Unhindered!" Another great lesson of your book that the gospel of our Lord Jesus Christ is so powerful that nothing can stop it; even though its preachers are martyred or imprisoned, that is no hindrance to the Word.[27] No barrier erected against The Message can stand; like water it seeps around and over and under all obstacles.

Lessons for Life

1. God can provide our needs through unlikely people in unlikely circumstances.
2. God is concerned about reaching government officials with the gospel. Are we?
3. Jewish evangelism should still be a priority.
4. The message we preach and teach is the kingdom of God and the Lord Jesus Christ, not "Christianity."
5. If we are faithful effective witnesses, God will bring people to us even if we cannot go to them.
6. Our "prison" may be the place of our greatest blessing and fruitfulness.
7. The Gentiles are still hearing and responding to the salvation of God to the ends of the earth.

---

27 *I suffer trouble like an evildoer, even unto bonds, but the word of God is **not bound*** (2 Tim 2:9 KJV).

BIBLIOGRAPHY

Partially Annotated

Commentaries:

Barclay, William. *The Acts of the Apostles,* The Daily Bible Study Series, Philadelphia: Westminster, 1976, Revised Edition. *Brief sermonic style with outstanding illustrations from the classical world.*

Bock, Darrell L. *Acts.* Grand Rapids: Baker Academic, 2007. *Very thorough, clear scholarly work which discusses every textual and exegetical issue, interacting with many significant recent scholarly writings on Acts.*

Boice, James Montgomery. *Acts: An Expositional Commentary,* Grand Rapids: Baker, 1997. *Sermonic style with excellent applications.*

Bruce, F.F. *The Acts of the Apostles: Greek Text with Introduction and Commentary,* 3rd Revised and Enlarged Edition, Grand Rapids: Eerdmans and Leicester England, Apollos, 1990. *One of the great scholars of the 20th century. Unsurpassed in meticulous linguistic and historical research.*

Fernando, Ajith. *Acts, The NIV Application Commentary,* Grand Rapids: Zondervan, 1998. *As the title implies, strong in application. Since Fernando is from Sri Lanka, many of his illustrations speak to the Asian context.*

Fitzmyer, Joseph A. *The Acts of the Apostles: A New Translation with Introduction and Commentary,* The Anchor Bible Vol. 31, New York: Doubleday, 1998. *Fitzmyer writes from a strong scholastic background, especially in Aramaic. He is Catholic (Jesuit) but often takes a fairly critical viewpoint.*

Haenchen, Ernst. *The Acts of the Apostles: A Commentary,* Philadelphia: Westminster, 1971. Translated from the 14th German Edition (1965). *A modern exemplar of German scholarship; he is very skeptical of the historical veracity of Acts.*

Hawthorne, Gerald F. *Philippians,* Waco Texas: Word Bible Commentaries, 1983.

Kidner, Derek. *Genesis,* London: Tyndale Press, 1967.

Kistemaker, Simon J. *Exposition of the Acts of the Apostles.* New Testament Commentary, Grand Rapids: Baker, 1990. *An excellent commentary with rich insights.*

Longenecker, Richard N. "Acts" in Vol. 9 of *The Expositor's Bible Commentary,* Frank E. Gaebelein, General Editor, Grand Rapids: Zondervan, 1981. *One of my top three. Strong in scholarly research, structural analysis, and exegetical insight.*

Marshall, I. Howard. *The Gospel of Luke: A Commentary on the Greek Text,* Grand Rapids: Eerdmans, 1978.

Marshall, I. Howard. *The Acts of the Apostles: An Introduction and Commentary,* Tyndale New Testament Commentaries, Leicester England: Inter-Varsity Press and Grand Rapids: Eerdmans, 1980. *Concise but thorough; never evades difficulties.*

Morgan, G. Campbell. *The Acts of the Apostles,* New York and London: Fleming H. Revell, 1924. *Excellent example of one of the master expositors of a previous generation; somewhat rambling sermonic style.*

Schnabel, Eckhart J. *Exegetical Commentary on the New Testament: Acts.* Grand Rapids: Zondervan, 2012. *An exhaustive 1162 page tour-de-force. Each chapter includes Literary Context, Main Idea, Translation with Exegetical Layout, Structure and Literary Form, Exegetical Outline, and Explanation of the Text. He deals with every significant Greek word and phrase. This is an abbreviated version of an Expanded Digital Edition available from Zondervan.*

Stott, John R. W. *The Message of Acts,* Leicester: Inter-Varsity Press, 1990. *Another of my top three. An excellent combination of strong scholarly background, judicious exegetical judgment, and the pastor's ability to summarize in expository points.*

Tannehill, Robert C. *The Narrative Unity of Luke-Acts: A Literary Interpretation,* Vol 2: *The Acts of the Apostles,* Minneapolis: Fortress, 1990. *Not a verse-by-verse analysis, but a broad overview of how the author (not necessarily Luke the companion of Paul) uses narrative (not necessarily factual) to promote his values and beliefs.*

Walker, Thomas. *The Acts of the Apostles,* Chicago: Moody, 1910.

Witherington, Ben III. *The Acts of the Apostles: A Socio-Rhetorical Commentary,* Grand Rapids: Eerdmans and Carlisle: Paternoster, 1998. *The third of my "top three." An 873 page goldmine of exhaustive scholarship that analyzes Acts according to the canons of ancient Greek rhetoric. Many extensive excurses on relevant topics.*

Other Works

Aland, Barbara, Kurt Aland, Johannes Karavidopoulos, Carlo M. Martini, and
    Bruce M. Metzger, *The Greek New Testament,* Fourth Revised Edition,
    Stuttgart: Deutsche Bibelgesellschaft, 1998.

Balz, Horst, and Gerhard Schneider, editors. *Exegetical Dictionary of the New
    Testament* (EDNT), translated from the German edition of 1978-80,
    Grand Rapids: Eerdmans, 1990.

Bauer, Walter. *A Greek-English Lexicon of the New Testament and other Early
    Christian Literature.* 3rd Edition (BDAG) revised and edited by Frederick
    William Danker, Chicago: The University of Chicago Press, 2000.

Boer, Hans. *Pentecost and Mission,* London: Lutterworth, 1961.

Bong Rin Ro. *Christian Alternatives to Ancestor Practices.* Taichung: Asia
    Theological Association, 1984.

Brawley, Robert L. *Luke-Acts and the Jews,* Atlanta: Scholars Press, 1987. *Defends
    Luke of the charge of anti-Semitism, taking a more balanced view of Luke's
    attitude toward the Jews.*

Chase, F. H. "On PRHNHS GENOMENOS in ACTS 1:18," *Journal of
    Theological Studies* (1912), 278-85.

Carson, Don, Douglas J. Moo, and Leon Morris. *An Introduction to the New
    Testament.* Grand Rapids: Zondervan, 1992.

Connolly, Peter. *Living in the Time of Jesus of Nazareth:* Jerusalem: Steimatzky
    Ltd., first published by Oxford University Press, 1983. *Loaded with
    wonderful original photographs, drawings, and maps.*

Derrett, J. D. M. "Ananias, Sapphira, and the Right of Property," in *Studies in
    the New Testament Volume I,* Leiden: Brill, 1977.

Dibelius, M. *Studies in the Acts of the Apostles,* translated from the German,
    London: SCM, 1956.

DuPont, J. "La structure oratoire du discours d'Etienne (Actes 7)," *Biblia 66*
    (1985), 153-167.

Edersheim, *Sketches of Jewish Social Life in the Days of Christ,* London: James
    Clarke, 1961. First published 1867.

Haraguchi, Teikichi. *Fukuin o Tsutaeta Michi,* ("Roads that Carried the
    Gospel"). Untranslated Japanese book published by Nazare Kikaku in
    Tokyo, 2004.

Harris, R. Laird, Gleason L. Archer, and Bruce K. Waltke, editors. *Theological
    Wordbook of the Old Testament,* Chicago: Moody, 1980.

Hay, D. M. *Glory at the Right Hand,* Nashville: Abingdon, 1973.

Hemer, Colin J. *The Book of Acts in the Setting of Hellenistic History,* edited by Conrad J. Gempf, Winona Lake: Eisenbrauns, 1990. *An unsurpassed defense of the historical accuracy of Acts.*

Hoehner, H. W. "Chronology," in *Dictionary of Jesus and the Apostles,* Edited by Joel B. Green, Scot, McKnight, and I. Howard Marshall, Downers Grove, IL: IVP, 1992.

Jensen, Irving. *Independent Bible Study,* Chicago: Moody, 1963.

Jeremias, Joachim. *Jerusalem in the Time of Jesus,* Philadelphia: Fortress, 1969.

Johnstone, Patrick and Jason Mandryk, *Operation World,* Carlisle: Paternoster, 2001.

Josephus, Flavius. *The Antiquities of the Jews,* c. 93-94 AD, and *The Wars of the Jews,* c. 78-79 AD, translated by William Whiston, 1737; from *Josephus: Complete Works,* Peabody MA: Hendrickson Publishers, new updated edition 1987.

Lidell, H. G. and R. Scott. *An Intermediate Greek-English Lexicon,* Oxford: The Clarendon Press, 7th edition, 1889.

Louw, Johannes P. and Eugene A. Nida, editors. *Greek-English Lexicon of the New Testament based on Semantic Domains,* 2 volumes, New York: United Bible Societies, 1989.

McRay, John. *Paul: His Life and Teaching,* Grand Rapids: Baker, 2003. *Writes from extensive experience of the archaeology and geography of the Bible lands. Presents a fresh chronology of the life of Paul integrating the data of Paul's epistles and the record of Acts.*

Moulton, J. H. and George Milligan. *The Vocabulary of the Greek Testament,* Grand Rapids: Eerdmans, 1985, first edition 1930.

Mowinkel, Sigmund. *He that Cometh,* Nashville: Abingdon, 1954. Translated from the German by G. W. Anderson.

Parsons, Mikeal C. and Martin M. Culy, *Acts: A Handbook on the Greek Text.* Waco, Texas: Baylor University Press, 2003.

Ramsay, William M. *St. Paul the Traveler and Roman Citizen,* updated and revised by Mark Wilson, Grand Rapids: Kregel, 2001. From the 15th edition published by Hodder and Stoughton, 1925. *One of the great historical and geographical studies of Acts in a very attractive modern edition with color photographs. Later commentators often react to Ramsay's bold conjectures on the life of Paul.*

Sanders, Jack T. *The Jews in Luke-Acts,* Philadelphia: Fortress, 1987. *Criticizes "Luke" as an anti-Semite.*

Shade, W. Robert III. PhD Dissertation "The Restoration of Israel in Acts 3:12-26 and Lukan Eschatology," Trinity Evangelical Divinity School,

Deerfield, Illinois, USA. Available from UMI Dissertation services, 300
N. Zeeb Road, Ann Arbor MI 48106, USA.

Tenney, Merrill C., General Editor. *The Zondervan Pictorial Bible Dictionary,*
Grand Rapids: Zondervan, 1963.

Uchimura, Kanzō. *How I Became a Christian: Out of My Diary,* Tokyo:
Kyōbunkan, 1971, from 1895 Japanese edition.

www.ingramcontent.com/pod-product-compliance
Lightning Source LLC
Chambersburg PA
CBHW030351130626
46549CB00004B/1444